Discovering
the Most
Amazing Book

Charles W Stebbing

Copyright © 2014 by Charles Stebbing.

Unless otherwise indicated, all Scripture quotations are from the New King James Version of the Bible. Copyright © 1982 by Thomas Nelson, Inc. Used by permission. All rights reserved.

| ISBN: | Softcover | 978-1-4990-9058-1 |
| | eBook | 978-1-4990-9059-8 |

All rights reserved. No part of this book may be reproduced or transmitted in any form or by any means, electronic or mechanical, including photocopying, recording, or by any information storage and retrieval system, without permission in writing from the copyright owner.

Any people depicted in stock imagery provided by Thinkstock are models, and such images are being used for illustrative purposes only.
Certain stock imagery © Thinkstock.

This book was printed in the United States of America.

Rev. date: 10/21/2014

To order additional copies of this book, contact:
Xlibris
0-800-056-3182
www.xlibrispublishing.co.uk
Orders@xlibrispublishing.co.uk
667139

Contents

Foreword 7

Introductory..9

Part One
The Bible: The Inspired written Word of God 13

Chapter One
The Bible – Origin, Authorship, Inspiration and Canonization 15

Part Two
The Bible: Composition and Message.......................................35

Chapter two
The Bible – Composition and Message.....................................37

Part Three
Survey of Old Covenant Books 93

Chapter Three
Survey of the Pentateuch 95

Chapter Four
Survey of the Historical Books..114

Chapter Five
Survey of the Poetical and Wisdom Books................................157

Chapter Six
Survey of the Major Prophets 176

Chapter Seven
Survey of the Minor Prophets 206

Part Four
Survey of New Testament Books...247

Chapter Eight
Differences between the two Covenants and
a Survey of the Gospels 249

Chapter Nine
Survey of the Book of Acts 292

Chapter Ten
Survey of Paul's Letters..314

Chapter Eleven
Paul's Letters to Individuals..355

Chapter Twelve
Survey of the General Letters..370

Chapter Thirteen
Survey of Revelation 396

Part Five
Bible Study 407

Chapter Fourteen
How to read and study the Bible..409

Addendum 421

Glossary 445

Bibliography..461

Foreword

This book is based on a discipleship course that we have done. The overwhelming interest of students from various age groups who signed up for the course was a clear indication that there is still a hunger for God's Word. That encouraged me to compile the course material into a book, in order to make it available to a wider audience.

The content of this book is not merely a personal opinion, it is rather an informed opinion because I have done much research to ascertain the facts. However, some information may still be tentative because we do not have full knowledge on everything that the Bible reveals, and opinions on subjects that are more difficult to interpret differ.

The purpose of this book is not merely to make information available, but to give the readers a workable knowledge of the Bible and to tickle their appetite to study and examine the Word of God for themselves. For that reason, I have kept the studies concise, not giving too much information but enough to arouse curiosity for further investigation.

The Bible is certainly the greatest tangible gift that God gave us. We should treasure it. Every person (including nonbelievers) should invest time in discovering the wonderful life-changing Revelation that this Amazing Book presents.

Charles Stebbing
Cork, Ireland
September 2014

Introductory

People are curious beings. They love to discover things. Naturally, the more wonderful and exciting the discoveries are, the more enjoyable. The greatest discovery that anyone can make is to discover one's Creator. Once you have found Him, then you will realize that everything you could possibly need in this life is in Him.

The starting place for discovering God, and for that matter, life, love, meaning, purpose, and truth is the Bible.

The Greatest Book

The only authoritative Resource that truly answers the greatest questions that people of all ages have asked is the Bible. "Where do we come from?" Where are we going?" "Why are we here?" "What will eventually happen with mankind?" "Is there something such as truth?", and, "How can we know the truth?" Because the Bible doesn't speculate, but reveals the truth about God, explains the origin of mankind, highlights the age-old problem of sin and suffering, and points clearly to the only way to salvation and eternal life.

The central, overarching theme of the Bible is mankind's need of salvation and God's provision of atonement in Jesus Christ. The unity and progress of Biblical revelation are convincingly demonstrated in the truth that Jesus Christ is the sum and substance of the revelation contained in the Bible. The person and work of Jesus Christ are promised, prophesied, and pictured in the types and symbols of the Old Covenant. The Four Gospels reveal Him in all His power, glory, and dignity; and the full meanings and applications of His life, death, and resurrection are explained in the Letters to the different churches. The glorious Second Coming of Christ and the restoration of all things are unmistakably foretold in the Book of Revelation.

The great purpose of the written Word of God is to reveal God, His redeeming love and plan of salvation for man to us (see John 1:1-18).

Because the Bible is a message from God, it has a "many layered message" – the message can be made applicable to an individual, a group of people, a society, a nation and even the whole world. The Bible's message is transcultural.

Moreover, the Bible itself declares that it will remain forever (Mark 13:31; Ps. 119:89); what a consolation! It is obviously the greatest Book ever written.

Amazing Facts About The Bible

The following are a few Amazing Facts about the Bible.[1]

- About fifty Bibles are sold every minute of every day of every week and month and year.

- The Bible is the most shop-lifted Book in the world.

- The first verse in the Bible contains seven Hebrew words (in the original language); the meaning of the number seven in the Bible is: completeness or perfection. The last word in the Bible is: Amen! So be it!

- The Bible is the oldest actual Book known to man, some parts of it are around 3500 years old.

- The Bible is old without growing older; it always remains new and fresh.

- The Bible has survived thousands of years of persecution and attempted destruction. Its "would-be" destroyers are gone, and yet the Bible still lives, and has even presided over some of their funerals.

---

[1] Taken from various resources on the internet, especially *YOUTUBE*

- The Bible is the most copied, translated and historically attested piece of literature that the world has ever known.

- The Bible is translated in over 2300 languages and dialects.

- The Bible was the first Book to be printed on a printing press.

- The Bible is the only "religious" Book in the world that tells of a Coming One and then records the fact of His coming, verified by history.

- The Bible declares the redemption of man by God Himself through Jesus Christ.

- The Centre of the Bible: the shortest chapter in the Bible is Psalm 117, the longest chapter is Psalm 119, the chapter between the shortest and longest chapters is Psalm 118. There are 594 chapters before Psalm 118 and there are 594 chapters after Psalm 118, add these numbers together and you will get 1188; Psalm 118:8 says: *"It is better to trust in the Lord than to put confidence in man."* What a verse for the days in which we live!

The Bible remains the most extensively printed, widely translated, and frequently read book in the world. Its words have been treasured in hearts of multitudes like none other. All who have received its gifts of wisdom and promises of new life and power were at first strangers to its redemptive message, and many were hostile to its teaching and spiritual demands. In every generation its power to challenge persons of all races and lands has been demonstrated. Those who cherish the Book because it sustains future hope, brings meaning and power to the present, and correlates a misused past with God's forgiving grace, would not long experience such inner rewards if Scripture were not known to them as the authoritative, divinely revealed truth. To the evangelical Christian, Scripture is God's Word, given in the objective form of propositional truths through divinely inspired prophets and apostles, and the Holy Spirit is the giver of faith through that Word. – Carl F H Henry

Scope and Purpose of this Book

Through the pages of this book you will gain a proper understanding of the Bible and the glorious message it proclaims. First and foremost you will learn that the message of the Bible is divinely inspired by God. This will lay a solid foundation for your faith upon which you can build your Christian life, and will also give you a greater appreciation for the Book of Ages. We will then look at the composition and message of the Bible by journeying chronologically through Biblical history and looking at a synopsis of every book of the Bible. This will help you to see how God worked in Old Testament times, and you will learn what changed with Christ's coming and why. We continue by looking at how to interpret the Bible properly and finish our exciting learning experience by considering how to read and study the Bible.

All this will strengthen your faith, you will experience greater confidence and have more knowledge when expressing your faith to others. It will enrich your life and even equip you for effective Christian living. Above all, you will have deepened in your love and appreciation for the Author of the most extraordinary Book.

An extensive addendum is added that consists of the following: a Suggested Chronology of New Testament Books, Outstanding Bible Books, Outstanding Bible Verses, Where to turn When ..., Scriptural answers concerning law keeping, and a Glossary to explain Biblical terms.

On your journey in discovering the most amazing book, you will stumble on many fascinating facts, and will certainly encounter the most amazing Person who ever lived as well as the amazing grace of God. Amen!

Part One

The Bible: The Inspired written Word of God

Chapter One

The Bible – Origin, Authorship, Inspiration and Canonization

The Origin of the Bible

From where did we get the Bible? Perhaps … long, long ago and far, far away a devoted Christian prayed to God asking Him, "Lord please give me your Word in written form, so that I can have a point of reference, read it, do studies, reflect on it, develop a better understanding of You and your plan for mankind." And then God dropped a Bible from heaven. No, the Bible has a very rich history.

The Bible originated in the heart of God – His desire, as a living and loving God, to reveal Himself and His plan and purpose to mankind.

Dividing the origin and history of the Bible into different stages, helps us to form a better understanding of how we eventually received the most amazing Book in our own language.

The First Stage

The Oral Tradition and Primitive writing period – from Adam to Moses. This was the period of storytelling and primitive writing. During this time God revealed Himself directly to people. We think of, for example, the instances when He revealed Himself to Adam, Enoch, Noah, Abraham and Moses. These revelations from God as well as cultural and historical material were transmitted orally from one generation to another. The oral records presumably originated soon after the actual events occurred.

Later, when primitive writing arose, many of these oral records would have been committed to writing. It is suggested that the transfer to written format may have happened earlier than we generally suppose.

Primitive alphabets are known to have circulated in the early second millennium BC, and with the discovery of the Palermo Stone we have evidence that the Egyptians wrote detailed historical records (in hieroglyphic text) at least as far back as 2600 BC, a time that predates Moses by about 1100 years. (The Palermo Stone is one of the seven surviving fragments of a stele known as the Royal Annals of the Old Kingdom of Ancient Egypt. The Palermo Stone is held in an Archaeological Museum in the city of Palermo, Italy, from which it derives its name.) The inscriptions on the Palermo Stone reach back towards the dawn of Egypt, naming kings from 3100 BC. So, we can suggest that key events and remembrances of early human history were preserved and passed down to later generations. We also suggest that God supervised these oral and written records so that reliable histories were preserved for inclusion in the Biblical record.

Furthermore, it is reasonable to say that writing was a well-developed art by the time of Joseph. He and his family would have had the opportunity to learn writing in Egypt. It is only credible to suggest that Joseph, as the chief bearer of Abraham's lineage, would have been keen to preserve his family's traditions and the experiences with and revelations from God of his ancestors. Thus, history and significant encounters and experiences with God, were preserved by recording it carefully, either orally and/or in writing.

As writing skills and material developed, and generations passed on, the need to write down the history and revelations of God became more evident.

The Second Stage

The writing down of God's revelations. Moses was the first person to receive a commandment from God to write down His words and revelations (Ex. 17:14; 34:27; Acts 7:38 compare with verse 22). Moses' inheritance as a Levite, the fact that he was commissioned by God, plus his upbringing and fine education in

Pharaoh's household, put him in a good position to write early history from a Hebrew perspective.

Many events in Exodus through Deuteronomy coincided with Moses' lifetime, and so he recorded that as an eyewitness. It is reasonable to suggest that Moses was able to write about historical events that took place long before his birth by drawing upon pre-existing sources (the preserved oral and written accounts), all while he was under the inspiration of the Holy Spirit. This model of research is supported by Luke 1:1-4. In Numbers 21:14, 15 we read that Moses refers back to the now lost *"Book of the Lord's Wars."* On the other hand, it is also reasonable to suggest that God could have revealed to Moses the historical events that predated him, particularly the Creation Account. So, we see that the Bible is not the product of divine dictation, but Bible composition involved both supernatural and natural means, which was supervised by God.

It has been argued that Moses could not have written the account of his own death. Deuteronomy chapter 34 contains an obituary (a notice of his death with a short account of his life) that was most probably written by his successor Joshua.

Moses was the first writer and after him all the other inspired writers of the Old Testament recorded what God said and revealed to them.

The Old Testament was written in Hebrew, with parts of the book of Daniel in Aramaic, and the New Testament in Greek (parts of the Gospel of Matthew are written in Aramaic).

The early writers wrote on papyrus and parchment. The papyrus, a paper-like material, was made from the sticky fibrous inner pith of the papyrus plant. The outer rind of the plant was first removed, and the sticky fibrous inner pith was cut lengthwise into thin strips of about 40 cm long. The strips were then placed side by side on a hard surface with their edges slightly overlapping, and then another layer of strips is laid on top at a right angle. While still moist, the two layers were hammered together, mashing the layers into a single sheet. The sheet was then dried under pressure. After drying, the sheet was polished with some rounded object, possibly a stone or seashell or round hardwood. Sheets were cut to size or glued together to create a longer roll. To form the long strip scrolls required, a number of such sheets were joined, placed so all the horizontal fibres parallel with the roll's length were on one side and all the vertical fibres on the other. Normally, texts were written on the lines following the fibres, parallel to the long edges of the scroll. Although relatively cheap, papyrus was fragile and not very durable.

Parchment, which was significantly higher in quality and durability, was made of animal skins (goats, sheep or calves). Those made of calf skin are called vellum. The animal skins were treated with lime, stretched and scraped to make it smooth and to get the correct thickness, and then dried under tension. These dried skins were cut to size and joined to form longer rolls.

The Third Stage

Handwritten Copies. There were no printing presses or photocopiers back then, all copying was done by hand. Thus, literary copying was an important skill in the ancient world. The handwritten copies are called Manuscripts (MSS). These copies were made in order to spread the Word. Copying was done by scribes and copyists, who took exceptional care when copying the scrolls, because they believed that the writings were authoritative and inspired by God.

Although they took utmost care in copying the scrolls minor mistakes, called variants, were made (these variants are minor and will never change the message of the Bible). These mistakes are things such as: an omitted letter or word, a misspelling, a duplicate line, and rearrangements of words. By comparing the many different manuscripts with each other these minor mistakes can be easily identified and eliminated.

We also suggest that scribes updated and edited the manuscripts to reflect contemporary word usage (see Judges 1:10, 11; 1 Samuel 9:9). These changes would have been undertaken with great care to preserve the meaning and intention of Scriptures.

There are many MSS of the Old Testament, perhaps over ten thousand including the very valuable Dead Sea Scrolls (found in 1947). The Dead Sea Scrolls include the earliest known surviving manuscripts of portions of the Hebrew Bible. One Scroll contains the book of Isaiah and it is reckoned to be approximately a thousand years older than most of the MSS of the Old Testament that we have.

The text of the Old Testament MSS is very accurate, because the Jews preserved and revised it since the earliest days. The Hebrew MSS were revised since the time of Ezra.

There are approximately 5700 MSS of the New Testament available; these are not complete New Testaments but portions and fragments of it.

The oldest MSS were written in capital letters with no spaces between letters, called uncials (meaning "inch-high," referring to the size of the letters). For instance: INTHEBEGINNINGWASGOD. What a joy to read, copy and translate! Only later, in the ninth century, cursive writing was used. The writers began a sentence with a capitol letter and left spaces between letters. The majority of MSS are written in cursive writing, known as minuscules (referring to the smaller letters that were used).

The Manuscripts of the Bible didn't contain chapter or verse divisions in the numbered form that we have today. The division of the Bible into the standard modern arrangement of chapters came much later. Cardinal Stephen Langton's (1150-1228) system of dividing the Bible into chapters was used to do the chapter divisions of the Bible (AD 1226). The division into verses was done by Cardinal Hugo De Santo Cato in the mid-16th century.

The making of handwritten copies was a laborious undertaking. The first Bible printed on a printing press, known as the Gutenberg Bible, was printed by Johannes Gutenberg in 1450. The Gutenberg Bible was also the first book printed on a printing press.

> The word "Scripture" means: holy writings.

The Fourth Stage

Translation. Before the existence of the New Testament there was already a need to translate the Hebrew Bible (Old Testament) into other languages. The earliest translation of the Hebrew Bible into Greek is the Septuagint (280 BC), also known as the translation of the seventy (since 70 scholars worked on the translation). This translation was made to serve the then "Greek world" during the Intertestamental Period (more about this later).

There are also other older translations such as the Coptic translation (4th century AD), the Latin Vulgate (late 4th century AD), the Armenian translation (5th century AD), the Syriac translation of the Gospels (5th century AD), and the Ethiopic translation (5th century AD). These older translations are also valuable resources in determining the original meaning of Scripture.

Later, English translations of the Bible followed: the John Wycliffe English New Testament (1380); the William Tyndale New Testament in 1525 and the Pentateuch in 1530; the Coverdale Bible, compiled by Myles Coverdale and published in 1535 was the first complete English translation of the Bible. The King James Bible, also known as the Authorised Version (AV) was finished in 1611. Today there are approximately 151 different English translations available.

As you can imagine, translating the Bible from the original languages is no easy task. While translating the Bible into German (1522), Luther said to one of his friends that he undertook a task that was far above his powers. Therefore, today, we should rejoice and be very thankful that we have the Bible in our own language. We should highly appreciate the written Word of God. Only God could have preserved His revelation to man in such an amazing way.

The Authorship of the Bible

Over and over, we are assured that the Bible is not merely a collection of human writings about God. Instead, it contains the words of God Himself, written through the pens of men, perhaps as many as forty over a period of 1500 to 1600 years. These men, with different backgrounds, were called and inspired by God to record what He wanted them to write down. They were kings, generals, fishermen, shepherds and priests. One was a physician. One was a tax collector. Some were wealthy while others were poor. Some were educated while others had no education.

There are three terms we need to understand when we talk about God writing the books of the Bible through the pens of men. The first one is **revelation**, derived from a Latin word, which means "unveiling." It indicates that God has taken the initiative to make Himself known. Revelation is the general term that covers all the ways that God reveals Himself and truth to man. We cannot discover

God by ourselves. What we know about God is only what He rev
about Himself. The second term refers to the process by which
God moved these men to write the different books of the Bible:
inspiration. This refers to what theologians call "Special Revelation."
The Bible is the Special Revelation of God to man. The third term is:
authority, the power or weight Scripture possesses because of what
it is, namely, divine revelation given by divine inspiration. Scripture
is authoritative and fully trustworthy because it is inspired by God.
So **Revelation** by **Inspiration** gives us **Authority**.

> *"Knowing this first, that no prophecy of Scripture is of any private interpretation, for prophecy never came by the will of man, but holy men of God spoke as they were moved by the Holy Spirit (2 Peter 1:20-21)."*

When the last words of the Book of Revelation were written, the
Special Revelation was complete. This kind of inspiration or Special
Revelation is no longer happening.

Now, after all, we can say that God is the First Author of the
Bible, while the men who wrote God's words down are the secondary
authors.

The Inspiration of the Bible

What is meant by Biblical inspiration?

Our view of the Bible is mostly determined by our belief as to its
inspiration. The word "inspiration" has more than one meaning.
For instance: we refer to the inspiration of poets and artists – that
inspiration which comes from the soul of the artist that inflames his
passion to express his feelings or thoughts in pure art. That is not
the same as Biblical inspiration.

The inspiration of the artist comes from his inner being; that is
to say, his soul and spirit. But the inspiration of the Bible is from
God – He is the source. In Biblical terms the word inspiration means:
"to breathe in." That is why the apostle Paul writes: *"All Scripture
is given by inspiration of God (God breathed), and is profitable for
doctrine, for reproof, for correction, for instruction in righteousness*

(2 Tim. 3:16)." The inspiration that the Bible writers received was a supernatural and special work of the Holy Spirit – it is that special work of the Holy Spirit that moved and led the writers to write down that which God revealed to them, and what they saw, heard and experienced. For instance, He gave them the thoughts and then also led them in their writing down of those thoughts. As we know words are merely expressed thoughts. Thus, the inspiration and leading of the Holy Spirit were not only extended over the thoughts but also over the words that they used. As somebody once said: "The Bible is God's thoughts clothed with vocabulary." The Holy Spirit led them in choosing the right words and gave them the thoughts and words after which they could express God's precise thoughts to man. The apostle Paul, for example, could declare that in communicating to others what God has revealed to him, he did not use *"words taught by human wisdom but ... taught by the Spirit* (1 Cor. 2:13)." This means that even the words and the writing down of those words are inspired. Thus, inspiration refers to the original Word that came directly from God by way of revelation to the writers, who then wrote it down as it was revealed to them.

We have to keep in mind that it does not mean that all the words in the Bible are the words of God, because in the Bible we also find the words of people. For instance, Paul says in 1 Corinthians 7:12: *"But to the rest I, not the Lord, say ..."* (here we can also keep the oral and written records in mind of which some writers made use). However, the whole Bible is God's Word in the sense that there is nothing in the Bible that God didn't want therein, and that nothing is excluded that God wanted to be in the Bible. Thus, the complete process of compiling the Bible by different authors is inspired and supervised by God. However, although everything in the Bible is inspired, we should take care not to look for inspiration in every loose standing word and letter, but in their correct context and meaning.

The Bible makes it clear that the writers were not like unconscious and passive objects, dictated by the Holy Spirit what to write down. No, the writers were not robbed of their own personalities. They wrote themselves within the framework of their own personalities, capabilities, talents, characters and styles. This is the reason why we find a variety of literary types in the Bible, namely, poetry, dramas, letters, history, prophecies and parables. Every writer reveals his own style and character. We can distinguish the differences between the books of Moses and Joshua, Samuel and David, Peter and Paul, and so on. Therefore, we believe that the Bible is organically inspired and not mechanically. (Organic inspiration means precisely what we just said: God used living human beings within the framework of their own individual personalities, abilities and styles.) In fact, the way in which God works in and through human beings is always in such a way that He will not annihilate man's self-activity.

By God's inspiration the mystery of the Triune God becomes clear and real, and Christ becomes a living and real Divine Person who came to pay the ultimate price for the redemption of mankind and the restoration of all things.

How Inspiration worked

There are different ways in which the Holy Spirit moved someone to write down the things that God revealed. The following are some examples:

- **Moses**. He had to record and write down, as an eyewitness, what he experienced and saw with Israel. Moses wrote down the history that he himself experienced. As we have seen, under the leading of the Holy Spirit Moses also made use of preserved oral and written records. Also, God could have revealed to Moses what He exactly wanted him to record, for instance the Creation Record.

- **The Prophets**. They supernaturally received messages from God and were then led by the Holy Spirit to write them down.

- **Luke**. He was inspired and led by the Holy Spirit to examine and research everything regarding the life and ministry of the Lord Jesus before he accurately wrote it down (Luke 1:1-4).

- **The Apostle Paul**. Under the inspiration of the Holy Spirit he wrote to different congregations as well as to individuals. And he also wrote down what Jesus Himself revealed to him, particularly the Justification by Faith message and the revelation regarding the Church (Acts 26:15-18; Eph. 3:1-7).

- **The Psalmists**. Under the inspiration and leading of the Holy Spirit they wrote from their own mental experience and brokenness songs of prayer, praise and worship.

These writers wrote in the time in which they lived, and spoke about circumstances of their time.

Reasons why we believe the Bible is the inspired Word of God

It is important to know *what* you believe, but it is equally important to know *why* you believe it. Given below are the reasons why we believe that the Bible is the inspired Word of God.

1. Prophecies concerning Jesus as the Christ

Recorded in the Old Testament we find predictions made by God's prophets that foretold every significant event concerning Jesus Christ as the Messiah. All these prophecies are fulfilled to the exact detail in the New Testament. When each one of these prophecies came true, the Bible says that it happened *"that the Scripture might be fulfilled."* There are about 330 prophecies in the Old Testament about Jesus Christ the Messiah.

The following diagram lists a few specific events concerning Jesus Christ and shown to be precisely fulfilled in every detail in the Gospel accounts of Jesus' life.

Prediction	When Predicted	Fulfilled
His birth of a virgin	Isaiah 7:14 (700 BC)	Matthew 1:24-25
His birth at Bethlehem	Micah 5:2 (700 BC)	Luke 2:4-7
His flight into Egypt	Hosea 11:1 (750 BC)	Matthew 2:15
His being anointed by the Holy Spirit	Isaiah 61:1 (700 BC)	Matthew 4:15-16
His being forsaken by His disciples	Psalm 88:8 (1000 BC)	Mark 14:50
His being rejected by the Jews	Isaiah 53:3 (700 BC)	John 1:11
His being condemned with criminals	Isaiah 53:12 (700 BC)	Luke 22:37
His being cursed on a tree	Deut. 21:23 (1400 BC)	Gal. 3:13
His hands and feet pierced	Psalm 22:16 (1000 BC)	Matt. 27:35
His being buried in a rich man's tomb	Isaiah 53:9 (700 BC)	Matthew 27:57-60
His rising from the dead on the third day	Hosea 6:2 (750 BC)	Luke 24:46

Jesus Christ and the Bible are both called the Word of God.

2. The History of the Nation of Israel

The Bible has predicted the course of Israel's history accurately for the past 3500 years. Here are only a few specific aspects of Israel's history predicted by the Bible long before they occurred:

- Enslavement in Egypt (Genesis 15:13)
- Deliverance with wealth from Egypt (Genesis 15:14)
- Possession of the land of Canaan (Genesis 15:18-20)
- Turning to idolatry (Deuteronomy 32:15-21)
- Assyrian captivity (Amos 5:27; 6:14; 7:17)
- Babylonian captivity (Jeremiah 16:13; 21:10)

- Destruction of the first Temple (2 Chronicles 7:19-22)
- Return from Babylon (Isaiah 6:11-13; 48:20)
- Destruction of the second Temple (Matthew 24:2; Luke 19:43-44)
- Scattered among all nations (Leviticus 26:33-34; Ez. 12:15)
- Persecution and oppression (Leviticus 26:36-39)
- Re-gathering from all nations (Isaiah 11:11-12; Zech. 10:9-10)

3. Claims from the Old Testament Authors

The Old Testament writers claimed to speak for the Lord more than 3800 times. The Bible shows us that the writers and prophets always acted in a way that clearly indicates that they were conscious of their specific calling from the Lord (Ex. 3; Isa. 6; Jer. 1; Jonah 1). Many times the writers state: *"Thus says the Lord," "The word of the Lord came to me"* and *"He said to me."* David could say: *"The Spirit of the Lord spoke by me, and His word was on my tongue* (2 Sam. 23:2)." Zechariah said: *"... hear the law and the words which the Lord of hosts had sent by His Spirit through the former prophets* (Zech. 7:12)."

We find these statements throughout the Old Testament as well as statements that clearly declare God as the speaker. The following are only a few examples:

- Genesis 1:3 – *"Then God said"* appears 9 times only in Genesis 1.

- Exodus 4:12 – *"Now therefore, go, and I will be with your mouth and teach you what you shall say."*

- 2 Samuel 23:2 – *"The Spirit of the Lord spoke by me, and His word was on my tongue."*

- Jeremiah 1:7 – *"And whatever I command you, you shall speak."*

- Ezekiel 1:3 – *"the word of the Lord came expressly to Ezekiel the priest."*

- Ezekiel 2:1 – *"So when I saw it, I fell on my face, and I heard a voice of One speaking. And He said to me, 'Son of man, stand on your feet, and I will speak to you."*

- Ezekiel 2:4 – *"Thus says the Lord God."*

- Micah 3:8 – *"But truly I am full of power by the Spirit of the Lord, and of justice and might, to declare to Jacob his transgression and to Israel his sin."*

- Zechariah 7:12 – *"... the words which the Lord of hosts had sent by His Spirit through the former prophets."*

4. The Testimony of the Bible's unity

Although the Bible consists of two Testaments, together they form a coherent whole. As someone once said: "The New is in the Old contained and the Old is in the New explained." When we consider the unity of the Bible we should realize that the two Testaments were written by forty different writers who came from different backgrounds and lived in different circumstances over a period of 1600 years. These writers were kings, fishermen, shepherds and priests. One was a physician. One was a tax collector. Some were wealthy while others were poor. Some were educated while others had no education.

Each Book of the Bible contributes to the one main theme: mankind needs a Saviour and Jesus Christ is the only Saviour.

The Scriptures clearly agree on every important area of belief. They agree on the Tri-unity of the Godhead, the fall of mankind and salvation by grace through faith. The unity of the Bible is a clear testimony that God inspired the Scriptures.

5. The Testimony from Jesus

Jesus believed that the Scriptures were from God. He called the Old Testament "the word of God" and said that *"the Scripture cannot be broken* (John 10:35)." Jesus spoke of even the least of the Biblical commandments as important, *"I tell the truth, until heaven and earth disappear, not the least smallest letter, not the least stroke of a pen, will by any means disappear until everything is accomplished* (Matt 5:19)." By quoting Scripture in response to Satan's temptation

(Matt. 4), Jesus demonstrated that the Old Testament Scriptures have authority. Jesus quoted frequently from the Old Testament, for instance: Matt. 4:6, 15; Mark 4:12.

6. The Belief of the Apostles

The apostles believed that the Old Testament was from God. Paul declared: *"All Scripture is God-breathed* (2 Tim. 3:16)." Peter wrote that prophecy did not come from *"the will of man, but holy men spoke as they were moved by the Holy Spirit* (2 Pet. 1:21)."

In first Corinthians 2:13 Paul said: *"These things we also speak, not in words which man's wisdom teaches but which the Holy Spirit teaches, comparing spiritual things with spiritual."* In the same book Paul wrote: *"the things that I write to you are the Lord's commandments* (1 Cor. 14:37)."

They frequently quoted from the Old Testament. For instance: Acts 13:22; 15:16 and 17. Also, in 2 Peter 3:15-16, Peter referred to Paul's words as Scripture, and Paul referred to Luke's Gospel as Scripture in first Timothy 5:18. Thus, the New Testament writers believed that both the Old and New Testaments were the inspired Word of God.

7. The Testimony of Millions of Christians

If the Bible is truly the inspired Word of God, then it should change lives. One man testified of how he had once been a thief who picked other people's pockets for a living. One day he picked a man's pocket and, to his disgust, found that he had stolen a pocket Bible instead of a wallet. Since he had the Bible, however, he decided to find out what it was about. He read how Jesus became a man and then died for the sins of all mankind. As he read, the Holy Spirit began to convict him. After just a few days, the thief believed in Jesus as Lord and Saviour, and his life was completely transformed. He returned what he had stolen and found a new occupation. The transformed life of every genuinely born-again believer is a testimony to the power of the inspired Word of God.

Millions of Christians will witness that the Bible has an extra-ordinary influence on their lives and that it is truthful – the One Book that really speaks in a fresh way daily into their lives.

8. Archaeology Confirms the Historical Accuracy of the Bible

The Bible is either true or it is not. And if it is true, then apart from what is said above, there must be evidence in history that will confirm its truthfulness.

We can state with all certainty that no archaeological discovery ever has contradicted any Biblical reference. In fact, Biblical archaeology confirms the historical accuracy of the Bible in phenomenal ways. It has become much easier to refute any false claim against the Bible by means of archaeology, because of the very many discoveries that have been made and those that are frequently being made. These discoveries include ancient Israelite places, situated exactly as described by the Bible as well as ancient non-biblical texts that refer to persons, events, and places which are also stated in the Bible.

The following are only a few of the significant discoveries archaeologists have made:

- Mernetah Stela – an engraved granite slab more than ten feet tall, found in AD 1896. It was carved in 1210 BC, and contains the oldest certain reference to "Israel."

- The Kurkh Monolith Stone found in Kurkh, Turkey (AD 1861). The Assyrians originally carved it in about 852 BC, and the writing on it refers to a battle involving king Ahab, who is also referred to in the Bible (see 1 Kings 16-22).

- The Moabite Stone was found in 1868 in the land of ancient Moabite, now modern Jordan. Inscribed on it in the Moabite language are references to Israelite king Omri and Moabite king Mesha, as well as the covenant name of God, YHWH.

- The ancient Egyptians cities, Pithom and Raamses, built by the Israelites (see Ex. 11:1), were found in AD 1833.

- Saul's mountain stronghold in Gibeah (see 1 Sam. 10:26) was discovered in 1922-23 by William F. Albright.

- The Chester Beatty Papyri were found in AD 1930, and they contain some of the oldest copies of portions of the Old and New Testament Books.

- The very significant Dead Sea Scrolls were found in 1947. These Scrolls contain manuscripts of every book in the Hebrew Bible except the book of Esther, and date back to the 2nd century BC.

> How can we really know that the Bible is the inspired Word of God? We find the answer in the words of Jesus: *"If any man wills to do, he will know* (John 7:17).*"* When you respond rightly to God's Word and do what it says, then you will certainly realize that it has to be His Word.

The Canonization of the Bible

The standard by which the Books of the Bible where chosen as inspired is called canonization. The word "canon" comes from the Greek word *"kanon"* which means "measuring reed." It denotes a standard that one uses to measure something.

It is important to realize that the canonization of the Bible was a laborious process of carefully and prayerfully scrutinizing the different books in order to determine if they were really inspired. Canonization was not a once off event.

The canonization of the Bible consisted of the following criteria:

1. An apostle or a close associate of an apostle had to be the author. For example, the Gospel of John was accepted because the apostle John wrote it. However, although the apostles did not write them, the gospels of Luke and Mark were accepted because Luke had travelled with Paul and Mark was a close associate of Peter (see 1 Pet. 5:13).

2. The content of the book had to agree with what the Church already knew to be Scripture. If there was any obvious conflict the book was not accepted.

3. The book had to be unanimously accepted by the Church. The Church as a whole had to recognize that God had inspired the book. If only a small portion of the Church believed that a book was inspired, then it was not placed in the canon.

DISCOVERING THE MOST AMAZING BOOK

4. The book had to have spiritual and devotional quality that revealed divine inspiration. In other words, it had to minister grace to the believer and change people's lives.

The Books that met this standard are seen as the inspired Word of God and were included in the canon of the Bible.

We find indications of collections of books already in the Old Testament: Exodus 24:4-7; Deuteronomy 31:24-26; Daniel 9:2 (refers to Jer. 25:12) and Isaiah 34:16.

Apparently Ezra and Nehemiah compiled the canonical books of the Old Testament (400 BC). In one of the Apocrypha Books (300 BC) we read of the three divisions of the Old Testament (Torah, Prophets, and Writings). So, it seems that the collection of Old Testament Books was already completed before 300 BC.

At the Jewish Council of Jamnia (AD 90) the Jews accepted the 39 Books of the Old Testament as canonical. In AD 170 Melito of Sardis also listed the 39 Books as inspired.

In AD 367 Athanasius gave a list of 27 Books of the New Testament which he believed were inspired. It was the collection of the 27 Books that we have today in our New Testament (only in a different order).

At the councils of Hippo (AD 393) and Carthage (AD 397) both the canons of the Old and New testaments, as we have them today, were accepted.

Now it is credible to say that just as God supervised the inspiration of the Bible He also supervised the canonization of the Bible – the 66 Books that are in the canon of the Bible are there by divine guidance.

We should realize and believe that the Bible is the infallible Word of God. That must form the solid foundation upon which we base our faith. Consider this: if any part of the Bible is doubtful, then that will make the whole Bible doubtful. Even if you don't understand parts of the Bible choose to wholeheartedly believe that the Bible is the authoritative written Word of God to mankind. The Bible should be the final authority on all matters of faith, doctrine, life and ministry. The rule that reigns is always: What does the Bible say?

There are also Apocryphal (meaning hidden or lost) books to the Old and New Testaments. The Apocryphal books were placed in the Septuagint merely as an addendum. Some of these books are accepted by the Roman Catholic Church as canonical, but they were never accepted as canonical by the Jews and were NOT included in the canon of the Protestant Bible. These books could be seen as merely ordinary writings of people, but NOT inspired by God. Although these books are not inspired they could serve us in determining historical events and social concerns of the time in which they were written.

The Old Testament Apocrypha was written well after the close of the Old Testament; they date from about the third century before Christ until roughly AD 100. The following are the fourteen Apocrypha books of the Old Testament:

1 Esdras

- 2 Esdras
- Tobit
- Judith
- Baruch (with the Letter of Jeremiah)
- 1 Maccabees
- 2 Maccabees
- Bel and the Dragon
- Prayer of Manasseh
- Susanna
- Additions to the Book of Esther
- Wisdom of Solomon
- Song of the Three Young Men
- Ecclesiasticus (Sirach)

Apart from the fourteen Apocrypha books in the Old Testament there were works produced by unknown authors from about the second century AD to perhaps as late as the ninth century. These writings were largely modelled after the New Testament Gospels and Letters, and sought to supplement, correct, or even replace established books of the New Testament.

The following are some of the New Testament Apocrypha:

- The Armenian Gospel of the Infancy
- Protevangelium of James
- Gospel of Thomas
- Gospel of Nicodemus
- Gospel of Bartholomew
- Gospel According to Peter
- Gospel of the Egyptians
- Acts of Paul
- Acts of Peter
- Acts of Andrew
- Acts of Philip
- Acts of Thomas
- Paul's Letter to the Laodiceans
- Apocalypse of Paul
- Apocalypse of Peter
- Apocalypse of Thomas

Part Two

The Bible: Composition and Message

Chapter two

The Bible – Composition and Message

As we know by now, the Bible is not simply one Book, but a collection of 66 Books, which form an entire library. The name Bible is derived from the Latin *Biblia,* which means books or collection of books. The Bible consists of an Old and New Testament; both are small libraries on their own. These Testaments are interdependent; each is incomplete without the other. Together they form a coherent whole – it has a unifying theme or storyline running from Genesis to Revelation. The Old Testament is also known as the Hebrew Bible and the New Testament is the Christian Scriptures originally written in Greek and some parts of Matthew in Aramaic.

> The Bible is more than a collection of texts, paragraphs, chapters, or even books; it is a spiritual organism, in which each part is related to, and is dependent on, every other part, the whole being pervaded by spiritual life. – Graham Scroggie

The Library of the Bible

The Old Testament consists of 39 Books, while the New Testament has 27 Books; altogether we have 66 inspired Books in the complete Bible. In the same way that a public library does, the Library of the Bible reflects the unique personalities, perspectives, and writing styles of the different authors as well as the different types of literature that they used.

The chronology of Old Testament history is different from the order in which the books appear. The order of the Books in the

Hebrew Bible is also different to that of our English Bibles. The Books in our English Bible (Protestant Canon) are arranged in terms of **Law**: Genesis to Deuteronomy (although these books are also regarded as history), then **history**: Joshua to Esther, then **poetry**: Job to Song of Songs, then **prophecy**: Isaiah to Malachi. The prophets are further divided into **Major Prophets**: Isaiah, Jeremiah, Ezekiel and Daniel, and the **Minor Prophets**: Hosea to Malachi. The terms "major" and "minor" do not refer to importance, but merely to the size of the books.

The order of the New Testament Books is also not chronological, but rather logical. We first have the **Gospels** (where we meet with the Saviour): Matthew to John, then the **early Church history** (where we find the response in faith of the first believers): Acts, then the **Letters of Paul to different early Christian churches** (doctrine, teaching to the churches): Romans to 2 Thessalonians, then Paul's **Pastoral Letters** to individual pastors (counsel to local church leaders): 1 Timothy to Philemon, then the General Letters, or Christian Hebrew Letters (mainly addressed to Hebrew Christians): Hebrews to Jude, and then the **end time events** (the unveiled purposes of God): Revelation.

However, although the Books of the Old and New Testaments are not in chronological order, it will never change the message of the Bible.

Covenant and Testament

Before we embark on our journey through Biblical history, also known as redemptive history, let us, in short, look at these terms: Covenant and Testament. Knowing the difference between these two terms will be helpful in understanding the message of the Bible, because the Bible is *per se* a Book of covenants.

The Difference between Covenant and Testament	
Covenant	**Testament**
Definition: A formal, solemn, and binding agreement between two or more persons to do or refrain from doing some act; a contract.	Definition: A will; a formal declaration, usually in writing, of a person's wishes to the disposition of his property after death.
The Hebrew term for covenant is *berit*, which means "to bond or fetter." In Biblical terms, covenant, emphasizes a **relationship** (e.g. Ex. 6:7) based, firstly on God's grace and, secondly on mutual agreement and commitments.	The Greek term for testament is *diatheke*, which means "will, testament;" some suggest that it could mean covenant also.
The Old Covenant primarily records God's relationship and dealings with the Jews. No death of a testator was involved in the establishment of the Old Covenant, so it cannot be a testament.	The New Testament can be seen as both a covenant and a testament, because: (1) by His death and resurrection Jesus established the New Covenant; and (2) after His death, resurrection, and ascension Jesus in the form of the New Covenant, left a glorious inheritance to all those who will believe in Him, and it is in writing.

Now after looking at the definitions of these two terms we realize that the major part of the Bible has been misnamed the "Old *Testament.*" Apparently when the Bible was translated into Latin the translators used the word *testamentum,* which could have meant either "covenant" or "testament."

The only place the term "Old Testament" is found in the Bible is in 2 Corinthians 3:14 (at least in the *New King James Version*). The term should have been translated as "Old *Covenant.*"

The terms covenant and testament are generally used interchangeably; for convenience sake we will do the same throughout our study.

A Short Chronological Survey of the Bible

A chronological survey of the Bible is important in order to gain a proper understanding of the Bible's message and the unfolding plan of Redemption. In this survey we will only touch on some of the main moments within Biblical history. Together with the synopses of the Bible Books this survey will certainly help to colour in the big picture of the message of the Bible. While walking through Biblical history we will come to realize that "all history is dominated by two facts, namely, man's sin and God's grace, and the very reason of history is the purpose of God to conquer sin by saving the sinner."[2]

Also, two life-altering events stand out in the history of mankind: (1) humanity's fall in the Garden of Eden and (2) Christ's coming to save fallen humanity.

Therefore, it is important to read the Old Covenant as history (His-story); God's dealings with the nation of Israel to work out the salvation of humanity. And while we read the Old Covenant we should keep the following in mind that will help us to interpret the message correctly: (1) God in His mercy and grace desires to be in a relationship with human beings; (2) therefore, He chose one man, Abraham, as the patriarch of the nation of Israel to work through in order to rescue mankind; (3) God knew that Abraham, his family, and their posterity as the solution-bearers were also part of the problem (because they were sinful), and that they would mess things up in all sorts of ways; (4) in God's dealings with Israel throughout Biblical history, we should realize that (a) the Israelites were sinful and often rebelled against God, (b) while God actually lovingly and graciously desires to save them and be their God, and (c) God as a righteous God had to deal with their sin. This will help us to realize that God is not an angry God who wants to punish people, but rather, people by their wrong choices and rebellion against God bring harm to themselves.

Biblical history spans the entire course of time from the creation of the universe, and all that is in it, to the era of the early Christian church in the first century.

The dates that we use are estimated and not precise.

---

[2]   Graham Scroggie, *The Unfolding Drama of Redemption*, p. 79.

❖ Beginnings: Creation 4000+ BC – 2100 BC

The Bible begins by introducing the Triune, Creator God to us, and then gives us an account of God's Creation. The Hebrew word used for God in Genesis 1:1 is *Elohim*, a plural pronoun suggesting the Trinity within the Godhead.

The first verse of the Bible is a foundational verse – it not only reveals the Triune, creative and miracle working God, but this one verse also refutes all of man's false philosophies regarding the origin and meaning of the world. Among many other things, it refutes atheism and evolution; the atheist says there is no God, but the Bible begins by declaring God as the Creator of the universe and everything in it. (This is one of the reasons why this most important book of the Bible is so much under attack.)

All that God created was "good;" however, human beings are distinguished from the rest of creation because they are created in the image and likeness of God. They were created to be God's representatives on earth, and to be in relationship with Him.

Adam was first created by God and then He made Eve to be Adam's wife and helper. Adam means man and Eve, "the mother of all living." God abundantly provided for them by placing them in a specially prepared garden called Eden (meaning Delight) where they enjoyed fellowship with God. God gave them only one command: they were not to eat from the tree of the knowledge of good and evil. Because Adam and Eve were created with innocence and freewill, God had to test their obedience. Freedom of choice untested is merely theory, not reality. Therefore, God allowed Satan in the form of a serpent to test them. Instead of trusting and obeying God they fell for the deception and lie of the serpent. This is called the "fall of man." Their sin brought a curse upon creation and they were cast out of Eden.

Now, paradise lost – sin, sickness, sorrow, hardship and even death entered the scene. But, praise God, He declared in Genesis 3:15: *"And I will cause hostility between you (the serpent) and the woman (Eve), and between your offspring (unbelievers) and her offspring (believers through Jesus). He (Jesus) will strike your (Satan's) head, and you will strike his heel (the crucifixion)."* This verse is known as the *protevangelium,* a Latin word, which means First Gospel. Both a gospel (good news) with a promise, and a curse proclaimed by God Himself. In the First Gospel there is a clearly discernible divine purpose and plan. God gave us a promise that He will send a Redeemer, and revealed His plan to defeat Satan and offer salvation to mankind through Jesus Christ. Genesis 3:15 proclaims the doom of the devil and the hope of mankind. In this verse we see two seeds: the serpent's, the children of unbelief; and the woman's, the children of faith. The seed of the woman is pre-eminently Christ through the line of Abraham, Isaac and Jacob (see Gal. 3:16). We read that the bruising of the one seed is to the head, which would be fatal, and to the heel of the other, which will not end in destruction. On the Cross Jesus Christ fatally wounded the devil, and there the devil's attempt to destroy Him failed completely (see Col. 2:15). The New Testament portrays Jesus Christ as the "Second Adam" whose obedience and sacrificial death on the cross undo Adam's disobedience (Rom. 15:12-21; 1 Cor. 15:45).

Thus, Genesis 3:15 gives us the unifying theme of the Bible – this prophetic and symbolic reference to Jesus Christ and His Cross carries in it the whole purpose, promise, and power of redemption. The rest of what is told through the Bible is seen as a footnote to this verse. From this verse onwards we can find pictures, types, shadows and prophetic predictions of Jesus Christ as the Redeemer basically on every page of the Old Testament – as salt is in seawater, so is Jesus in the Old Testament.

The reality of the Fall makes redemption a necessity – there can be no redemption if there is no sin. However, the redemption of mankind is not of necessity, but of grace. God is under no obligation to save mankind, He does so by His grace alone.

Immediately after Adam and Eve had sinned *"the eyes of both of them were opened, and they knew that they were naked; and they sewed fig leaves together and made themselves coverings* (Gen. 3:7)." They became self-conscious and attempted to put themselves right in relation to one another and God. In verse 8 we read that *"Adam and his wife hid themselves from the presence of the Lord God among the trees of the garden,"* because of their guilt and fear of punishment. Later in verse 21 we read that *"the Lord God made tunics of skin and clothed them."* The covering of fig leaves can never do justice for man's naked sinfulness before God. Adam and Eve's attempt to cover themselves speaks of man's own "good" and self-centred attempts to justify himself before a holy God. The prophet Isaiah declares: *"All our righteousnesses are like filthy rags (64:6)."* In verse 21 we see for the first time that sacrifice, the shedding of blood is needed to cover sin. The animals from which the skins were taken had to be killed – sacrificed. Also, the innocent suffered for the guilty. The covering of the skins symbolizes atonement. This gracious act of God was typical and prophetic of the (innocent) Sacrifice that was to be eventually offered on the Cross.

As we journey through Biblical history, we see that sadly, the curse of sin was passed down to all of mankind. While he was warned by God not to allow sin to reign in his life, Cain was the first man who let sin reign in him; he was *"of the wicked one* (1 John 3:12)."* His attitude towards God in his weak and unthankful offering and the killing of his innocent brother revealed the seed of the serpent. In his deed of murdering his brother, the real nature of the wicked one, as "a murderer from the beginning," had come openly to light: so that already there had sprung up that contrast of two distinct seeds within the human race, which runs through the entire history of humanity.[3]

Another son was born to Adam and Eve, and because they regarded him as taking the place of murdered Abel they called him Seth, which means "appointed." Abel is seen as a type of the Lord in His death, while Seth typifies the Lord in His resurrection.

With Cain and Seth, two great civilizations developed on earth. We are introduced first to the Cainite civilization which centred on Cain's lineage – a godless and lawless civilization that was progressive in industry and art, but divorced from God (speaking of the seed of the serpent). Side by side with the Cainite culture a Sethite civilization developed, which centred on Seth, Enoch, Methuselah, and Noah – godly men, who sought to walk with God (see Gen. 4:26).

However, even Seth's posterity had backslidden: *"the sons of God (Sethites) saw the daughters of men (Cainites), that they were beautiful; and they took wives for themselves of all whom they chose* (Gen. 6:2)."* (Cain's lineage was that of the serpent and Seth's that of the woman; they were not supposed to mingle, as the Church is not supposed to mingle with the world.)

---

3   Keil & Delitzsh, *Commentary on the Old Testament, Genesis*, e-Sword

> When we consider the meaning of the different names in the lineage of Adam through Seth, in Genesis 5, we see the promise of the Redeemer revealed:
>
> 1. Adam – Man
> 2. Seth – Appointed
> 3. Enosh – Mortal
> 4. Cainan – Sorrow
> 5. Mahalalel – The blessed God
> 6. Jared – to come down
> 7. Enoch – Teaching
> 8. Methuselah – His death shall bring
> 9. Lamech – The despairing
> 10. Noah – Comfort
>
> Thus: Man appointed to mortal sorrow, the blessed God [will] come down teaching, His death shall bring the despairing comfort.

After about 1500 years of human history, sin increased in such a wicked way that God planned to destroy everyone on earth (Gen. 6:1-7). However, in the midst of all the wickedness there was one man, Noah, who found grace in the eyes of the Lord because he was a just man who walked with God (Gen. 6:8, 9). Because of Noah's righteousness, God made a covenant with him and his family. He instructed Noah to build an Ark to save his family and pairs of every kind of animal. Then God caused it to rain for forty days and forty nights – the Flood. In the story of the Flood we find a picture of salvation. Because of Noah's faith, God saved him from destruction. And if we have faith in God, we, too can be saved from destruction.

After the floodwaters subsided, Noah and his family left the Ark to start a new humanity. *"God blessed Noah and his sons, and said to them: 'Be fruitful and multiply, and fill the earth* (Gen. 9:1)." Noah's three sons, Shem, Ham and Japheth, became the fathers of a new race. In Genesis 10, which is known as the "Table of Nations," we find the names of all the descendants of the three sons of Noah.

Noah's descendants did multiply. And in Genesis 11:1 we read that everyone spoke a single language. Verse 2 continues and tells us that they journeyed from the east and that they settled on a plain in the land of Shinar; and from what follows it is clear that they intended to remain there. They decided to build a city, and a tower that could reach the heavens, a testimony to their own greatness. This really speaks of their open rebellion against God, their independence and false security, and their trying to approach God on their own self-serving terms to grab divine power. Herein we see that the flood had destroyed sinners but not sin.

God confused them by giving them different languages, making it virtually impossible for them to continue with their great project. As a result, the people soon dispersed and spread out over all the earth, which is what God had commanded them to do in the first place. If God had left them to do as they intended, what would have been the course of human history? God's intervention at Babel preserved a line which eventually led to Calvary and redemption for mankind.

The following diagram explains the significance of the Tower of Babel, looking at it in contrast to the Day of Pentecost, which is its counterpoint.

Genesis 11	Acts 2
Babel, the city built by people	Jerusalem, the city built by God
The people reached for heaven	God the Holy Spirit descended from heaven
One language spoken by everybody	Sixteen different languages spoken by different people
God confused them by giving them different languages; the result was they were scattered	People came from all over; it was the unifying event establishing the Church of Christ

❖ God's Chosen Family: 2100-1800 BC

Again, with each generation after Noah, people drifted further and further from God (this shows us the power that sin has on man). Then God chose a man named Abram (father of elevation), a descendant of Noah's son Shem, in order to ultimately redeem and bless mankind.

The ancestral history of Israel begins in *"Ur of the Chaldeans* (Gen. 11:28),*"* the southernmost part of Mesopotamia near the Persian Gulf. (Ur was located in present-day Iraq.) The Chaldeans were idolaters, worshipping the celestial bodies, mainly the moon.

From Ur, Abram's father, Terah, moved his family to the city of Haran on the bend of the Euphrates River in north-western Mesopotamia (which means "the middle of the rivers," *meso* – "middle" and *potamia* – "rivers," referring to the Tigris and Euphrates Rivers). Abram called by God from a heathen nation, migrated from Haran and eventually settled in southern Canaan (modern Israel), near Hebron.

In His sovereign wisdom God called Abraham and told him to leave his home country and go to a new land (Canaan) that He would show him. Abraham responded in faith to God's call. Hebrews 11:8 says: *"By faith Abraham obeyed when he was called to go out to the place which he would receive as an inheritance. And he went out, not knowing where he was going."* That's faith! The apostle Paul says, *"we walk by faith, not by sight* (2 Cor. 5:7).*"*

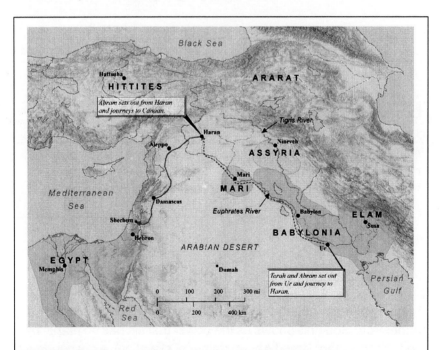

Diagram 1
Abraham Travels to Canaan (Used by permission, David P Barrett, www.biblemapper.com)

God promised to bless Abraham, to make him into a great nation, that his descendants would be as many as the dust of the earth (Gen. 13:16), and that through him all the families on the earth will be blessed. God sealed His promise with signs – circumcision and He changed both Abram's name and his wife's name. Abram became Abraham which means "father of a multitude," and his wife's name Sarai was changed to Sarah, which means "princess or fruitful."

Abraham became the great patriarch of Israel, the only man ever to be called a "friend of God." As somebody once said: "Abraham is one of the greatest men God ever made." He was a man of great faith also known as the father of faith – the first man that the Bible mentions who truly believed in God. This man is referred to more in the New Testament than any other Bible character, always in conjunction with faith. Abraham is the walking definition of faith. Although Abraham was a man of faith, he also made mistakes, for instance, he lied about his wife. This shows us that Abraham was a sinner just as we are, and that a person of faith is not exempted from the possibility of sinning. However, in different ways his faith was challenged and disciplined to the point of his perfect surrender to all the will of God.

In Genesis 15 we read that God cut a covenant with Abraham as a sign and seal of His commitment to fulfil His promise. In the cutting of the covenant we see that: (1) blood must be shed in order to cut or seal a covenant; (2) the innocent has to suffer in being (3) a sacrifice in order to (4) bring salvation to the guilty.

However, when the answer of the promised son was slow in coming, Sarah gave Abraham her servant Hagar, thinking that she shall obtain children by Hagar. A son was born to Abraham by Hagar, who was named Ishmael (Gen. 16:1-4, 15). From this situation we learn that often if God's promise is slow in coming, then we tend to do things (mistakenly) in order to help God.

> Hagar was Sarah's Egyptian slave woman that Abraham obtained during his visit to Egypt (Gen. 12:10; 16:1). God has set us free from Egypt, enslavement to sin. Thus, in Christian terms, Hagar represents a "worldly attachment" that Abraham was not supposed to bring out of Egypt – when God has delivered you from "Egypt," don't bring "attachments" with you, *Let us lay aside every weight and the sin which so easily ensnares us* (Heb. 12:2)."

Because God had promised Abraham a legitimate son by his wife, Sarah, Abraham continued to place his trust in God. After an agonizing time of waiting, and an interplay of different circumstances, God finally gave Abraham and his wife, their promised son, Isaac. The Bible says that Isaac was born *"in the set time of which God had spoken to him [Abraham]."* This shows us that there is always a set time for God's purposes to be accomplished (and God doesn't need our help to fulfil His promises). Abraham was 100 years old and Sarah was 91. They named the boy Isaac, meaning "laughter" because both Abraham and Sarah initially laughed at the idea that they would have a child in their old age. Apparently Abraham's laugh indicated delight, but Sarah's doubt.

It is known that Ishmael is the founder of the Arab nation and Isaac became one of the patriarchs of the Jewish nation. To this very day, the Arabs remain enemies of the Jews (Gen. 17:15-22; 21 21:1-5; Gal. 4:21-31).

> Ishmael represents the factor of faith that the greatest enemy of God's best is something good.

As we have mentioned, circumcision was one of the signs of God's covenant with Abraham. From then on, all male descendants of Abraham (through Isaac) were circumcised at eight days of age, as a sign that they were part of God's people (Gen. 17:1-14). Circumcision was a requirement for the Jews, but the apostle Paul made it abundantly clear that other peoples did not need to follow this requirement (Rom. 2:25-29; 4:9-12; Gal. 5:2-6).

A few years later God tested Abraham's faith by telling him to sacrifice Isaac. This was the ultimate demonstration not only of Abraham's faithful trust in God but also his complete self-surrender unto God. As someone once said: "In your surrender [unto Christ] you will find victory." Abraham's faith had been disciplined, and we can suggest that in his will Abraham had sacrificed Isaac before they reached the mountain. Isaac was the son of promise, the only son born to Abraham and Sarah, the only visible hope that God would fulfil his promise to bless Abraham with a multitude of descendants.

Now, Abraham took Isaac up on the mountain believing that God would provide a lamb. And He did, at the last moment, when Abraham proved his faith-obedience, God provided a ram as a substitution for Isaac's life (see Gen. 22:1-19). In the same way, God sent His promised Messiah (Son) to die as a sacrifice in our place (Heb. 10:10). Also, Isaac is known as the submissive son who was willing to be sacrificed, a type of Jesus who was completely submissive to the will of God the Father.

Abraham also made sure that the promised line of redemption was safeguarded. He arranged that a wife for his son Isaac should be found who was of the family of his brother Nahor who settled in Mesopotamia. *"And I will make you swear by the Lord, the God of heaven and the God of earth, that you will not take a wife for my son from the daughters of the Canaanites, among whom I dwell, but you shall go to my country and to my family, and take a wife for my son Isaac* (Gen. 24:3, 4)." The Canaanites had been cursed (Gen. 9:25) and the Covenant could not be fulfilled in their line.

Later, Isaac's wife, Rebekah, gave birth to twin boys, Esau and Jacob. Although Esau was the elder of the two brothers, God purposed that Jacob should take precedence over him: *"the older shall serve the younger* (Gen. 25:23)." Esau sold his birthright to Jacob for a bowl of soup. Rebekah and Jacob then tricked his father into granting him the blessings that belonged to Esau. However, the way in which the birthright and the blessing were obtained was wrong – Esau was indifferent to his birthright and Jacob coveted it, and Isaac planned that Esau should have the blessing (Gen. 27:1-4), while Rebekah plotted to get it for Jacob (Gen. 27:6-10). All this made necessary the severe disciplining of Jacob to become the man God wanted him to be for carrying forward His redeeming purpose. As we have seen: God's purposes must be fulfilled in God's time, and in God's way.

Being afraid of his brother, Jacob fled to the homeland of his ancestors (Mesopotamia) where he lived with and worked for his uncle Laban. While working for Laban, Jacob married his daughters Leah and Rachel. They and their servants bore Jacob twelve sons, who founded the twelve tribes of Israel: Reuben, Simeon, Levi (whose tribe became the priestly tribe), Judah (from whom Jesus was descended), Issachar, Zebulun, Dan, Naphtali, Gad, Asher, Joseph and Benjamin (Gen. 35:23-26). He eventually reconciled with his brother Esau and returned to Canaan. On the way he encountered God face-to-face at Penuel (Gen. 32:30, 31). God changed Jacob's name to Israel. Jacob means "one who grabs by the heel or supplanter (self-reliant, self-seeking)," and Israel means "prince of God" (based on Gen. 32:28, some suggest Israel means "one who struggles with God"). The name Israel, for the Jewish nation, is actually from the new name God gave to Jacob at the ford of Jabbok. This explains why Jacob's descendants are often called the children of Israel. His twelve sons became the ancestors of the twelve tribes of Israel. God reaffirmed to Jacob the covenant that He made with his father and grandfather.

"Israel [Jacob] loved Joseph more than all his children, because he was the son of his old age (Gen. 37:3)." Because of that Joseph's brothers hated him. And when Joseph told them the dreams he had of becoming master over them, they hated him even more. Driven by hatred and jealousy his brothers plotted against him to kill him, but they eventually sold him to slave traders headed to Egypt (Gen. 37:12-36). However, God was with Joseph and blessed him even while he was a slave in Egypt. Through a complicated interplay of circumstances, Joseph was brought before Pharaoh to interpret his dreams. With God-given wisdom, Joseph explained to Pharaoh that the dream predicted seven years of abundance followed by seven years of famine. Joseph even suggested a plan to prepare for the coming events. After that, Pharaoh made Joseph second in command of all of Egypt. During the famine, Joseph's brothers were forced to travel to Egypt to buy grain from Joseph. When they first journeyed to Egypt to buy grain, Joseph recognized them, but his brothers did not recognize their long-lost brother.

With their second visit to buy grain, Joseph could not restrain himself and eventually he revealed his identity to them. His brothers were understandably shocked and troubled, but Joseph responded to them with these comforting and revealing words: *"But now, do not therefore be grieved or angry with yourselves because you sold me here; for God sent me before you to preserve life … And God sent me before you to preserve a posterity for you in the earth, and to save your lives by a great deliverance. So now it was not you who send me here, but God …as for you, you meant evil against me; but God meant it for good, in order to bring it about as it is this day, to save many people alive* (Gen. 45:5, 7; 50:20)." The message of Joseph's story is summed up in one verse in the New Testament: *"And we know that all things work together for good to them that love God, to them who are called according to His purposes* (Rom. 8:28)." Joseph's story boldly underscores the providence of God. God is sovereign over the circumstances of our lives, and there is no situation so bad that He cannot redeem and bring good from it. In the account of Joseph we also identify the intimate relationship between divine sovereignty and human responsibility.

Moreover, Jacob's much-loved son, Joseph, is a type of Jesus, the Son of God's love. By "type" we mean that Joseph's life "foreshadowed" what was going to happen with Jesus.

The following chart indicates the many parallels between Joseph's life and that of Jesus Christ.

Parallels between Joseph's life and that of Jesus		
1. The beloved Son	Genesis 37:3	Matthew 3: 17
2. Hated by his brothers	Genesis 37:4	John 15:25
3. His kingship rejected	Genesis 37:8	Luke 19:4
4. Conspired against	Genesis 37:18	Matthew 27:1
5. He was stripped of his clothes	Genesis 37:23	Matthew 27:28
6. Sold for silver	Genesis 37:28	Matthew 27:15
7. Went into and came out of Egypt	Genesis 37:36	Matthew 2:14, 15
8. Two others were bound with him, one of whom was saved, while the other was destroyed.	Genesis 40	Luke 23:32-43

9. Hard to find anything negative against Joseph's character; Jesus was sinless	Genesis 40:15	John 8:46
10. Released by the King	Psalm 105:20	Acts 2:24
11. Godly wisdom	Genesis 41:39	Colossians 2:3
12. All power given unto Him	Genesis 41:55	Matthew 28:18
13. To be obeyed	Genesis 41:55	John 2:5
14. Served all nations	Genesis 41:57	Isaiah 49:6
15. Not known by his brothers	Genesis 42:8	John 1:10, 11
16. Made known through an interpreter	Genesis 42:23	John 16:13, 14
17. A fruitful bough	Genesis 49:22	John 15:5
18. All of God	Genesis 45:8	Acts 2:23

In the end of the day, Joseph convinced his entire family, including his father to move to Egypt. Now we realize that Jacob gave Israel their name and Joseph saved them from starvation preserving the line of covenant promise from destruction. At every turn in the line of the promised Redeemer, we see God turning the wickedness of man to account for the fulfilment of His redeeming purpose and promise.

The sons of Israel and their families stayed in Egypt for about four hundred years, and their numbers grew greatly.

[Job probably lived during the time of the patriarchs (Abraham, Isaac, and Jacob). Thus, fitting into this time-period in Biblical history. The book of Job tells us about the severe sufferings of the man Job and how he remained steadfast in his faith in spite of all his troubles. In the end he acknowledges the sovereignty of God in his life and receives back much more than he had before his trials.]

The following chart gives us some fascinating facts about the patriarchal family.

Some Fascinating Facts about the Patriarchal Family

1. God called Abraham from a heathen people, the Chaldeans, so that he would have had no natural or moral right on Him. In this we also see that God is sovereign in whom He chooses, and well able to transform a "heathen" into "a friend of God."

2. Abraham's faith was disciplined so that he could eventually surrender himself fully onto God. And as someone once said: "Abraham blazed tracks which his followers trod."

3. Out of Abraham's life and faith three great men of faith rose to prominence and purpose – Isaac, Jacob and Joseph.

3. The Bible doesn't say too much about Isaac, the promised son, but he was the necessary link between Abraham, the root of the nation of Israel, and Jacob the father of the twelve sons, whose descendants became the nation of Israel. Isaac was also typical of the promised Messiah:

   (a) He was predicted before he was born
   (b) He was supernaturally begotten
   (c) He was the "only" son of the covenant
   (d) He was the sacrificial lamb
   (e) In that Isaac was made the type of Abraham's spiritual descendants: Christians, as contrasted with his descendants under the law, the nation of Israel (see Gal. 4:21-31).
   (f) Isaac is a picture of the man of rest, also typifying Christ, our (perfect) Man of rest.

4. Jacob's life is an example of a spiritual man, a man of faith, because he earnestly sought God and spiritual values and blessings. He also represents fruitfulness, his twelve sons became the heads of the twelve tribes of Israel.

5. Joseph is a type of Christ in his life of suffering and glory. In Joseph we have faith, sonship, service, and reigning blended together.

6. These men were chosen, tested and trained in order to be the patriarchs of God's chosen people.

❖ The Birth of the nation Israel: 1800-1406 BC

Before we look at the Exodus, the following questions remain: Why did the Israelites not go back to their own land after the famine was over? And, why did a loving God allow His people to live in slavery for approximately 400 years?

The reasons are obvious:

1. The suffering from slavery under the Egyptians was foretold by God to Abraham many years before it actually happened. *"Know certainly that your descendants will be strangers in a land that is not theirs, and will serve them, and they will afflict them four hundred years. And also the nation whom they serve I will judge; afterward they shall come out with great possessions (Gen. 15:13-14)."*

2. God further revealed to Abraham: *"But in the fourth generation they shall return here, for the iniquity of the Amorites is not yet complete (Gen. 15:16)."* God had to wait until the Amorites became so bad that it would be an act of justice and judgment to remove them from the Promised Land and let the Israelites in.

3. Goshen, where they settled, was a fertile piece of land in the Nile delta; food was in abundance to feed a growing nation.

4. While in slavery, they learned about the horrors of slavery – physical slavery is a by-product of spiritual slavery. And, if there is no slavery, then there is no need for a deliverer and deliverance. The Egyptian slavery of Israel typifies the slavery of human beings to the enemy of their souls, the devil, and their need of a Deliverer and deliverance.

The Book of Exodus records the story of the Israelites' deliverance from Egyptian slavery and their journey to Mount Sinai. This took place approximately 1440 BC.

> The Israelites were literally in slavery; without Christ, we are spiritually in slavery to our sin. Moses is a type of Jesus Christ, our great Liberator.

Many years after Joseph's death a new Pharaoh arose in Egypt who did not know of all Joseph had done. He oppressed and used the Israelites as slaves, because he was afraid they might rebel against him. The cry of the enslaved Israelites *"went up to God* (Ex. 2:33).*"* God had not forgotten His covenant with Israel's patriarchs. To save His chosen people God had to raise up a strong leader. Moses, one of the greatest leaders of all God's people was that leader. The interesting parallel that both Moses and Christ faced the threat of death as infants, and both were saved to accomplish a great redemption and establish a blood covenant between God and His people, identifies Moses as a type of Christ. Moses' name is mentioned more than seven hundred times in the Bible; a clear indication of the prominence and importance of this outstanding leader of God.

When we consider the life of Moses in three periods of forty years, we realize how God prepared Moses to be the deliverer of His people. In the first forty years the main lesson God taught Moses was: "Moses, you are nobody."

Through the interplay of some unusual circumstances Moses was raised in the palace of Pharaoh (see Ex. 1-2:10). Perhaps it was because of this that he could have thought that he was somebody special (because he was actually a prince in the household of Pharaoh). But around the time that he was forty years old, God apparently succeeded in convincing him that he was really nobody (see Ex. 2:11-15). When Moses failed to deliver the people by killing an Egyptian, God showed him that he is nobody and that deliverance does not come by human power or might.

In the second forty year period of Moses' life, God had to take Egypt out of Moses before he could use him to bring His people out of Egypt. After Moses killed the Egyptian, he fled to the land of Midian where he lived for forty years. Eventually, Moses got married and tended the sheep of his father-in-law. One day he led the flock to the back of the desert and came to Horeb, where he had an encounter with God – he saw an acacia bush burning with fire but it was not consumed. Because of the intense heat in that desert, these bushes usually catch fire and will be consumed in a few seconds. However, this time the bush was not consumed; it kept burning. When Moses *"turned aside and see this great sight, why the bush does not burn ... God called to him from the midst of the bush and said, 'Moses, Moses!' And he said, 'Here I am.' Then He said, 'Do not draw near this place. Take your sandals off your feet, for the place where you stand is holy ground.' Moreover He said, 'I am the God of your father – the God of Abraham, the God of Isaac, and the God of Jacob ...* (Ex. 3:4-6)." In this passage, God goes on to tell Moses that the important thing is not that he (Moses) has seen the problem of the slavery of Israel. The important thing is not his compassion or desire to do something about this slavery. God tells Moses at the burning bush: (1) what really matters is that the God of Moses has seen the problem and He will do something about that problem and (2) "Moses you are now somebody because I have chosen you and I am with you." (The bush burning without being consumed is also a picture of the Christian who is filled with the presence and fire of the Holy Spirit, but not consumed [burned out] by it, and the fact that we need the power of the Holy Spirit to fulfil our God-given callings.)

During the third forty year period of Moses' life, after he had been prepared, God used him to deliver the Israelites from Egypt. Now, under the strong leadership of Moses and favoured by God's intervention through an extraordinary series of events – among other things, the ten plagues and the passing through the Red Sea on dry land – the Israelites were miraculously delivered from Egypt.

Moses and his older brother Aaron repeatedly asked Pharaoh to let the Israelites go. Each time Pharaoh refused, God sent a plague upon the Egyptians. The "Passover" was instituted to protect the Israelites from the last plague, the killing of all the first born in Egypt. An unblemished lamb was sacrificed and eaten by each Israelite family, and the blood was sprinkled on the doorposts as a sign to the destroying angel to "pass over" that house (Ex. 12:1-23). Jesus is our "Passover lamb," seeing that we are saved from death by His blood (1 Cor. 5:7; 1 Pet. 1:19). The Israelites also ate unleavened bread because there was no time to let the dough rise. When Pharaoh discovered that his firstborn son was dead, he ordered the Israelites to leave that same day (Ex.12:29-39).

> Why specifically ten plagues? God revealed His person and power through them; it shows us that God is sovereign over Pharaoh and the gods of Egypt. As God says in His own words: "*I will get glory over Pharaoh and all his host, and the Egyptians shall know that I am Lord* (Ex. 14:4)."

The Israelites travelled by divine guidance, God guided them by a pillar of cloud during the day and a pillar of fire during the night (Ex. 13:20-22). This cloud was obviously perceptible to Israel, and it took two different forms. By day it was a cloud, giving shadow from the heat of the sun. By night it was a pillar of fire, giving both light and warmth in the darkness and coldness of the night. By day and by night it provided Israel with divine direction and guidance. When we read Exodus 14:24 we realize that God was present in the cloud. The cloud had a very different meaning for and effect on the Egyptians. For the Egyptians, *"it was a cloud of darkness,"* but to Israel it *"gave light at night* (Ex. 19:20)." This Cloud is a type or picture of the baptism in the Holy Spirit, because:

- God was present in the cloud that came down over the Israelites from above, out of heaven. In the same way, the baptism in the Holy Spirit is the presence of God Himself coming down from heaven over the person who trusts God for this baptism, enveloping and immersing him or her.

- The cloud was not merely an invisible influence, but it was perceptible. The baptism in the Holy Spirit is also perceptible, and the effects it produces can be both seen and heard.

- The cloud provided shadow from the heat by day and light and warmth by night. By means of the baptism in the Holy Spirit the Christian is empowered to overcome "heat" and "darkness" and also receives warmth and comfort from the Holy Spirit.

- The cloud gave the Israelites divine direction and guidance. The Holy Spirit provides leading and divine guidance to the Christian.

- The cloud gave light to the Israelites but was darkness to the Egyptians. The baptism in the Holy Spirit brings divine light to the Christian, but this supernatural experience remains something dark, incomprehensible and even fearful to the unbeliever.

- The cloud came between the Israelites and the Egyptians, separating and protecting God's people from the Egyptians. The baptism in the Holy Spirit decisively separates the Christian from the world and protects him from the sinful influences of the world (in the sense that the Holy Spirit empowers him not to give in to the pressures of the world).

As soon as the Israelites had gone, Pharaoh changed his mind, took his army and pursued after them. The Israelites feared greatly, but Moses said to them: *"Fear not, stand firm, and see the salvation of the Lord, which He will work for you today. For the Egyptians that you see today, you shall never see again. The Lord will fight for you, and you have only to be silent* (Ex. 14:13-14)." The cloud of the Lord moved in between the Egyptian army and Israel, to separate and protect God's people from their enemies. God told Moses to lift up his staff and stretch his hand over the sea and divide it. The Lord then drove the sea back by a strong east wind and made the sea dry land, and the waters were divided. The Israelites miraculously passed through on dry ground (Ex. 14:15-22). The Egyptians who pursued the Israelites were all drowned by the waters that came together again (Ex. 14:23-31).

The passing through the Red Sea is a type or picture of Christian baptism in water, because:

- Israel's passing through the Red Sea was made possible only through a supernatural provision of God's power. Christian baptism in water has been made possible only through the death and supernatural resurrection of Jesus Christ.

- Hebrews 11:29 says: *"By faith they [Israel] passed through the Red Sea as by dry land, whereas the Egyptians, attempting to do so, were drowned."* The waters were opened and closed by an act of faith on the part of Moses, and Israel was able to pass through by faith. One of the main conditions for Christian baptism is faith. Once a person believes that Jesus Christ is the only Saviour then he can be baptized. Baptism is based on faith: *"he who believes and is baptized will be saved* (Mark 16:16)."* The Egyptians who attempted to pass through the Red Sea, without faith, were not saved but destroyed.

- Israel followed their new leader through the water, to live by new laws (values) and to proceed to a new destination. Christians, in faith-obedience, follow Jesus through the baptism in water into a new destination, living a new life with a new set of values.

The Israelites escaped into the desert of the Sinai Peninsula. Finally they came to Mount Sinai where God, through Moses, gave them the Ten Commandments and other instructions.

We summarize the main purposes of the Law as follows: (1) to single Israel out as God's covenantal people and to preserve them – the Ten Commandments could be seen as their constitution and then God also gave them many prescriptions as to righteous living in order to protect themselves and others, and to receive material blessings. The detailed commandments governed both their civil and religious matters – it gave them guidance in how to keep the Ten Commandments. The Apostle Paul says: *"We were kept under guard by the law, kept for the faith which would afterward be revealed* (Gal. 3:23)."* The law kept Israel as a special nation, separated from all other nations, by their distinct commandments, and preserved them for the special purposes for which God had called them. (2) The law with all its sacrificial commandments and ceremonies reminded the Israelites of their sinfulness and God's holiness. It showed them that they were unable to make themselves righteous before God by their own efforts. (3) Related to the previous point, the law with all its sacrificial commandments and ceremonies foreshadowed Christ and directed their attention to the promised Messiah as the ultimate sacrifice and Saviour (Gen. 3:15; Heb. 10:1-4). In faith they were supposed to look forward to the promised Messiah. The New Covenant tells us: *"Therefore the law was our tutor to bring us to Christ, that we might be justified by faith* (Gal. 3:24)."* Also, an example of direct prophecy, within the framework of the law is found in Deuteronomy 18:18-19, where God said to Israel through Moses: *"I will raise up for them a Prophet like you from among their brethren, and will put My words in His mouth, and He shall speak to them all I command Him. And it shall be that whoever will not hear My words, which He speaks in My name, I will require it of him."* In the sacrifices and ordinances of the law many types foreshadowed Jesus Christ as the Saviour who was to come.

> Through Moses God gave the Israelites what any emancipated people need: leadership, government (or law), and worship.

God also gave Moses instructions for building the Tabernacle, also known as the Tent of Meeting/Worship – the centre of their camping activity, personal, social and religious. The fact that the Tabernacle was to be put at the centre of the camp illustrates to us what Scripture teaches: God is to be central, at the centre of our lives.

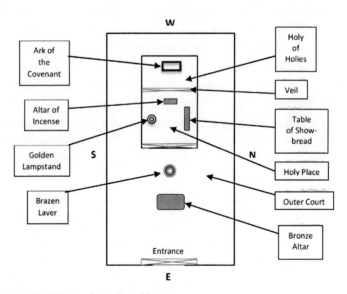

Diagram 2: The Tabernacle in the wilderness

The Bible dedicates fifty chapters to the Tabernacle of Moses. That shows us the important spiritual significance of the Tabernacle, the full meaning of which is found only in the New Testament. The Tabernacle with all its furnishings, sacrifices and ceremonies is a

DISCOVERING THE MOST AMAZING BOOK

type of Christ and His work of atonement (Heb. 10:20). It was the place where God met with the Israelites (Ex. 25:22; 29:42, 43); now He meets us in Christ (2 Cor. 5:19). It was the place where God lived among His people (Ex. 25:8; 29:45, 46); today He lives with us in Christ (Matt. 1:23; John 1:1, 14). The Tabernacle was the place where God received the sinner (Lev. 1:4); now God receives the sinner in Christ (Eph. 1:6). It was the place where God forgave the sinners (Lev. 4:20, 26, 31, 35; 5:10, 16, 18; 6:7); now, after the crucifixion, sinners receive forgiveness for their sins in Christ (Eph. 1:7).

Furthermore, there was only one entrance to the Tabernacle; Jesus is the Door, the only entrance to eternal life and the only way to God (John 10:9; 14:6); the Brazen Altar speaks of *Regeneration*; the Laver of *Purification* (Sanctification); the Lampstand of *Illumination*; the Shewbread (pronounced showbread) of *Fellowship and Sustenance*; the Altar of Incense of *Intercession*; the Ark of *Representation*; all of which are to be found in Jesus Christ only, the Word who *"became flesh and did tabernacle among us* (John 1:14 *YLT*)."

By day the Tabernacle was covered by the cloud of God's glory, and appearance of fire by night (Num. 9:16).

Today, in the Christian age, every Christian is a priest, and the whole Church *"a royal priesthood* (1 Pet. 2:9)." However there is no "class of priests" in the Christian Church, and there is no distinction, such as "high priest", and "priest," as in the Old Covenant. Jesus Christ is the only High Priest, and in Him are fulfilled both the Aaronic and Melchisedecan priesthoods of intercession and benediction.

Together with the giving of the Law, and the institution of the Tabernacle, we find the ordination of the priesthood (Ex. 28-29). The special function of the priests was related to the law. Since the law was civil and religious, their function was twofold: first, to declare, interpret, and teach the law; and second, to tend to the sacrificial duties in the Tabernacle. The priesthood was the prerogative of the tribe of Levi, and it was handed down from father to son. Aaron, Moses' brother was the first high priest (in that sense a type of Christ). The whole idea of priesthood reminds us of the sinfulness of man and the need for mediation.

After the Israelites had camped at the foot of Mount Sinai for a year, God directed them towards the Promised Land (Canaan). While in the wilderness of Paran God told Moses to send out twelve spies into Canaan. The spies returned with a report that the land *"truly flows with milk and honey* (Ex. 13:27)" and that it was fruitful. However, ten of the spies were intimidated by the inhabitants and believed Israel could not conquer Canaan. But, Joshua and Caleb were full of faith and certain that Israel was well able to take the land. The Israelites believed the ten spies and refused to take possession of the land. Because they failed to trust in God for victory, He judged them "according to the number of the days in which you spied out the land, forty days, for each day you shall bear your guilt one year, namely forty years, and you shall know My rejection (Num. 14:34)." Israel wandered in the wilderness until that entire generation had died, except for Joshua and Caleb. Despite their continual grumbling, complaining and unfaithfulness God still, in His grace and mercy, miraculously provided for them, among other things, manna and water from a rock. "Manna" is a type of Christ – He is our Bread from heaven.

By weeping (Num. 11:10; 14:1), wailing (Num. 11:4, 13), murmuring (Num. 14:27), grumbling (Num. 14:2), complaining (Num. 11:1; 14:2), and quarrelling (Num. 20:3, 13) you can go around in circles in your Christian life, not experiencing the blessing of God; rather, by faith in the finished work of Christ, possess your "Canaan."

Once, when the Israelites were complaining and grumbling, they were punished for it by being bitten by poisonous snakes. God in His mercy told Moses how to help the people. Moses made a bronze snake and put it on top of a pole. If those who were bitten by the snakes looked at the bronze snake on the pole, they lived (Num. 21:4-9). In the same way we too obtain deliverance from sin and death, and receive life by looking in faith at Jesus lifted up on the cross (John 3:14-15).

At the end of thirty eight years a new generation of Israelites came to Kadesh-Barnea, heading towards the Promised Land again. They set up camp on the plains of Moab. The Promised Land was just across the Jordan to the west. Before the Israelites entered the Promised Land, Moses spoke one last time to the people. This speech is recorded in the Book of Deuteronomy. Moses reviewed the history of Israel and the law. Because of Moses' act of disobedience (see Numbers 20:7-12) he could not enter the Promised Land, however, God told Moses to climb Mount Nebo, and from there he could see the Promised Land. Moses died just before the Israelites entered the land and God Himself *"buried him in a valley in the land of Moab* (Deut. 34:6)."* Now, Joshua, who was commissioned by Moses, led Israel into the Promised Land.

The watershed of Israel's history was the Exodus from Egypt. Even today the Jewish people understand their vocation and destiny in the light of this revealing event which made them a nation and became their undying memory.[4]

Just as Christians remember Jesus Christ as their Saviour in the celebration of the Lord's Supper, so Jews recall and make contemporary the Exodus as they celebrate the Passover.

❖ Possessing the Promised Land: 1406-1050 BC

Under the capable leadership of Joshua, the Israelites crossed the Jordan. Joshua was a well-trained leader. He witnessed the miracles God performed in delivering Israel under the leadership of Moses. Before Moses died, he laid his hands on Joshua and the Spirit of God came upon him, enabling Joshua to lead Israel (Deut. 34:9).

With the crossing of the Jordan we again see an extraordinary demonstration of God's power when we take Him in faith at His Word: *"And it shall come to pass, as soon as the soles of the feet of the priests who bear the ark of the Lord ... shall rest in the waters of the Jordan, that the waters ... shall be cut off, the waters that come down from upstream, and they shall stand as a heap. So it was ... as those who bore the ark came to the Jordan, and the feet of the priests ... dipped in the edge of the water ... that the waters ... stood still, and rose in a heap very far away* (Joshua 3:13-16)." Apparently the river Jordan was in flood the season when Joshua and his people had to cross it. God said that He will stop the flow of the water. Joshua, the priests and the people had to take God at His Word – the river didn't stop to flow until the priests had put their feet into the water. Faith is persistent!

---

4   Anderson Bernhard W, *The Living World of the Old Testament*, p. 9

> The Biblical symbolism of crossing the Jordan for the Christian is: death to self.

After Israel crossed over the Jordan on dry land they camped in Gilgal, on the east border of Jericho. When the kings of the Amorites and Canaanites heard what the Lord had done *"their heart melted; and there was no spirit in them any longer* (Joshua 5:1)." At Gilgal God removed the reproach of Egypt from Israel.

The Canaanites were wicked and worshipped many different gods. The war between Israel and Canaan was God's judgment on the Canaanites and His reclaiming of the land.

> The Promised Land for the Christian is not a place but a Person: Jesus Christ.

The Israelites first conquest was Jericho; by means of God's plan and power they conquered the city of Jericho. After they had marched seven times around the city as the Lord had commanded, they blew the trumpets and shouted. Jericho's walls fell down, and they marched in (Joshua 6:1-21). A harlot named Rahab had hidden two Israelite spies in the city earlier, based actually on her faith in God, for she said to them, *"I know that the Lord has given you the land* (2:9)." She let the spies down by a scarlet rope through the window, because her house was on the city wall. After the city fell she was rewarded by being spared (Joshua 2:1-21; 6:22-25). The scarlet cord, which provided safety for Rahab and her house, portrays deliverance and safety through the blood of Jesus (Heb. 9:19-22). Hebrews 11:30-31 refers to her as one of the people of faith in the Old Testament. Rahab amazingly became an ancestor of Jesus Christ (Matt. 1:5).

Through their military campaigns the people of Israel learned a crucial lesson under Joshua's capable leadership: victory comes through faith in God and obedience to His word, rather than through military skill. We also learn that since the battle is the Lord's, only His methods will bring success. The entire conquest of the land occurred over many years, but they never fully completed it; most of the tribes failed to take over their territories. God had commanded the Israelites to completely drive out the Canaanites, but they were

DISCOVERING THE MOST AMAZING BOOK   65

satisfied to simply live alongside them. The idolatry of the Canaanites was a snare to the Israelites for centuries to come.

Don't compromise with sin, it will weaken your faith, then you will not be able to walk in the victory that God has for you. The world, the flesh and the devil are enemies of your faith.

Joshua failed to raise up a legacy of leadership. Therefore, after he died, God repeatedly raised up leaders, called judges, to deliver His people from oppression. The most famous of these judges, or deliverers were Gideon, Barak, and Samson. During this time (the period of the Judges), they had to wage ceaseless wars of defence to maintain their hold on the Promised Land. The Judges account tells us how much of the land was not conquered. Israel's oppression was typically a direct result of their sin. Often Israel turned away from God to the gods and idols of their neighbours. So God allowed His people to fall into the hands of their oppressors. This cycle of sin, oppression, and deliverance occurred throughout the time of the judges. During this time Israel was a group of tribes, each one governed itself. They also experienced conflict among themselves as the tribe of Benjamin was almost completely wiped out by the other tribes in a bloody civil war. The period of the judges was a spiritually dark, chaotic, and volatile time for Israel, because: *"In those days there was no king in Israel; everyone did what was right in his own eyes* (Judges 21:25)."

When Jesus is not the King over your life, then you can expect all sorts of trouble.

In the midst of chaos and tragic life circumstances during the days of the judges, we do find love, hope and provision. The Book of Ruth tells the story of David's great-grandmother who was not an Israelite, but a Moabite. She believed in the true God and because of her faithfulness in a time of national unfaithfulness, God rewards her by giving her an Israelite husband, a son, and a privileged position in the lineage of David and Jesus Christ (Matt. 1:5). The Book of Ruth presents a cameo story of love, devotion, grace, providence and redemption in the midst of challenging times; it foreshadows redemption in Christ (see the synopsis on the Book of Ruth).

With the judges failing, we will now see a definitive change in the history of the Israelites: from Theocracy (God ruling His people) to Monarchy (God's people ruled by native kings). The following chart gives us an outline of this era and will help to more easily understand and remember the three different periods of the Monarchy.

The Age of the Monarchy 1050-586 BC			
The United Kingdom	The Divided Kingdom		The Surviving Kingdom
Saul, David and Solomon	North: Israel Jeroboam to Hoshea	South: Judah Rehoboam to Ahaz	Judah alone Hezekiah to Zedekiah
120 Years 1050-930 BC	208 Years 930-722 BC		136 Years 722-586 BC
1 Samuel 8-1 Kings 11 1 Chron. 10-2 Chron. 9	1 Kings 12-2 Kings 18:12 2 Chronicles 10-28		2 Kings 18:13-25:21 2 Chronicles 29-36:21
Prophets: Samuel	**Prophets:** Elijah Elisha Micaiah Amos Hosea	**Prophets:** Joel Isaiah* Micah Habakkuk Zephaniah Jeremiah * Isaiah prophesied to Judah and briefly to Israel	
Take notice: the Prophets referred to are only those who prophesied during the era of the Monarchy; see page 51 for other Prophets.			

❖ The United Kingdom: 1050-930 BC

This is a most important period in Biblical history for the following reasons:

1. The establishment of the kingly rule was in God's purpose for Israel (see Deut. 17:14-20; 1 Kings 11:32) and it is part of God's plan of redemption.

2. It is a leap forward in the development of Israel as the Messianic Nation.

3. It gives us the founding of Israel's kingdom, a picture of God's kingdom – how God wants to set us apart unto Himself and reign in love and righteousness over us.

4. King David, in his testings, triumphs, testimonies, zeal for the house of God, his combining of the offices of prophet, priest, and king, is a forerunner of King Jesus. David and his reign look forward to the coming of the Messiah King. Also David is the embodiment of Israel's dreams.

5. And, naturally, it all confirms the truthfulness of the Prophetic Word.

First Samuel records the beginning of the United Kingdom – from judges to kings, covering three major leadership changes – Eli, Samuel, and Saul.

The immediate backdrop to the beginning of the United Kingdom finds Israel in a spiritually dark place, because of the failure of the judges. And First Samuel opens with Elkanah's family. One of his wives, Hannah, was barren. One day, while her family was worshipping God, she wept and prayed fervently to God for a son. The old priest Eli thought that she was drunk, *"put your wine away from you,"* he told her (1 Sam. 1:14). After Hannah explained her situation to him, Eli pronounced a blessing on her and said that God will answer her prayer. And He did. Hannah conceived and gave birth to a son whom she called Samuel, because the Lord heard her request.

After Samuel was weaned, Hannah took him to the tabernacle and literally gave him to God by presenting him to the priest, Eli.

Here Samuel's name, meaning "heard of God," proved to be fitting, because when he was a small boy being raised by Eli in God's presence, he heard the voice of the Lord (chapter 3). Samuel grew up to be a judge, but he was also a very significant prophet (keep his name in mind), *"none of his words [fell] to the ground. And all Israel ... knew that Samuel had been established as a prophet of the Lord* (3:19, 20)." In fact, he was the first of the Order of the Prophets, a writing prophet, and he established a school of prophets (10:5; 19:20). The priest Eli failed both as a priest and father, and Samuel succeeded him to become the final judge, priest and prophet of Israel. Samuel proclaimed the word of the Lord during a time when the Word was rare and he was respected as a prophet.

Samuel was gentle and remained faithful to God and the people of Israel to the end of his life. He is seen as one of the most gentle and loyal characters in the Bible.

When Samuel grew old and the Israelites saw that his sons did not have the integrity of their father, they told Samuel that they wanted to have a king like all the other nations (1 Sam. 8:1-5). God told Samuel not to take this rejection personally, but to agree to their request and to warn them of the problems earthly kings could bring upon them. The people were really rejecting the Lord, preferring a human king in the place of having God as their King (although this change was necessary, because it was to bring to power David and eventually the Messiah, it was wrongly conceived and entered upon).

Saul became the first king of Israel. Thus began the kingdom of Israel. Sadly, Saul proved to be disobedient; he did not have a heart for doing God's will. His life is one great warning. After Samuel anointed Saul, God changed his heart (10:9). Saul even prophesied with a band of prophets when God's Spirit came upon him. However, it becomes evident as we study Saul's life that he lost his spirituality. He did not repent after sinning on several occasions. So, after some years, Samuel had to tell Saul that God had rejected him from being king of Israel.

> *"But the Lord said to Samuel, 'don't look at his appearance or at his physical stature, because I have refused him. For the Lord does not see as man sees; for man looks at the outward appearance, but the Lord looks at the heart* (1 Sam. 16:7).'"

However, Saul's son Jonathan had tremendous faith in God. While leading his armour-bearer in a daring attack on the Philistines, he said: *"For nothing restrains the Lord from saving by many or few* (14:6)." The two of them killed about twenty Philistines, and God honoured his faith and courage by sending a panic attack throughout the rest of the Philistine army. Jonathan later became one of David's best friends.

God chose a man after His own heart to replace Saul: David (1 Sam. 13:14). David was an unlikely choice. The youngest and least of eight brothers (does this sound familiar), he was not even considered at first. But soon after Samuel anointed David to be the next king, David demonstrated that he was indeed specially chosen by God: for he slew the Philistine giant Goliath when Israel's soldiers, including his brothers, were too afraid to face the giant in battle. David afterward became a great soldier and king. Soon after becoming king, David recaptured the ark of the Lord with great rejoicing which had been previously seized by the Philistines – David had a passion for the presence of God and he knew that if he desired to be a good king, leading the people of God well, he needed to live within the realm of God's presence (the ark symbolizes the presence of God with His people in the Old Testament). Although he was far from perfect, David was the best king Israel ever had. After sinning he always would repent and renew his relationship with God. Because of his submissive and tender heart towards the Lord, God could work through him. David was also a musician and poet, and wrote many of the Psalms. God promised David that his throne would be established forever; this promise was fulfilled in Jesus Christ, whose kingdom will never end. Jesus descended from David (Matt. 1:1), and was called the "Root of David."

The next king was David's son, Solomon. At first, Solomon looked like the kind of man God could use. God told Solomon to ask from Him whatever he wanted and He will give it to him. He prayed for discernment and an understanding heart to rule God's people with justice. God gave him the wisdom he asked for as well as wealth and honour (1 Kings 3:5-14). Solomon built the temple for the Lord that his father David had dreamed of building.

Sadly and tragically Solomon drifted from God and surrendered to his lusts, marrying seven hundred wives and keeping another three hundred as concubines. These women worshipped idols and *"his wives turned away his heart* (1 Kings 11:3)" joining them in their pagan worship.

His latter years were plagued by foreign and domestic troubles. The sin of Solomon brought chaotic consequences upon the chosen nation. Because he didn't remain faithful, God warned through the prophet Ahijah, *"Behold, I will tear the kingdom out of the hand of Solomon and will give ten tribes to you [Jeroboam] (but he shall have one tribe for the sake of My servant David, and for the sake of Jerusalem, the city which I chosen out of all the tribes of Israel),* (1 Kings 11:31, 32)." We should immediately notice: (1) a Righteous God does not tolerate sin; (2) the preciseness of the prophetic Word of God; and (3) in His grace and sovereignty God preserved the royal line of David in order to accomplish His purpose for the eventual salvation of mankind.

The United Kingdom lasted for 120 years, during which three kings ruled, each for 40 years: Saul, David, and Solomon.

❖ The Divided Kingdom: 930-722 BC

In spite of occasional hostility, the nation remained united under both David's wartime rule and Solomon's peaceful leadership. However, soon after Solomon's death, Israel became a divided kingdom.

Solomon's son Rehoboam followed him as the fourth king of Israel in 930 BC. The people of Israel demanded that Rehoboam grant some reprieve from the heavy tax burden placed on them by his father (Solomon taxed the people heavily in order to maintain his wealthy lifestyle and many women). Under the influence of his young counsellors he foolishly vowed to tax the people even more. Furthermore, as we have seen, the Lord became angry with Solomon because of his sins, and warned him that He would surely tear the kingdom away from him (1 Kings 11:9-11). The king with a divided heart caused the kingdom to divide.

Ten of the twelve tribes of Israel refused to submit to Rehoboam. Only the tribes of Judah and Benjamin remained loyal. The kingdom of the nation of Israel was torn into two. From then on the kingdom established by the ten northern tribes, under Jeroboam, was called Israel, and the kingdom in the south that continued to be ruled by Davidic kings was called Judah. The division between these two kingdoms was very real, and they often fought wars against each other. The period of the Divided Kingdom continued for approximately 208 years.

The following chart shows us three distinct periods that we can identify between Israel and Judah during the Divided Kingdom era, and the kings that ruled during those periods. Also see the chart on the next page listing all the kings of both kingdoms.

Three Periods during the Divided Kingdom between Israel and Judah			
Kingdom	First Period (60 years of War)	Second Period (75 years of Alliance)	Third Period (75 years of War)
Israel	Jeroboam-Omri	Ahab-Jehoahaz	Jehoash-Hoshea
Judah	Rehoboam-Asa	Jehoshaphat-Joash	Amaziah-Ahaz

Altogether twenty kings ruled in Judah. Twelve of these kings – Rehoboam-Ahaz – ruled during the era of the Divided Kingdom. Eight kings – Zedekiah-Hezekiah – ruled during the period known as the Surviving Kingdom, when the Northern Kingdom was exiled by Assyria and Judah survived as a single kingdom.

The Books of Kings and Chronicles deal with the kings and their kingdoms. We will meet with some of these kings when we look at the Synopses of these books in the next chapter.

The Northern Kingdom never had a single good king. Of the many kings Israel had, none of them worshipped God; they were all evil (the one more wicked than the other). Their first king set up two golden calves, one at Bethel and the other at Dan. The people (later called Samaritans) worshipped these idols instead of the true God at the temple in Jerusalem. This was one of the reasons why the Jews despised them in Jesus' day (John 4:9, 19-24). One of the most notorious kings of Israel, Ahab, was married to a foreigner, a heathen Canaanite, named Jezebel. She is reckoned among the wickedest of women; her character was "uniformly and consistently wicked." Both Ahab and Jezebel hated Elijah, a powerful prophet of God at that time. Elijah and his successor, Elisha, performed many miracles, by which they showed that God was the true Lord.

The Northern Kingdom existed for approximately two hundred years. The wicked and unspeakably cruel Assyrians (modern Syria) conquered the Northern Kingdom and took the ten tribes into captivity.

This was done in two stages: Galilee, northern and eastern Israel were overrun by Tiglath-Pileser III of Assyria in 734 BC. The rest of Israel were captured by Sargon in 722 BC. Many Israelites were killed and exiled to faraway lands, and other foreign people were brought in to diffuse the possibility of a unified revolt. (The Jews of the Northern Kingdom intermarried with Gentiles, and their descendants had become known as Samaritans, living in Samaria). The Bible makes it very clear that this exile was a direct result of the wickedness and idolatry of the people of Israel.

Kings of the Divided Monarchy			
(Dates are approximate and may vary from other sources)			
Israel (Northern Kingdom)		**Judah (Southern Kingdom)**	
Jeroboam 1	930-909 BC	Rehoboam	930-913 BC
Nadab	909-908	Abijah	913-910
Baasha	908-886	Asa	910-869
Elah	886-885	Jehoshaphat	872-848
Zimri	885 (7 days)	Jehoram	848-841
Omri	885-874	Ahaziah	841
Ahab	874-853	Athaliah (Queen)	841-835
Ahaziah	853-852	Joash	835-796
Joram	852-841	Amaziah	796-767
Jehu	841	Uzziah	792-740
Hehoahaz	814-798	Jotham	750-732
Jehooash	798-782	Ahaz	735-715
Jeroboam 2	793-753	Hezekiah	729-686
Zechariah	753 (6 mths)	Manassah	696-642
Shallum	752 (1 month)	Amon	642-640
Menahem	752-742	Josiah	640-609
Pekahiah	742-740	Jehoahaz	609
Pekah	740-732	Jehoiakim	608-598
Hoshea	732-722	Jehoiachin	598-597
		Zedekiah	597-587/6

❖ The Surviving Kingdom: 722-586 BC

The Southern Kingdom, Judah, survived the time of the Divided Kingdom, and lasted for another hundred and thirty six years after the Northern Kingdom was destroyed by the Assyrians. Eight kings – Hezekiah through Zedekiah – ruled in Judah before it was finally conquered and exiled by Babylon. Of these eight kings only two were good – Hezekiah and Josiah.

Hezekiah did not follow the evil example of his father, Ahaz, whose reign was one unbroken course of sin, and his son [Hezekiah] inherited the consequences. Instead, he led the nation in a restoration to righteousness (2 Kings 18-20; 2 Chronicles 29-32) – he removed idols, restored worship in the temple, sacrificed offerings for sin, and participated in thanksgiving celebrations. Hezekiah not only brought in spiritual reformation, but strengthened the nation politically and economically as well. He also built up an army to protect the city from enemies and exhorted the people to trust in the Lord for divine protection (2 Chronicles 32:6-8).

In 701 BC, Sennacherib, king of Assyria threatened Jerusalem, mocked the God of Judah, led his army in to Judea, capturing many strong cities in the kingdom of Judah, and demanded that Judah surrender to his powerful army. The prophet Isaiah prophesied that Judah would be delivered and encouraged king Hezekiah to trust in the Lord. King Hezekiah and the nation prayed, and in response to their prayer, God sent an angel who killed 185,000 soldiers and leaders in the Assyrian camp (2 Kings 19:35; Isaiah 37:36). An embarrassed and defeated Sennacherib returned to his country, and soon after, while he was worshipping his false god, two of his sons struck him down with the sword (2 Kings 19:37).

In 2 Kings 20:1-11 we are told of Hezekiah's severe sickness and how the prophet Isaiah told him to set his house in order and that he would die. Hezekiah turned his face to the wall, wept, and prayed. God graciously answered his prayer and added fifteen years to his life.

Manasseh, Hezekiah's son, began ruling with his father in 696 BC. After Hezekiah's death, ten years later, Manasseh turned out to be a very wicked king who rejected righteousness and promoted and practiced all sorts of idolatry, he even filled the streets of Jerusalem with innocent blood (2 Kings 21:16). *"Manasseh seduced Judah and the inhabitants of Jerusalem to do more evil than the nations whom*

74 CHARLES STEBBING

the Lord had destroyed before the children of Israel (2 Chronicles 33:9)." The Lord warned Manasseh, but he didn't listen. Therefore the Lord caused and allowed the captains of the army of Assyria to take him in chains to Babylon. The Bible tells us when Manasseh saw his affliction, he repented and implored the Lord to help him. God graciously saved Manasseh and brought him back to Jerusalem. Upon his return, Manasseh removed the idols and altars from God's temple and rebuilt the altar of the Lord. Manasseh even commanded the people to serve the one true God (2 Chronicles 33:10-16).

After Manasseh died, his son Amon became king. He led the kingdom Judah away from God by promoting and practicing idolatry. Amon ruled for only two years before he was killed by his own officers.

Amon's son, Josiah, was made king by the people of Judah when he was only eight years of age. Second Chronicles 34:3 tells us that at the age of sixteen, Josiah sought the God of his father David and at age twenty *"he began to purge Judah and Jerusalem of the high places, the wooden images, the carved images, and the molded images."*

In the eighteenth year of his reign, king Josiah led a campaign to repair and restore the temple. A book of the Law was discovered by Hilkiah the priest and when the Law was read to the young king, he was deeply moved. Then he commanded Hilkiah to inquire from the Lord concerning the words of the book that was found. Hilkiah went to the prophetess Huldah and the Lord gave her a word that judgment was coming for Judah because of their idolatry. However, she said that the Lord would delay his judgment to spare Josiah because his heart was tender and he humbled himself before God. King Josiah led Judah back to God, restored true worship and kept the Passover; he brought about a spiritual revival in Judah. As a result, his reign was quiet and peaceful.

In 609 BC, Pharaoh Necho II of Egypt marched his army north to fight with his allies, the Assyrians, against the Babylonians who were a threat to Egypt. Necho had to pass through territory controlled by the kingdom of Judah, and he requested permission from king Josiah. Josiah refused permission, and although Necho did not want to fight Judah, king Josiah engaged in battle with him, known as the Battle of Megiddo. Josiah was fatally wounded and died shortly afterwards. Judah fell under Egyptian control and influence.

King Josiah had three sons, and each in time ruled over Judah. Not one of them followed in the footsteps of their father. After Josiah's untimely death, the people made his son Jehoahaz king. His ungodly reign only lasted three months before he was deposed and carried off to Egypt by king Necho II on his return from battle in Syria (this was after the Battle of Megiddo). Necho of Egypt placed Jehoahaz's brother Eliakim on the throne and changed his name to Jehoiakim, *"who did evil in the sight of the Lord* (2 Chron. 36:5)." He was the king who imprisoned the prophet Jeremiah.

In the meantime Babylonia, simply known as Babylon (modern Iraq), grew in prominence and became a world power to reckon with. Jeremiah (46:2) records the decisive battle of Carchemish where Pharaoh Necho II was defeated by king Nebuchadnezzar of Babylon in 605 BC. It was in the fourth year of Jehoiakim's reign that Nebuchadnezzar, king of Babylon, invaded Judah, and control of Judah passed from the Assyrian-Egyptian alliance to that of Babylon. In that same year (605 BC), the first of three exiles took place when king Nebuchadnezzar of Babylon subdued Jerusalem and took prominent citizens of the city as captives to Babylon, including Daniel and his three friends – Shadrach, Meshach, and Abednego.

Nebuchadnezzar made Jehoiakim a vassal (puppet) king to him. He turned and rebelled against Nebuchadnezzar (2 Kings 24:1). Not long afterward, Jehoiakim was killed and his son, Jehoiachin, became king and reigned for only three months. He also *"did evil in the sight of the Lord, according to all that his father had done* (2 Kings 24:9)."

In 597 BC, Nebuchadnezzar again invaded Judah, marched his army to Jerusalem, and Jehoiachin surrendered. Nebuchadnezzar took Jehoiachin, his servants, princes and officers as captives, he also confiscated the treasure of the house of the Lord, including all the gold articles of the temple, and he carried into captivity all Jerusalem: all the captains and all the mighty men of valour, ten thousand captives (2 Kings 24:10-14) – including Ezekiel.

Nebuchadnezzar then made Mattaniah, Josiah's youngest son, his puppet-king and changed his name to Zedekiah. He was the last king of Judah, but his reign was merely as a servant to the Babylonian kingdom. Zedekiah was most likely Josiah's worst son. He rebelled against the Lord and Nebuchadnezzar (2 Chron. 36:13). Even all the leaders of the priests and the people transgressed more and more; they defiled the house of the Lord. God sent them warnings by His messengers, because He had compassion on them, but they despised His words, and scoffed His prophets, until the wrath of the Lord arose against His people, till there was no remedy (2 Chron. 36:15-17).

After Zedekiah foolishly rebelled against the king of Babylon (2 Kings 24:20), Nebuchadnezzar laid siege to Jerusalem. In 586 BC, Babylon finally attacked the city of Jerusalem. This was the final blow. Zedekiah tried to escape. The Babylonians pursued and overtook him. His sons were killed before his eyes, and his own eyes were put out and he was deported to Babylon (2 Kings 25:7). The Babylonians completely destroyed the Temple, burned Jerusalem, broke down the walls all around Jerusalem, and took most of the survivors into exile, thus leaving the once proud nation in ruins.

God used the Babylonians (also known as the Chaldeans) to execute his judgment on Judah.

Lessons from the history of both good and evil kings

The era of the kings is not merely historical, we do learn many theological and doctrinal lessons from this time-period in Biblical history. For instance:

❖ The sovereignty of God – He does as He wills, and even uses human beings in spite of their mistakes.

❖ That God, as a righteous God, has to deal with sin.

❖ Sin has consequences, sometimes severe consequences.

❖ A righteous God demands obedience; sinful human beings cannot obey God fully; they need a Saviour, a Divine Person who can fulfil all the righteous demands of God on their behalf.

❖ The grace of God – He graciously saves and heals those who do not really deserve it (2 Kings 20:1-11).

❖ God will forgive anyone who genuinely repents, even the worst of sinners (2 Chron. 33:13).

❖ Faith in God leads to obedience and righteous living, which in turn command God's blessing.

❖ The Babylonian Exile: 586-538 BC

The Bible is clear that the Babylonian exile was God's judgment upon the idolatry of Judah – God caused and allowed the captivity to cleanse Judah from idolatry. The prophets warned the Judeans, but they didn't listen.

As we have seen, the Babylonian captivity of Judah took place in three stages:

605 BC	Some captives, mostly prominent citizens, including Daniel were taken.
597 BC	About ten thousand captives were taken, including Ezekiel.
586 BC	Jerusalem was burned; most of the survivors were taken, except the poor.

The Babylonian captivity of Judah was not nearly as brutal as that of the Assyrian captivity of Israel. The Judeans were, for the most part, allowed to maintain their cultural and religious distinctiveness. And it was during the exile that the people of Judah first came to be referred to as Jews (from the term Judeans).

However, the exile had a major impact on virtually every aspect of Israelite life. Only the poor were left in Judah, and the ritual sacrificial system had essentially ceased. At the same time, many of those taken into exile became somewhat prosperous and even occupied positions of significant political power in the Babylonian government. Daniel, for instance, was a close advisor to several Babylonian and Persian rulers.

In the meantime, the mighty Medo-Persian Empire (modern Iran) from the north was growing, and they eventually conquered Babylon (539 BC) and nearly everything else in the then known world. Now the Jews were under Persian rule. God directed the new emperor, Cyrus the Great, to decree that any Jew who wanted could return to their land to rebuild the Lord's temple. We read of this in the Books of Ezra and Nehemiah (also see 2 Chronicles 36:22-23).

Praise God for His mercy, the Exile did not last forever, only about seventy years as promised by God by the mouth of His prophet, Jeremiah. The Lord had punished them, yet He still loved them, and had set Himself to deliver them once again. Note, how the Sovereign Lord God moved a pagan ruler to release His people.

❖ Return and Diaspora: 538-5/6 BC

The Judeans were taken into captivity in three stages, they returned also in three stages:

The Return from Babylon		
First Stage	Second Stage	Third Stage
Under **Zerubbabel** In 538 BC	Under **Ezra** In 458 BC	Under **Nehemiah** In 445 BC

This was also an important time-period in the history of the Jews, because it meant that they had to re-establish as a people in their own land.

Around 538 BC the first group of Jews, about fifty thousand, returned home to the land of Israel under the leadership of Zerubbabel (Ezra 2). They rebuilt the sacrificial altar and later began to rebuild the temple. However, the work on the temple had ceased for sixteen years because of opposition and the people's personal affairs. During this time God raised up the prophets Haggai and Zechariah to encourage the people to continue rebuilding the temple.

In 458 BC, Ezra led the second group back to Jerusalem. This second group consisted of 1700 men and 5,000-10,000 women and children (Ezra 8:1-14, 18-21).

Although Israel continued to enjoy relative religious freedom under the Persians, many individuals, including some leaders abandoned their faithfulness and commitment to God. Ezra, a priest, taught the Jewish law and confronted them with their sin. He led some reforms that dealt with the sin of intermarriage with foreign women who enticed their Jewish husbands into idolatry. During this same period the story of Esther, the Jewish queen of Persia, took place. She was used by God to save the Jewish people from a plot to destroy them.

Later in 445 BC Nehemiah, a contemporary of Ezra and cupbearer to the Persian king, was granted permission to return to Jerusalem with a third group of Israelites. His concern for the welfare of his people prompted him to take bold action. Nehemiah challenged his countrymen to arise and rebuild the shattered wall of Jerusalem (Neh. 6:15-16).

DISCOVERING THE MOST AMAZING BOOK

However, not all the Jews returned to the Promised Land. Over the decades in exile, many had largely integrated with the societies in which they were living and married with the local foreign people. Over time the Hebrew language came to be replaced by Aramaic (the dominant language of their exile) as the spoken language of the Jews. This large population of Jews living permanently outside the Promised Land is often referred to as the Diaspora ("scattering").

The Book of Nehemiah together with the prophetic Books of Haggai, Zechariah and Malachi conclude the history of the Jewish people within the Old Testament.

Prophets of the Old Testament and Times they Prophesied			
Prophet	**Age**	**Year/s**	**To Whom**
Samuel	Early prophets	1050-1000 BC	Judah (S K) and Israel (N K)
Elijah	Early prophets	875-848 BC	Israel
Elisha	Early Prophets	848-797 BC	Israel
Joel	Early prophets	837-800 BC	Judah
Micaiah	Early prophets	849 BC	Israel
Jonah	Assyrian Age	770 BC	Nineveh
Amos	Assyrian Age	760 BC	Israel
Hosea	Assyrian Age	760-730 BC	Israel
Isaiah	Assyrian Age	740-700 BC	Judah
Micah	Assyrian Age	735-700 BC	Judah
Nahum	Babylonian Age	650 BC	Nineveh
Habakkuk	Babylonian Age	630 BC	Judah
Zephaniah	Babylonian Age	627 BC	Judah
Jeremiah	Babylonian Age	627-580 BC	Judah
Daniel	Babylonian Age	605-530 BC	Babylon
Ezekiel	Babylonian Age	593-570 BC	Captives from Judah
Haggai	Persian Age	520 BC	Judah
Zechariah	Persian Age	520-518 BC	Judah
Obadiah	Persian Age	500 BC	Edom
Malachi	Persian Age	443 BC	Judah

❖ The Intertestamental Period

The Old Testament ends around 430 BC, with the prophet Malachi. The time between the last recorded events of the Old Testament and the first recorded events of the New Testament are referred to as the Intertestamental Period (also known as the period of the Second Temple). A period of approximately four hundred years during which the voice of prophecy was known to be silent.

This period forms the backdrop to the New Testament; it sets the scene for the life and ministry of Jesus Christ.

A brief look at a few events from the Old Testament will help us to better understand the time between the two Testaments. There are references to this period in the Book of Daniel. Daniel predicted the rise and fall of great empires (these predictions of Daniel are once again evidence of how precise and authoritative the prophetic word of God is). The best known is Nebuchadnezzar's dream of a vast image, whose head was made of gold, breasts and arms of silver, belly and thighs of bronze, legs of iron and feet of mixed iron and clay (Dan. 2). Then (in the dream) a stone hit the feet, and the whole image was smashed into pieces. Daniel interpreted the dream as referring to successive empires. These great empires did follow one another. They provided the setting within which God's plan of redemption was acted out. The Babylonian kingdom (head of gold) lasted from 605-539 BC, the Medo-Persian Empire (the breast and arms) from 539-331 BC, the Greek Empire (belly and thighs of bronze) from 331-165 BC, the Maccabean Period (which is seen as part of the Greek Empire) 165-63 BC, and the Roman Empire (the legs) from 63 BC on into the Christian era.

We have already seen that during the Babylonian exile some Jews intermarried Gentiles which gave rise to the Samaritans. And that the common language in Israel changed from Hebrew to Aramaic. In Daniel eight we read of a powerful ram, charging west, north, and south, with no beast able to stand before it. Being two-horned, it represents the Medo-Persian Empire (8:20). The Medo-Persian Empire conquered the Babylonian empire and the Jews were allowed to go back to Jerusalem. The inspired Word of God in the Old Testament ends around 430 BC with the prophet Malachi, but the return and diaspora do not end with the book of Malachi, it actually continues through the 400 years. Many people mistakenly

Daniel says, *"... a male goat came from the west, across the surface of the whole earth (8:5)."* This is *"the kingdom of Greece (8:21),"* the rise of the Greek empire under Phillip of Macedon. The goat from the west "had a large horn" between its eyes, with which it struck the ram and broke its two horns. This prominent horn was Alexander the Great (356-323 BC), son of Phillip. The rise to power of Alexander the Great is perhaps the single most significant event that happened during this period. He defeated the Persian army in 331 BC. As Daniel says, *"The male goat grew very great (8:8),"* referring to his military conquest through which he has conquered the then known world; in today's terms, through Afghanistan as far as India. Having studied under the Greek philosopher, Aristotle, Alexander promoted the Greek language and culture throughout his conquered lands. *"But when he became strong, the large horn was broken;"* for he died in 323 BC, and in its place four prominent horns grew up, because Alexander's empire continued under the rule of his four generals, who split it into four kingdoms. They were Cassander, Lysimachus, Ptolemy and Seleucus.

Seleucus, founder of the Seleucid dynasty, who is referred to as *"king of the north"* in Daniel 11:6, ruled in Syria. Ptolemy, founder of the Ptolemaic dynasty, referred to as "king of the south (Dan. 11:5)," claimed both Egypt and Judea. These two kingdoms dominated the fortunes of Israel for about three hundred years: *"They brought untold miseries upon the world (1 Maccabees 1:9)."* They fought back and forth and Israel was caught in the middle.

Politically, little changed for the Jews under Greek rule. Culturally, however, they became more influenced by Greek (Hellenistic) civilization. (The process of "Greek-izing" the world became known as *hellenizing*, since the Greeks called their land *Hellas* and themselves *Hellenes*.) The Ptolemaic dynasty promoted Greek thought and language by all possible means in order to preserve and

82 CHARLES STEBBING

strengthen their empire culturally. (During the time of the Greeks the focus was on culture not politics.)

Although the Jews resisted adapting to Greek religion, they couldn't escape all aspects and the force of Hellenistic influence. Koine (common) Greek became the trade language of the empire. For this reason the Hebrew Bible (Old Testament) was translated into Greek (known as the Septuagint), and came to be widely used by Jews everywhere. During this period, a sizeable Jewish community grew in Egypt and Alexandria became an influential centre for Judaism.

In 198 BC, the Seleucids overthrew the Ptolemies in Judea. So, Judea came under Syrian rule. During this time, certain segments of Jewish society became increasingly attracted to Greek culture. (Remember, the Seleucid dynasty was also Greek and promoted Greek culture and language forcefully.)

Initially the Seleucids were tolerant towards the Jews, but that soon changed. Antiochus Epiphanes (175-164 BC) tried to destroy the Jewish religion (Judaism) completely and everyone who resisted him – he desecrated the Temple by offering a pig and putting an altar to Zeus in the temple, forbade sacrifices to God, destroyed all copies of Scripture that could be found, outlawed circumcision, forced Jews to eat pork, cancelled Sabbaths and feast days and instituted pagan worship (see Daniel 8:9-12). Apparently Antiochus gave himself the name "Epiphanes" meaning "god manifest."

Some Jews resisted Antiochus while others attempted to conciliate with him. These two groups were known as the Hellenists and the Hasidim. The Hellenists embraced and promoted Greek culture, while the Hasidim, which means "pious ones," closely practised Jewish law and were the forerunners of the Pharisees. In the subsequent revolt, Mattathias the Hasmonean, an elderly patriotic priest with unbound courage, and his sons provided leadership for the Hasidim.

The conflict in Judea finally reached boiling point when Mattathias strongly resisted Antiochus Epiphanes. He refused to offer a required pagan sacrifice. This led to organized resistance, known as the Maccabean Revolt, when Mattathias killed a Hellenistic Jew and the king's officer who invited him to offer a sacrifice to an idol. After this,

Mattathias and his five sons fled to the wilderness of Judea from where they would wage a war against the Seleucid dynasty.

After Mattathias' death in 166 BC, his son Judas who was nicknamed Maccabeaus, meaning "the hammer" or "eradicator," led an army of Jewish dissidents to victory over the Seleucid dynasty in guerrilla warfare. Judas was a warrior of amazing military genius who won battle after battle against all odds. He captured Jerusalem in 165 BC, purified and rededicated the temple. Judas and his brothers continued the now more ambitious struggle, with the goal of not only gaining religious freedom, but also complete political independence from the Seleucids.

In 152 BC, Jonathan, Judas' brother and successor, became both military governor and high priest. In 143 BC, Jonathan's brother Simon, who succeeded him, finally achieved political freedom and took the title of king. Now the priestly and civil authority was united in one person, thus the line of Maccabean, also known as Hasmonean (the Maccabees' family name), priest-rulers was established who for the next hundred years governed an independent Judea. The Sadducees supported Hasmonean rulers as both kings and priests, whereas the Pharisees insisted that a true king could only be a descendant of David and a priest could only be a descendant of Aaron.

The Maccabean military campaigns also expanded the borders of the Jewish state north and south until it nearly reached the size of the Davidic and Solomonic kingdoms in the ninth century BC.

During the Maccabean period all rulers came from the same family, and they became progressively dictatorial, corrupt, immoral, and even pagan.[25] Although independent, Judea was still beset by infighting by various Israelite factions. Different separatist groups also existed during that time. It was during this time that groups such as the Pharisees and Sadducees rose to prominence.

The independence of Judea under Hasmonean rule was short-lived and disastrous. The Hasmonean dynasty came to an end as a result of internal strife between leaders. Rome was invited to help settle the internal struggle. The Roman General Pompey, of the growing Roman Empire, laid hold of the opportunity, and decided to resolve the unsettled situation in Judea by making Judea part of the

---

[5]   Scott Julius J, *ESV Study Bible*, p. 1784.

Roman Empire. In 63 BC Pompey sacked Jerusalem. Judea could offer little resistance and became a Roman protectorate, and Jewish independence was lost again. Rome inaugurated Antipater as ruler over Judea. Antipater's son, Herod the Great, followed him as king of the Jews, and it was under his rule that Jesus Christ was born – ushering in a new era in Biblical history. The Romans continued to occupy Israel throughout all of the New Testament history.

Now, we can agree that: through four centuries of conflict, opposing religious polarities – paganism and Judaism – and political power struggles, God prepared the world around Israel for the coming of the promised Saviour and His gospel of salvation. Furthermore, the Greek empires gave the then-known world a common language, Greek, while later the Roman Empire provided a strong government as well as a remarkable road system. All of this allowed the rapid spread of the Good News of Jesus Christ.

❖ Jesus Christ: 5/6 BC-AD 30

In the midst of this incredibly complex interplay of religion, political struggle, and social change, God did indeed send His Son, the long awaited Messiah *"in the fullness of time* (Gal. 4:4)." The time was properly "ripe" for the Messiah to appear, because many, like the prophetess Anna, were eagerly *"looking for redemption in Jerusalem* (Luke 2:38)." As someone said: "Before the Bread of Life could be given the world had to become very hungry, and before the Water of Life could be supplied mankind had to become very thirsty; but 'when the fullness of the time was come' there came the Bread and Water."

DISCOVERING THE MOST AMAZING BOOK

85

"He was born in an obscure village, the child of a peasant woman. He grew up in another village, where He worked in a carpenter shop until He was thirty. Then for three years He was an itinerant preacher. He never wrote a book. He never held an office. He never had a family or a home. He didn't go to college. He never visited a big city. He never travelled two hundred miles from the place where He was born. He did none of the things that usually accompany greatness. He had no credentials but Himself. He was only thirty-three when the tide of public opinion turned against Him. His friends ran away. One of them denied Him. He was turned over to His enemies and went through the mockery of a trial. He was nailed on a cross between two thieves. While He was dying, His executioners gambled for His garments, the only property He had on earth. When He was dead, He was laid in a borrowed grave through the pity of a friend. Nineteen centuries have come and gone, and today He is the central figure of the human race. All the armies that ever marched, all the navies that ever sailed, all the parliaments that ever sat, all the kings that ever reigned, put together, have not affected the life of man on this earth as much as that solitary man." From Dr. James Allen Francis' book, *"One Solitary Life"* as cited by *Joy!*

The New Testament opens with His virgin birth to Mary. Jesus' birth was the moment in history when *"the Word became flesh (John 1:14)."* The birth of Jesus Christ took place in the final years of Herod the Great, probably around 6 or 5 BC. (The odd phenomenon of Jesus being born "BC" is due to a miscalculation by a monk named Dionysius Exiguus in AD 526. Jesus was born when the Jewish nation was part of the Roman Empire, and in the empire, years were counted from the founding of the city of Rome. When the Roman Empire fell and Christianity became the universal religion in what had once been the Roman Empire, Emperor Justinian requested Dionysus to make a new calendar. This calendar was to replace the Roman calendar, and it counted years from the birth of Christ. The new calendar divided history into the years before Christ (BC) and after the birth of Christ [AD, which stands for Anno Domini, "in the year of the Lord."] However, long after the Christian calendar had replaced the Roman calendar it was discovered that Dionysus had made a mistake. He had placed the birth of Christ four to seven years later than the founding of the city of Rome).[6]

---

[6] Hampton Henry Halley, *Halley's Bible Handbook*, 2000, p. 533

John the Baptist came to announce the arrival of the Saviour Jesus Christ, who is the fulfilment of God's promises to Abraham and David, and, of course, Genesis 3:15. He is the One through whom the whole world will be blessed. He is the Eternal King from David's house. He is the One who died for all mankind's sin, reconciles man to God and He is the Restorer of everything. He is the Establisher and Fulfilment of the New Covenant – a Covenant that does not require the keeping of laws or good works, but is based on the amazing grace of God.

Now everyone who believes that He is the Saviour, can be saved from the power of sin and eternal damnation, by grace through faith not of works (Eph. 2:8-9). Jesus Christ is the ultimate fulfilment of all God's promises.

The Jews under the rule of the Roman Empire expected a political messiah that would liberate them from Roman law and re-establish their hold on the land. But, the long anticipated Messiah, Jesus Christ, came as the Saviour to set people free from the bondages of sin and self so that they could establish a relationship with God. He came to bring the spiritual kingdom of God to earth. He came to destroy the works of the devil and eventually He will restore all things to His eternal purpose (1 John 3:8; Acts 3:19-21).

The four Gospels tell of Jesus' extraordinary life, powerful ministry, horrific death on the cross and glorious resurrection. We read of the most amazing life ever lived: how He came to reveal God and His plan for man to us; how He demonstrated God's love to mankind, how He, through His life of sinless perfection, fulfilled the law of the Old Testament; how He lived out the values of the kingdom of God; and how He came to give us the Gospel. As we have seen before, every prophecy that was prophesied about Him in the Old Testament was precisely fulfilled.

During the 40 days following His resurrection, He appeared to His disciples and other people on different occasions, confirming that He had been supernaturally raised from the dead. His resurrection is the most monumental event in history. Jesus Himself said: *"After three days I will rise* (Matt. 27:63)."* The apostle Paul said: *"And if Christ is not risen, then our preaching is empty and your faith is also empty* (1 Cor. 15:14)."* He did rise! His resurrection confirms that He is the Glorious Risen Saviour. All the persons in the Bible that were brought back to life, such as Lazarus, were merely resuscitated and not resurrected – they came back to life only to die again. But Jesus Christ of Nazareth died and was resurrected to live forever. Therefore, we have a Gospel and we can truly believe in Him as the only Risen Lord and Saviour.

In Luke 24:49 Jesus gave His disciples instruction to *"tarry in the city of Jerusalem until you are endued with power from on high"* (referring to the promised Holy Spirit). He then ascended into heaven as His disciples watched, where He sits at the right hand of the Father until He will return in glory for His Church.

❖ The Church: AD 30-Present

AD 30 during the feast of Pentecost, fifty days after Jesus' resurrection and ten days after His ascension into Heaven, the promised Holy Spirit was poured out upon His disciples. They proclaimed the great works of God in languages that they did not even know. The outpouring of the Holy Spirit and the corresponding co-operation of the Holy Spirit in the ministry of the Apostles point clearly to the dawn of a pertinent new era.

The Church was a mystery (i.e., hidden, not revealed) in the Old Testament. It was first prophesied to Peter in Matthew 16:18. In its revealed form, as the body of Christ, it could not exist before the resurrection of Christ (Eph. 1:20-23; Hebr. 9:15-17). Our Lord declared that the kingdom, which includes the Church, will come with power (Mark 9:1). Later He confirmed with His disciples that the "power" will be received when the Holy Spirit is poured out (Acts 1:8). Seeing that the Holy Spirit was poured out on the day of Pentecost it is viewed as the moment of the real establishment of the New Testament Church – it was established in the power of the Holy Spirit. So, we suggest that the New Testament Church was established during the outpouring of the Holy Spirit on the day of Pentecost, in Jerusalem (approximately) 30 AD.

Sadly, there are many different opinions concerning "church," because of a great variety of churches that demonstrate considerable differences of lifestyle, reflecting their differing views of the nature and purpose of the Church. Most people's understanding of "church" is determined by their personal experience of Church. However, to correctly understand the concept of "church," it is imperative to see it from the point of view of God's intention with it – what is God's Vision and Purpose for the Church.

The Greek word translated as "Church" is *ekklēsia*. The noun *ekklēsia* is derived from a verb that means "to call out." The concept is indicative of a group of people that is formed as a result of their calling out of a larger group of people (the world). It signifies a group of people that is called for a specific purpose. Christians are called out of the world by faith in Jesus Christ. The Church is speaking of a community of people who believe in Jesus Christ and are in a special relationship with God, and they express Him in society.

The word *ekklēsia* really means "assembly." The word was not invented by the New Testament writers; they simply gave special meaning to it. In the secular Greek in New Testament times the word *ekklēsia* had a very specific meaning: a **governmental assembly**. As we know "assembly" means: a group (or body) of people assembled (brought or put together) for a specific purpose. This picture portrays wonderfully the concept of the Body of Christ.

The New Testament reveals to us that it is in and through the Church that all God's intended purposes will be fulfilled (Heb. 10:5-7). God uses the Church and by His working through the Church He reaches out to the sinful world and brings the Christians to maturity in Christ (Acts 1:8; Eph. 4:12-16; Col. 3:10; Rom. 8:28-30). He is going to use the Church to meet His desire for His Son's bride (2 Cor. 6:14; Eph. 5:32). God uses the Church to reveal and demonstrate the dynamic principles of His kingdom – the Church gives expression to the values and standards of the kingdom; the Church reflects the Gospel that she proclaims. He uses the Church to bring back humanity in a righteous relationship with Him and to restore the priestly function (1 Pet. 2:5-9; 1 John 1:3). God is going to use the Church to fulfil His desire for manifold seed and sinless posterity (Rev. 12). The Church, with different ministries and spiritual gifts, is God's final instrument to fulfil His intended purposes in the world.

There are approximately eighty different pictures in the New Testament that identify and define the New Testament Church. These different pictures should give us a better understanding of the purpose of the Church. In the letters of the apostle Paul, the Church is called, among other things:

- **The Bride of Christ** – the apostle Paul tells us that the relationship between a man and his wife symbolises *"Christ and His church* (Eph. 5:32)." See also Second Corinthians 11:2. Our loyalty to Christ will be tested during our "engagement" here on earth. The bride should be committed to the Bridegroom. The bride of Christ should reflect and manifest the glory of the Bridegroom.

- **The Temple of the Holy Spirit** – the born-again believers are also called a temple of God in which the Holy Spirit dwells (1 Cor. 13:16, 17). Seeing that God is omnipresent, He indwells the individual Christian as well as the corporate Church – a body of people: living stones in a living temple (see 1 Peter 2:5).

- **A family** – there exist many family pictures that are used in connection with the Church. For example, the apostle Paul sees the Church as a family when he tells Timothy to act as if the members of the Church are members of a larger family (1 Tim. 5:1-2). Also see Matthew 6:9, Ephesians 2:18-19; 3:14-15 and Heb. 2:10-12.

  A family is a family because it has a shared life-source – the Father. You cannot claim to be God's child if you do not acknowledge His other children as your brothers and sisters. Thus, God's fatherhood has relational implications in two directions: vertical and horizontal.

  As a family, the Church is a place of love, acceptance, joy, sharing, caring, learning, and purpose; a refuge from the stresses of life and the world; and an oasis where you are strengthened in your walk with the Lord. There should be mutual acceptance – Jesus calls us His brothers (and sisters), because God calls us His sons and daughters.

- **The Lords Army** (2 Cor. 10:3-6; Eph. 6:10-18; 2 Tim. 2:3-4) – this calls us to attention that we are in a spiritual war. The essential feature of the Lord's army is to manifest His victory. The Lord's Army should demonstrate His invincible power. The Lord Jesus is the Victor and we are supposed to be victorious in Him. In our relationship to the Commander in Chief it is required of us to live disciplined lives and to be completely obedient to His commands.

- **The Pillar and Ground of truth** (1 Tim. 3:15); that is to say, the source and support of all realistic knowledge of life. It is especially important that the present-day Church will live up to the real meaning of this picture. In the contemporary postmodern context of relative opinions and everything goes, the Church should be solid in her proclamation of the truth of God's Word; there is no room for compromise, because God never compromises. It is only when we proclaim the truth in a fallen world that people will receive freedom (John 8:32, 36).

- **The Body of Christ** (Eph. 4:16; Heb. 10:5-7). Probably the most significant picture of the Church. Human beings relate to the world they live in through their bodies. It is in our bodies that we get things done in a world of time and space. Similarly, Christ relates to the world through His Body, the Christians – the Church. The born-again believers as the Church of Christ are the instruments by which He works out His redemptive purposes in this fallen world; by the body of Christ He manifests Himself. We are His eyes, ears, mouth, heart, hands and feet in this fallen world.

  A body is a **unit** with different members that have **different functions** that **work together**. The members are **correctly connected** to the body as well as the Head and they are **interdependent**. The body of Christ is not a group of separated, isolated individuals. **We belong to one another and depend on each other**. When one member suffers everyone else suffers (see 1 Corinthians 12:12-27).

Fittingly, the Book of Acts records the first thirty years of the early Church. By reading through Acts we identify the supernatural element of the Church and we see that Jesus Christ continues His ministry through the life and ministry of the Church. We come to realize the power of God's grace and His Spirit – that ordinary people did extraordinary things by the grace and power of God's Spirit. Many signs and wonders are being referred to in the Book of Acts.

More importantly we read of the love of God in action – how the first converts to Christ were committed to love and care for each other. They even demonstrated the love of God to their enemies and were willing to die for the name of Jesus.

God allowed persecution so that the Gospel of Jesus could spread and the Church could grow. Acts 6-9:31 tells us that persecution of the Church leads to expansion. We read that as the persecuted disciples moved out they took the Gospel with them. If you throw a rock into a pond of water, the rock will cause a circle of waves (spirals) to go out in all directions. These waves will continue, moving further away from where they started. So it was with the Church. The rock was thrown into the pond on the Day of Pentecost. Acts 1:8 describes three stages in which the witness of the Church, and of course, the Church itself expanded. The Church began in Jerusalem and Jesus' followers began witnessing there (Acts 1-7), then they took the Gospel to the districts of Judea and Samaria and throughout Israel (Acts 8-12) and then the Gospel was spread throughout the Roman Empire and to Rome itself (Acts 13-28). And today the Church is spreading literally to *the end of the earth* (Acts 1:8)."

Jesus Christ of Nazareth is both the foundation and the head of the Church, and He says: *"I will build My church, and the gates of Hades shall not prevail against it* (Matt. 16:18)." Church history confirms this truth. The Gospel message is increasing and the Church is growing; nothing can stand against the moving forward of the Church, simply because it is His Church. Yes, we can declare: "all over the world the Spirit is moving." And Jesus is accomplishing His purpose in and through His Church.

Today, we are part of the same Church that was established about AD 30. We have the same commission, the same grace, the same Spirit, and the same spiritual gifts. The Book of Acts has 28 chapters. However, the book doesn't end there; we are writing the subsequent chapters of the Acts of the Holy Spirit in and through the Church of Christ.

The Church of Christ is called, commissioned and anointed to continue the ministry of Jesus on this earth in the power of the Holy Spirit. And you are part of that Church.

A Basic Biblical Timeline

The following timeline is obviously not to scale and the dates are approximate.

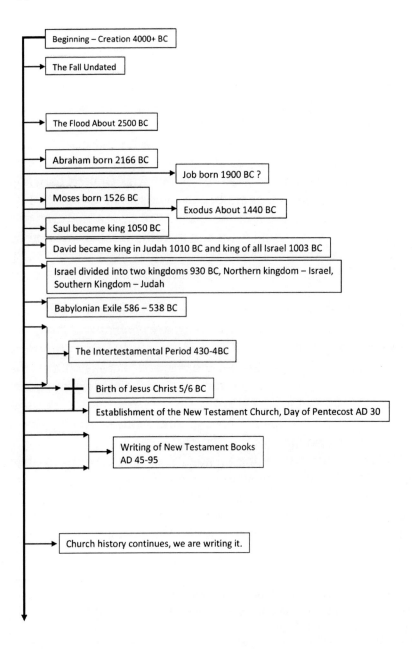

Part Three

Survey of Old Covenant Books

Chapter Three

Survey of the Pentateuch

Introductory

The main message of the Old Covenant can be summarized in a few words. It cries out: we desperately need a Saviour! And, Jesus is coming!

As we have seen, the Old Covenant contains the Creation Account (Gen. 1-11), God's calling of one man, Abraham, to establish the lineage from which the Messiah would be born, the covenant God made with the people of Israel at Mount Sinai (Ex. 19:5), and God's revelations to and dealings with Israel. The Old Covenant is seen as the **promise** – God's promise of a Messiah (Gen. 3:15) from the House of David (2 Sam. 7:12-16) and a New Covenant (Jer. 31:31); and the New Testament is the **fulfilment** of that promise.

The Old Covenant is not "old" because it is ancient, but by contrast to the New Covenant which we call the New Testament. The "old" does not mean that we do not make use of it any more. Some parts of it were only applicable to the Jewish people, for instance: the sacrifice of animals and circumcision. However, it is good to understand and believe the Old Covenant's message. We can learn from the history and experiences of Israel with God – what God is like and how He wants to interact with mankind (see 1 Cor. 10:1-11). In fact, Israel could be seen as a microcosm of humanity – they too have a fallen nature, our struggles through life could be compared to their struggles, they were in need of God, we are too.

The Apostle Paul says: *"For whatever was written in former days was written for our instruction, that we through the endurance, patience and comfort of the Scriptures might have hope (Rom. 15:4)."* The Old Covenant must be viewed and interpreted in the marvellous bright light of the New Covenant. It should be read through the lens of the Messianic promise and the God-unveiling events that point to the New Covenant.

The Division of Old Testament Books

Jewish tradition divides the Old Covenant into three parts: The Law, The Prophets and The Writings. The Hebrew names for these divisions are: *Torah, Nebiim, Ketubim.* The first letters of these – T, N, K – are used to form the name, which the Jews use, for the complete Hebrew Bible: *Tanakh.*

For the purpose of our study, we divide the Old Covenant into four groups of books: The Pentateuch (the Law), The Historical Books, The Poetical and Wisdom Books, and the Prophets.

We will do a swift-paced walk through each book, which will show us how each book is put together and how each one relates to the whole. This will also lay the necessary groundwork for further study.

The Pentateuch

The first five books of the Bible are known as the *Pentateuch,* meaning "five rolls," which is derived from the meaning of the two Greek words: *pente* (five) and *teukhos* (roll or case), referring to the five rolls or cases in which the five scrolls were placed. Hebrew tradition treats the first five books not as separate independent books, but as a unit, and the Jews refer to it as the *Torah* (meaning "instruction" or "teaching").

GENESIS

Author
Traditionally Moses, based on the testimony of Scripture and the absence of any plausible alternatives.

Date
Approximately 1440 BC

Main Theme
God's Sovereignty in Creation, Judgment, Election, and Salvation

Key Verse
"In the beginning God created ... (Gen. 1:1)."

Key Phrase
"In the beginning"

Key Words
Beginning, Create, Covenant and Genealogy

Setting
The beginning of Biblical history; the geographical setting is mostly Mesopotamia within the Fertile Crescent.

Purpose
To record God's creation of the universe, His plan for mankind and the chosen man through whose lineage the Messiah would be born.

Synopsis
The Book of Genesis is the foundational book of the Bible; it lays the foundation for all God's revelation, it explains the origin of everything and gives us, at least in germ form, every leading fact, truth and revelation. The Book of Genesis must be the most important book of the Bible – if we remove it from the Bible, then the rest of the Bible will be incomprehensible. The Book of Genesis provides the context and sets the stage for the rest of Scripture.

Genesis appropriately means "origin" or "beginning," because it is all about origins: the universe, life, mankind, marriage, sin, Israel, and God's plan for mankind.

The Book of Genesis was written purposefully as an historical account. Moses structured the book by eleven separate units, each beginning with the words *"this is the genealogy of"* or *"this is the history of"*.

The eleven separate units, which form the Book of Genesis, are:

1. The Introduction to the Generations, the Creation Account (1:1-2:3)
2. *"The history of the heavens and the earth"* (2:4-4:26)
3. *"The genealogy of Adam"* (5:1-6:8)
4. *"The genealogy of Noah"* (6:9-9:29)
5. *"The genealogy of the sons of Noah"* (10:1-11:9)
6. *"The genealogy of Shem"* (11:10-26)
7. *"The genealogy of Terah"* (11:27-25:11)
8. *"The genealogy of Ishmael"* (25:12-18)
9. *"The genealogy of Isaac"* (25:19-35:29)
10. *"The genealogy of Esau"* (36:1-37:1)
11. *"The history of Jacob"* (37:2-50:26).

We can also divide the Book of Genesis into two main sections. Genesis 1-11 covers approximately 2000 years and deals with the Primeval History. The first 11 chapters reveal the person, character, power and purpose of God, the source of life and the created order; the nature of humankind as being distinct from the rest of creation; the problem of sin; and the promise of Redemption – it's a frame of reference to understand God's gracious plan for mankind.

The first 11 chapters are also dominated by four momentous events which form the basis for the rest of Biblical history:

1. **Creation**: God is the sovereign Creator of the universe. He created time, space and matter to provide a world in which human beings, who are the pinnacle of His creation, can live and be in relationship with Him.

Day	Created	Genesis
1	Light (day) and Darkness (night); established the day-night cycle	1:3-5
2	Hydrosphere and Atmosphere	1:6-8
3	Fertile earth, sea, plants, and trees	1:9-13
4	Light bearers, son, moon, and stars	1:14-19
5	Fish and Birds	1:20-23
6	Animals and Man	1:24-31

2. The Fall: Although originally good, the creation became subjected to corruption as a result of the sin of Adam and Eve.

3. The Flood: As humanity multiplied, sin also multiplied until God was compelled to destroy the human race with the exception of Noah and his family.

4. The nations: Although there is only one human race originating in Adam and Eve, God divided the single culture and language of the post-flood world, and scattered the peoples over the face of the earth, thus creating many different nations.

Towards the end of Genesis 11 we are introduced to Abraham, "the father of all who believe," with whom God made a covenant so that He could ultimately bless and save mankind.

Genesis 12-50 covers approximately 350 years and tells us about four great men, the History of the Patriarchs – Abraham, Isaac, Jacob and Joseph (Joseph is not really seen as a patriarch, because the Covenant was not confirmed with him, however, he inherited it). About half of the Book of Genesis tells us about the first three men to whom God gave the promises that underlie the formation of the Hebrew nation – focusing on Abraham and Jacob. (Remember, the amount of time dedicated to a subject tells us of the importance of that subject.)

A quarter of the Book of Genesis (fourteen Chapters) is concerned with Joseph, son of Jacob, because his story is necessary for the completion of Jacob's story; he is the link between the family and the nation, between Canaan and Egypt, and between a nomad and a civilised mode of life. Joseph is the most perfect anticipation of Jesus who was to be the Seed of the woman, and the fulfilment of the Messianic prophecy.

Genesis 12-50 chronicle the patriarchs and their families' stumbling attempts at following God faithfully and also detail God's gracious and miraculous interventions on their behalf and His patience with their failures. Genesis concludes with Abraham's descendants living in Egypt. They have taken their name, the people of Israel, from the name God gave to Jacob, whose sons gave their names to the twelve tribes of Israel.

Noteworthy

The Book of Genesis had always been under constant attack, because: (1) it reveals God as the Creator of the universe and everything in it; and (2) it prophecies the downfall of Satan.

The Creation account in the Book of Genesis is the only authoritative record of the Creation that we have, and it reveals God as a God of plan and purpose, the Source of life, wisdom, and beauty.

Genesis chapter 1 reveals God as the all-powerful Creator God who created the universe and all that is in it in six consecutive days, and climaxes with the creation of man. While Genesis chapter 2 reveals God as the covenant-keeping personal God, and focuses on the creation of man on the sixth day, and climaxes with the marriage of man.

Genesis 18 reveals to us that Jesus had lunch with Abraham in real Bedouin hospitality, and a serious discussion about Sodom. "Three men" came to visit Abraham. One of the three was called "the Lord;" the other two were angels. After they had lunch, the two angels moved on to Sodom to destroy it (Gen. 19:1, 13), while the Lord and Abraham were in conversation. Throughout Genesis 18 Abraham speaks with the Lord as Someone he already knows, because the Lord appeared to him before (Gen. 12:7; 17:1). All the appearances of the Lord in, most likely, angelic form in the Old Covenant are appearances of the pre-incarnate Christ. In John 8:56 Christ says strikingly: *"Your father Abraham rejoiced to see My day, and he saw it and was glad."* Some scholars will say that the word "it" is incorrect. It should be "Him." Abraham saw Him – the pre-incarnate Christ. The Jews were kind of insulted when Jesus told them about Abraham; they argued that He was not yet fifty years of age so how could He have seen Abraham. By His statement in John 8:58 Jesus clearly reveals His deity and the possibility that He could have seen Abraham.

Personal Application

Like every other Christian you should have a Biblical worldview. What is a worldview? A worldview could be defined as: a set of culturally structured assumptions, values, and beliefs which we hold that make up our outlook on the nature of the world and how to live in that world; it provides the foundation on which "we live and move and have our being." We make use of the word "assumptions," because our view of viewing reality is not necessarily correct, we may be wrong in some of our considerations.

The humanistic worldview is by far the most dominant worldview today which is responsible for creating this anti-God, post-Christian and postmodern culture. The humanistic view embraces naturalism that denies the existence of God and maintains that everything, including human beings, are merely material (thus human beings evolved from animal life and are "rational animals").

A Biblical worldview see life and the created world around us through the "eyes" of God. Only God sees everything absolutely – precisely the way that things are. That makes a Biblical worldview imperative. Your values and beliefs should be based on what the Bible says.

A Biblical worldview declares, among many other things, that:

- The God of the Bible is the One True God eternally existing in three Persons – God the Father, God the Son, and God the Holy Spirit.

- God is the Grand Designer of the universe, and He is Sovereign in Creation, Judgment, and Calling.

- Human beings are created in the image and likeness of God to be in relationship with Him (man did not evolve). This makes human beings unique – they are primarily spiritual beings with the ability to communicate with God.

- As the Book of Genesis reveals, man failed (sinned, even in the midst of an ideal environment), however, God is divinely gracious.

- In the same way as Abraham, human beings who put their trust in God and respond in faith to Him will be justified; all that God expects of us is to believe Him and to surrender ourselves unto Him.

- God has a plan, which is revealed through the Bible, to redeem man eternally and to restore all things to His intended purpose.

Invest time alone with God in prayer, praise & worship, and Bible study, so that you can arrive at a scriptural knowledge of Him, and of yourself and your ways. Trust Him to touch your heart, and allow Him to change your views so that they will fit into His viewpoint.

EXODUS

Author
Moses who is the central figure of the Exodus. Jesus Himself confirms the Mosaic origin of the book (Mark 7:10; 12:26; Luke 20:37; John 5:46, 47).

Date
About 1400 BC

Main Theme
Deliverance and Redemption by Blood

Key Verse
"So I have come down to deliver them out of the hand of the Egyptians, and to bring them up from that land to a good and large land, to a land flowing with milk and honey ... (3:8)."

Key Phrase
"Let My people go"

Key Words
Deliver, Sacrifice, Sign, Tabernacle, and Sanctuary

Setting
In the wilderness during Israel's wanderings

Purpose
To record Israel's deliverance from Egypt and development as a nation.

Synopsis

Exodus means "exit," "departure," or "going out." The Book of Exodus, starting with the word "now," is a continuation of the Genesis account, dealing with the development of a small family group of seventy into a large nation of two to three million. The Hebrews lived in Egypt for 430 years most of the time in slavery. Their exponential growth became a threat for their masters, who abused them cruelly.

Exodus records how God raised up Moses to be the leader and deliverer of His chosen people. And tells us of their journey from Egypt to Mount Sinai to receive the Ten Commandments, the cornerstone of God's covenant with Israel. The first five commandments guided their relationship with God, while the last five their relationship with people. Out of these commandments flow many chapters of other commandments, statutes and regulations, which would have helped the Israelites to keep the Ten Commandments.

After the Israelites accepted the covenant, God gave clear instructions on building the Tabernacle (moveable tent), where His presence could be seen as a cloud by day and fire by night – a daily reminder of fellowship possible through His redemptive work and God's desire to dwell among His people.

We can divide the Book of Exodus into three major sections:

1. The Miraculous Deliverance of Israel (1:1-13:16)

This section tells us about the slavery of the Israelites in Egypt, how God prepared Moses to be the deliverer of His people, and how the God of Israel had a resounding victory over Pharaoh and the gods of Egypt.

2. The Miraculous Journey to Sinai (13:17-18:27)

In this part of the Book of Exodus we read about four major events that took place during Israel's journey to Sinai: (1) the Israelites experienced God's awesome delivering power (13:17-15:21); (2) they experienced God's supernatural ability to provide for His people (15:22-17:7); (3) they received protection from their enemies, the Amalekites (17:8-16); and (4) Moses appointed ruling elders to help him to guide the people and to keep peace among them (18:1-27). These events emphasize God's care for His people.

Although the Israelites had experienced a miraculous deliverance from Egypt and journey to Sinai, they were quarrelsome and discontent.

3. The Miraculous Revelations at Sinai (19:1-40:38)

In this section of the book we identify three major events: (1) the giving of the Ten Commandments and those instructions that explained how these commandments were supposed to be expressed in the lives of the Israelites (19:1-23:19); (2) detailed instructions concerning the building of the Tabernacle, its furnishings, and the duties of the priests and the people (25:1-31:18; 35:4-40:33); and (3) the worshipping of the golden calf and the consequences thereof (32:1-35).

Noteworthy
Exodus begins in darkness and gloom, yet ends in glory – it begins by telling how God came down in grace to deliver the enslaved Israelites, and ends by declaring how God came down in glory to dwell in the midst of a redeemed people.

Personal Application
God is faithful to His covenant and well able to deliver. You are redeemed by the blood of Jesus; He has delivered you from your spiritual bondage. Now you should be the instrument through which somebody else can receive deliverance.

LEVITICUS

Author
Moses (Fifty-six times the Book of Leviticus states that God imparted these laws to Moses.)

Date
About 1400 BC

Main Theme
Holiness in Worship and Life based on God's Holiness

Key Verse
"Be holy, because I am holy (Lev. 11:44)."

Key Phrase
"I am the Lord your God"

Key Words
Holiness (152 times, more than in any other book of the Bible), Sanctify, Offering, Sacrifice

Setting
In the wilderness during Israel's wanderings

Purpose
To reveal God's perfect holiness, to serve as a handbook for the priests and Levites outlining their duties in worship and to serve as a guidebook of holy living for the Hebrew people.

Synopsis
The English title of the book, which is adopted from the Latin Vulgate version, is a bit misleading, because it does not particularly address the Levites, but Leviticus deals with all of Israel approaching the holy God and responding to His holy presence.

Leviticus is God's guidebook to His newly redeemed people, showing them how to worship, serve, and obey the holy God, who has just established His presence among them in the Tabernacle.

"In the Book of Exodus, Israel was redeemed and established as a kingdom of priests and a holy nation. In Leviticus Israel is taught how to fulfil their priestly call. They have been led out from the land of bondage in Exodus and into the sanctuary of God in Leviticus. They moved from redemption to service, from deliverance to dedication."[7]

Leviticus underscores God's holiness; it is filled with rules and regulations for sacrifices, offerings, priestly duties, various types of impurity, and the celebration of religious festivals. The sacrificial system highlights human sinfulness and points prophetically to Jesus' eventual once-for-all atonement. The sacrifices proclaimed only one way to God – the way He prescribes. The system of law constantly reminded the Israelites that God's covenant with them carries expectations and consequences.

We can divide Leviticus into two major sections:

1. Worshipping a Holy God in the Old Covenant (1:1-17:16)

The first seventeen chapters primarily deal with the sacrificial system of worship and reconciliation to God when they had violated the covenant. In this section we find specific instructions for the different offerings, the priests, the people, and the altar. These instructions taught the Israelites about the nature of God, the seriousness of sin, and how to worship Him.

2. Living a Holy Live in the Old Covenant (18:1-27:34)

The last ten chapters deal primarily with how God's chosen people are to deal with one another. In this section we find the standards for the people, the rules for the priests, and the different seasons and festivals. These standards, regulations, and ceremonial feasts were to separate the Israelites from the pagan nations around them.

The content of Leviticus covers approximately a month, between the erection of the Tabernacle (Ex. 40:17) and the departure from Sinai (Num. 10:11).

---

[7] *Nelson's Complete Book of Bible Maps & Charts*, p. 39

Noteworthy
A renowned Bible scholar once said that in Leviticus the Holy Spirit is not once mentioned, because all here relates to Christ, and it is the Holy Spirit's work to glorify Him. Also, no other book in the Bible contains so many direct messages from the Lord as Leviticus. "The Lord spoke," "said" or "commanded," are met with 56 times; "I am the Lord," 21 times; "I am the Lord your God," 21 times; "I am" 3; and "I, the Lord, do," twice.[8]

Personal Application:
God is holy; if we want to fellowship with God we need to be holy. In Jesus we are sanctified – set apart from sin and the world to live saintly lives in fellowship with God. Our daily lives should reflect God's holiness.

NUMBERS

Author
Moses (Eighty references in Numbers claim that the Lord spoke to Moses.)

Date
About 1400 BC

Main Theme
Israel's Wilderness Wanderings and Journey to the Promised Land

Key Verse
"Only do not rebel against the Lord (Num. 14:9)."

Key Phrase
"Tabernacle of Meeting"

Key Words
Census, Murmuring, Purity, Tabernacle

Setting
In the wilderness during Israel's wanderings

---

[8] Robert Lee, *The Outlined Bible*

Purpose

To record the two numberings of the Israelites and to describe their experiences as they wandered in the wilderness.

Synopsis

The title of the Book of Numbers comes from the Septuagint and relates to the two censuses listed in the book. The Hebrew title is a better summary of the book: "In the Wilderness," because it primarily deals with Israel's wilderness wanderings.

The Book of Numbers stretches over almost thirty-nine years and continues the account of the Exodus. It begins with Israel still at Sinai. The Israelites' entry into the Wilderness of Sinai is recorded in Exodus 19:1, and they leave Sinai at Numbers 10:11. Numbers then records the Israelites wanderings round Kadesh-Barnea, and finally their arrival in the plains of Moab in the fortieth year.

We can divide Numbers into three main parts:

1. Preparing for the Journey (1-10:10)

The introductory part finds the Israelites camped at Sinai, dealing with the preparation for the journey and receiving different instructions.

2. Wrong Approach and Wanderings in the Wilderness (10:11-25:18)

The second part records the events of the lengthy wilderness wanderings, and describes the perishing of the generation that experienced the Lord's deliverance from Egypt. This part of the book highlights the complaints, rebellion, and disobedience of the first generation that led to their deaths.

3. At the Doorway to the Promised Land (chs. 26-36)

This part tells us of the new generation at the doorway to the Promised Land. It informs us about the census of the new generation of Israel, (ch. 26), the inauguration of Joshua as the new leader (27:12-23), instructions concerning offerings (chs. 28-30), and instructions concerning the apportionment of the land among the tribes of Israel after they have entered the Promised Land

By the grace of God, the wilderness experiences prepared a nation, the new generation, to possess the Promised Land – one way or the other, God's purposes will be accomplished.

Noteworthy
This book warns us: "Beware of unbelief." Although there was failure in the wilderness wanderings, from Sinai to Kadesh, we see Israel in glorious victory in Moab.

The repeated failure of God's people to keep their covenant is central to this Book. "The people who trusted God to bring them *out* of Egypt failed to trust Him to get them *into* Canaan."[9] This highlights the problem of sin and the need for a Saviour. The Israelites complained, challenged Moses' authority, they gave in to fear, the spies gave a false report, rebellion and unbelief were the order of the day, they worshipped Baal and even Moses disobeyed God.

The Book of Numbers illustrates both the kindness and severity of God – God is loving and forgiving, but as a righteous God He has to judge sin. It also teaches that God's people can move forward only if they put their trust in Him. Further, Numbers testifies to the grace and mercy of God, and points forward to the divine grace to be displayed and received in Jesus Christ.

Personal Application
Praise God, Jesus took our judgment upon Himself.

While it may be necessary to pass through wilderness experiences, one does not have to live there. In the face of trials and tests yield to the Holy Spirit and follow His leading – we are not poorly led. Also, trust Christ who has delivered you from "Egypt" as your Provider – He is our daily bread and spiritual drink (John 6:32, 33; 1 Cor. 10:4).

---

[9] John Phillips, *Bible Explorer's Guide*, p. 159

DEUTERONOMY

Author
Moses (forty references that Moses wrote the book are included in Deuteronomy); the final summary was most likely written by Joshua after Moses' death.

Date
About 1400 BC at the end of the forty-year period in the wilderness

Main Theme
Obedience brings Blessing, Disobedience brings Cursing

Key Verse
"Love the Lord your God with all your heart ... (Deut. 6:5)."

Key Phrase
"You shall remember the Lord your God"

Key Words
Covenant, Obey, Remember, Blessed, Cursed

Setting
Moab, the east side of the Jordan, just before the Israelites entered the Promised Land

Purpose
To remind the Israelites of the faithfulness of God, what He had done for them and to encourage them to rededicate their lives to Him so that they can go and possess the Promised Land.

Synopsis
Deuteronomy means "second law," coming from two Greek words, *deutero*, which means "second" and *nomos*, which means "law." However, the book is more accurately described as a renewing of God's covenant with Israel; an expansion of the original covenant given on Mount Sinai, and a second reading as well as a ratification (acceptance) of that covenant. The setting of Deuteronomy is clearly

the plains of Moab. After the forty years in the wilderness, a new generation waited to enter Canaan, a generation that had to hear the covenant and renew its agreement. What God had promised to Abraham, Isaac and Jacob was about to come true. Deuteronomy is a proclamation of a second chance for Israel.

Deuteronomy is the last of the five books of Moses, which contains three long speeches or farewell addresses of Moses to Israel in covenantal form as they prepare to enter the Promised Land. Moses was now 120 years old, entering the last week of his life, and he was well aware of the present generation's weaknesses, and what was lying ahead for them. The Israelites faced a turning point in their history – entering the Promised Land, new enemies, temptations, new leadership and maybe excitement mingled with uncertainty. Therefore, Moses reminded the Israelites of the Lord's faithfulness and challenged them to be faithful and obedient to their God as they possess the Promised Land. Moses encouraged them thirty-five times *"go in and possess"* the land. He reminded them thirty-four times that it *is "the land the Lord your God gives you."* Deuteronomy is a very personal and emotional book for Moses, because he experienced a strong sense of anticipation for the Israelites. He appealed to the people like a dying father to his children.

Strikingly, Moses was the first to prophesy the coming of the Messiah, a Prophet like Moses himself (18:15). And notably, Moses is the only person with whom Jesus ever compared Himself: *"For if you believed Moses, you would believe Me; for he wrote about Me. But if you do not believe his writings, how will you believe My words* (John 5:46, 47)?" Jesus often quoted from Deuteronomy. He quoted Deuteronomy 6:5 when He stated the greatest commandment. When Jesus was tempted by the enemy in Matthew 4, He quoted exclusively from Deuteronomy (8:3; 6:13, 16; and 10:20).

Deuteronomy's message is so powerful, it is quoted over eighty times in the New Testament.

The Book of Deuteronomy follows the structure of an ancient Near Eastern international treaty, known as "suzerain treaty." (Suzerain Treaty was made between a suzerain king, the greater, more powerful king, and the vassal or lesser king, which in basic terms said that if the conquered behaved themselves, the king would protect them and provide for them, but if they misbehaved, he would punish them.) In fact, the structure of Suzerain Treaties dating from around the time of Moses compare the best, especially to Deuteronomy. Most likely Moses saw and studied these treaties when he was educated in Egypt. Therefore Moses presented the covenant to Israel in a form of a treaty. This is also strong evidence that Deuteronomy was written at the suggested time (1400 BC).

As such, Deuteronomy first gives a historical prologue, chapters 1-3, in which Moses recaps what has happened from Sinai to that present moment; this is, in part, an appeal to the Israelites to learn from previous failures; then in chapters 4-11 general exhortations and basic stipulations are made. The centre of the Book, chapters 12-26, is the section of detailed stipulations, rather than a simple rehearsal of Sinai, this expands on the Ten Commandments' provisions giving instruction for all areas of life. Chapters 27-30 prescribe the covenant ratification with its attendant curses and blessings. Chapters 31-33 provide for succession of leadership and continuation of the treaty; Joshua is designated to lead the people into the Promised Land. Chapter 34 tells of Moses' death and divine burial.

Noteworthy
We find the following in Deuteronomy: (1) the first mention of death by hanging on a tree (21:22, 23); (2) the only reference in the Old Testament referring to the burning bush recorded in Exodus 3, which led to Moses' call and Israel's deliverance (33:16, "Him who dwelt in the bush"); (3) the prophetic declaration about the coming Great Prophet (18:15-19).

Deuteronomy boldly underscores the faithfulness of God – to His purpose, promise, and His people in bringing them into the Promised Land.

Personal Application
"I have set before you life and death, blessing and cursing; therefore choose life, that both you and your descendants may live (30:19)." In the New Covenant, choose Jesus; He became a curse on behalf of mankind by His crucifixion (Gal. 3:14) and He is life, eternal life (1 John 5:12). As well, Jesus says: *"I have come that they may have life,*

and that they may have it more abundantly (John 10:10)." Your faith in Christ and His work of atonement remove the curse from your life.

The Book of Deuteronomy is also a plea for obedience based on the motives of love and faith (loving God is a major theme of Deuteronomy).

Furthermore, Deuteronomy's principles can be applied to relationships in general and each person's relationship with God:

- Be exclusively loyal to the Lord – He is the only God and Saviour.

- Do not imagine God as less than He has revealed Himself to be.

- Honour God and be in harmony with Him in all we do and say.

- Daily rest in God spiritually, in faith – He is in control although it sometimes doesn't look like it.

- Respect those representing God and His authority, beginning with our parents.

- Respect human life – created in the image and likeness of God – and His authority over it.

- Respect marriage and the family; do not violate the commitment, but be faithful.

- Respect what belongs to others and their well-being.

- Respect the reputation of others, value justice and speak truth.

- Do not let selfishness rule and hurt others; deal with heart attitudes and desires; trust the Lord to provide.[10]

---

[10] Roger Cotton, *Pentateuch,* p. 141

Chapter Four

Survey of the Historical Books

The Historical Books chronicle Israel's history from the first days of conquering Canaan, through the spiritually trying times of the judges and kings and the divided nation, to the Israelites exile and return. They cover about seven hundred years in the history of the Israelites. The major events covered by these books are:

1. The settlement of the Israelites in the Promised Land after their escape from Egypt and their years of wandering in the wilderness

2. The transition from rule by judges to rule by kings

3. David's anointing as king of the United Kingdom

4. The division of the nation into the Northern and Southern kingdoms

5. The destruction of the Northern kingdom

6. The captivity and return of the Southern Kingdom

Let's look at the different Historical Books, starting with Joshua.

JOSHUA

Author
Uncertain, based on Joshua 24:26, Joshua could have written portions of the book; most probably the book was composed in its final form by a later scribe, but was founded on recorded documents written by Joshua.

Date
1400-1375 BC

Main Theme
The Conquest and Settlement of the Promised Land

Key Verse
"Be strong and courageous ... for the Lord your God will be with you (Joshua 1:9)."

Key Phrase
"All came to pass"

Key Words
Courage, Obedience, Covenant

Setting
Canaan, the Promised Land, which is modern-day Israel

Purpose
Recording the history of Israel's conquest of the Promised Land

Synopsis
The title of this book is appropriately named after its central figure, Joshua. His original name was *Hoshea,* which means "salvation" (Num. 13:8), but Moses changed it to *Yehoshua,* "Yahweh is Salvation" (Num. 13:16). The shorter version is Yeshua, the Hebrew equivalent of the name "Jesus." In Joshua's role of triumphantly leading the Israelites into their inheritance, he foreshadows Jesus who will bring *"many sons to glory* (Heb. 2:10)." Joshua's name is

symbolic of the fact that although he is the leader of the Israelites, the Lord is the real Conqueror.

Joshua begins where Deuteronomy ends, and so forms a link between the Pentateuch and the rest of Israel's history. As the Israelites prepare to take possession of the Promised Land, their loyalty to God is tested.

The theme of conquest and occupation pervades the Book of Joshua. This book chronicles the period from Israel's entrance into Canaan through the conquest, division, and settlement of the Promised Land. And declares and demonstrates God's faithfulness.

We can divide Joshua into four sections:

1. Preparing for the Inheritance (1-5)
The Lord gave Joshua the call and encouraged him as the new leader of Israel. Joshua prepared Israel militarily and spiritually before they, by faith, crossed over the Jordan on dry land. In chapter five the Commander of the Lord's army appeared to Joshua.

2. Possessing the Inheritance (6-12)
The conquest opens with an unorthodox but resounding victory over Jericho; their next battle, against Ai, resulted in humiliating defeat. While God used Israel to bring judgment on Canaan, He at times used others to bring judgment on Israel; after they've confessed their sin, His blessing is restored. Three major military campaigns took place – Joshua first established the Israelites in the central part of Canaan, then conducted campaigns in the southern and northern parts of Canaan in order to complete the possessing of the inheritance. A careful study of Joshua's military campaigns shows that he had a carefully planned strategy of conquest – divide and conquer.

3. Distributing the Inheritance (13-21)
After the conquest of the Promised Land under Joshua, the land was assigned to the sons of Israel. Thus the long-promised and anticipated inheritance was made tangible, yet more local battles must be fought for them to fully occupy.

4. Joshua's Final Discourse and Death (22-24)

Joshua challenges the Israelites not to forsake the Lord, who remained entirely faithful. He rehearsed the mighty acts of God on Israel's behalf and encouraged the leaders to remain faithful. Joshua pledged: "As for me and my household, we will serve the Lord (24:15)." The Israelites willingly reaffirmed their covenant with God.

Noteworthy

The Canaanites represent our lusts, besetting sins and spiritual enemies.

Personal Application

The battle is the Lord's, only His methods will bring success; you must know the Commander (Jesus) and follow Him; faith is the victory; you must surrender to Jesus in order to be victorious and to lead others you must follow Him.

JUDGES

Author
Unknown

Date
About 1050-1000 BC

Main Theme
No God, No Peace; the Book of Judges illustrates the sad results of Israel's disobedience; man's proneness to wander from God

Key Verse
"In those days Israel had no king; everyone did as he saw fit (21:25)."

Key Phrase
"And the Spirit of the Lord came upon"

Key Words
Did Evil, Cried Out, Delivered, Judged, Spirit of the Lord

Setting
Canaan

Purpose
To tell about Israel's repeated departures from God and consequent failures

Synopsis
The Book of Judges stands in stark contrast to Joshua. In Joshua obedient Israel conquered the land through trust in God, while in Judges, disobedient and idolatrous Israel, was repeatedly oppressed by their enemies.

The title of the book describes those who ruled after Joshua – Judges, a word that refers not so much to those who preside over trials at a court, but rather to those raised up by the Spirit of God to deliver Israel from foreign oppression and to establish and maintain domestic law and order, and adherence to covenant principles. It covers about 350 years.

The purpose of the Book of Judges is threefold: (1) historical – to record the history of Israel between Joshua and Samuel, providing a link between the conquest of Canaan and the monarchy; (2) theological – the book underscores the principles of obedience (brings peace and life) and disobedience (brings oppression and death), and points to the need of a Deliverer; (3) spiritual – it reveals the faithfulness of God to His covenant. Whenever the Israelites repented and turned from their evil ways, the Lord always forgave them and raised up Spirit-empowered judges to deliver them from their oppressors (although not all the judges were morally strong, and the people often turned back to idolatry).

As we have learned in the Book of Joshua, God had instructed Israel to remove all their enemies from the land, but they failed to fully obey. Some Canaanites remained in the land and caused God's people many troubles. And because Joshua failed to raise up a legacy of leadership, there was no strong leader with vision to lead the people of God effectively.

The following outline shows us:

1. The conditions in the time of the judges (1:1-3:6)

    A. Areas not conquered (1:1-2:5)
    B. Israel's cycle of failure (2:6-3:6)

2. The six major judges who delivered Israel (3:7-16:31)

    A. Othniel – delivered Israel from Mesopotamia (3:7-11)
    B. Ehud – from Moab (3:12-30)
    C. Deborah and Barak – from Canaan (4-5)
    D. Gideon – from Midian (6-8)
    E. Abimelech – known as the anti-judge, because he was the opposite of the other judges God appointed (9)
    F. Jephthah - from Ammon (10:6-12:7)
    G. Samson – from Philistia (13-16)

3. A time of confusion (17-21)

    A. Micah and his idolatry (17)
    B. The Danites and their relocation (18)
    C. Sin and civil war (19-21)

Noteworthy
The Book of Judges contains: (1) the oldest known parable in the world (9:7-15); (2) a great battle-song (ch. 5); and (3) the first record in history of the emergence of a woman into prominence and leadership of a nation (ch. 4).

Personal Application
Know this: sin separates you from God. Remain committed to the Lord. The Lord is your Judge – your Deliverer – well able to save and set you free from sins that bind. He will empower you with His Holy Spirit to live a victorious life, and use you to bring deliverance to those who are bound in sin and despair.

RUTH

Author
Unknown

Date
Between 1050 BC and 500 BC

Main Theme
Redemption based on God's Grace, and Sovereignty

Key Verse
"Your people will be my people and your God my God (1:16)."

Key Phrase
"that you may find rest"

Key Words
Sovereignty, The Almighty, Redemption, Kinsman

Setting
A dark and chaotic time in Israel's history when people lived to please themselves, rather to please God.

Purpose
To show that in a decaying society there can be people who remain truthful to God and to foreshadow Jesus our Kinsman Redeemer

Synopsis
While the Book of Judges ends on a negative note, Ruth presents a positive story of romance and redemption, by the grace of God, in the midst of tragic life circumstances. Compared to the Book of Judges, Ruth is like an oasis in the desert. The Book of Ruth beautifully portrays love, devotion, and redemption set in the distressing period of the Judges (1375-1050 BC), because we read: *"In the days when the judges ruled … (Ruth 1:1)."* Ruth covers about 30 years.

Because of famine in Israel, Naomi and her family moved to Moab. While there her husband died, her two sons married, and then her sons also died. Naomi was left with her two daughters-in-law, both Moabites.

When Naomi decided to return home to Bethlehem, her daughter-in-law, Ruth, made a pledge of loyalty: *"Entreat me not to leave you, or to turn back from following after you; for wherever you go, I will go; and wherever you lodge, I will lodge; your people shall be my people, and your God, my God. Where you die, I will die and there will I be buried. The Lord do so to me, and more also, if anything but death parts you and me* (1:16, 17)." Naomi agreed and Ruth travelled with her to Bethlehem. There they hoped to reclaim the family property.

Naomi loved and cared for Ruth. And, obviously, Naomi's life was a powerful witness to the reality of God. Ruth was drawn to her and the God she worshipped.

Naomi is a picture of a child returning to her father's house. Ruth represents those people who are not part of God's family – Gentiles. "The Moabite, shut out by Law (Deut. 23:3), is admitted by grace." Ruth was a foreigner, since her husband died and she had no children. As a foreigner Ruth could glean (gather grain left by the reapers) in the fields during harvest time (see Lev. 19:9-10).

God's providence led Ruth to glean in the field of Boaz, a man of great wealth, who was a relative of her deceased father-in-law. He noticed her and made arrangements for her protection and provision.

At Naomi's direction, Ruth presented herself to Boaz with the risky request to marry her. Since Ruth was married to a Hebrew man, as a result of that marriage, she was brought into the family of God, the Hebrew nation. However, since they had no children and her husband died, Ruth was no longer a member of the family of God. The law in Deuteronomy 25:5-10 stated that she could go to a kinsman of her husband, and ask him to marry her. Take notice: the woman has to propose not the man – romance in reverse. If he refused, she could bring the matter to the elders.

The man who agreed to marry such a woman did two things: First, he bought her back (redeem her) by paying any debts she owed. Secondly, as a responsible male relative he married her and fathered a son to continue the family name. Establishing the relationship of marriage brought her back into God's family. Boaz accepted the obligations of that custom, because he obviously loved her. God gave Boaz and Ruth a son, whom they named Obed, which means "servant" or "worshipper." He became the grandfather of David, which put Boaz and Ruth in the blood line of Jesus Christ. Thus, through Jesus Christ, God's mercy and grace in Ruth's life extends all the way to believers today.

While Ruth is a type of the Gentiles, Boaz, the kinsman redeemer, is a type of Christ. This story is a picture of God's grace for the prodigal child who was coming home, and God's grace for the person who is coming to Him for redemption.

Furthermore, when we first meet Ruth, she is a destitute widow. We follow her as she joins God's people, gleans in the grain fields, and risks her honour at the threshing floor of Boaz. In the end, we see Ruth becoming the wife of Boaz. What a picture of how we come to faith in Christ. We begin with no hope and are rebellious aliens with no part in the kingdom of God. Then as we risk everything by putting our faith in Christ, God saves us, forgives us, rebuilds our lives, and gives us blessings that will last through eternity. Boaz redeeming Ruth is a picture of Christ redeeming us.[11]

The concept of the kinsman redeemer is an important portrayal of the work of Christ. The kinsman redeemer must:

1. Be related by blood to those he redeems (Deut. 25:5, 7-10; John 1:14; Rom. 1:3) – Jesus became part of the human race to redeem us.

2. Be able to pay the price of redemption (Ruth 2:1; 1 Pet. 1:18, 19) – because Jesus is the sinless God-Man, he is the only One who paid the price for redemption in full by His blood. He paid the debt that we owe in full.

3. Be willing to redeem (Ruth 3:11; Matt. 20:28; John 10:15, 18; Heb. 10:7) – Jesus loves us so much that He was more than willing.

Noteworthy

Ruth is the only book in the Bible which is completely devoted to a woman (though two books are named after women: Ruth and

---

[11] Dr. James C Galvin, *Book Outlines, Blueprints* in *Chronological Life Application Study Bible*, p. 185

Esther). Further, the Book of Ruth is seen as an appendix to the Book of Judges.

> **Redemption** means: "to buy back" and "to bring back." Boaz redeemed Ruth in two ways: (1) he bought her back when he paid all her debts; (2) then he established a relationship with her that brought her back into the family of God.
>
> In the same way Jesus redeemed us: (1) when He paid the debt for our sins in full on the Cross; (2) when He initiated and established relationship with us, He brought us back into the family of God.

Personal Application

Jesus is our Kinsman Redeemer, we should be in love with Him, appreciate Him and be fully committed to Him. Also, we should embrace the beauty of commitment and friendship and the values of family commitment.

1 & 2 SAMUEL

The previous three Old Testament History Books: Joshua, Judges, and Ruth, are also known as "The Allegorical History Books" because of the examples and warnings they provide. When we come to First Samuel, we begin the next section, of the History Books, which are known as "The Kingdom Literature History Books." This section includes First and Second Samuel, First and Second Kings, and First and Second Chronicles. All these books are "kingdom literature" because they tell us about the kings and kingdom of Israel.

The Books of First and Second Samuel were originally one book in the Hebrew Bible known as "The Book of Samuel" or simply "Samuel," but were divided when they were translated into Greek. Thus the Septuagint and Protestant Canon divide Samuel into two books, this introduces an artificial division into what is actually one continuous account.

1 SAMUEL

Author
Uncertain, most likely Samuel supplied or wrote some of the material for 1:1-25:1; some suppose that Abiathar the priest wrote 1 Samuel.

Date
Between 931 and 722 BC

Main Theme
The early history of Israel, including the failure of the priestly office in Eli, the founding of the prophetic office in and judgeship of Samuel, and the forming of the princely (or kingly) office in Saul, as well as the preparation of David for kingship

Key Verse
"Appoint a king to lead us, such as all the other nations have (1 Samuel 8:5)."

Key Phrase
"pray to the Lord"

Key Words
Prayer, Prayed

Key Persons
Samuel, Saul, David

Setting
Israel, during the transition in leadership from judges to kings

Purpose
To record the life of Samuel, Israel's last judge and Saul's kingship (Israel's first king) as well as the choice and preparation of David, Israel's greatest king

Short Synopsis
First Samuel describes the transition of leadership in Israel from theocracy under the judges to monarchy under the kings. It covers the ninety-four-year period from the birth of Samuel to the death of Saul and much of it deals with the conflicts Israel had with the Philistines. First Samuel also provides a historical link between the Book of Judges and the Books of the Kings. The content of First Samuel may be grouped around the names of the three great personages found in the book – Samuel, Saul, and David.

We divide 1 Samuel into three main parts:

1. Samuel, the Last Judge and First Prophet (1:1-7:17)
The book begins with the background and birth of Samuel who was not only the last judge of Israel, but also priest and prophet. He was dedicated to God's service by his mother, Hannah. As a small boy he lived with and was trained by the priest Eli. As a child he even *"ministered to the Lord before Eli the priest* (2:11)," in a time that the Word of the Lord was rare (3:1). While Eli's sons were wicked (2:12-17), *"Samuel grew in stature, and in favour both with the Lord and men* (2:26)."

God warned Eli twice that He was going to destroy his household. The Philistines crushed Israel in battle, stole the Ark, and killed both Eli's sons. Eli was so shocked when he received the devastating news of the capture of the Ark and the death of his two sons that he fell backward, broke his neck and died (ch. 4).

We have seen that the form of government (theocracy) under the Judges had been a failure. And the priesthood had also failed as Eli and his sons proved. So Samuel succeeded Eli. Samuel's integrity and loyalty served Israel well – he was respected as a prophet and leader, and through this dark and dangerous period of Israel's history, Samuel led the people to a place of dignity and power. His prophetic ministry led to a revival in Israel, the return of the Ark of the Covenant, and the defeat of the Philistines (ch. 7).

2. The Reign of Saul Israel's First King (8:1-15:35)

When Samuel was old and his sons proved to be unjust judges, the people of Israel requested a king *"like all the nations* (8:5)." (Israel was not supposed to be "like all the nations," they were chosen and called by God to be His people.) *"But the thing displeased Samuel when they said, 'Give us a king to judge us.' So Samuel prayed to the Lord (8:6)." "And the Lord said to Samuel, 'Heed the voice of the people in all that they say to you; for they have not rejected you, but they have rejected Me, that I should not reign over them (8:7)."* Under God's instructions Samuel anointed Saul as king. He was a handsome and charismatic man. Despite early promise Saul did not have the godly character to be a successful king. As someone said: "His ego was as large as his stature." In Saul God gave the people *their* king (the establishment of a kingly rule was in the Divine purpose, however, not based on the terms of the people). Saul was on different occasions disobedient to God. Because of his disobedience, God told Samuel to tell him *"your kingdom shall not continue. The Lord has sought for Himself a man after His own heart (13:14)."* Saul's pride became his downfall. Israel had rejected the Lord in asking for a king, now their king is rejected by the Lord.

3. Saul's Decline and David's Rise (16:1-31:13)

hile Samuel's life gives us a positive example of a godly leader, Saul's life manifests much bad fruit – no fear of God, pride, jealousy,

DISCOVERING THE MOST AMAZING BOOK 127

plain disobedience, and even rebellion against God. Outwardly Saul was the ideal king, but not inwardly; physical appearance could be misleading.

In 1 Samuel 16:1 to 17:58 we read how David increased in prominence. David, the youngest and least of Jesse's sons, was chosen by God to be the next king (16:12). Samuel privately *"anointed him in the midst of his brothers; and the spirit of the Lord came upon David from that day forward (16:13)."*

It took a long time, though, for David to become king. Most of First Samuel tells us about David in "God's seminary of preparation." David soon began serving Saul as a musician and armour-bearer. After killing Goliath, David became increasingly popular in Israel, and Saul grew dangerously jealous. As Saul jealously and murderously pursued him, David went through all kinds of trials that taught him to trust and obey God no matter what. It was during this period of David's life that he wrote many of his emotionally laden and spiritually rich Psalms, perhaps seventeen of them. These Psalms reveal David's distress, and fear; his belief that he was not to blame, and his confidence that God would ultimately deliver him. Everything he experienced made him fit for God's purposes for his life (see Romans 8:28).

David's life was the exact opposite of Saul's. Although a man with mistakes, the dominating characteristic of David's life was obedience. Where Saul's life was disintegrating because he had divorced himself from God by his disobedience, God brought everything together in David making him a great king.

First Samuel concludes with the fierce battle against the Philistines; the deaths of Saul's sons and Saul's death by suicide.

Despite the many less-than-positive events in and the tragic ending of First Samuel, three theological emphases do emerge from this book: (1) the ancient promise of God that kings would issue from the Patriarchs (Gen. 17:6; 35:11) is fulfilled; (2) the book reveals the error of attempting to run ahead of the promises of God and to bring to pass with human effort what only God can and should do; (3) the book teaches the principle that the all-wise and all-powerful God is sovereign and when nations or individuals submit to His dominion, there is great blessing.[12]

---

[12]   Dyer and Merrill. *Nelson's Old Testament Survey*, pp. 205-206

Noteworthy

First Samuel makes many remarkable contributions: (1) it first gives and uses the title *"Lord of hosts* (1:3);" (2) The name "Messiah" is first found in 1 Samuel 2:10, *"His anointed,"* literally means: "His Messiah;" (3) the term "Ichabod," meaning the glory has departed, is first mentioned in 1 Samuel 4:21; (4) 1 Samuel 5:1-4 tell us that evil cannot stand in the presence of a Holy God; (5) 1 Samuel 9:9 gives us the former name of a prophet, "seer;" (6) David first described a king as *"the Lord's Anointed* (24:6)"; and (7) The Holy Spirit is prominent in this book: (a) He is seen as the author of prophecy (10:6) and channel of regeneration and a new heart (10:9, 10), (b) the author of holy and righteous anger (11:6), (c) the inspirer of courage and prudence of speech (16:13 with 18), and (d) He preserves us from evil (16:14).

Failure is everywhere in this book: Eli failed both as priest and father; Samuel failed with his sons, who did not have the same spiritual integrity as their father; and Israel's first king, Saul failed. However, we find great consolation when we recognize the glorious work of the Holy Spirit (as mentioned above), the power of prayer (1:27; 7:5), and the revelation of the promise of the Shepherd-King (David prefigures Jesus Christ as the Shepherd-King).

Furthermore, in the life and ministry of Samuel, a man of "wonderful integrity" and "splendid loyalty," we see God's hand at work – he was asked (by his mother) from God, given by God, dedicated to God, and he lived for God.

Personal Application

As God is at work in history, so He is at work in your life. Submit yourself to the Kingship of Jesus; allow Him to rule your life.

We learn from the small boy Samuel that God speaks to us in a familiar and recognizable "voice," not in a scary unfamiliar voice – when God called Samuel, he thought it was Eli who called him. God spoke to Samuel in a "voice" that was familiar to him so that he would not be frightened. Samuel was accustomed to hearing Eli's voice; therefore when God called him, it sounded like Eli.

Men look at the outward appearance, but God looks at the heart (16:7); if the intentions of your heart are pure, don't let man be your judge. Be obedient to God, it is better than sacrifice (15:22, 23), and is always worthwhile. God is concerned about your heart and your actions – they are interrelated. Your actions reflect your character.

We learn from David's early life that the difficult circumstances in life and the times of waiting often refine, teach, and prepare us for the future responsibilities God has for us (Rom. 8:28).

2 SAMUEL

Author
Unknown, possibly Abiathar the priest, or Nathan and Gad, two of David's contemporaries

Date
Between 931 and 722 BC

Main Theme
King David, forerunner of the Messiah

Key Verse
"The God of Israel said, the Rock of Israel spoke to me: 'He who rules over men must be just, ruling in the fear of God (2 Samuel 23:3)."

Key Phrases
"before the Lord," "enquired of the Lord"

Key persons
David, Nathan, Absalom, Joab, Bathsheba
Setting
Israel, under the kingship of David

Purpose
To record the history of King David's reign showing us his rise and fall and the consequences of his sin

Synopsis

When both Saul and Jonathan are killed in battle, the stage was set for David to become king.

Second Samuel records David's ascendance to the throne and the forty years of his reign (1010-970 BC). It highlights David's reign, first over the territory of Judah (7 years), and then over the entire nation of Israel (33 years); it also tells us of his sins of adultery and murder, and the shattering consequences of those sins upon his family and the nation. Also First Chronicles tells us in part of David's reign. Therefore one must read both books in order to be able to form a better and more complete picture of David's life and rule.

We can divide Second Samuel into three parts:

1. The Triumph of David (chs 1-10)

Second Samuel begins with the report of Saul and Jonathan's death, and how David lamented over them (1:17). After David "enquired of the Lord," he was directed to Hebron where he was anointed as king over Judah. Ishbosheth, a son of Saul, was crowned as king by Israel (not Judah) wanting to maintain the line of Saul on the throne. This shows us the sharp clash between the will of man and the will of God. Israel and Judah were at war and there was a power play by the house of Saul in the persons of Ishbosheth, and Abner, Saul's commander in chief of the armies. Abner joined forces with David for he said: *"if I do not do for David as the Lord has sworn to him – 'to trandfer the kingdom from the house of Saul, and set up the throne of David over Israel and over Judah, from Dan to Beersheba (3: 9, 10).'"* Abner was later murdered and so was Ishbosheth.

It took David seven and a half years to unify the nation under his leadership. 2 Samuel 3:1 reveals the reason to us: *"Now there was a long war between the house of Saul and the house of David. But David grew stronger and stronger, and the house of Saul grew weaker and weaker."* The will of God did prevail (man's will was for Saul, and God's will was for David).

In 2 Samuel 5 David made a covenant with the elders of Israel and he was anointed as king over all of Israel and the Word says that David *"became great and the Lord God of hosts was with him (6:10)."* God broke through in David's warfare against the Philistines (5:20) and David triumphantly *"drove back the Philistines from Geba as far* as *Gezer* (5:25)." He then brought the Ark of the Covenant back to Jerusalem, the capital of his rule, and thus unifies the political and religious life of the nation. 2 Samuel 7 tells us about the covenant that God made with David: *"Your throne shall be established forever* (7:16)," introducing the theme of the coming King and Messiah.

King David triumphed over his enemies (chs. 8 and 10) as a type of Christ Who *"disarmed principalities and powers, He made a public spectacle of them, triumphing over them in it* (Col. 2:15)."

David took the fractured kingdom that Saul left behind, and built a strong, united kingdom. By his victories over the enemies of Israel, David actually completed the conquest of the Promised Land begun by Joshua, he expanded the borders of the kingdom.

Note: It is necessary to mention the importance of the first ten chapters of Second Samuel; each part showing a little more clearly the Messianic Plan or God's Plan of Redemption. As Scroggie rightly says: "they show that the Messianic Kingdom (yet to come) will be united and not divided (v. 1-5); that it will have a Theocratic Centre (v. 6-10); that in that Centre the Presence of God will be specially manifested (ch. 6); that the Kingdom will be secure in perpetuity (7:12-16); and that all its enemies will be eliminated (chs. 8 and 10)."

2. The Transgressions of David (ch. 11)
When David was at the zenith of his reign he fell into sin. David, although mighty king and warrior, was merely human. He committed adultery with Bathsheba and organised the murder of her husband, Uriah. After Bathsheba's mourning over Uriah was over, she became the wife of David and gave birth to a son.

3. The Troubles of David (chs. 12-24)
Although David repented deeply (see Psalm 51) after the prophet Nathan confronted him, the consequences of his sin are clear: *"The sword shall never depart from your house* (12:10)." The following is a summary of David's troubles as a result of his great sin: (1) The child that Bathsheba bore to David died (12:15); (2) Amnon, David's son, found guilty of incest (13:1-20); (3) Absalom, another son of David, killed Amnon (13:21-36); (4) Absalom fled from home, and didn't see his father for five years (13:37-39); (5) Absalom returned,

rebelled, and treacherously seized the kingdom (15:1-12); (6) David had to flee (15:13-16:14); (7) Ziba deceived David, and Shimei cursed him (16:1-4; 5-13); (8) Joab murdered Absalom (18:9-33); Sheba's rebellion (20:1-22); and (9) the judgment on David's sin of numbering Israel and Judah (24:10-17).

Noteworthy
In 2 Samuel 5:2 we find the first instance that a ruler is likened to a shepherd, *"You shall shepherd my people Israel."*

It is in 2 Samuel 23:2 that David claimed divine inspiration for his Psalms, and that even his words came from God.

David combined the three offices of prophet, priest, and king. He was anointed as king, he functioned as prophet in chapter 23 and in chapter 24:25 he functioned as priest. These were again combined in Jesus the Christ, and again combined in the Spirit-filled Church, in whose members the Spirit of prophecy resides (Acts 2:14-21) and who are *"kings and priests to our God* (Rev. 1:6; 5:10)."

Personal Application
Remain patient while you depend on God for the fulfilment of His promises; through times and seasons of "testing" God disciplines our faith. Always respond in faith to God, and in challenging times "enquire of the Lord." Also, remember sin has consequences.

1 & 2 KINGS

Along with 1 & 2 Samuel, the Books of Kings and Chronicles highlight three phases in Israel's history: the United Kingdom, the Divided Kingdom, and the Surviving Kingdom. We could refer to 1 and 2 Kings as "The Rise and Fall of the Hebrew Nation."

The Books of Kings are written in the form of selective historical narrative. Their content is taken up by the summary of individual kings' careers, consisting of the name of each king, what kingdom he ruled (Israel or Judah), the date of his accession to the throne, the length of his reign, his religious and other policies, the details

of his death, and the name of his successor. Also First and Second Kings present God as the Lord of history. They demonstrate God's providential working in and through the lives of the Israelites for His redemptive purpose, and the necessity of obedience to God's covenant and the serious consequences of disobedience. First and Second Kings should not only be seen as mere history, they rather interpret history along theological lines, showing what happens when political and religious leaders foolishly choose to worship false gods instead of wisely choosing to worship the one true God.[13]
These books vividly illustrates to us what Samuel warned the Israelites about earthly kings.

The Books of Kings cover a span of about four hundred years (970-560 BC).

1 KINGS

Author
Unknown, attributed to Jeremiah

Date
Between 560 and 538 BC

Main Theme
The political history of Israel, focusing on the reigns of different kings from the time of Solomon to the captivity of the Jewish people by the Babylonians.

Key Verse
"Who is able to govern this great people of yours (1 Kings 3:9)."

Key Phrase
"as David his father"

Key Words
King, House, Prophet

---

[13] Iain W Provan. Introduction to 1-2 Kings in ESV Study Bible, p. 589

Key Date
931 BC, the year the kingdom was divided

Setting
The once great nation of Israel turned into a land divided, not only physically, but spiritually as well.

Purpose
To show the causes of the establishment and decline of the kingdom; it points out that, when faithful to God, Israel flourished, but when Israel departed from Him their morals and their kingdom declined. The Book of Kings was written to move the exiles to reflect on their history and return to the Lord.

Synopsis
The main events of First Kings are David's death, Solomon's reign, the division of the kingdom, and Elijah's ministry. First Kings covers the 120 years from the beginning of Solomon's reign in 971 BC through Ahaziah's reign ending in 851 BC.

First Kings divides naturally into two main parts:

1. The United Kingdom (1:1-11:43)
The years of the United Kingdom are seen as the glory years. The first half of First Kings records the golden era of Solomon's reign, his wealth, wisdom, and the monumental accomplishment of building the temple. However, his disobedience in marrying foreign pagan wives turned his heart away from the Lord and led him into idolatry, which set the stage for the division of the kingdom.

2. The Divided Kingdom (12:1-22:53)
The years of the Divided Kingdom are seen as the declining years. This part of the book is hard to follow because the author switches back and forth between the Northern Kingdom of Israel and the Southern Kingdom of Judah, tracing their histories simultaneously. There were nineteen kings in the Northern Kingdom (Israel), all of them wicked. The Southern Kingdom (Judah) had nineteen kings and one queen, only eight of them were good. First Kings records the first nine kings in Israel and the first four in Judah.

The following outline of the Divided Kingdom recorded in First Kings shows us the different kings listed in this Book:

The Divided Kingdom (12:1-22:53)

    A. The revolt and reign of Jeroboam in Israel (12:1-14:20)
    B. The reign of Rehoboam in Judah (14:21-31)
    C. The reign of Abijam in Judah (15:1-8)
    D. The reign of Asa in Judah (15:9-24)
    E. The reign of Nadab in Israel (15:25-32)
    F. The reign of Baasha in Israel (15:33-16:7)
    G. The reign of Elah in Israel (16:8-14)
    H. The reign of Zimri in Israel (16:15-20)
    I. The reign of Omri in Israel (16:21-28)
    J. The reign of Ahab in Israel (16:29-22:40)
    K. The reign of Jehoshaphat in Judah (22:41-50)
    L. The reign of Ahaziah in Israel (22:51-53)[14]

Noteworthy

1 and 2 Kings were originally one book, which formed a sequel to 1 & 2 Samuel.

The failure of the prophets, priests, and kings of Israel points to the necessity of the coming of Jesus Christ and the redemption of man.

In 1 Kings the central prophet is Elijah.

Personal Application

God controls human affairs. If you respond rightly to God, you will certainly enjoy the great benefits of a relationship with Him. But if you don't, then you will experience God's discipline. Revere God. Human beings are sinful, but God is gracious to forgive and redeem those who will repent and turn to Him.

---

[14]   Larry D Powers, Book Outlines, 1 & 2 Kings, *Spirit Filled Life Bible*, p. 483

2 KINGS

Author
Unknown, attributed to Jeremiah

Date
Between 560 and 538 BC

Main Theme
Lessons from the Ruin of Israel and Judah

Key Verse
"Know now that nothing shall fall to the earth of the word of the Lord which the Lord spoke concerning the house of Ahab; for the Lord has done what He spoke by His servant Elijah (10:10)." (This is actually applicable to every king.)

Key Phrase
"Man of God (36 times)," "according to the Word of the Lord (24 times)"

Key Words
King, House, Prophet

Setting
The same as First Kings: the Divided Kingdom

Purpose
The author answers the looming question of why both the northern and southern kingdoms had been taken captive. He writes with a prophetic perspective to show that this punishment by captivity to foreign pagan nations was the inevitable consequence of the persistent violation of God's covenant with them.

Synopsis
Second Kings continues with the tragic history of the Divided Kingdom with Ahaziah on the throne of Israel, and Jehoshaphat is king of Judah. It covers about 285 years.

The book can be divided into two parts. The first part continues recording the kings of the Divided Kingdom and ends with the captivity of Israel to Assyria. The second part is taken up by the Surviving Kingdom, Judah, and ends with the captivity of Judah to Babylon.

The following outline gives us a glimpse of the content of the book and the different kings reigning:

1. The Divided Kingdom (1:1-17:41)

A. The reign of Ahaziah continues in Israel (1:1-18)
B. The reign of Jehoram in Israel (2:1-8:15)
C. The reign of Jehoram in Judah (8:16-24)
D. The reign of Ahaziah in Judah (8:25-9:29)
E. The reign of Jehu in Israel (9:30-10:36)
F. The reign of Queen Athaliah in Judah (11:1-16)
G. The reign of Joash in Judah (11:17-12:21)
H. The reign of Jehoahaz in Israel (13:1-9)
I. The reign of Jehoash in Israel (13:10-25)
J. The reign of Amaziah in Judah (14:1-22)
K. The reign of Jeroboam 2 in Israel (14:23-29)
L. The reign of Azariah in Judah (15:1-7)
M. The reigns of Zechariah, Shallum, Menahem, Pekaniah, and Pekah in Israel (15:8-31)
N. The reign of Jotham in Judah (15:32-38)
O. The reign of Ahaz in Judah (16:1-20)
P. The reign of Hoshea in Israel (17:1-5)
Q. The captivity of Israel to Assyria (17:6-41)

2. The Surviving Kingdom, Judah, (18:1-25:30)

A. The reign of Hezekiah (18:1-20:21)
B. The reign of Manasseh (21:1-18)
C. The reign of Amon (21:19-26)
D. The reign of Josiah (22:1-23:30)
E. The reign of Jehoahaz (23:31-34)
F. The reign of Jehoiakim (23:35-24:7)
G. The reign of Jehoiachim (24:8-16)

H. The reign of Zedekiah (24:17-20)
I. The fall of Jerusalem (25:1-7)
J. The captivity of Judah to Babylon (25:8-26)
K. The release of Jehoiachim (25:27-30)

Noteworthy

Second Kings vividly illustrates the need for Jesus Christ as our reigning King.

The tragic sentence: *"Did evil in the sight of the Lord"* and its equivalent are referred to 21 times.

Prominence is given to the Lord's anger (13:3; 17:18; 23:26; 24:20) and wrath (22:13, 17; 23:26).

Elisha was the central prophet in Second Kings. The first half of the book is largely taken up with his ministry of 66 years. Second Kings records sixteen miracles of Elisha, while Elijah performed only eight. This is significant when we consider the double anointing that Elisha asked for.

Personal Application

Be zealous for God with your whole heart. Let the Word of God be the final authority in your life. Be courageous and proclaim the truth, as Elijah and Elisha did.

1 & 2 CHRONICLES

These two books were originally a single volume. The translators of the Septuagint divided them into two parts and gave them the titles "The First Book of Things Omitted" and "The Second Book of Things Omitted." The "Things Omitted" refer to the things omitted from Samuel and Kings. The title "Chronicles" comes from Jerome in his Latin Vulgate Bible. Apparently he meant this title in the sense of "The Chronicles of the Whole of Sacred History."

These books cover much the same historical ground as the other books of Israel's kingdom (2 Samuel, 1 & 2 Kings), but they were written after the Babylonian captivity, and they concentrate mostly on Judah. The two books of Chronicles present the history of Israel from the viewpoint of the priests rather than the prophets, focusing on the religious (or spiritual) history of Judah, and not the political history. They were written primarily to interpret for the returned remnant the significance of their history and to show that, although the throne of David was gone, the royal line remained.

1 CHRONICLES

Author
Ezra

Date
430 BC (recording events that happened much earlier)

Main Theme
Encouragement, hope, and instruction from Judah's spiritual heritage; the temple in Jerusalem is the major unifying theme of First and Second Chronicles.

Key Verse
"His throne will be established forever (17:14)."

Key Phrase
"You reign over all"

Key Words
King, House, David, Jerusalem, Priest

Setting
The specific background of First and Second Chronicles is the period after the Exile; these books were written to the exiles who returned from captivity. During this time period the then known world was under the control of the powerful Persian Empire.

Purpose
To unify God's people; to trace the Davidic line and to teach that genuine worship ought to be the centre of individual and national life. First Chronicles was written to encourage those who had returned

to Jerusalem. The remnant that was left needed encouragement to keep their faith alive in the midst of hard circumstances.

Synopsis
The whole book of First Chronicles, like Second Samuel, is dedicated to the life and reign of David.

We can divide First Chronicles into two main divisions. The first section is taken up by nine chapters of genealogies. It begins with Adam and proceeds all the way through the Exile to those who returned to Jerusalem.

One might think that genealogies are boring and unimportant. Well they might be boring to read, but are certainly very significant: (1) they form a foundation for the account that follows; (2) in the case of first Chronicles, they trace the royal line of David that is the recipient of the promises of the Davidic Covenant, and (3) underscore the need for racial and religious purity; (4) they prove God's faithfulness and sovereignty in preserving that specific line; and (5) they give a sense of identity, heritage, and destiny to those who belong to those lines.

The second section of First Chronicles (chs. 10-29) records the events and accomplishments in the life and reign of David. Chapter 10 gives us David's affirmation as king. In chapters 11 and 12 David becomes king over all Israel and took the city of Jerusalem from the Jebusites making it his capital. The joyful bringing of the Ark of the Covenant to Jerusalem is dealt with in chapters 13 to 17. David's military exploits are recorded in chapters 18 to 20, and the preparations for the building of the temple are taken up in chapters 21 to 27. The closing two chapters of First Chronicles record David's last days.

Noteworthy
Both books of Chronicles purposefully magnify God and give Him His rightful place in Israel.

There is a clear resemblance in style and language between the two books of Chronicles and those of Ezra and Nehemiah, consequently the authorship is ascribed to Ezra. The books of Samuel and Kings are concerned with both kingdoms, Judah and Israel, while Chronicles deals only with Judah.

In trying to understand both books of Chronicles, it is important to know that these books are not mere repetition of the same material as recorded in Second Samuel and the books of Kings, but they rather have a priestly and spiritual perspective.

First Chronicles is more concerned with the Temple and its rituals than the wars of the kings, and centres on the priestly worship of Judah.

The activities of the Lord on behalf of His people are prominent in this book (4:9, 10; 5:20-22; 11:14; 12:18; 14:2, 11, 15; 18:13).

Both books of Chronicles demonstrate God's keeping of His covenant promises in preserving the Davidic line through the centuries. Special attention is also given to the tribe of Levi, because of the priestly focus of Chronicles.

Personal Application

Know and believe that God is a promise-making and promise-keeping God. Learn from the failures of the Israelites, in order not to make the same mistakes (1 Cor. 10:11; Heb. 4:11).

2 CHRONICLES

Author

Ezra

Date

About 430 BC (recording events that happened much earlier)

Main Theme

Same as First Chronicles: Encouragement, hope, and instruction from Judah's spiritual heritage; the temple in Jerusalem is the major unifying theme of First and Second Chronicles.

Key Verses

"if My people who are called by My name will humble themselves, and pray and seek My face, and turn from their wicked ways, then I will hear from heaven, and will forgive their sin and heal their land (7:14)."

Also, *"So they rose early in the morning and went out into the Wilderness of Tekoa; and as they went out, Jehoshaphat stood and said, 'Hear me, O Judah and you inhabitants of Jerusalem: Believe in the Lord your God, and you shall be established; believe His prophets, and you shall prosper (20:20)."*

Key Phrase
"Prepare his heart to seek God (30:19)."

Key Words
King, House, David, Jerusalem, Priest

Setting
The same as First Chronicles: The specific background of First and Second Chronicles is the period after the Exile; these books were written to the exiles who returned from captivity. During this time period the then known world was under the control of the powerful Persian Empire.

Purpose
To reunite the nation around the true worship of God after the Captivity.

Synopsis
Second Chronicles continues the history of First Chronicles and recounts the downfall of the Davidic dynasty from Solomon to the Exile. It covers a period of 440 years.

We can divide Second Chronicles into two major parts. The first part (chs. 1-9) records the reign of Solomon. Chapter 1 tells us that Solomon *"was strengthened in his kingdom and the Lord his God was with him and exalted him exceedingly (1:1)."* God blessed Solomon with wisdom to rule His people (1:10) and verses 13-17 give us a glimpse of his wealth, *"the king made silver and gold as common in Jerusalem as stones (1:15)."* The greater part of the account emphasises the construction of the temple (chs. 2-7). The wealth, wisdom and glory of king Solomon are again emphasised in chapters 8 and 9. However, the history of king Solomon ends abruptly, making no mention of the king's sin and failure as is recorded in 1 Kings 11.

The second part (chs. 10-36) begins with the revolt against Rehoboam, Solomon's son and successor, and the division of the kingdom (see 1 Kings 11:36-12:24). Rehoboam reigned, for seventeen years, over Judah the southern kingdom on which the second part of Second Chronicles focuses almost exclusively. Second Chronicles 10:1-36:11 trace the reigns of Judah's twenty rulers.

The following chart indicates the reigns of the different kings and their characters.

Kings of Judah			
King	Years of Reign	Character	2 Chronicles
1. Rehoboam	17	Bad	10:1-12:16
2. Abijah	3	Bad	13:1-22
3. Asa	41	Good – reforms	14:1-16:14
4. Jehoshaphat	25	Good – reforms continued	17:1-20:37
5. Jehoram	8	Bad	21:1-20
6. Ahaziah	1	Bad	22:1-9
7. Athaliah	6	Bad	22:10-23:21
8. Joash	40	Good – reforms	24:1-27
9. Amaziah	29	Unstable	25:1-28
10. Uzziah	52	Unstable	26:1-23
11. Jotham	16	Good	27:1-9
12. Ahaz	16	Bad	28:1-7
13. Hezekiah	29	Good – reforms	29-32
14. Mannasseh	55	Bad	33:1-20
15. Amon	2	Bad	33:21-25
16. Josiah	31	Good - reforms	34:1-35:27
17. Jehoahaz	3 months	Bad	36:1-4
18. Jehoiakim	11	Bad	36:5-7
19. Jehoiachim	3 months	Bad	36:8-10
20. Zedekiah	11	Bad	36:11-21

Second Chronicles ends with the fall of Jerusalem and the captivity of Judah (36:17-21), and the decree by Cyrus, king of Persia, for the release and return of Judah to rebuild the temple (36:22-23).

Noteworthy

Second Chronicles parallels First and Second Kings and serves as their commentary. Both First Kings and Second Chronicles begin with Solomon. Second Chronicles was written after the exile and highlights the importance of the Temple and the religious festivals of Judah. Thus, believing in and worshipping God is central to this Book.

Second Chronicles omits entirely the history of the Northern Kingdom, because of its false worship and refusal to acknowledge the temple in Jerusalem and, of course, God's promise was in the Davidic line from the tribe of Judah.

Second Chronicles 9:29 and 12:15 indicate that there were written accounts available (now lost) about the kings of those days. Most likely the authors of the books of Kings and Chronicles, under the guidance of the Holy Spirit, made use of those written accounts to compile their Books.

Personal Application

Seeking, believing, trusting, obeying, serving, worshipping, and loving God are the lifeblood of a spiritual and victorious Christian.

The temple is prominent in Chronicles. In the New Testament Christians are the temple of God, the dwelling place of the Holy Spirit (1 Cor. 3:16; 6:19). Think of it – you are a temple of God, His dwelling place. Covet the presence of God.

Be careful not to make any ungodly allegiance. Maintain a heart that is fully committed to the Lord.

Guard against pride when you have experienced success.

Trust the Lord in battle and stand still to see His deliverance – victory in spiritual battles manifests as we put our faith in the Lord and His victories.

Develop a lifestyle of praise, it is a mighty effectual spiritual weapon.

Differences between the Books of Samuel and Kings and that of Chronicles	
Samuel-Kings	**Chronicles**
• Prophetic Perspective	• Priestly Perspective
• Political History	• Religious History
• Wars Prominent	• Temple Prominent
• Record of both Nations	• Record of Judah
• Continuing History of Nation	• Continuity of David's line
• Man's Failure	• God's Faithfulness

EZRA AND NEHEMIAH

These two books were originally united in one book in the Hebrew text, and in the Greek Septuagint, but they were separated in the Latin translation, and English translations also treat them as separate.

The books of Ezra and Nehemiah, together with Esther are known as "The Post-captivity History Books."

EZRA

Author
Ezra

Date
538-445 BC

Main Theme
Restoration – the restoration of the temple and the restoration of the people, spiritually, morally and socially

Key Verses
God's sovereign command to Cyrus, king of Persia, to build Him a house in Jerusalem (1:1-4)

Key Phrases
"The Word of the Lord," "the Hand of the Lord," "the house of the Lord"

Key Words
Build, Built, Finished

Setting
Persia to Jerusalem, rebuilding of the temple in the context of the Persian Empire

Purpose
To record the return of a remnant of the exiles to rebuild the temple and to return to the Word of the Lord, also demonstrating God's faithfulness to His promises and people

Synopsis
The Book of Ezra continues where Second Chronicles ends, showing us how God fulfilled His promise to return His people to the Promised Land. It covers about 81 years.

God had promised through the prophet Jeremiah (25:12) that the Babylonian exile would last only 70 years. God faithfully kept His promise, and in His ordained time He stirred the heart of Cyrus to issue an edict for the exiles to return with purpose (1:1-4). He then faithfully provided zealous and capable leaders (Zerubbabel and Ezra) to lead His people and to accomplish His ordained purpose. Ezra tells us of two returns from Babylon – the first under Zerubbabel and the second under Ezra.

Therefore, we divide the Book of Ezra, and likewise the purpose of God, into two main segments or phases:

1. The Return under Zerubbabel and the Temple Reconstruction Program (chs. 1-6), covering twenty-three years. The first post-exilic return was under Zerubbabel. He was joined by 49897exiles to journey back to Jerusalem. After arriving, they built the altar so that they could offer sacrifices unto God (3:2). After that they began to lay the foundation of the Temple (3:10). They soon met opposition from local inhabitants who strongly campaigned against them so that the work on the temple was discontinued until the second year of the reign of king Darius (ch. 4). During this time, the prophets Haggai and Zechariah encouraged and helped the people (5:1, 2). Their prophesying proved to be successful, *"they [the Jews] prospered through the prophesying of Haggai the prophet and Zechariah the son of Iddo* (6:14)." Eventually king Darius issued a decree that the work should proceed unhindered (ch. 6).

2. The Return under Ezra and Reformation under Ezra (chs. 7-10)
After a fifty-eight year gap, Ezra led a second group of Jews, 1754, from Persia to Jerusalem. Armed with authority, decrees and money, Ezra's task was to administer the law of his God and the law of the king (chs.7-8). Upon arriving, he learned that the Jews were unfaithful to God, they strayed from His Word, and intermarried with their pagan neighbours. Ezra was astonished, he tore his garment and robe, and plucked out some of the hair of his head and beard; he wept and prayed for the nation (ch. 9). The people were deeply moved (10:1). Ezra's humble example of repentance affected a great many of the populace and leading priests; it led to a radical reformation.

Zerubbabel rebuilt the temple and Ezra rebuilt the spiritual life of the Jews.

Noteworthy
Ezra means "help." Mostly an unsung hero of the Bible, however, he was a very devoted priest, scribe and spiritual leader who served God faithfully. The Bible declares that Ezra was an *"expert in the words of the commandments of the Lord* (7:11)" and he *"had prepared his heart to seek the Law of the Lord, and to do it* (7:10)." Tradition says that Ezra wrote most of First and Second Chronicles, Ezra, Nehemiah, and Psalm 119 and that he led the council of 120 men who compiled the canon of the Old Testament. Certainly, he should be remembered and his fitting example should be followed.

God's sovereignty – He can work His will even beyond civil government – he moved Cyrus and Darius in order to accomplish His purpose.

148

This book records how, mainly through Ezra's ministry, the Word of God gained for the first time in the history of Israel and Judah its rightful place.[15]

Furthermore, Ezra foreshadows Christ by the life he lived and the roles he fulfilled. The following stand out:

1. As one who *"had prepared his heart to seek the Law of the Lord, and to do it* (7:10)," Ezra reminds us of Christ's description of Himself as the One who ardently obeys the Father (John 5:19).

2. As *"the priest* (7:11)," Ezra foreshadows Christ's role as the *"great High Priest* (Heb. 4:14)."

3. As the great spiritual reformer who calls Israel to repentance (ch. 10), Ezra foreshadows Christ's role as the One who transforms Israel's spiritual perspectives, including a call away from dead traditionalism and moral impurity (Matt. 11:20-24; 23).[16]

Personal Application
Know that God will fulfil His Word. In the face of opposition, trials and tests, be faithful to God. The world seeks to oppose, discourage and frustrate the purposes of God, however, God will have His way.

NEHEMIAH

Author
Probably Nehemiah, the main character of the book (tradition has it that Ezra wrote both the books of Ezra and Nehemiah which was one book in the original Hebrew)

Date
About 423 BC

---

[15] Robert Lee, *The Outlined Bible*

[16] Gary Matzdorf, *Spirit-Filled Life Bible*, p. 657

Main Theme
Godly leadership, unity in purpose (cooperation), how to handle opposition to success

Key Verses
"... though some of you were cast out to the farthest part of the heavens, yet I will gather them from there, and bring them to the place which I have chosen as a dwelling for My name (1:9)."

Also, *"... Do not sorrow, for the joy of the Lord is your strength (8:10)"*

And, *"Stand up and bless the Lord your God forever and ever! Blessed be your glorious name, which is exalted above all blessing and praise (9:5)!"*

Key Phrase
"Remember me, O my God, for good"

Key Words
Prayer and Work

Setting
Persia to Jerusalem, rebuilding the wall of Jerusalem

Purpose
To recount the rebuilding of the wall of Jerusalem and restoring the people

Short Synopsis
Nehemiah was a contemporary of Ezra and cupbearer to the Persian king Artaxerxes. He led the third and last group of Jews to return to Jerusalem after the Babylonian exile, about twelve years after Ezra's reformation. This book covers 25 years.

The Book of Nehemiah opens with the disturbing news, which Nehemiah received from fellow Jews who reported that the wall of Jerusalem is broken and gates are burned with fire, and the people in Jerusalem are in great distress. Rebuilding the walls of Jerusalem and helping the people living there became Nehemiah's burden. King Artaxerxes noticed that something was wrong with Nehemiah. When he asked him what it was that concerned him, Nehemiah replied: *"Why should my face not be sad, when the city, the place of my fathers' tombs, lies waste, and its gates are burned with fire (2:3)."* The king gave Nehemiah permission to go to Jerusalem and also letters of authority that granted him safe passage.

We divide the Book of Nehemiah into two main divisions:

1. The Rebuilding of the Wall (chs. 1-7)

Nehemiah challenged his countrymen to arise and rebuild the broken wall of Jerusalem. He organised the people into groups and assigned them to specific sections of the wall (ch. 3). The construction project was not without opposition – insults, threats, and sabotage from without and abuse from within. However, Nehemiah employed strategies to render the enemies powerless – prayer, encouragement, guard duty, and consolidation (ch. 4); he even confronted the offenders face to face (ch. 5). Praise God, under Nehemiah's powerful leadership and God's grace, the wall was finished in only 52 days. Even Nehemiah's enemies *"perceived that this work was done by God* (6:16)."

2. The Restoration of the People (chs. 8-13)

The enemies inside the wall were exposed and taken care of properly and firmly. Ezra and Nehemiah worked together to establish the people in the covenant of God again. The law was read publicly in chapter 8 and they celebrated the Feast of Tabernacles (8:13-18). The people confessed their sin personally and corporately (9:1, 2), and the Levites encouraged the people to praise God and they reflect on the goodness and faithfulness of God (9:5-38). The covenant was renewed and the people committed themselves to separate from the Gentiles in marriage and to obey God's commandments (9:1-10:39). In the last chapter we read of the reforms Nehemiah instituted during his second term as governor.

The Book of Nehemiah completes the historical account of God's people in the Old Testament.

Noteworthy

Nehemiah means "Yahweh Comforts."

The book begins and ends with prayer. Nehemiah discloses our daily practical walk in faith with God.

While Ezra deals with the rebuilding of the temple, Nehemiah tells us about the rebuilding of the wall of Jerusalem. Without walls, Jerusalem was vulnerable and could not be considered a city.

Nehemiah was twice appointed as governor of Judah – his first term spanned twelve years (5:14).

Nehemiah used the influence of his office, as governor, to support Ezra in helping to restore the spirituality of the people, and to bring moral reform.

Sanballat, and Tobiah are typical "manifestations" of the enemy that try their best to frustrate the work of the Lord and His purposes for our lives, but as we known: God's purposes will stand, and nothing or no one will change or reverse it.

The high priest Eliashib sadly fell because of his worldly alliance (13:4, 28).

Most probably the prophet Malachi also prophesied during this period, providing additional moral and spiritual support and direction.

The methods that Nehemiah adopted were effective only because of the quality of his character. The following are some outstanding qualities of Nehemiah:

- He was a man of prayer (1:4, 6; 2:4; 4:4, 9; 5:19; 6:14; 13:14, 22, 29)
- He identified with his people in their sorrows and sins (1:4-6)
- He had a genuine concern for the welfare of others (2:6)
- He had keen insight and foresight, and was a strategist (2:8, 11)
- He inspired others to work (2:17, 18), and led by example (4:23)
- He was empathetic; he sympathized with others (4:10-12; 5:1-5)
- He was vigilant (4:9)
- He gave God the glory (7:5)
- He showed courage in the face of danger (6:11), and refused to compromise; he "contended with the nobles of Judah (13:17)."
- He dealt drastically with offenders (8:28)

The Book of Nehemiah contains many (more than 100) leadership principles; it is a handbook on spiritual leadership.

Personal Application

When you stand for the truth, you will experience resistance and when you do something in the name of the Lord, you will experience opposition. Be, as Nehemiah, zealous and courageous, and don't compromise; God will overcome any opposition to His work.

When God has called you to do something for Him, in the face of challenges and opposition, persevere, press in and on, don't give in or up or compromise, finish your mission; *"So the wall was finished (6:15)."* Remember: the test of spiritual leadership is the achievement of its objective.

The enemy will also oppose restoration in your life, but be like Nehemiah remain zealous and focused while you trust prayerfully in God.

Refuse evil alliances, but cooperate well with spiritual people that God puts in your path in order to accomplish His purposes.

Always give God the glory for success and favour.

Some thoughts about prayer: United prayer demonstrates our corporate dependency on God; Fervent prayer displays our desperation to see change; and Persevering prayer demonstrates both our determination to achieve our end results and our faith in God.

ESTHER

Author
Unknown, possibly Mordecai (see 9:20)

Date
About 465 BC

Main Theme
God's Care for His People under Gentile rule

Key Verse
"Yet who knows whether you have come to the kingdom for such a time as this (4:14)?"

Key Phrase
"Esther won favour in the sight of all who saw her (2:15)"

Key Words
Humility, Interdepence, the Fear of the Lord

Setting
The geographical setting is Susa, the Persian capital. It was during the time between the first return under Zerubbabel and the second return under Ezra that Esther, a beautiful orphaned Jewess, became the queen of the Persian king Ahasuerus, God used her to save His people.

Purpose
To demonstrate in a fascinating way God's sovereign rule over the destiny of the Israelites and other nations in general; and to relate how God's people were preserved during perilous times.

Synopsis
The Book of Esther tells us about the character and conditions of the captivity; it unveils a segment of Jewish history during the Jewish captivity in Persia. The events described in Esther took place between 483-473 BC, and fit in between chapters 6 and 7 of Ezra.

As we know, not all the Jews returned to Jerusalem, very many of them remained in Babylon while many must have been born there too. And the Jews were treated fairly well in the glorious Persian kingdom; many rose to high official positions, many were wealthy and possessed their own property (all reasons why they didn't want to return to Jerusalem). Yet they lived in danger – a despotic king could turn against them overnight and change their position from prosperity to peril. The Book of Esther reminds us of this.

We can divide the Book of Esther into two main sections:

1. The Threat to the Jews (1:1-4:17)
During a lengthy festival made by king Ahasuerus of Persia to show off his glorious kingdom, his wife, queen Vashti, rebelled and refuse to obey her husband. The king got furious and on recommendation of his advisors he deposed Vashti. He later began to miss her. His

advisors suggested that he should choose a new beautiful queen from the virgins of his kingdom. Among those selected was a young Jewish girl, Esther, who was adopted by her cousin Mordecai (2:7). Esther was taken to the king and he loved her *"more than all the women, and she obtain grace and favour in his sight more than all the maidens, so that he set the royal crown on her head and made her queen instead of Vashti* (2:17)."

One day Mordecai, who was an attendant in the king's court, overheard two guards, plotting to kill the king. Through Esther, Mordecai reported the plot to the king, and those guards were hanged. Thus Mordecai has spared the king's life (2:21-23).

Sometime afterward, king Ahasuerus promoted Haman to be the second-most powerful individual in the kingdom, directly under himself, and commanded that the other nobles bow down to Haman. Mordecai refused. This made Haman very angry, and he sought to destroy not only Mordecai but all the Jews, the people of Mordecai. Declaring that the Jews did not obey the king's laws, Haman convinced the king to sign a law to destroy them all (3:8-11). Neither the king nor Haman knew that Queen Esther was a Jew.

God's plan and purpose were to work through Esther. Via her maids Esther found out that Mordecai was in sackcloth and ashes. And she sent one of the king's attendants to go to Mordecai to find out what exactly was going on. Mordecai sent word with the attendant, warning Esther that she was also in danger and he charged her to go to the king to plead for mercy for her people, even though she risked her own life by doing so. Mordecai indicated that God may have made Esther queen *"for such a time as this* (4:14)."

Esther told the attendants to tell Mordecai that he should gather all the Jews together and fast for three days for her, then she will go to the king (4:17).

2. The Triumph of the Jews (5:1-10:3)
Esther arranged two private dinners with the king and Haman to reveal Haman's plot. While Haman was making further plans to hang Mordecai, the king could not sleep and he asked for the book of memorable deeds. King Ahasuerus found out that Mordecai had not been rewarded for discovering the plot on the king's life. The king asked Haman, *"What shall be done to the man whom the king*

delights to honour?" Haman, not knowing that the king referred to Mordecai, suggested that the man should be clothed with royal apparel, a crown should be set on his head and he should ride on one of king's horses. So for Mordecai's reward, the king commanded Haman to honour Mordecai by doing what he suggested, bringing him through the open square of the city.

At the second dinner Esther told the king that she was Jewish and that Haman desired to kill the Jews. The king was very displeased about this, because Esther obtained favour in his sight. He commanded that Haman should be hanged on the gallows that he made for Mordecai.

Because the law did not allow king Ahasuerus to change the original edict, a new edict was issued allowing *"the Jews who were in every city to gather and defend their lives; to destroy, to slay, and wipe out any armed force that might attack them ... and to take the enemies' goods for spoil* (8:11)." The Jews did defend themselves successfully. *"And many from the peoples of the land became Jews, for the fear of the Jews had fallen upon them* (8:17)." In one day the Jews killed seventy-five thousand of their enemies (9:16).

In chapter nine of Esther we read of the establishment of the Purim Festival – on the day that they were to be annihilated, the Jews celebrate their deliverance, annually commemorated to this day. In Old Testament times, people cast a *pur,* or lot, to make choices. The word *purim* means "two or more lots." The Jews called their feast Purim to remind them that although Haman had used a *pur* to choose a day to destroy them, God was faithful and delivered them (9:19-28).

The Book of Esther ends by telling us that Mordecai was next to king Ahasuerus and great among the Jews, a man who sought the welfare of his people and spoke peace to the whole nation.

Noteworthy

The name of God does not appear in Esther, however the theme of God's providential protection of His people pervades this book.

There's no mention of prayer, but fasting is prominent.

Esther is never quoted in the New Testament. However, many Jews treat this book as a most sacred book, and we do learn much from it.

The importance of unity – individual and corporate success depends to a large extent on unity – cooperation with God firstly, then with those He wants you to work with

The Book of Esther shows us how God destroys those who try to harm His people, and that God's sovereign purposes will ultimately prevail.

Personal Application

Esther and Mordecai demonstrate a classic example of teamwork. And, even though you are only one person, you can make a great difference.

If you ever feel rejected, unworthy or that you are not meant to live now, remember this: you are born for a time such as this (see Acts 17:26)! And God does have a plan for your life.

God put Esther in a position to save a nation. He can put you in a position to save others, if you are willing.

Victory is certain when you remain obedient to God. Submit to God's plan even if it is challenging, like Esther, so that His purposes can be accomplished.

Like Mordecai, seek the welfare of others and speak peace and the truth in love to everyone.

Chapter Five

Survey of the Poetical and Wisdom Books

The poetical and wisdom literature consist of the following books: Job, Psalms, Proverbs, Ecclesiastes, and Song of Songs. These books reflect the typical poetical writing styles of the Old Testament era and relate God's wisdom to the great issues of life.

Poetry is seen as the language of the heart. By giving us five sacred poetry books, God ministers to our hurting hearts.

JOB

Author
Unknown

Date
Several factors argue for a patriarchal date (2000-1800 BC): (1) Job does not refer to any of the miracles during the Exodus or the Law of Moses; (2) Job's long life, he lived another 140 years after the events described in his book (42:16); (3) Job acted as high priest in his family, which was not allowed by the Law of Moses; (4) the measurement of Job's wealth in livestock; (5) Eliphaz was a descendant of Esau's eldest son called Eliphaz, who had a son called Teman (Gen. 36:10, 11; Job 4:1).

However, most scholars today date the book between the time of king Solomon and the Exile, and some suggest that it could have been written the same time as the Book of Isaiah.

Main Theme
The Problem of and Perseverance in Suffering

Key Verse
"I know that my redeemer lives (19:25)."

Key Words
Trial, Comfort

Setting
Most probably during the times of the patriarchs; it has been said that Job was a descendant of Nahor, Abraham's brother, and that he was a wealthy farmer living a semi-nomadic life-style in the land of Uz (a large area east of the Jordan, present day North Arabia). Job *"was blameless and upright, and one who feared God and shunned evil* (1:1)." God allowed satan to test this man, not because of his unrighteousness, but in spite of his righteousness.

Purpose
To reveal to us, not only the problem of suffering, but what we should learn from it – the sovereignty of God over all creation. Also demonstrating to us the battle between good and evil.

Synopsis
The Book of Job tells us of a saint that suffered severely. We may rightly say: If ever there was a suffering saint on earth, then it was Job. He lost everything in an agonizing way – his wealth, family, and health. Then he wrestles with the age-old question: Why? "If God is good and loving, why does He allow people to suffer?"

The Book of Job has been fittingly described as "a gripping drama of riches-to-rags-to-riches," a thought-provoking account of suffering and divine sovereignty, and a picture of persistent faith that endures.

By dividing the Book of Job into four sections, we will be able to get a handle on the content of the book.

1. Job is Tested (1:1-2:13)

Chapters 1 and 2 give us the backdrop to the story. The righteous Job was blessed by God with many children and great wealth. The one who accuses the children of God falsely and seeks to destroy their lives, satan, presented himself to the Lord, and claimed that Job served God only because of his blessings. When God allowed satan to test Job, Job lost all his children and possessions in tragic ways. In spite of these horrendous circumstances Job remained faithful to God. Satan presented himself a second time to the Lord and the Lord challenged and allowed him to test Job again severely by attacking his health. This time, even Job's wife suggested that he should curse God and die (2:9). But, *"In all this Job did not sin with his lips* (2:10)." Tormented as he is, Job expressed genuine steadfast faith in God.

2. The Discussions between Job and His Three Friends (3:1-31:40)

Three friends, Eliphaz, Bildad, and Zophar, came to mourn with Job and to comfort him (friends is a term used for those showing a solemn, covenant relationship). They were heartbroken. They sat with Job in silent grief for the first seven days; they comforted Job with their presence.

Note that Job 4-27 contains three cycles of six speeches. First, Eliphaz speaks and Job responds; then Bildad speaks and Job answers; then Zophar speaks and Job answers him. The final cycle is incomplete (chs. 22-26) because the final speech of Zophar is omitted.

Job cursed the day of his birth, longed for rest and lamented his sufferings – this began a dialogue between Job and his friends. Apart from encouraging Job to remain positive and strong, Eliphaz argued that Job's sickness must be a result of his sin. Bildad concluded that Job was suffering because of his sins and that his children had died because of their sins (8:1-7). He also said that Job was a sinner. Zophar suggested that man cannot really know why he suffers, but said that contemplating it is an intelligent and pious thing to do (11:7-12). He joined his two friends, agreeing with them that the source of Job's dilemma has to be sin in his life. All three of these "Job's comforters" tried to convince Job to repent. They moved around the circle doing this nearly three times (taking up three quarters of the book). Their "comfort" did not serve Job well – they insisted that he was a sinner in need of repentance, while he was fully convinced that he was righteous.

All three friends were wrong, suffering is not always a direct result of personal sin. Suffering could have many causes. Often we don't know the cause of our suffering. No one, not even Christians, are exempt from it. So we don't have to add to the pain by blaming ourselves or feeling guilty, thinking that some hidden sin is causing the trouble.

In the end of the day, these three friends *"ceased answering Job, because he was righteous in his own eyes* (32:1)."

3. The Young Elihu's Challenge to Job (32:1-37:24)

A fourth friend, Elihu, much younger than Job and his friends, *"was aroused against Job ... because he justified himself* (32:2)." He was also aroused against Job's three friends, *"because they had found no answer, and yet had condemned Job* (32:3)." The young man eventually spoke and explained that he has refrained from speaking because he is younger than them. However, Elihu, decided to speak because: (1) he realized that wisdom comes from the Holy Spirit regardless of age, and (2) he realized that they are never going to resolve the dilemma because they are asking the wrong question. Elihu challenged Job to see the greatness of God and His perspective on suffering. He argued that God had a higher purpose in Job's suffering. Elihu made the point that God is greater than we are, and no one has the right to question Him for what occurs. Some things done by God remain incomprehensible to man. Elihu proclaimed the justice, goodness and majesty of God, and condemned self-righteousness. He summoned Job to fear God (37:24).

4. God Answers Job (38:1-41:34)

"Then the Lord answered Job out of the whirlwind ... (38:1)." The Lord revealed His omnipotence to Job. God is Almighty and in control (even if it doesn't look like it), and only He understands why good people suffer.

After Job received the amazing revelation of and from God he cried out: *"Behold, I am vile; what shall I answer you? I lay my hand over my mouth (40:3)."* When Job came face-to-face with God, he came face-to-face with his own self-righteousness.

From 40:6-41:34 God rebuked Job's presumption of His injustice and again revealed His omnipotence to him.

5. Job's Response and Restoration (42:1-17)
Job responded in humility and repented; he saw God now completely differently because of God's personal revelation to him. Job said: *"I have heard of You by the hearing of the ear [hearsay], but now my eye sees You. Therefore I abhor myself, and repent in dust and ashes (42: 5-6)."*

God then vindicated Job before his three friends by rebuking them because they did not speak correctly of Him, as Job did. He also gave them instruction to bring offerings to Job who, acting as their priest, will sacrifice to God for them *"for the Lord had accepted Job (42:9)."* *"And the Lord restored Job's losses when he prayed for his friends. Indeed the Lord gave Job twice as much as he had before (42:10)."* Because of his humility, Job was fully reconciled with God. Suffering is never easy, but the result is often a deeper relationship with God. When we endure the testing of our faith, then we will experience God's great rewards.

Finally, satan was (and always is) wrong. God is always right; He is sovereign and His ways are incomprehensible.

Noteworthy
There are thirty references to God as "Shaddai" – the Almighty. Job did not merely believe in God, he believed that God is the Almighty God with whom nothing is impossible.

The Book of Job throws light on the mystery of suffering – having some understanding of the age-old message of the Book of Job will help us in handling unfair suffering.

Scientific facts that are listed in the Book of Job were only discovered by man in the sixteenth century onwards. For example:

- Long before it was discovered that air had weight (16th century), Job said: *"To establish a weight for the wind (28:25)."*

- Science discovered in AD 1650 that white light is made of seven colours, which can be "parted" from the white. Job says: *"By what way is light diffused … (38:24)?"*

Concerning the Book of Job, American Astronomer, Charles Burckhalter, once said: "The study of the Book of Job and its comparison with the latest scientific discoveries has brought me to the matured conviction that the Bible is an inspired book and was written by the One who made the stars."[17]

Personal Application

We all can, to a certain degree, identify with the sufferings of Job; his life is an example of the unfairness and incomprehensibleness of trails and tests that human beings have to face in this fallen world. Suffering is a product of a fallen world; a corrupted nature makes no exceptions for nice people.

Suffering never originates in God, but He allows it. Most of the time we do not understand why. However, He could allow suffering to test and reveal our character (also see Deut. 8:2, 3). We learn from the sufferings of Job that God permitted it: (1) to reveal Job's character; (2) to bring out a hidden sin, of which Job was unconscious, namely – self-righteousness (32:1); and (3) to serve as a lesson to others.

When somebody else suffers, be cautious not to criticize too freely. Often, like Job's sorry comforters, we have insufficient data.

When you face suffering in your life, remember: don't lose faith in God, see God for who He is; your Redeemer lives and is working on your behalf. Your responses to suffering can give it either a positive or negative meaning.

When your life is built on God, then you will be able to endure. No matter what happens, trust God. Your persevering faith will ultimately cause you to triumph and God will restore to you far more than you have lost or suffered.

In one of the Beatitudes Jesus encourages us: *"Blessed are those who mourn, for they shall be comforted* (Matt. 5:4)."

---

[17] As cited by Ray Comfort, *Scientific facts in the Bible*, 17

PSALMS

Author
A variety of authors – David wrote seventy-three of the Psalms, while Asaph (David's chief musician) is credited with twelve and the sons of Korah with eleven. Scholars believe Hezekiah wrote ten Psalms, Moses wrote Psalm 90, Ezra wrote Psalm 119, and Solomon wrote two (Psalm 72 and 127). Many of the Psalms are anonymous and were most likely written by some Levites or David himself could have written some of these anonymous Psalms.

Date
Span of authorship stretches from 1400 to 420 BC, reflecting about 1000 years of Israel's history

Main Theme
Fellowship with the Lord in the beauty of holiness in Prayer, Praise and Worship

Key Verse
There could be various key verses, however, in my opinion, the following three do stand out – *"Give unto the Lord glory due to His name; worship the Lord in the beauty of holiness (29:2)."* And, *"Praise the Lord, O my soul, and forget not all his benefits (103:2)."* And, *"Let everything that has breath praise the Lord (150:6)."*

Key Words
Worship, Praise, Rejoice, Mercy

Setting
The Book of Psalms covers a time-span of about a thousand-years of diverse periods in Israelite history – the time of Moses, the life and times of king David, the rule of Hezekiah, and during the leadership of Ezra and Nehemiah. The geographical, religious, social and political conditions, and events during these different periods in Israel's history form the setting of the different individual Psalms.

Purpose

The collecting and recording into book form and the setting to music of the different Psalms were done to serve as the temple hymnbook for Tabernacle and Temple worship, as well as private devotion.

Synopsis

While the Hebrew title of the Book of Psalms, *Sepher Tehillim*, means "Book of Praises," the Greek title, *Psalmoi*, suggests a poem that is to be accompanied by a stringed instrument.

The Book of Psalms is a collection of 150 spiritual songs, poems and prayers, which was originally in five sections or smaller books.

Various scholars have suggested that the themes of these five smaller books correspond with the five books of the Pentateuch, and thus, the whole Book of Psalms forms a typical poetical Pentateuch:

- Book 1 (Psalms 1-41), mainly written by David, tells much about man and creation as does Genesis.

- Book 2 (Psalms 42-72), mainly written by David and the sons of Korah, speaks about deliverance and redemption, and corresponds with Exodus.

- Book 3 (Psalms 73-89), mainly written by Asaph or his descendants, often refers to sanctuary, the presence of God, and worship, and corresponds with Leviticus.

- Book 4 (Psalms 90-106), mainly written by unknown authors, tells us about the coming kingdom, God's dealings with His people before any kings reigned, wilderness wanderings of Israel and triumph, and corresponds with Numbers.

- Book 5 (Psalms 107-150), mainly written by David, expresses thankfulness and praise for God's faithfulness and His Word, and corresponds with Deuteronomy.

The Book of Psalms consists of different types of Psalms that focus the reader's thoughts on God in praise and worship. We could group the different types of Psalms as follows:

Psalm Type	Basic Characteristics	Examples
Messianic Psalms	Describe some aspect of the Messiah's person, sufferings and ministry	Psalm 22
Psalms of Lament	Expressing grief or regret; speaks of moments of desperation and despair; prayer for God's deliverance	Psalms 3; 4; 6; 38-40; 42; 63; 130
Imprecatory Psalms	Calls for God's judgment on His enemies or those of His people	Psalm 35; 69
Hymns	Songs of praise and thanksgiving to God for who He is and what He has done; usually these psalms are exuberant	Psalms 9
Psalms of confidence	Express trust in God's faithfulness and power	Psalm 16
Psalms of remembrance	Express thankfulness for what God did in the past	Psalm 78
Penitential	Confess sorrow for sin, appeal to God for grace and forgiveness	Psalms 39; 51
Wisdom Psalms	Emphasize wise living by contrasting between righteous and wicked patterns of living and their consequences	Psalms 1; 37; 119
Royal Psalms	Portray the reign of the earthly king and the heavenly King of Israel	Psalms 2; 18; 45; 89

The Psalms were written out of deep emotional experiences – joy and sorrow, despair and triumph, hope and fear, love and hate, peace and war – the lows and highs of human experience can be found in them. Further, many Psalms contain a prophetic element, particularly of the Eternal King.

Noteworthy
The Book of Psalms is the largest and perhaps the most widely used book in the Bible.

The word "Hallelujah" translated as "praise the Lord" appears twenty-eight times in the Bible, and twenty-four of those are in Psalms.

The New Testament quotes 186 times from the Book of Psalms – far more than it quotes any other Old Testament book.

The Book of Psalms contains both the longest chapter (Psalm 119) and shortest chapter (Psalm 117) of the Bible.

Psalms 14 and 53 are similar.

An outstanding and predominant theological emphasis of the Book of Psalms is its God-centeredness.

Characteristics of Hebrew Poetry	
Hebrew poetry is not based on rhyme. It is based on parallel lines or thoughts, and the term describing this is parallelism. There are at least four types of parallel poetry in Hebrew Scripture:	
Type	**Definition and Example**
Synonymous parallelism	Occurs most often and is the best known. It is defined as the repetition of the same thought in two different phrases, using two different sets of words. The two parts basically reflects the same idea. For instance Psalm 2:1, "Why do the nations conspire and the people plot in vain?"
Antithetic Parallelism	Expresses the same thought, but from two different and often opposite perspectives. Psalm 37:21, "The wicked borrow and do not repay, but the righteous give generously." The book of Proverbs primarily uses this type of Hebrew poetry.
Synthetic parallelism	In this type of parallelism the second phrase completes or supplements the first. Psalm 19:10, "They [the ordinances of the Lord] are more precious than gold, than much pure gold."

Chiasm	The word "chiasm" comes from the Greek letter "chi" which is written like the letter "x." Chiasm occurs when two successive lines of poetry reverse the order in which parallel themes appear, criss-crossing each other. Psalm 18:20, "The Lord has dealt with me according to my righteousness; according to the cleanness of my hands he has rewarded me." The whole of Psalm 1 illustrates chiasm in a longer portion of poetry.

Personal Application

The Psalms teach us how to act and react in good times and in bad times. Since they express the full range of human experiences (deepest feelings and needs) in a very personal and practical way, the Psalms serve as great consolation in times of need and help us to express our love, praise and prayer wholly and exuberantly in good as well as bad times. They help us to relate to God both spiritually and emotionally, and tell us much about God. The Psalms serve as great comfort for the lonely and brokenhearted, they strengthen the weary and instruct us in the way of wisdom and righteousness, and encourage us to turn our eyes up towards God in times when we feel downcast. The Psalms instruct and encourage us to pray. In the Psalms we find Spirit-breathed direction of how to thank, praise and worship God in any and all circumstances.

Many references to Christian doctrines are to be found in the Book of Psalms – the love and faithfulness of God, the sinfulness of all mankind, man's need of God and of salvation, confession of sin, the forgiveness of sin by His grace, and the appropriate conduct of believers.

---

[18] Arnold and Beyer, as cited by Global University, *Old Testament Survey*, 130

PROVERBS

Author
Solomon (influenced by the psalm-writing of his father), with Agur (Proverbs 30) and King Lemuel (31:1-9), and others (Proverbs 22:17 and 24:23)

Date
About 950 BC with portions added around 700 BC during the time of king Hezekiah (see Proverbs 25:1).

Main Theme
The nature of true wisdom: *"The fear of the Lord is the beginning of knowledge, but fools despise wisdom and instruction (1:7 also 9:10)."*

Key Verse
"The Lord gives wisdom, and from His mouth comes knowledge and understanding (2:6)."

Key Phrase
"the fear of the Lord"

Key Words
Wisdom, Knowledge, Understanding, Righteous, Instruction

Setting
From the reign of king Solomon to that of king Hezekiah

Purpose
To record the sayings of the wise: *"to know wisdom and instruction, to perceive the words of understanding, to receive the instruction of wisdom, justice, judgment, and equity; to give prudence to the simple, to the young man knowledge and discretion – a wise man will hear and increase learning, and a man of understanding will attain wise counsel, to understand a proverb and an enigma, the words of the wise and their riddles (1:1-6)."*

Synopsis

The Hebrew word for "proverb," *mashal,* generally means "wise speech, parable, proverb, or wise saying." But it has a deeper meaning: "to rule or to govern." These wise sayings, reminders and admonitions provide profound advice to govern our lives in a godly way.

The Book of Proverbs provides wise instructions for God's people so that they can successfully handle the practical and sometimes challenging affairs of everyday living. It covers a wide spectrum of topics: how to relate to God, how to build healthy human relationships, wise sayings to youth, how to discipline children, self-control and resisting temptation, marriage, seeking truth and wisdom, and it all boils down to the most fundamental instruction – righteous living before a holy and righteous God.

The proverbs consist of a combination of poetry, parables, short stories, thought provoking questions and wise sayings.

Wisdom as used in Proverbs refers to the ability to judge and act according to God's directives, and it is personified to act as God's dynamic Word personally communicating to us (in the New Testament Jesus becomes the Wisdom and Word of God).

The Book of Proverbs could be outlined as follows:

1. The Purpose and Theme (1:1-7)
2. A Father's Invitation to Wisdom (1:8-9:18)
3. The Main Collections of Solomon's Proverbs (10:1-22:16)
4. The Proverbs of Solomon copied by Hezekiah's men (25:1-29:27)
5. Proverbs of Agur (30:33)
6. Proverbs of King Lemuel (31:1-9)
7. Proverbs about the Virtuous Wife (31:10-31)

Noteworthy

Proverbial teaching is one of the most ancient forms of instruction.

The topical method is the best way of studying the Book of Proverbs. For instance, search and write down all that Proverbs has to say on wise men, the heart, the righteous, pride, humility, fools, and so on, then you will receive much instruction.

Some proverbs use numbers for emphasis: *"These six things the Lord hates, yes seven are an abomination to Him* (6:16);" *"There are three things which are too wonderful for me, yes, four which I do not understand* (30:18)."

Often the author of Proverbs contrasts two opposite ideas with each other in order to clarify and emphasize his wise instruction, for instance:

Wisdom versus Folly
Righteousness versus Wickedness
Pride versus Humility
Good versus Evil
Life versus Death

Some proverbs are very direct: *"Go to the ant, you sluggard! Consider her ways and be wise* (6:6)."

Personal Application
Fear the Lord, then you will live wisely; it is the first and controlling principle of wisdom. In this sense, to fear God means: to believe in Him, respect, honour and obey Him. Another word for fear is "revere" and it is related to the word "revelation." One can only revere God if you have a revelation of God. Study the Word of God, listen to the Holy Spirit and pray that God will give you a fresh revelation of Himself.

Appreciate wise instruction, embrace the discipline of instruction and follow it diligently.

ECCLESIASTES

Author
Traditionally Solomon after he had turned away from God

Date
Uncertain, possibly 930-450 BC

Main Theme
A Quest for Something of True Value in this Life

Key Verse
"This too is meaningless, and grasping for the wind (6:9)."

Key Phrases
"grasping for the wind," "Under the sun"

Key Words
Vanity (meaningless)

Setting
The Book of Ecclesiastes speaks of a time during which traditional solutions to life's great questions, particularly the meaning of life, have lost their relevance.

Purpose
To emphasize that independently of God, life is full of weariness and disappointment

Synopsis
The Hebrew title of the book is *Qoheleth*, which means "teacher" or "preacher." In the Septuagint, the Hebrew *qohuleth* was translated into a Greek word with the same meaning: "ecclesiastes." The word "ecclesiastes" is derived from *ekklesia* ("assembly") and means "one who addresses an assembly."

The Book of Ecclesiastes contains an account of intense search for meaning and satisfaction in life, particularly in view of all the injustice, life's uncertainties and foolish things of this world that we don't always understand.

Although the preacher sounds a bit negative and pessimistic at times, he is honest and doesn't try to destroy all hope, but directs us to the only One who can really bring fulfilment and satisfaction into our lives. In fact, the preacher reminds us that everything temporal must be seen in the light of the eternal.

We divide the Book of Ecclesiastes into three parts:

1. The Preacher's Problem (1:1-11)
The preacher reflects on the apparent futility of life from a very pessimistic viewpoint.

2. The Preacher's Experiences in Life (1:12-11:6)
He shares his experiences and experiments in life, touching on wisdom, pleasure, materialism, religion (without God), wealth, and morality, but nothing satisfied him.

3. The Preacher's Conclusion and Solution to the Problem (11:7-12:14)
In his conclusion the preacher boils it all down to: *"Fear God and keep his commandments, for this is man's all* (12:13)." When we revere and obey God then He enables us to keep everything else in the proper perspective that will give eternal significance to our lives.

Noteworthy
You must see and grasp the "big picture" of the message of Ecclesiastes before it can be understood in part – the preacher who is backslidden struggles to find something of true value in his life. When you are backslidden, then you are blinded by different concerns of life, you cannot see clearly and cannot discern correctly.

Ecclesiastes contains statements that are contradictory to what the rest of the Bible teaches (1:15; 2:24; 3:3, 4, 8, 11, 19, 20; 7:16, 17; 8:15). However, it is still indispensable because it is filled with wisdom and encourages us to constructive action, contentment, and wise living (understand the purpose of the book).

The Book of Ecclesiastes contains remarkably accurate scientific statements (1:6, 7; 3:11, 21; 8:8; 12:6, 7).

Personal Application
For the unbeliever life does not really make sense. However, realize that life is meaningful when you believe as a Christian that: *"in Him we live and move and have our being* (Acts 17:28)." Your life is meaningful and purposeful in God. He is the sovereign source of everything that you may need.

All is not vanity, because truth exists. God is the Absolute Truth in the universe; His Word is truth (John 17:17); and Jesus Christ is *"the way, the truth, and the life* (John 14:6)." Without Christ, who is the personification of truth and the source of eternal life, life is empty, meaningless and unsatisfactory. But, once you are in Christ, united with Him, then you can *"have life ... more abundantly* (John 10:10)."

All the negative remarks relating to the futility of life are there for a purpose: to lead you to seek fulfilment and happiness in God alone. Most of life's questions can only be answered in Jesus Christ, for only Christ can provide ultimate satisfaction, peace, joy, and wisdom.

Stop searching after foolish things. We are accountable to God. The preacher's advice is clear and wise: *"Fear God and keep His commandments, for this is man's all (12:13)."* In New Testament terms: believe in God, respect and honour Him with your life, and though there are many unanswered questions, trust Him fully, He is in control and His intended purposes for your life will stand and nothing or no one will change or reverse it.

Christians are not merely "under the sun," we are seated with Christ in the heavenlies far above principalities and powers (Eph. 2:6, 1:21).

No one can find any lasting enjoyment without God.

SONG OF SONGS

Author
Solomon

Date
Between 970 and 931 BC

Main Theme
The Quest for Authentic Love

Key Verse
"My lover is mine and I am his (2:16)."

Key Phrase
"my beloved"

Key Word
Love

Setting
The reign of king Solomon, most probably when he was still a young man, before he was overtaken by his own lusts after wealth and women.

Purpose

To demonstrate the basis of godly love – covenant love

Synopsis

Based on its first line this book is known by the titles "Song of Songs" and "Song of Solomon." "Song of songs" reflects the Hebrew superlative and could be interpreted as "the greatest song" or "the most beautiful song."

The Song of Songs is a moving love poem, featuring the love dialogue between a young Shulamite woman and her lover (king Solomon). They describe in intimate detail their feelings for each other and their desire to be together – it is an intimate story about pursuing love, expressing love, and enjoying love.

There are different interpretations to this book: the literal and the allegorical. Some say it is a literal story about marriage, depicting the ideal love relationship in marriage. Others view it as a picture of God's love for Israel in the Old Covenant, and Christ's love for His Church in the New Covenant. Both views are applicable (its principles and lessons can be applied both naturally and spiritually): on the one hand we see the expression of pure intimate love within the context of the bonds of marriage, and on the other hand we learn about God's overwhelming love, especially in Christ, for His people. The bride is seen as the Church and the Lover as Christ.

However, we must be careful: looking for allegories in Scripture could be risky, because we can create meanings that God never intended. We should use allegorical interpretations only when Scripture itself uses allegory, such as in Paul's reference to Hagar and Sarah in Galatians 4.[19]

Noteworthy

It is one of the most misunderstood books of the Bible, because it is an oriental poem as well as a parable; therefore there are many figures of speech which should be correctly interpreted.

The Jews reckon it amongst the holiest of books. They compared Proverbs to the outer court of the Temple, Ecclesiastes to the Holy

---

[19] Global University, *Old Testament Survey*, p. 145

Place, and the Song of Solomon to the Holiest of all. It was sung annually on the eight day of the Passover feast.[20]

The most explicit statements on sex can be found in this book, which disturb and discomfort some. But we should keep in mind that this book upholds the fact that sex between a husband and wife is a gift of God, and Song of Songs affirms and encourages the celebration of sexual relations within sacredness of marriage. A married couple honours God when they love and enjoy each other.

Personal Application

You are loved by God! See life, sex and marriage from His point of view.

In a world that is permeated by lust and fierce sexual temptation, you should abandon yourself to the Lover of your soul (Jesus Christ) and, if married, to your spouse. This book encourages you to love God and your spouse wholeheartedly and passionately, enjoying them every moment of the day.

The Song of Solomon also shows us that the love we share with Christ is unselfish, intimate, mutual, satisfying, non-threatening, edifying, fruitful, liberating, and unquenchable.

---

[20] Robert Lee, *The Outlined Bible*

Chapter Six

Survey of the Major Prophets

There were prophets right through Old Testament times, from Moses on. We divide them in two groups. Some were Oral Prophets, such as Samuel, Nathan, Elijah, Elisha, Jehu, Shemaiah, Iddo, Oded, Azariah, Hanani, and Micaiah. Others are called Writing Prophets, such as Isaiah, Jeremiah and all those whose writings are included in the Old Testament.

Furthermore, there are two common methods used to divide the Old Testament's Prophetic Books. One way is to divide the prophets chronologically, in the historical time in which they lived and prophesied to their respective kingdoms. This chronological pattern divides the books as follows: prophets during the divided kingdom, prophets before the exile, and prophets after the exile. In addition, during the Divided Kingdom, prophets to Israel are distinguished from prophets to Judah.

The second method is to distinguish between the Major Prophets and the Minor Prophets (major and minor refer to the general length of the books rather than to the prophets themselves). We will follow this second method, seeing that the Prophetic Books appear in this order in our Bibles.

The following chart shows us the Prophets of the Old Testament, to whom they prophesied and during which times (note: all the early Oral Prophets are not listed).

Prophets of the Old Testament and Times they Prophesied			
Prophet	**Age**	**Year/s**	**To Whom**
Samuel	Early prophets	1050-1000 BC	Judah (S K) and Israel (N K)
Elijah	Early prophets	875-848 BC	Israel
Elisha	Early Prophets	848-797 BC	Israel
Joel	Early prophets	837-800 BC	Judah
Micaiah	Early prophets	849 BC	Israel
Jonah	Assyrian Age	770 BC	Nineveh
Amos	Assyrian Age	760 BC	Israel
Hosea	Assyrian Age	760-730 BC	Israel
Isaiah	Assyrian Age	740-700 BC	Judah
Micah	Assyrian Age	737-690 BC	Judah
Nahum	Babylonian Age	650 BC	Nineveh
Habakkuk	Babylonian Age	630 BC	Judah
Zephaniah	Babylonian Age	627 BC	Judah
Jeremiah	Babylonian Age	627-580 BC	Judah
Daniel	Babylonian Age	605-530 BC	Babylon
Ezekiel	Babylonian Age	593-570 BC	Captives from Judah
Haggai	Persian Age	520 BC	Judah
Zechariah	Persian Age	520-518 BC	Judah
Obadiah	Persian Age	500 BC	Edom
Malachi	Persian Age	443 BC	Judah

> What is a prophet in Old Testament terms? The word "prophet" means "one who speaks for God." They received messages from God which they communicated to the people. These prophets spoke for God in two ways: (1) they "told forth" the Word of God, which means they preached the Word that they received from God to the people; and (2) they also "foretold," or predicted events that were in the future.
>
> Their ministry of the Word of God consisted mainly of two elements: (1) **warning** about judgment on sin, and (2) **encouragement** that if the people trust and obey God then they will experience His blessing, or encouragement that God will eventually save them, such as the seventy year captivity of the Southern Kingdom that God promised would come to an end.

In this chapter we will be looking at the Major Prophets: Isaiah, Jeremiah, Ezekiel and Daniel. Of the four Major Prophets Isaiah and Jeremiah were Pre-exile Prophets, meaning they prophesied before the exile took place, and Ezekiel and Daniel were Exilic-prophets, meaning they were part of the exile and prophesied during the exile.

The Major Prophets

ISAIAH

Author
Isaiah. Based on a presupposition that predictive prophecy is not possible some argue that Isaiah did not write the entire book. They argue that Isaiah only wrote chapters 1-39 and another person wrote chapters 40-66. They call this section Second Isaiah and insist that since these chapters deal with events that took place long after Isaiah's death, such as the Babylonian captivity of Judah, the return from Captivity, and the rise of Cyrus who decreed the return from Captivity, these chapters were later written and attached to Isaiah. Still there are others suggesting that a third person wrote chapters 55-66. However, divine inspiration of Scripture and the supernaturalism of prophecy make the unity of single authorship

of Isaiah more than possible. Furthermore, key words, phrases, thoughts, characteristic expressions, references to landscape and local colouring are similar throughout the book, which further support single authorship.

Date
About 700-690 BC

Main Theme
Salvation

Key Verse
"Holy, holy, holy is the Lord Almighty (6:3)."

Key Phrase
"The Holy One of Israel" (25 times)

Key Words
Salvation, Redeemer, Righteousness, Peace, Comfort

Setting
Isaiah prophesied during the reigns of *"Uzziah, Jotham, Ahaz, and Hezekiah, kings of Judah* (1:1)." His ministry took place from about 740-690 BC. During this time-period Judah's history was marked by increase of wealth and military strength which produced pride and false security; foreign trade fostered an inclination to idolatry, which led to the introduction of foreign superstitions and a decline in moral standards. By Isaiah's time Judah fell into unbelief and moved from independence under God's power to aligning herself with the promises, and fears, of pagan powers. On the other hand Assyria began to make itself strongly felt in the regions of Western Asia. In Isaiah's time both Assyria and Babylonia became dominating factors in the history of the ancient world, while Egypt to the south was already a powerful nation. (These three great powers were in contest for world supremacy back then.) Also Israel and Judah laid between the great Assyrian and Egyptian Powers, which affected Judah in a major way.

180 CHARLES STEBBING

In order to understand the message of Isaiah we should be reminded of three crises that took place in his day: (1) the Syro-Ephraimitic War (734-732 BC), during the reign of Ahaz; (2) the exile of the Northern Kingdom by Assyria (722 BC); and (3) the invasion of Judah by Sennacherib, king of Assyria, in 701 (Is. 36:1); while king Hezekiah prayed to God for help, Isaiah had a revelation that God will deliver Judah, and the prophecy was fulfilled (ch. 37). The political and religious aspects during these crises are important factors in the understanding of Isaiah.

Isaiah prophesied during the last years of the Northern Kingdom but ministered to the Southern Kingdom which was following in the sins of her neighbour to the north. After Samaria and the Northern Kingdom fell, he warned Judah of judgment not by the Assyrians, the most immediate threat, but by Babylon. Isaiah indicated that because of Judah's sins, Babylon would conquer the nation (39:5-7). About one-hundred years after Isaiah's death, this captivity took place (586 BC). God showed Isaiah the sorrows of the captivity and that He would raise up a leader named Cyrus to assist the Jews (44:28-45:13). This prophecy was fulfilled in the days of Ezra – about 150 years later (again the precise fulfilment of the prophetic Word). Isaiah also prophesied many details about the coming Messiah, His glory and ministry.

Purpose
Isaiah prophesied to make God's displeasure with and judgment upon sin known in Judah, Israel and the surrounding nations. Thus, he declared the need of repentance and turning in faith and obedience to God, and he reminded the people of the promises of the covenant-keeping God, laying a foundation for hope and faithfulness.

Synopsis
"Isaiah" means "Yahweh is salvation," which is very suitable because this was the main subject that he was commissioned to proclaim.

The first half of the Book of Isaiah (chs. 1-35) contains severe denunciations, and warnings of judgment as he calls Judah, Israel, and the surrounding nations to repent of their sins. Isaiah also warned the people of God about the invasion and captivity by the Assyrians. Because of the pronouncement of judgment we have many "woe oracles" in this section of the Book (5:8-22; chs. 28-33). We also find prophecies of the coming Messiah in the first part of Isaiah: the virgin birth of Jesus Christ, the Messiah (7:14-16); the eternal government and peace of the promised Messiah (9:6, 7); and we find a "prophetic preview" of the Messiah in 11:1-5, He will be the Perfect expression of the Spirit of God.

In chapters 36-39 we have accounts from the reign of Hezekiah which appear to form a transition between the book's first and second parts; the focus shifts from a world dominated by Assyria to one dominated by Babylon. Here we read of the invasion of Judah by Sennacherib, king of Assyria, and how God delivered Judah, and Hezekiah's healing and sin.

The second part of the book (chs. 40-66) is filled with prophecies of comfort, hope and salvation as God gave assurance that Judah's captivity will come to an end. We can divide this last part of Isaiah into four section: (1) Chapters 40-48 speak prophetically of Israel's restoration and the dominant key word is "comfort"; (2) The Suffering Saviour is vividly and dramatically portrayed in chapters 49-53; (3) Israel's promise of redemption, an invitation to abundant life, salvation for the gentiles, and the blessings of true worship are described in chapters 54-59; and (4) the prophecies of Israel's future glory (chs. 60-66).

The Book of Isaiah is shaped and dominated by his vision of God's glory, sovereignty and holiness (see chapter 6 of Isaiah). Thus, the central theme of the book could be seen as God Himself. Isaiah defines everything by its relation to God.

Noteworthy
Isaiah is seen as the greatest of the Hebrew prophets, the foremost man in the nation in his time, and possibly, after David, the most conspicuous personage in the history of Israel; and, perhaps, more than any other prophet, he has powerfully influenced both Jews and Christians for over two-thousand-seven-hundred years.[121]

Isaiah was from Jewish nobility. He was related to king Uzziah and king Joash through his father. Since he ministered to several kings, his royal heritage was good preparation for the ministry to which God called him.

---

[21] Graham Sroggie, *The Unfolding Drama of Redemption*, pp. 322, 333

The Book of Isaiah is like a miniature Bible – it has 66 chapters (the Bible has 66 books); it divides into two main sections (the Bible is divided into two main sections, the Old and New Testaments); the first 39 chapters of Isaiah are filled with judgment upon immoral and idolatrous people (reminding us of the Old Testament that has 39 Books, and revealing the true condition of man and the solution man can find in God); and the final 27 chapters declare a message of hope and consolation (reminding us of the New Testament that has 27 Books; there are salvation, comfort and hope in the Saviour of Whom Isaiah prophetically spoke).

Isaiah has been called: "The prince of prophets," "The fifth evangelist," "The prophet of redemption," and "the prophet's prophet" (because John the Baptist preached one of Isaiah's prophecies [Luke 3:4; Is. 40:3]). And the book of Isaiah has been called: "The Gospel according to Isaiah," and "The Gospel of the Old Testament."

Seventeen chapters of Isaiah contain prophetic references to Christ, and Isaiah is directly quoted 21 times in the New Testament, more than any other Old Testament prophet.

Tradition tells us that Isaiah was martyred during the reign of the wicked Manasseh, Hezekiah's son. Many believe that the clause "sawn in two" in Hebrews 11:37 is a reference to Isaiah's death.

Personal Application
The prophetic warnings and promises of salvation of Isaiah are applicable to every nation, group of people and individuals.

Isaiah prophesied extensively about the coming Messiah. Thank God! Your Saviour has come, and he is coming again! Believe in God's redemption through Jesus.

God is still calling: *"Whom shall I send? And who will go for us* (Is. 6:8)?" What is your response?

As Isaiah, have a high view of God. If not, study the Bible prayerfully, and ask God to give you a fresh revelation of Himself.

JEREMIAH

Author
Jeremiah

Date
About 585-580 BC

Main Theme
The certainty of God's judgment; failure to repent will lead to destruction; but obedience to God's will bring blessing.

Key Verse
"'For I will restore health to you and heal you of your wounds,' says the Lord (30:16)."

Key Phrase
"rising up early and speaking"

Key Words
Forsake and forsaken, Backslider and backsliding, Return, Repentance, Restoration

Setting
Jeremiah ministered about 100 years after Isaiah whose ministry saved Jerusalem from Assyria. Jeremiah tried his utmost to save Jerusalem from Babylon, sadly he failed, because of the hardened hearts of the Judeans. As a pre-exilic prophet, Jeremiah's ministry began during the reign of Josiah and he ministered through the reign of Zedekiah. His prophetic ministry lasted nearly fifty years (627-580 BC). He was a contemporary of Zephaniah, Nahum, Habakkuk, Daniel, and Ezekiel.

The wicked king Amon, Manasseh's son, had left king Josiah, who was a good king, with a frightful heritage of wickedness and iniquity. However, great reform took place during Josiah's reign (2 Kings 23). Workmen who were rebuilding the temple discovered several scrolls of the Book of the Law. The reading of the Law again resulted in confession of sin and destruction of both idols and idolatrous priests. The reform introduced by king Josiah called for the centralization of worship in the Jerusalem temple. Idolatrous worship at the "high places" was outlawed. Judah rose to the occasion with king Josiah.

After Ashurbanipal, the last great king of Assyria died (627 BC), Assyria was weakening and king Josiah was expanding his territory to the north. Babylonia joined forces with Media and became a powerful threat to both Judah and Egypt. In 609 BC Pharoah Necho of Egypt marched north to the aid of the Assyrians. King Josiah went out against him. Necho insisted that he had no intention to fight against Josiah and that God was with him in this battle. Josiah would not turn back from engaging him in battle; he disguised himself and was shot with an arrow. Sadly the good king died at the age of thirty nine in the battle of Megiddo (2 Chron. 35:20-27).

With the death of king Josiah Judah's hope also died. Josiah was followed by his son Jehoahaz who reigned for only three months; then Jehoiakim came to the throne, and with him the days of wickedness and idolatry, of injustice and cruelty were revived. Jeremiah witnessed the folly and wickedness of Jehoiakim and warned him to no avail.

The sin of Judah was gross – deceit, idolatry and injustice were rampant – for the Word says: *"The sin of Judah is written with a pen of iron; with the point of a diamond it is engraved on the tablet of their heart, and on the horns of your altars (17:1)."* And they said: *"That is hopeless! So we will walk according to our own plans, and we will every one obey the dictates of his evil heart (18:12)."* It was during these days and circumstances that Jeremiah acted as God's prophet to the nations.

Jeremiah's ministry could be divided into three stages: (1) from 627-605 BC he prophesied while Judah was threatened by Assyria and Egypt; (2) from 605-586 BC he proclaimed God's judgment while Judah was threatened and besieged by Babylon. From 586 to about 580 BC he ministered in Jerusalem and Egypt after Judah's downfall.[22]

---

[22] *Nelson's Complete Book of Bible Maps and Charts*, p. 215

Purpose

"I ordained you a prophet to the nations (1:5).*"* God called and ordained the then young Jeremiah to warn Judah of judgment upon their sin and about the coming Babylonian invasion. Jeremiah and Baruch recorded God's message for that time and God's message for the future of Israel as well as other nations (especially in the light of the New Covenant).

Synopsis

Jeremiah is called the "weeping prophet" and the "prophet of the broken-heart," because God gave him a prophetic revelation of the impending and catastrophic fall of Jerusalem – he knew what horrendous circumstances were awaiting his people, but they took no notice of his warnings – it grieved him deeply (9:1). He was tender-hearted and patriotic; withdrawn from the crowds to fulfil his calling purposefully as a prophet, a dedicated and humble person (15:15-18).

It is difficult to outline Jeremiah's book, because "people do not cry in outline form."[23]

The broken-hearted prophet wrote a broken book. His Book is mainly a composition of different prophecies, prayers, and sobs, which are not in chronological order, but are mostly topical. However, many have found great encouragement and consolation through this book, especially chapters 31 and 33.

We could divide the Book of Jeremiah into four main sections:

1. The Call and Commission of Jeremiah (ch. 1)

God called Jeremiah to be a prophet when he was still young. Jeremiah argued that he could not speak because he was only a youth, but the Lord assured him that He was with him. The Lord touched his mouth and said: *"I have put My words in your mouth* (1:9).*"* Jeremiah's task was clear: *"to root out and pull down, to destroy and to throw down, to build and to plant* (1:10).*"*

The Lord equipped and encouraged Jeremiah to fulfil his calling, and promised to protect him (1:11-19).

---

[23] Calvary Academics, Old Testament Survey Part 3, p. 16

2. Jeremiah's Prophecies to Judah (2:1-45:5)

This section presents prophecies about judgment: oracles against kings, prophets and people, and prophecies regarding the Babylonian Exile, and the hateful treatment of Jeremiah by fellow citizens, we frequently read of his despair and his struggles with God over his persecution (chs. 2-29). In the midst of the doom of God's judgment we find what some call "the Book of Comfort" (chs. 30-33); comforting the people by telling them that a remnant will be saved (31:1-22), the people will experience prosperity in Judah again (31:23-30), the promise of the New Covenant (31:31-40), and the assurance of the people's return to Judah (32:26-44).

3. Historical Appendix (34:1-45:5)

The following are included in this section: the warning to king Zedekiah that he will be taken as a captive to Babylon (34:1-7), and his proclamation of freedom to all slaves (34:8-22), the example of the Rechabites (35:1-19), the trials and sufferings of Jeremiah (36:1-32), Jeremiah's imprisonment (37-38), the fulfilment of the prophecies concerning the fall of Jerusalem (37), Gedaliah made governor and his assassination (40, 41), the flight to Egypt forbidden by the Lord (42), Jeremiah was forced to go Egypt for a time (43), by the mouth of Jeremiah God's warning that He will cut off all of Judah in Egypt (44), and the Lord assured Baruch that he will escape with his life (45).

4. Jeremiah's Prophecies to Gentiles (46:1-51:64)

In this section of the book we find Jeremiah's oracles against foreign nations: Egypt, the Philistines, Moab, the Ammonites, Edom, Damascus, Kedar and Hazor, Elam, and Babylon.

5. Historical Appendix on the Fall of Jerusalem (52:1-52:34)

In this final chapter the Fall of Jerusalem and the Babylonian Captivity are reviewed.

Noteworthy

Because of his unwelcome message of judgment to be brought about through Babylonian invasion, Jeremiah was a hated man and his message was rejected by most: his fellow citizens conspired against him (11:18), his own family turned against him (12:6), he was

Discovering the Most Amazing Book 187

threatened and imprisoned several times (37:11-15; 38), he was thrown into a cistern (38), and king Jehoiakim was openly hostile to him, he destroyed one of Jeremiah's scrolls by cutting off a few columns at a time and throwing them into a fire (36:23). Although everyone was against Jeremiah, God was with him.

Jeremiah's closest friend and associate was his scribe Baruch to whom Jeremiah dictated his words (36:27). Most likely Baruch put Jeremiah's book in its final form shortly after Jeremiah's death (585-580 BC).

God gave Jeremiah unique commands. The demonstration of these commands, called "symbolic act preaching" vividly described what the Lord wanted to communicate to the people. For instance, God commanded him not to marry or have children (16:1, 2) to illustrate his message that judgment is pending and that the next generation would be wiped out. Some other commands that the Lord gave Jeremiah to illustrate His message were: the ruined sash (ch. 13), the potter and the clay (ch. 18), the broken flask (ch. 19), the yoke of straps and crossbars (ch. 27), and the purchase of a field (ch. 32).

It is by the Prophet Jeremiah that God gave the promise of the New Covenant (31:31-34), which was explicitly expressed by Jeremiah and it is at the heart of his prophecy. The passage is quoted in its entirety in the New Testament (Heb. 8:8-12; 10:16, 17).

Chapter 52 is a supplement to the Book of Jeremiah, and is almost identical to 2 Kings 24:18-25:30; probably not written by Jeremiah.

Jeremiah was martyred in Egypt.

Personal Application
Do you sometimes feel too young or inadequate to act as a minister of our Lord Jesus? Read what God told the young Jeremiah in 1:7-10.

Be successful in God's eyes by being committed to Him, the truth, and the calling on your life, while you pray for your enemies (in the face of fierce testing and trials; Jeremiah was successful, because he remained faithful to God and spoke what God told Him to say, both negative and positive).

When you proclaim the Gospel to a fallen world, then many can turn against you and others don't respond; don't be discouraged, but rather be committed and keep on warning people of their sinful ways and their need to turn to God.

LAMENTATIONS

Author
Jeremiah (see 2 Chronicles 35:25)

Date
587 BC

Main Theme
The misery and suffering that sin brings; there is future hope if confession and repentance occur

Key Verses
"Through the Lord's mercies we are not consumed, because His compassions fail not. They are new every morning; great is Your faithfulness (3:22, 23)." Also, *"Let us search out and examine our ways, and turn back to the Lord (3:40)."*

Key Phrase
"the Lord's mercies"

Key Words
Sin, Sorrow, Prayer, Faithfulness

Setting
After the third siege and fall of Jerusalem; Judah experiencing the horrors of the destruction of the City of Jerusalem and the temple

Purpose
To portray: the chaos and suffering that the sin of Judah brought on them; that the Lord is righteous in His punishments, and that there is always hope in God for restoration, because He is always faithful to His Word (remember the covenant that God made with Israel, in virtue of their own agreement: if you obey Me then I will bless you, if you don't obey Me, then I will punish you).

Most likely copies were made of Lamentations; some were taken to Egypt, and others sent to Babylon for the exiles to memorize and sing.

Synopsis

The Book of Lamentations has been described as a "tearstained portrait of the once proud Jerusalem," "a funeral song written for the fallen city of Jerusalem." The city and the temple have been sacked completely, reduced to rubble by the invading Babylonians.

Jeremiah's two books focus on the one subject – the fall of Jerusalem. In the Book of Jeremiah the faithful prophet predicted the fall of Jerusalem, and in Lamentations he looks back on it.

In obedience to God and with great humiliation and determination, the patriotic prophet had warned the people, but they couldn't care less and continued in their sin. Since God is righteous, He has brought about His promised punishment.

Although Lamentations is considered one of the Prophetic Books, its message is contained in a collection of five poems, which are known as laments (cries of anguish and sorrow). In this five-poem lamentation, the prophet expresses his deepest feelings as a witness of the horrific event that took place and all its consequences.

The Book of Lamentations is divided into five sections by the five poems as follows:

1. The Destruction of Jerusalem (1:1-22)

Reflecting deeply on the horrendous misery that the sin of the people brought upon themselves; Jerusalem is graphically represented as a weeping woman; Jeremiah grieves deeply because of the destruction of Jerusalem and the devastation of his people; the first poem ends with a prayer, an appeal to the Lord, *"See, O, Lord that I am in distress ... (1:20)."*

2. God's Anger at Sin (2:1-22)

In the second poem the city of Jerusalem is vividly portrayed as a veiled woman mourning sorrowfully in the midst of the ruins; the devastation of Jerusalem is attributed to the anger of God; His warnings are justified. This poem concludes with a desperate cry to the Lord (1:20-22).

3. Hope in the Midst of Affliction (3:1-66)

In the depths of Jeremiah's grief, he realized that it is only by the mercy of God that they are not completely consumed (a remnant survived); there is still hope, because God's mercies are new every morning and His faithfulness is great. In this poem the prophet identifies himself with his people, sharing in their misery and sorrow. The third poem also ends with a prayer (3:55-66).

4. Devastation, the Result of Disobedience (4:1-22)
The fourth poem represents Jerusalem as gold that is dimmed, changed and degraded; the horrors of the siege are highlighted and the sins of the people, the prophets and priests are judged by God; the hopes of the people were dashed; Edom will also be judged for her cruel deeds against Judah (1:21-22). The fourth poem does not end with a prayer, however, the fifth poem is one long earnest appeal to the Lord for restoration.

5. Jeremiah's Prayer for Restoration (5:1-22)
The prophet reviews their pitiful state and need for restoration, and this poem ends with a final, desperate plea for repentance, restoration and renewal that can only come from the sovereign Lord.

Noteworthy
It has been suggested that the last chapter of Jeremiah should be read as an introduction to Lamentations. The Septuagint adds the introduction: "And it came to pass, after Israel was led into captivity and Jerusalem was laid waste, that Jeremiah sat weeping, and lamented this lamentation over Jerusalem, and said ..."

Chapters 1, 2 and 4 are in acrostic form in the original Hebrew (in our English translation it is not obvious). The Hebrew alphabet has twenty-two letters, and each verse of these poems begins with one of the twenty-two letters of the Hebrew alphabet in order. For instance, Lamentations 1:1 begins with aleph, the first letter of the Hebrew alphabet, and Lamentations 1:2 begins with beth, the second letter of the Hebrew alphabet. It continues in this pattern so that Lamentations 1:22 begins with taw, the last letter of the Hebrew alphabet. Chapter 3, which has 66 verses, follows the same pattern, but here three verses per letter – in other words, the first three verses begin with A, the second three with B, and so on. Thus twenty-two groupings of three verses each that give us 66 verses in all. This form of Hebrew poetry was adopted in part as an aid to memory. Chapter 5 does not employ the acrostic form.

The Book of Lamentations is read, to this day, by Jews in their synagogues on the ninth day of the fourth month, the day of fasting that commemorates the fall of the temple (Jer. 52:6).

The Book of Lamentations presents a Road to Renewal:

1. Sin leads to Suffering (1:8), which causes sorrow;
2. Sorrow (in the right attitude) leads to Repentance (1:20), which centres on prayer;
3. Prayer unleashes Hope (3:19-24) that stimulates faith;
4. Faith encourages and brings Renewal (5:21),

Personal Application

Are you moved by compassion because of all the injustice, poverty, sin, and affliction in the world? Reflect on Lamentations and learn from Jeremiah. Are you in need of "restoration?" Put your hope and trust in the Lord, He is faithful.

EZEKIEL

Author
Ezekiel

Date
593-573 BC

Main Theme
The Destruction and Restoration of Jerusalem

Key Verse
"I, the Lord, have spoken and have done it (17:24)." Also a key expression: *"They will know that I am the Lord"* (62 times)

Key Phrases
"Thus says the Lord" (120 times), *"the Glory of the Lord"* (14 times in the first 11 chapters), and *"son of man"* (90 times)

Key Words
Judgment, Blessing, Responsibility

Setting
Ezekiel spent his childhood in the days of the revival brought about by the reformation of king Josiah, and his training was in accord with the days of reform in Judah. He upheld what he had learned from the reformation as a safeguard against religious syncretism (11:12; 20:32).

Ezekiel was most likely a student of Jeremiah, or he at least heard Jeremiah preach and was influenced by the older prophet's ministry. For example, look at the similarities in the following references:

Ezekiel	Jeremiah
7:26	18:18
12:02	5:21
13:16	6:14
20:4-31	7:21-26; 11:1-8; 16:10-13
22:17-22	6:27-30
33:1-9	6:17

At the age of twenty-five Ezekiel was exiled, together with ten thousand Judeans, to Babylon in 597 BC, 11 years before the fall of Jerusalem. He was a younger contemporary to Jeremiah, and prophesied during the time of national despair in Babylon: (1) to assure the exiles of God's ultimate control and sovereignty, and (2) to proclaim God's judgment on Judah. He was the only prophet who ministered directly to the captives. His ministry began when he was thirty, five years after his exile (1:2), and lasted for about twenty years (593-571 BC).

False prophets led the captives to believe that Jerusalem would not be destroyed, and they would soon be restored to their beloved city and land. Jeremiah heard of this and wrote a letter to the elders and people who were carried away to Babylon, explaining to them God's perspective on their situation (Jer. 29). Ezekiel began his ministry the following year, endorsing what Jeremiah had said and, in the midst of great opposition, trying to convince the people that they need to repent and return to the Lord before they can ever expect to return to Jerusalem. And there was no way to avoid the Babylonian captivity and destruction of Jerusalem.

Purpose

Ezekiel's ministry has a threefold purpose: (1) to proclaim God's judgment on Judah (Ez. 1-24) and the nations (25-32), (2) to explain why God caused and permitted Judah's captivity, and (3) giving the people hope of restoration and blessing (33-48).

Note: Most prophets' ministry in the Old Testament followed a threefold pattern or purpose:

(1) Judgment on Judah or Israel;
(2) Judgment on the nations; and
(3) The hope and encouragement of future restoration and blessing. But the manner in which the prophets handle these subjects differs.

Synopsis

Ezekiel's name means "God strengthens," which is indicative of his mission and ministry (see 3:8, 9), and also, to a large extent, of his character, stern and strong, although he was not lacking in tenderness. We recognize the strength of God in the ministry of Ezekiel as he, in the midst of idolatry and all sorts of sin, proclaimed a prophetic message of God's judgment on sin and of God's unending, unbreakable covenant with His people.

The Book of Ezekiel belongs to the genre of "apocalyptic" writings, as Daniel and Revelation do. The word "apocalypse" means "to pull back the veil" or simply "unveiling," so that people can see things they otherwise would not be able to see. This type of literature is characterized by symbolism, visions, allegories, parables, and symbolic actions. Ezekiel is led by God to make use of many of these avenues of expression to emphasize his message.

The Book of Ezekiel can be divided into four main sections:

1. The Call and Commission of Ezekiel (chs. 1-3)

His call to prophetic ministry is accompanied by an impressive vision of God, symbolizing God's omnipotence, omniscience, and omnipresence. There were four living creatures, identified as cherubim (10:20). Cherubim are seen as guardians of the holiness of

God (Rev. 4:6-9). Each had four faces, a lion's, king of the beasts; an ox's, king of cattle; an eagle's, king of birds; and a man's, crown of all creation. This is a revelation of God's omnipotence. The vision has reference to the attributes of God, yet these attributes are centred and summed up in the Person of Christ, as we will see in the Gospels.

The burning coals coming from the midst of the four living creatures anticipated the judgment upon Jerusalem.

Ezekiel also saw with these living creatures wheels full of eyes round about them, which is a revelation of God's omniscience, Who sees the end from the beginning; and these wheels, with the living creatures, moved rapidly between earth and heaven, which is a revelation of God's omnipresence.

Above the four living creatures was a firmament and above the firmament a throne of blue sapphire with the appearance of a man high above it, revealing God's majesty and holiness.

The glory of the Lord appeared like a bright fire and a glowing rainbow to Ezekiel. The glory of the Lord refers to God in all His fullness, especially as He interacts with man (Ex. 33:17-34:9). The rainbow symbolizes God's never-ending faithfulness.

Ezekiel ministered to a backslidden and idolatrous nation. For the prophet to fully understand the sinfulness and depravity of Israel, it was essential that he had a proper revelation and understanding of God's sovereignty and holiness. Chapter 1 details Ezekiel's vision of the omnipotent, omniscient, omnipresent, and righteous God. With this understanding, he would have a true perspective of his calling to minister to the "rebellious house" of Israel (2:8).

The commission of Ezekiel was not easy, he was sent to minister to a rebellious nation, to "stubborn and obstinate" people (2:4), who were unfaithful. However, his message was faithful (2:5-3:3). His message was delivered to him in the form of a scroll, which he was commanded to eat. In his mouth the scroll was "sweet;" the Word of God is sweet when it is received in the right attitude. Eating the scroll signifies that before the prophet can deliver the message it must first become part of him.

2. The Judgment on Judah (chs. 4-24)
Ezekiel then begins to hear regularly from the Lord and faithfully proclaims a series of judgments against Judah. He employs many

symbols, including dramatic symbolic acts to seize the attention of the people. He also proclaims in detail startling visions, endeavouring to bring to an end the sin and rebellion of his people – God will bring judgment on all who do not repent. The departure of the glory of God symbolized the certainty of judgment (8:1-11:25).

Does Ezekiel 28 refer to satan? In the light of the immediate historical and cultural context Ezekiel 28 primarily refers to the king of Tyre, whose chief sin was pride – believing himself to be a god. Verse 12 specifically refers to the King of Tyre.

3. The Judgment on the Gentiles (chs. 25-32)
Ezekiel emphasized the certainty of God's judgment on the nations surrounding Israel. Their involvement in Jerusalem's destruction, or their plans to benefit from it, will not go unpunished. By following the nations in a clockwise circuit, it shows the full circle of judgment on them: Ammon, Moab, Edom, Philistia, Tyre, and Sidon (chs. 25-28). The prophecies of judgment on the nations conclude with Egypt, a nation that would continue to exist, but will never recover to its former glory (29:15); Babylonia will plunder Egypt, both Egypt and her allies will fall.

4. The Future Restoration and Blessing of Israel (33-48)
After the fall of Jerusalem, Ezekiel's first statement was that the wicked left in Judah would be destroyed (vv. 23-29). Chapter 34 calls the irresponsibility of the kings and priests, who have exploited the people, to repent. Ezekiel 35 declares the doom of Edom that saw an opportunity to take the land. Chapters 36 and 37 proclaim a hopeful future for Israel – the land of Israel will be re-inhabited; it will one day become like the Garden of Eden, and the vision of the dry bones predicted the national resurrection of scattered Israel by the Spirit of the Lord (Ez. 37); their return to their own land, and the reign of an everlasting king called "David" (vv. 24-26). This is a clear forecast of the conversion of the Jews to Christ.

Ezekiel 38 and 39 deal with prophecies concerning Gog and Magog – Gog and his allies attacking Israel, the judgment on Gog, his armies destroyed and his burial (38:1-39:16). Who are Gog and Magog? Much has been speculated about the prophetic meaning of these terms. Gog is apparently a leader or king who appears only here and in Revelation 20:8. If Gog refers to a person, then Magog could simply mean "land of Gog," because the Hebrew prefix *ma* can mean "place of." It is generally accepted that Gog is the chief ruler, or prince, over the geographical areas Meshech and Tubal. These areas were located in what are now the countries of Russia, Turkey, and Iran. In Revelation 20:7-10 Gog and Magog are used to represent all nations in satan's final and furious attack on the people of God.

The glorious restoration is further predicted as Ezekiel returns in a vision to the fallen city and is given detailed specifications for the reconstruction of the city, the temple, and the land (chs. 40-48).

Chapters 40-48 are hard to interpret and has been the section of various interpretations:

- Some hold that its prophecies were fulfilled in the return and rebuilding of Jerusalem during the times of Zerubbabel, Ezra, and Nehemiah.

- Others believe that both Israel and the Church are implicated and that those promises are to be fulfilled in the Millennium Kingdom.

- While others reckon these prophecies are being fulfilled now in the present reign of Christ over His church.

- A fourth view combines aspects of the first and third views.

- A fifth view argues that this section should only be interpreted symbolically, and not literally; it expresses the purity and vitality of the ideal place of worship and those who will worship there.

Noteworthy

Ezekiel was both a prophet and a priest (1:3). His priesthood is clearly reflected within the book: he revered the temple (7:22; 24:19-21); he was concerned for the "holy things" of the sanctuary (22:8, 26); he insisted that offerings should be presented to Yahweh alone (16:18-19; 24:1-14) and he urged obedience to the priestly office.

Ezekiel stands out among the prophets as the "Prophet of the Spirit." The Spirit of the Lord fell upon him (11:5), entered into him, took him up, and lifted him up (2:2; 3:12). Woe is pronounced against the prophets who do not prophecy by the Spirit. Also, the restoration and regeneration of Israel by the Spirit of the Lord in the latter days are promised. There are about twenty references to the Spirit in his book.

Ezekiel ministered in unusual ways; he is known as the Prophet of "Dramatic Acting." He was led by God to make use of symbolic acts to communicate his prophetic messages. For example, he built a model of the siege of Jerusalem using a clay tablet, a ramp and battering rams, and an iron pan, portraying the siege of Jerusalem (4:1-3); he lay on his side illustrating the captivity of the Northern and Southern Kingdoms, and to bear the iniquity of Israel (4:4-8); he ate, by measure, defiled bread with limited water supply to illustrate that the children of Israel will not only be forced to eat rations of defiled bread during their time of captivity, but will suffer from a lack of proper food and water (4:9-17). Ezekiel also packed his bags, dug through a wall with his hands, and carried his belongings out with his face covered to illustrate the people's exile (12:1-16). The prophet ate his food with fear and trembling to demonstrate the Jews' despair (12:17-20). Ezekiel's ministry of symbolic acts emphasized the perils of sin and God's judgment upon it, and it served as a kind of "shock treatment" to convict the demoralized remnant of Judah who were in Babylonian captivity of their sinfulness.

Some of Ezekiel's visions are mentioned in the book of Revelation:

- The cherubim (Ezekiel 1; Revelation 4)
- Gog and Magog (Ezekiel 38; Revelation 20)
- Eating the scroll (Ezekiel 3; Revelation 10)
- The New Jerusalem (Ezekiel 40-48; Revelation 21)
- The river of the water of life (Ezekiel 47; Revelation 22)

Each of the three great Prophets emphasized one Person of the Trinity: Jeremiah is seen as the Prophet of the Father, Isaiah as the Prophet of the Son, and Ezekiel as the Prophet of the Spirit.

Personal Application
Understand that you cannot be saved by another's righteousness or be judged for another's sin. Each individual is responsible for his or her individual sin (18:2-4). In the New Covenant sin is judged in Jesus Christ, therefore you need to accept and embrace Christ as your Saviour.

Gain a vision of God's greatness, majesty, and holiness as you face the struggles of daily life. Know that hope and restoration are always available in God.

DANIEL

Author
Daniel

Date
About 537 BC

Main Theme
God is sovereign, He controls the destiny of all nations.

Key Verse
"There is a God in heaven who reveals secrets [mysteries] (2:28)."

Key Phrases
"Ancient of Days," "Son of Man," Jesus' favourite self-designation

Key Words
Kings, Kingdoms, Visions, Dreams

Setting
Daniel, whose name means "God is my Judge" was born to nobility, during the reign of king Josiah, probably about the time of the great reformation under Josiah (623-622 BC). Thus he grew up in a time of religious revival, which definitely influenced him and moulded his character.

When he was about seventeen, Daniel, along with other Jews, were carried off to Babylon in the first captivity (exile) under Nebuchadnezzar in 605 BC. The vast and diverse Babylonian Empire required skilful administration. Captives who were educated or possessed needed skills became the manpower of the government. From among the sons of Judah, Daniel, Hananiah, Mishael, and Azariah were taken to serve in the palace (1:6). Daniel's outstanding character and natural abilities, and God's hand on his life propelled him into a position in the palace as a counsellor to King Nebuchadnezzar and governor of the Babylonian Empire. Later in 539 BC, when the Persians, under Cyrus the Great, took control of Babylon, Daniel continued to serve as an official in the Persian government.

Daniel lived through the entire period of the Babylonian Exile (605-538 BC), and through the first couple of years of the Persian Empire. His book spans over a period from Nebuchadnezzar's first invasion of Jerusalem (605 BC) to the third year of Cyrus in 536 BC (Daniel 10:1), covering the reign of two kingdoms, Babylon and Medo-Persia, and four kings: Nebuchadnezzar (2:11-4:37); Belshazzar (5:1-31); Darius (6:1-28); and Cyrus (10:1-11:1). It was during this time-period in Jewish history and circumstances that Daniel was sovereignly used by God to fulfil His purposes.

Purpose
To reveal God's steadfast love for His people, to support them in their difficult decision to continue to be loyal to Him, and to encourage the people that their captivity would end and that the future would be much brighter.

Synopsis
Daniel, the "Apocalypse of the Old Testament" is written in two languages – Hebrew and Aramaic. The Hebrew of Daniel 2:4 says: *"Then the Chaldeans spoke to the king in Aramaic,"* and from this point until 7:28 the text is in Aramaic.

Daniel is divided into two distinct parts:

1. Mainly Historical (chs. 1-6), written by Daniel in the third person. The first chapter of Daniel begins with the siege of Jerusalem by Nebuchadnezzar, marking a great date in Jewish history, because then commenced the 70 years of captivity which Jeremiah had predicted (29:10). Chapter one also gives us a glimpse of the young Jewish nobleman and his three friends who were deported to Babylon to serve before the king. Chapters 2 and 4 recount the dream of Nebuchadnezzar and its interpretation by Daniel.

Nebuchadnezzar's Great Statue (2:31-33)	
Part of the Statue	**Interpretation**
Golden Head	Babylon
Silver Chest and Arms	Medo-Persia
Bronze Belly and Thighs	Greece
Iron Legs and Feet	Rome

In Nebuchadnezzar's dream a *"stone was cut out of the mountain without [human] hands, and it broke in pieces the iron, the bronze, the clay, the silver, and the gold ... (2:45)."* The stone (or rock) that had destroyed the statue grew into a great mountain and filled the whole earth. Daniel identified the stone as the coming kingdom of God, its development into a huge mountain symbolizes that it will be universal (see also 7:13-14, 18, 27). This kingdom will be of divine origin, eternal, triumphant and certain to come.

Daniel's three friends' test of faith, which culminated in the fiery furnace is recorded in chapter 3. King Belshazzar's feast, the writing on the wall, and the king's fall are described in chapter 5. Chapter 6 tells us about the plot against Daniel and his own test of faith in the lions' den, and how he was miraculously saved.

2. Profoundly Prophetical (chs. 7-12), written by Daniel in the first person.
The second half vividly retells the visions given to Daniel, involving much symbolism. Some of these visions are linked to the past (see Intertestamental Period), while others have reference of what is yet to

come. In chapter 9 we have Daniel's great prayer for his people and the Seventy-Weeks Prophecy (see explanation below). Daniel's vision of the final conflict is recorded in chapters 10 and 11. Then Daniel concludes with the promise of resurrection to glory or doom (12:1-4), and, though we don't know the exact time, the end is certain (12:5-13).

We should celebrate this: the Babylonians, Medo-Persians, Greeks, and Romans came and have gone, but "the Ancient of Days" did establish His eternal kingdom through the "Son of Man," and we are part of it.

The Beasts from the Sea (7:3-8) correspond with the Statue of Nebuchadnezzar	
The Lion ((7:4)	Babylon
The Bear (7:5)	Medo-Persia
The Leopard (7:6)	Greece
The Unidentified Beast (7:7-8)	Rome

Explanation of the Seventy Weeks Prophecy (Dan. 9:24-27)
This is one of the most amazing prophecies in the Bible, and obviously hard to interpret (or is it?). There are various suggested interpretations of this passage, and many suggest that it contains a multi-level prophetic fulfilment. Most of the suggested interpretations are not satisfying.

A complete exploration of the meaning of the "seventy weeks" falls outside the scope of this book, we will merely touch on the subject by referring to the most plausible view.

We break this prophecy down as follows:

1. Background
Remember, this prophecy was received by Daniel towards the end of the <u>seventy</u> year captivity in Babylon. The Lord was revealing to Daniel, "just as the captivity lasted seventy years, the time between the captivity and the coming of the Messiah, who would establish the Eternal Kingdom of God as revealed in the dream of Nebuchadnezzar, would be seventy weeks, or four hundred and ninety years."

2. The Period of Time (9:24a)

The "seventy weeks" are also referred to as "seventy sevens" or "seventy sets of seven." Each day of these 70 weeks represents one year. So, it means 70 x 7 = 490 years. These seventy weeks of years would be broken down like this: seven weeks or 7 x 7 = 49 years; sixty two weeks or 62 x 7 = 434 years; and one week or 7 years.

(The concept of "sevens" of years must have been familiar to Daniel and his Jewish audience, because the sabbatical year observance was based on this premise, see Leviticus 25:1-7; 26:33-35; 2 Chronicles 36:21; also see Numbers 14:34 and Ezekiel 4:6).

3. The People (9:24b)

"For your people [the Jews] and your holy city [Jerusalem]." Clearly the Jews and the city Jerusalem. Here we can also keep in mind that salvation was for the Jew first (Rom. 1:16).

4. The Purpose (9:24c)

"To finish the transgression, to make an end of sins, to make reconciliation for iniquity, to bring in everlasting righteousness, to seal up vision and prophecy, and to anoint the Most Holy." Who can do all this? There is only One that can and only One that did all these things.

5. The Commencement of the Seven Weeks (9:25a)

"Know therefore and understand, that from the going forth of the command [decree] to restore and build Jerusalem ..." That means that this prophecy should be dated from the time King Cyrus issued the decree that the Jews could return to rebuild Jerusalem. There were three such returns, but the principal one was in 458 BC.

Verse 25 continues stating, *"Until Messiah the Prince there shall be seven weeks and sixty-two weeks."* Now, if you take the sixty-two weeks plus seven, and multiply that by seven, then you get 483 years. Move 483 years forward in history, then you will reach the year AD 26. (Remember, there is no zero AD – the year after 1 BC is AD 1; one year must be subtracted.) Most scholars will agree that AD 26 was the year Jesus Christ began His ministry.

6. Events of the First Sixty-nine Weeks (9:25b-26)

"The street shall be built again, and the wall, even in troublesome times." Jerusalem was rebuild, including the wall "in troublesome times." We have seen in the book of Nehemiah that he had much opposition from within and outside the camp opposing him in rebuilding the wall.

"And after the sixty-two weeks Messiah shall be cut off, but not for Himself." Jesus' crucifixion did occur after "sixty-two weeks." This allows for Jesus' death in AD 30. And Jesus did not die for Himself – He died horrifically, paying the ultimate price to make salvation possible to all of mankind.

7. The Events of the Seventieth Week (9:27)

"Then he shall confirm a covenant with many for one week; but in the middle of the week He shall bring an end to sacrifice and offering." There was to be a final week of years, or seven years, to complete the 490 years. We have determined that the 69 weeks brought us to AD 26, when Jesus' ministry began. In the seventieth week, the week after "the sixty-two weeks" and "seven weeks," *"He shall confirm a covenant with many for one week"* – it was during this week of years that Jesus Christ personally revealed God's plan of salvation to man which is embodied in the New Covenant. However, Jesus ministered for only three and a half years. *"But in the middle of the week He shall bring an end to sacrifice and offering."* By His death and resurrection, (in the middle of the week), Jesus brought "an end to sacrifice and offering," and He sealed the New Covenant with His blood (see Heb. 8:7-13; 9:16-10:18).

Although many could disagree about the details, it is an amazing prophecy of the precise time of the coming and the crucifixion of the Messiah, establishing the New Covenant about which Jeremiah prophesied, and the beginning of the eternal Kingdom of God of which Nebuchadnezzar had a vision.

In summary

The seven week prophecy reveals the following to us:

1. Jerusalem will be restored and rebuilt within the first seven weeks of years.

2. The Messiah will be revealed in the 69th week.

3. He will come *"to finish the transgression, to make an end of sins, to make reconciliation for iniquity, to bring in everlasting righteousness, to seal up vision and prophecy, and to anoint the Most Holy."*

4. He will be *"cut off"* after the 69th week.

5. In the middle of the seventieth week, by His death and resurrection, *"He shall bring an end to sacrifice and offering"* – He will fulfil the Old Covenant, and establish and seal the New Covenant in His blood.

Note: there are two more events that are revealed in the seven weeks prophecy.

- In verse 26 we have the following parenthetical statement: *"And the people of the prince who is to come shall destroy the city and the sanctuary. The end of it shall be with a flood, and till the end of the war desolations are determined."* This statement refers to the second destruction of Jerusalem and the temple, which took place in AD 70 under the Roman Emperor, Titus. The Roman war against Jerusalem lasted three and a half years.

- In verse 27 we read, *"And on the wing of abominations shall be one who makes desolate, even until the consummation, which is determined, is poured out on the desolate."* After the death of the Messiah something abominable will be set up that will desolate the temple area, and it will remain until the end. The Dome of the Rock (built in AD 688) which is on the area where the sacrifices took place is an abomination that makes the temple area desolate (making it unclean).

Noteworthy
Daniel never claimed to be a prophet, and the Old Testament does not present him as such. Nor is he placed in the Hebrew Bible among the prophets, but is included in the Writings. However, the Book of Daniel presents a sweep of profound prophetic history, and our Lord refers to him as *"Daniel the prophet* (Matt. 24:15)."

Daniel's prophecies are among the most remarkable in the Bible. For instance, the sequence of empires predicted in chapters 7 and 8, and Daniel's seventy weeks of years (ch. 9).

Striking revelations of Jesus Christ are found in Daniel:

- Christ's Kingdom (2:34-35, 44-45)
- The Fourth Man in the furnace (3:25, 28)
- Daniel's Protector from the lions (6:22)
- One who looked like a man (8:15-17)
- The Anointed One, the Ruler (9:25-26
- The Man dressed in linen (10:4-6; 12:6-7)

The Book of Daniel contains three of the most well-known stories of the Bible, and for that matter, in all literature: Shadrach, Meshach, and Abed-Nego in the fiery furnace, the handwriting on the wall, and Daniel in the lions' den.

Daniel is one of the few well-known Biblical characters about whom nothing negative is written. He was a man of faith, prayer, courage, consistency, and lack of compromise. Ezekiel mentioned Daniel three times as an example of righteousness.

Personal Application

God is sovereign, He is in control, His intended purposes will be accomplished; nothing and no one will change or reverse it.

Daniel is the ultimate example of separation to God (see 1:8-16 and 6:4-24) – by the born-again experience you are separated to God.

Dare to be a Daniel – be a person of faith, courageous, consistent, given to prayer and one who does not compromise with the world.

Even if you are facing a "fiery-furnace" testing, the Lord's protection, purpose, and deliverance will be there.

Chapter Seven

Survey of the Minor Prophets

The twelve Minor Prophets can be, for convenience sake, divided into two groups: nine Pre-exile (who delivered their messages prior to the Babylonian captivity), and three Post-exile (who ministered after the Babylonian captivity).

The Minor Prophets

We will look at the Minor Prophets in the sequence that they are listed in our Bible and not in their chronological order.

HOSEA

Author
Hosea

Date
About 750 BC

Main Theme
Return to the Lord

Key Verse
"But you must return to the Lord (12:6)."

Key Phrase
"A lack of knowledge"

Key Words
Harlotry, Judgment, Love, Mercy

Setting
Chapter 1:1 gives us not only the date, but the historical setting of Hosea: by naming the kings of the Southern Kingdom, Judah (Uzziah, Jotham, Ahaz, and Hezekiah), and the king of the Northern Kingdom, Israel (Jeroboam II) who ruled during the time of his ministry. Hosea ministered to the Northern Kingdom that was enjoying a temporary period of political and economic prosperity under Jeroboam II (782-753 BC). However, moral corruption and spiritual adultery permeated the lives of the people. And after Jeroboam died in 753 BC reversal of political and economic prosperity quickly set in. Within fifteen years of his death, four of Israel's kings were murdered (Zechariah, Shallum, Pekahiah, and Pekah). Confusion, corruption and decline characterized the last years of the Northern Kingdom. And the Assyrian Empire became a major threat under Tiglath-Pileser II (745-727 BC) who strengthened his empire and began his conquest of northern Israel during the reign of Pekah (2 Kings 15:29). Eventually Assyria carried off the last king of Israel together with many of his people into exile (722 BC).

Hosea, God's "living sermon," warned Israel of imminent danger and divine judgment, but the people had passed the point of no return; they refused to listen to him.

Purpose
In the midst of spiritual adultery, corruption, violence, disregard for God and His covenant, and trusting in political alliances rather than in God, Hosea demonstrates that God still loves His people dearly and they need to return to Him. He also emphasizes God's obligation to judge those who reject Him.

Synopsis
God instructed the prophet Hosea to marry an unfaithful woman, whose name was Gomer. Hosea illustrated his message by living it out, and shared a part of God's heartache, sorrow, and pain. His own marriage became a vivid illustration of the unfaithfulness of God's people and the faithfulness of God. In Hosea's life, Gomer represented Israel and

Hosea represented God. Gomer committed physical adultery just as Israel committed spiritual adultery against God.

Even the names of their children were prophetic signs to Israel. The name of their first child, Jezreel (1:4), means "God scatters;" the second child's name, Lo-Ruhamah (1:6), means "no mercy;" and the third child's name, Lo-Amni (1:9), means "not my people." On the other hand, Hosea means "Yahweh is Salvation."

Hosea's message reflects Israel's Baal worship. Baal means "husband" or "lord," and his worship involved fertility rites that included ritual prostitution. Baal was the other lover to whom the unfaithful Israel often turned.[24]

Three recurring themes in Hosea's message as he attempts to call Israel to repentance are: God strongly dislikes the sin of His people; divine judgment is certain; but God still steadfastly loves you.

We divide the Book of Hosea into two main sections:

1. Israel's Spiritual Adultery against God as Illustrated in Hosea and Gomer's Marriage (chs. 1-3)
Hosea's marriage to Gomer was a painful object lesson. Gomer lost interest in Hosea and prostituted after other lovers, reflecting Israel's spiritual decline and darkness. God's marriage to His people does not depend on their faithfulness but on His. He promises to punish them for their unfaithfulness, however, He will have mercy on them, and they will return to Him.

2. God's Message for Israel: The Unfaithfulness of Israel and Her Inevitable Punishment (chs. 4-14)
The righteous God makes it abundantly clear that there is an impending judgment on both Israel and Judah. The sins of Israel are listed (7:1-8:14), and the forms of judgment are specified (9:1-10:15). However, God confirms His love for Israel, *"When Israel was a child I loved him* (11:1)." His love is persistent in spite of the peoples sinning and resisting, *"How can I give you up* (11:8)." Because Israel doesn't heed God's call to repent, but rather sin *"more and more,"* her judgment will be relentless. However, in His divine love He promises *"I will heal their backsliding* (14:4)."

---

[24] *Nelson's Complete Book of Bible Maps and Charts*, p. 244

Noteworthy

Hosea is the only one of the writing prophets that came from the Northern Kingdom, Israel.

Hosea has the same name as Israel's last king, Hoshea, although the English Bible spells them differently, and his name relates to Joshua and Jesus.

Personal Application

God kept His part of the covenant; Israel failed to keep hers. The sinfulness and unfaithfulness of Israel should remind you of your own, and your desperate need of "Hosea" (Salvation). Jesus is our salvation; He is faithful. The New Covenant is an agreement between God the Father and God the Son (as we will see when we journey through the New Testament); Jesus upholds the New Covenant and He will grace you to be faithful. Commit yourself to Him alone.

People need not only to hear about the love of God, but to see it demonstrated through our lives. Realize that your life is the most powerful sermon that only you can preach. Your life should reflect the undiluted love of God to a world that is desperately hungry for authentic love, which is only to be found in God. Ponder on this: "If God loves a people and the prophet hates those same people, how can God use the prophet to proclaim His love to them?"

Know this: *"the ways of the Lord are right; the righteous walk in them, but transgressors stumble in them (14:9)."*

JOEL

Author

Joel

Date

835-805 BC. However, scholars are of two opinions regarding the date of Joel. Some suggest that the book was written about 400 BC after Judah's Babylonian exile, when Judah no longer had a king. Most conservative scholars are in favour of a later date: 805-835 BC. The restoration of worship by the high priest Jehoiada during the reign of king Joash (2 Kings 11; 2 Chronicles 23:16) is ascribed by some to the ministry of Joel.

Main Theme
The Need and Importance of Repentance

Key Verse
"I will pour out My Spirit on all flesh (2:28)."

Key Phrase
"The Day of the Lord"

Key Words
Repent, Judgment

Setting
Joel was probably one of the first of the Writing Prophets who ministered in Judah during the reign of king Joash also known as Jehoash (2 Kings 11 and 12). He prophesied to Judah at a time of great natural disasters – an enormous locust plague, famine, fire, the sun turning dark, and the moon turning to blood. It was so disastrous that Joel saw it as a prophetic sign of God's judgment; a foreshadowing of the Day of the Lord.

Purpose
The prophet drew his lesson from the awful natural disasters: To point out the need for righteous living, and to exhort the people to national repentance. The purpose of Joel's prophecy is fourfold:

1. To explain why disaster had come (the locusts and famine)
2. To warn of an even greater danger (the army that was ready to march on Judah from the north)
3. To call the people of Judah to repent wholeheartedly
4. To prophecy about the future Day of the Lord that would bring restoration and blessings for some, and judgment for others.[25]

---

[25] Global University, *Old Testament Survey*, p. 167

Synopsis

The Book of Joel is an appeal from the Lord to the people to seek Him through repentance; those who respond to His appeal will share in His glory, those who deny Him will be judged.

Moses warned the Israelites: *"You shall carry much seed out to the field but gather little in, for the locust shall consume it."* And, *"Locusts shall consume all your trees and the produce of your land* (Deut. 28:38, 42)." Such a day has dawned. The invading locust army, together with drought and fires, is seen as a warning of approaching divine judgment, out of which came the urgent call from God for wholehearted repentance. It foreshadows the coming Day of the Lord (which involves judgment on unbelievers). His message was concise and clear: "If you think the plague of locusts is bad, wait until you see the final judgment of the Lord."

The Book of Joel naturally divides into two sections:

1. The Present Day of the Lord (Historical) – Judgment of God and the prophet's call to repentance (1:1-2:16).
The devastating locust invasion is the occasion for the prophet's call to repentance. Joel vividly warned the people of divine judgment and challenged them to repent and return to God wholeheartedly.

2. The Future Day of the Lord (Prophetical) – Restoration and Blessing to Israel, Judgment to the nations (2:18-3:21).
As with all prophets, Joel did not only announce judgment, he also proclaimed God's promise of deliverance and restoration, and gave the people hope. God used Joel to assure the people that He will bring material and spiritual blessings to those who belonged to Him and that their enemies would be judged. A particular spiritual blessing is the outpouring of the Holy Spirit, seen in Peter's declaration of the fulfilment of Joel 2:28-32 (see Acts 2:14-21).

Noteworthy

We know very little of Joel other than what the first line of his book states: *"Joel the son of Pethuel."* Herein he is distinguished from other men with the same name. "Pethuel" means "the openheartedness or sincerity of God." And Joel means "Jehovah is God." Joel most likely lived in Jerusalem.

Joel gives us the first clear prophetic word on the outpouring of the Holy Spirit upon all flesh, which took place on the day of Pentecost. And the future judgment on the nations.

Joel has been called "the prophet of Pentecost," and "the prophet of Worship revival." He was a clear, concise, and uncompromising preacher of repentance.

Personal Application
The Holy Spirit has been poured out. Are you baptized in the Holy Spirit? He wants to walk alongside you, to equip and empower you for your Christian service.

As a Christian you have the wonderful privilege of experiencing salvation, and you have the responsibility of proclaiming the Gospel. Just as Joel was, you are a prophetic voice calling non-believers to repentance, proclaiming the grace of God and extending the hope of salvation from the terrible Day of the Lord.

Worship the Lord alone as your God.

AMOS

Author
Amos

Date
760-750 BC

Main Theme
The Impending Judgment on Israel

Key Verse
"But let justice run down like water, and righteousness like a mighty stream (Amos 5:24)."

Notable Phrase
"For three transgressions"

Key Words
Punishment, Justice, righteousness

Setting
Although Amos was from Tekoa in Judah, he prophesied mainly to the Northern Kingdom, Israel, during the latter years of the capable king Jeroboam II's reign. This time was marked by prosperity, which increased religious corruption, and the immorality and injustice of the people; the nation of Israel had become lax in their faithfulness to God and casual about sin.

Purpose
Amos preached against the excessive pursuit of luxury, self-indulgence, oppression of the poor, and hypocrisy by calling for social justice for the poor and faithful godly living, and he warned the Israelites of impending judgment.

Synopsis
With divinely given insight Amos saw the corruption, deception, and trappings of that prosperous era. His message of doom reminded the people that God is righteous and holy, and that they had failed Him. Instead of worship, righteous living, and love and concern for one another, they had become cruel, selfish, and rebellious.

The Book of Amos falls into five sections:

1. Judgment of Surrounding Nations (1:1-2:3)
The first verse introduces Amos and the setting of the book to us. Then Amos pronounces judgment on six nations surrounding Israel – Damascus, Gaza, Tyre, Edom, Ammon, and Moab. These nations occupied territory that belonged to Israel.

2. Judgment of Judah and Israel (2:4-16)
Where sin is concerned, God is no respecter of persons. He now turns to His people and pronounces punishment on them, because they have despised the law of the Lord (v. 4), sell people into slavery (v. 6), trampled on the head of the poor (v. 7), and they were guilty of incest, drunkenness and possibly ritual prostitution (vv. 7, 8).

3. Three Oracles against Israel (3:1-6:14)

Each of these three oracles begins with hear and gives authority to the prophet's message. The oracle in chapter 3 shows us that privilege brings responsibility. Chapter 4 makes it clear that God's discipline should lead to repentance. In chapter 5 we have an oracle on "seeking the Lord" – God is with those who seek Him, and against those who seek evil. From chapter 5:18-6:14 we have an oracle of "woe," with the assurance that God will raise up a nation against Israel.

4. Visions concerning Israel's Judgment (7:1-9:10)

In this section we find five visions of judgment on Israel:

i.   Locusts (not sent – Amos prayed and God relented) (7:1-3)

ii. Fire (not sent – again Amos cried out to God and He relented) (7:4-6)

iii. Plumb line – symbolic of God's standard; a plumb line is used in the building trade to measure the vertical uprightness of a wall; Israel had been built "true" to God's standard; now she will be measured by that same standard; she is not in an upright relationship with God anymore (7:7-9)

iv. Basket of ripe fruit – the ripeness of Israel's judgment; her judgment is long overdue (8:1-14)

v.   The Lord by the altar – destruction of the sinful kingdom is ordered; none will escape (9:1-10)

5. Future Restoration of Israel (9:11-15)

The promise of a bright future; some refer to it as "the Messianic hope." This refers to the coming of the Messiah; through His resurrection the fallen "tabernacle of David is raised up," and now all the nations (Gentiles) are included in God's blessings as promised to Abraham (Gen. 12:3). (Also see Acts 15:15-17.)

Noteworthy

Amos means "burden-bearer," and his life exemplifies it: he bore the burden of God's call to speak prophetically to the nation of Israel who had sinned consistently against God and failed to repent from their sins. He also bore the burden of identifying with poor people in their struggles and difficult times in life.

Although Amos was only a shepherd and tender of sycamore trees (a wild fig only eaten by the poor; it had to be bruised or punctured before it would ripen), his book portrays him as a good communicator and a model worker for God.

The earthquake of which Amos speaks in verse 1, must have been of exceptional severity, because Zechariah refers to it nearly 300 years later as an event well remembered (Zech. 14:5).

Personal Application
God uses "ordinary" people to do extra-ordinary things, such as Amos.

A few questions to reflect on when you read through Amos. Do you have God's viewpoint in focus? Who is your God, or what is your god? Are you indifferent to others? Do you care for the poor? Are you complacent?

OBADIAH

Author
Obadiah

Date
The background of Jerusalem's destruction and captivity by the Babylonians in 586 BC places the date of Obadiah's prophecy shortly after 586 BC.

Main Theme
God's Judgment on Edom

Key Verse
"As you have done, it shall be done to you (v. 15).

Key Phrase
"Day of the Lord"

Key Words
Pride, day, cut off

Setting
The Edomites were descendants of Esau (Gen. 25:19-27:45), Jacobs brother, and thus, blood relatives of Israel. They were (like their father Esau) rough, fierce and proud warriors; resentful, and ever seeking to harm Jacobs' descendants. Edom and Israel have a long history of animosity, dating back to Edom's refusal to let Moses and the people traverse their land on Israel's way to Canaan. Instead of helping their relatives when Nebuchadnezzar destroyed Jerusalem and took the people into captivity, they rejoiced over Judah's downfall and cruelly took part in the plundering; capturing and delivering fugitives to the enemy. Psalm 137:7, Lamentations 4:21, 22, and Ezekiel 25:12-14 decry the participation of the Edomites in the destruction of Jerusalem.

Purpose
Obadiah proclaims God's message to the Edomites, because of their pride, indifference, treachery and cruelty towards their relatives in Judah, they are doomed and will be destroyed.

Synopsis
The Book of Obadiah presents a twofold message: the fall of Edom and the exaltation of Israel.

We divide Obadiah into two sections:

1. The Destruction of Edom decreed (vv. 1-16)
Verse 1 announces the decree of the Lord to destroy Edom. The Lord makes it clear that they are deceived by their pride, He despises them and will bring them down vv. 2-4). The completeness of their destruction, the treachery of their allies, and the failure of their wisdom and might are certain.

The reasons for their judgment are clear: violence and unbrotherly conduct towards Judah (vv. 10-16). Seven times Obadiah charged them: *"You should not have* (vv. 12-14). What the Edomites sowed, they will reap (v. 15).

2. The Exaltation of Israel (vv. 17-21)

There shall be no survivor for the house of Esau, but the house of Jacob (Israel) will be restored and exalted in the coming Day of the Lord.

Noteworthy

Obadiah is the shortest book in the Old Testament.

After Israel's restoration, Cyrus, king of Persia, overcame the Edomites and slaughtered thousands of them. They received another crushing defeat by the Jews, under the Maccabees, and in 70 AD they were completely destroyed by the Romans.[26]

Personal Application

"God resists the proud, but gives grace to the humble (1 Pet. 5:5)."

You are God's child, under His love and protection – He will undertake for you as you trust Him.

Love your neighbour, and do unto others as you would have them do unto you.

JONAH

Author

Jonah

Date

About 760 BC

Main Theme

God is the God of the Jew and the Gentile

Key Verse

"I know that You are a gracious and merciful God, slow to anger and abundant in lovingkindness, One who relents from doing harm (4:2)."

Key Phrase

"three days and three nights" (the prophetic sign of the prophet Jonah)

---

[26] Robert Lee, *The Outlined Bible*

Key Words
Arise, Prepared, Relent

Setting
Jonah, the son of Amittai, lived in the village of Gath Hepher, located about four miles northeast from what was later the city of Nazareth, in Galilee. Jonah's name and place of birth identify him as the prophet of Israel in the days of king Jeroboam II (2 Kings 14:23-25). His ministry must have played an important role in the exploits of king Jeroboam II under whose reign, as we have seen before, Israel grew in prosperity.

Because of internal strife and wars with revolting provinces, the Assyrian Empire was weaker during Jonah's time. Thus, this weaker and depressed state of Assyria contributed much to the readiness of the people to hear Jonah's message.

Purpose
To demonstrate God's love and mercy for all people; He is willing and desirous to save even heathen nations if they repent (see Rom. 3:29); God's love is infinite and universal; therefore His concern is for all. Also to foreshadow the death, burial, and resurrection of Christ.

Synopsis
The Book of Jonah is unique among the prophets of the Old Testament. It is different from all other prophetical books in that it has no prophecy that contains a message; the historical events are the prophetic messages. As we have seen, the historical events in Jonah proclaim mainly a twofold message: God's loving desire to save all kinds of people, which was not understood by Jonah, but is fully revealed in the New Testament; and the prophetic sign of Jonah foreshadowing Christ's death, burial, and resurrection.

We divide the content of the book into two main sections:

1. Jonah's First Commission (1:1-2:10)
God instructed Jonah to go to the great city Nineveh, the capital of the worst enemies of the ancient Jews, the Assyrians, to call the people to repentance. He disobeyed God and tried to run away from his calling by travelling the opposite direction to Tarshish (about 4000

km west from Judah, modern south-western Spain) – he tried to get as far away from Nineveh as he possibly could. Jonah knew enough about the character of God to know that if he responded to God's call, his enemies would be saved.

In spite of Jonah's wilful disobedience, God did not discard or destroy him. Instead God disciplined him by sending a great wind on the sea that bombarded the ship Jonah was on. According to beliefs of that time, particularly of heathen nations, such weather phenomena indicated that the gods were angry and punishing someone for inappropriate behaviour. The sailors cast lots to determine who made the gods angry. The lot fell on Jonah, and he admitted his guilt. At Jonah's insistence and after they had cried out to the Lord, they threw Jonah overboard. Immediately, the raging sea became calm, and the sailors feared the Lord, God of Israel, exceedingly and worshipped Him (1:4-16). It is striking how these sailors, lacking of past experience with the true God, immediately came to faith in Him and displayed more sensitivity to God than Jonah did.

The Lord had prepared a large fish to swallow Jonah. Naturally, he was gripped by fear; he prayed to the Lord from inside the belly of the fish; he obviously regretted his disobedience and repented – Jonah turned from "I will not" to saying three times to God "*I will* (vv. 4, 9)." God forgave Jonah, and directed the fish to vomit Jonah onto dry land (2:1-10).

Herein we see that God's purposes will not be frustrated; His plans will be established, no matter what. He is sovereign and in control even making use of the elements to fulfil His purposes, and to display his absolute, yet loving guidance.

2. Jonah's Second Commission (3:1-4:11)

Out of God's perfect patience Jonah heard Him call a second time. This time Jonah obeyed God and went to Nineveh, a journey of about 800 kilometres. When he arrived, he proclaimed the message that God gave him; the Ninevites believed in God, repented, and turned to God. As a result, God spared the people. This is viewed as "the greatest evangelistic crusade in the history of God and man."

Jonah did not respond well to this; instead of being ecstatic that an entire city turned to God, he was displeased and became angry (4:1). He desired condemnation for the Assyrians, not mercy. Jonah was full of prejudice. But God made it clear to Jonah that He is sovereign and His lovingkindness is available to everyone, not only to the Jews, when they turn to Him in repentance. In spite of Jonah's anger, God gave him an object lesson. He caused a plant to grow over Jonah's booth to shelter him from the hot sun. This pleased Jonah greatly. But then God sent a worm to destroy the plant. The next day the sun beat down on the head of Jonah. Then Jonah went into another outburst of anger and self-pity, wishing he was dead. But the Lord said to Jonah, *"You have had pity on the plant for which you have not labored, nor made it grow, which came up in night and perished in day. And should I not pity Nineveh, that great city, in which are more than one hundred and twenty thousand persons who cannot discern between their right hand and their left – and much livestock (4:10-11)?"* The Lord was challenging the misplaced values and priorities of the very prejudiced Jonah. In the end of the day, the Lord was patient and merciful to him, in the same way that He was patient and merciful to Nineveh.

Noteworthy
Jonah's prophetic ministry began after the time of Elisha, and just before the time of Amos and Hosea.

Many destructive critics consider the Book of Jonah as fiction, not as a historical account. However, 2 Kings 14:25 proves Jonah as a historical person, and in Matthew 12:39-41 Jesus affirms that Jonah and his ministry are factual and historic. The answer to the question about the "great fish" is obvious: Can God work miracles or not? Scripture makes it clear: *"Now the Lord had prepared a great fish to swallow Jonah (1:17)."* It was a sovereign work of God for His purposes. And, a large whale, such as a sperm whale can easily swallow a man whole, particularly under instruction of God.

Two plagues (765 and 759 BC), and a solar eclipse (763 BC) may have prepared the people for Jonah's message of judgment.[27]

In the light of the little that we now know about the Assyrian Empire and Israel, we can understand why Jonah didn't want to go to Nineveh: (1) There was a bit of nationalistic pride; Israel was God's chosen people; and (2) the brutal cruel Assyrians were not only their enemies, but practiced paganism; most likely in Jonah's

---

[27] *Nelson's Complete Book of Bible Maps & Charts,* 256

opinion they didn't deserve God's love and forgiveness, they rather ought to be destroyed.

This short Book of Jonah is filled with God's miraculous providence: He sent the great storm, prepared the great fish, directed the great fish to vomit Jonah onto dry land, prepared a plant to cover Jonah, sent a worm to destroy the plant, and He appointed a scorching east wind to discomfort Jonah.

Apparently Jewish tradition has the following opinions about Jonah: (1) he was the widow's son of Zerephath, whom Elijah raised from the dead (1 Kings 27:17-24); (2) he was the "servant" who accompanied Elijah when he fled from Jezebel (1 Kings 19:3); and (3) that he was the young man whom Elisha sent to Ramoth Gilead to anoint Jehu King of Israel (2 Kings 9:1-10).These legends hold no substance.[28]

Personal Application

God desires to extend His love and grace through you to a love-hungry world; make yourself available to God and join Him in His ministry to people who need His love.

Is it possible that your prejudice and maybe strong dislike concerning some unloving, ungodly and wicked sinners are blocking the love and salvation that God wants to share with those people?

Remember: you cannot hide or run away from God; you cannot frustrate God's purposes.

Often the opportunities that God brings into your life are accompanied by great challenges; if you remain faithful to Him, and follow His leading, then you will be successful.

God will use circumstances to guide you into His will if you are unwilling to follow Him.

---

[28] Graham Scroggie, *The Unfolding Drama of Redemption*, p. 334

MICAH

Author
Micah

Date
From about 735-700 BC

Main Theme
Micah means "Who is like Jehovah," and it is written over all the pages of this book, while his message centres on social injustice, true worship, false security and judgment on sinful practices.

Key Verse
"And what does the Lord require of you but to do justly, to love mercy, and to walk humbly with your God (6:8)?"

Key Phrases
"Daughter of Zion" and *"Hear now"*

Key Words
Sin, Remnant, Compassion, Mercy

Setting
Micah primarily prophesied to Judah, although he also addressed Israel (the Northern Kingdom) and predicted the fall of Samaria (1:6).

The first verse of the book gives us the setting. Micah prophesied during the reigns of the following kings of Judah: Jotham (740-731 BC), Ahaz (731-716 BC), and Hezekiah (716-686 BC).

During this time-period idolatry on "high places" was introduced in Judah by Samaria. True temple worship of the Lord declined and it was now in competition with idolatry (1:5). Micah's strong denunciations of idolatry and immorality suggest that his ministry mainly preceded the religious reforms of king Hezekiah (although, it is likely that these reforms were mere form-religion, and superficial; it did not bring permanent results).

The days of Micah were marked by social and religious injustice and corruption: the fields of the poor were coveted and taken by

DISCOVERING THE MOST AMAZING BOOK   223

force (2:2:1-2), the poor were robbed (2:8), women were cast out of their houses (2:9), the people were under the powerful control of false prophets (2:11) who prophesied for reward (3:6, 11), the priests taught for reward (3:11), corrupt business ethics were practised (6:11), and judges judged for a bribe (7:3).

Additionally, the Assyrian Empire rose to the pinnacle of its power and was a constant threat to both Israel and Judah. The Northern Kingdom, Israel, was exiled and destroyed in 722 BC by Assyria. And in 701 BC Sennacherib invaded Judah, the Southern Kingdom; divine intervention prevented the desecration of Jerusalem (see 1 Kings 17-19).

Purpose
To reveal the incomparability of the compassionate and merciful God, and to expose sinful practices, such as social injustice and idolatry; warning of judgment unless the people turn back to God. However, Micah holds out the hope and promise of deliverance and restoration after judgment.

Synopsis
Like Amos, Micah was burdened by the abusive treatment of the poor. He rebuked anyone who would use social status or political power for personal gain. Like other prophets, Micah placed the blame for the moral and spiritual corruption of the people of God on the spiritual and political leaders of both the Northern and Southern Kingdom, and prophesied God's judgment with vivid imagery. Through it all Micah proclaims God's righteous demands for His people: *"To do justly, to love mercy, and to walk humbly with your God (6:8)."*

We divide the Book of Micah into three sections that basically consists of three sermons:

1. Micah's First Sermon (1:2-2:13)
The first message of Micah is addressed to all the people, and he laid out God's case against them for their evil practices; their idolatry and ruthless exploitation of the poor and powerless. Because God's people were choosing not to follow His ways, He warns them of a future punishment: *"Behold, against this family I am devising*

disaster, from which you cannot remove your necks; nor shall you walk haughtily for this is an evil time (2:3)."

God's warning of impending judgment obviously referred to the Assyrian and Babylonian conquests and captivities. These captivities were God's chastisement of both Israel and (later) Judah, and were an expressing of His righteousness and holiness.

However, Micah preached at the end of his first message hope and certain restoration: *"I will surely assemble all of you, O Jacob, I will surely gather the remnant of Israel (2:12)."* God will always save a faithful remnant of His people; we see this throughout the history of Israel.

2. Micah's Second Sermon (3:1-5:15)

In his second message, Micah addressed three levels of leadership or government: the priests, the prophets, and the political rulers. All three levels of this God-ordained leadership structure were corrupt to the core (see 2:11; 3:6, 11; 6:11; 7:3). If leadership is corrupt by not following God's instructions, then spiritual and moral decline are quite evident.

Again, Micah offered hope of restoration, including the glorious messianic prophecies (see 5:2-5). Where human government had failed in Jerusalem (representing the Southern Kingdom) and Samaria (representing the Northern Kingdom), the Messiah's reign will not fail, and He will bring true peace to His people. (As we know human government always fails; therefore we all look forward to the Day when Jesus Christ, the Messiah, the perfect Priest, Prophet, and King, will reign in ultimate authority, righteousness and love.)

3. Micah's Third Sermon (chs. 6 and 7)

Micah represents, in his third message, an allegorical court case between God and man, by preaching *"Hear now what the Lord says ... for the Lord has a complaint against His people, and He will contend with Israel (6:1, 2)."* As the prophet presents God's case against Israel, God reminds Israel of His mighty acts on their behalf, bringing her up out of Egypt sending Moses, Aaron, and Miriam before them. Yet, the Lord is righteous and cannot ignore their injustice, violence, greed, and idolatry, He has to bring judgment upon them. God also showed Micah that no person is righteous, and man cannot do anything to atone for his sins. It is only by the grace of God that the contrite of heart is granted forgiveness for his sins.

Micah concludes his third message by assuring Israel that God will forgive and restore the faithful remnant that will turn back to Him.

Noteworthy

As one of the eight century prophets, during the time when Assyria was a dominant world power, Micah is the slightly younger contemporary of Jonah, Hosea, Amos, and Isaiah.

The Book of Micah has a striking resemblance to Isaiah. It has been said that both Micah and Isaiah's ministry influenced the character, conduct, and work of king Hezekiah.

Micah gives a clear and precise prediction of the birth place of the Messiah (5:2). Additionally, he gives vivid descriptions of the righteous reign of Christ over the world (2:12, 13; 4:1-8; and 5:4, 5).

Micah was quoted on three significant occasions: (1) In Jeremiah 26:18, by the elders of the land; that saved Jeremiah's life; (2) in Matthew 2:5, 6 confirming the birth place of the Messiah; and (3) by our Lord Himself when He sent out His twelve disciples (Matt. 10:35, 36).

Personal Application

The God of Micah's message is a God of compassion and of merciful love. This means you cannot earn, win, or achieve God's love by a positive performance – it is only extended by grace – you also cannot lose God's love by a negative performance. Properly understood, the message of the prophets is a message of hope that is built on the foundation of the love and grace of God. However, the love and grace of your heavenly Father is perfectly balanced with His justice – a justice that could only be satisfied by the payment of His Son's perfect death, so that we might enjoy that perfect love and grace of God for eternity.[29]

---

[29] Calvary Academics, *Old Testament Survey Part 3*, p. 71

NAHUM

Author
Nahum

Date
Nahum's prophecy must have been written after 663 BC, the year the Egyptian capital Thebes, (known as *No Amon* in Hebrew), was destroyed (mentioned in 3:8), and **before 612 BC**, the date of Nineveh's destruction.

Main Theme
The Power and Wrath of God demonstrated in the Destruction of Nineveh

Key Verse
"The Lord is slow to anger and great in power, and will not at all acquit the wicked (1:3)."

Key Phrase
"utter end"

Key Words
Evil, Cut Off

Setting
The repentance of Nineveh, in response to the preaching of Jonah, did not last long. About forty years after Nineveh's repentance the Assyrians conquered the Northern Kingdom, Israel, and took those ten tribes captive.

The repentance of the Ninevites had been replaced by a complete and deliberate apostasy from God (see 2 Kings 18:29-35; 19:10-13). They returned to their habits of violence, merciless brutality, idolatry, and arrogance (their cruelty was indescribable and their barbarism was unprecedented; everybody feared their brutality). In 701 BC they laid siege to Jerusalem, and as we have seen, God intervened and saved Jerusalem. About seventy years after this event Nahum prophesied, under the inspiration of God, the coming judgment and extinction of Nineveh.

Purpose
To proclaim God's judgment on and victory over Nineveh

Synopsis
Jonah's ministry to the Ninevites resulted in repentance. It shows us that God gave them an opportunity. However, they turned back to their old ways, and approximately 120 years later the prophet Nahum proclaimed the doom and destruction of Nineveh.

Nahum means "comfort;" his message of doom for the Assyrians must have been a source of comfort to the Judeans who had suffered under their cruelty.

We divide the brief book of three chapters into three sections:

1. God Decreed Nineveh's Doom (ch. 1)
In chapter 1 Nahum contrasts God's wrath with His goodness (v. 3) – although God will judge Nineveh, He will show mercy to Judah. He vividly describes and praises God's power and wrath, in terms of His judgment against Nineveh that opposed Him, and also His compassionate vindication of *"those who trust in Him* (v. 7)."

In verse 9 Nahum prophesied that the Lord will not allow Assyria to defeat His people again.

2. The Destruction of Nineveh Described (ch. 2)
In vivid detail Nahum described Nineveh's destruction, but gave Israel hope *"the Lord will restore the excellence of Jacob* (v. 2)." Nothing will be able to save the city; the Lord declares: *"Behold, I am against you ...* (v. 13)."

3. The Reasons for and Certainty of Nineveh's Extinction (ch. 3)
In his final chapter Nahum listed, in graphic fashion, the reasons why the wrath of God will be poured out over Nineveh. It was a bloody city, full of lies and robbery, and countless corpses of those they had slain, it hosted a multitude of harlotries, and the list continues.

Ancient history tells us that the Assyrians skinned their captives alive, and after they had conquered a city, they would massacre half the population, and place a huge mound of skulls at the gate of the city to terrorize those they permitted to live.

Again the Lord said: *"Behold, I am against you ... (v. 5)."* And in the final verse Nahum prophesied: *"Your injury has no healing, your wound is severe. All who hear news of you will clap their hands over you ... (v. 19)."* The ruin of Nineveh would be a source of comfort to all nations who were living in fear of the Assyrians. The fall of Nineveh has been described as the one great "At Last!"

Noteworthy
Nineveh, the capital of the mighty Assyrian Empire, was known as the Queen City of all the earth; the prophet Nahum predicted that this great Queen City would be annihilated. And it was. Nahum's prophecy was fulfilled in painful detail when the combined forces of Babylon and Medes completely destroyed Nineveh in 612 BC. Its ruins can still be seen today on the Tigris River, opposite the city of Mosul, Iraq.

Personal Application
God is sovereign even over those who think they are invincible. God's goodness and justice will prevail.

Examine yourself, is your life in line with God's will, are you with or against Him? Return, realign, and reprioritize if necessary.

Put your trust in God alone and be confident that His power and justice will work on your behalf – He will keep you safe.

The message of Nahum should prompt you to a renewed zeal for evangelistic outreach (read 1:15).

HABAKKUK

Author
Habakkuk

Date
About 607 BC

DISCOVERING THE MOST AMAZING BOOK

Main Theme
"The just shall live by faith"

Key Verse:
"The just shall live by faith (2:4)."

Key Words
Faith, Why? Woe

Setting
Habakkuk lived during one of Judah's most critical periods, and ministered during the "death throes" of the nation. The first verse of his book tells us about the burden which the prophet saw. Chapter 1 verses 2-4 speak of exceedingly bad conditions of the people, a time after the untimely death of king Josiah. Habakkuk prophesied during a period when the country had fallen from the reformation in king Josiah's reign to wickedness, injustice to the poor, and the collapse of the legal system. Additionally, the world around Judah was at war with Babylon rising to power over Assyria and Egypt. Judah was on the brink of being taken captive by Babylon.

Purpose
To warn the Judeans of the approaching judgment, and to encourage the righteous to *"live by faith."* And to believe His prophets, such as Isaiah and Jeremiah; that God will eventually save them and bring them back to their land. (The words "the righteous shall live by faith" would have resonated well with the righteous people in Judah.)

Synopsis
The Book of Habakkuk is a dialogue between the prophet and God. Habakkuk saw the rapid decline of Judah's moral, civil, and spiritual condition and that troubled him deeply. The first two chapters of the Book centre on Habakkuk's complaints and the Lord's answers. The last chapter stands in stark contrast to the first two: after Habakkuk heard from God he rejoiced by writing a psalm of faith.

We divide the Book of Habakkuk into two main sections:

1. Habakkuk's Questions (1:1-2:20)

Judah's wickedness had increased to the point where Habakkuk could not stand it any more. His first question to God was: How can God allow Judah to continue in her wicked ways (1:2-4)? God's response emphasized His sovereignty; He is aware of the situation and He will use the Babylonians (Chaldeans) to punish Judah (1:5-11).

Habakkuk's second question to God was: How can God use a wicked nation to punish His people (1:12-2:1)? God replied to him that He will punish Babylon too, but in the time and place of His choosing (2:2-20); again God declared that His sovereign purposes would be accomplished.

Habakkuk continues by pronouncing a series of woes – judgments – that will eventually befall the wicked Babylon.

2. Habakkuk's Prayer and Praise to God (3:1-19)

Habakkuk began his prophecy with despair, but he concludes it with a psalm of faith, praise, worship, and hope. He showed the people of God (of any generation) how to focus on that which honours God and how to turn mourning into rejoicing.

The difference between the beginning of the book and the end is striking. Although the Babylonian invasion will surely bring destructive results (3:17), the prophet of faith declares: *"Yet I will rejoice in the Lord, I will joy in the God of my salvation. The Lord God is my strength; He will make me walk on my high hills (3:18-19)."*

Habakkuk was a:

- Man with a burden
- Man with a vision
- Man with a prayer
- Man with a song

Noteworthy

Habakkuk is viewed as the grandfather of the Reformation. The apostle Paul learned the doctrine of justification by faith from Habakkuk and Luther learned it from Paul.

Paul quoted Habakkuk 1:5 in his warning to the unbelieving Jews in Antioch (Acts 13:41), and the key verse of Habakkuk, *"But the just shall live by faith,"* Paul quoted twice (Rom. 1:17; Gal. 3:11). The author to the Hebrews also quoted this verse (Heb. 10:38).

Habakkuk has been called "the prophet of faith," and also "the agnostic prophet" – he cried out to God with his "why" questions.

Habakkuk was not only a prophet, but possibly also one of the Levitical members of the choir (3:19b).

Personal Application

Suffering could be disciplinary (especially in the context of Israel's rebellion against God) – God could allow suffering in your life to serve a higher purpose.

When you struggle with penetrating questions, don't be afraid to ask God for answers. Write down what God reveals to you, hold fast to His promises in faith, knowing and believing that they will come to pass (2:2, 3).

Always remember: the righteous does not live by feelings, or sight, or under circumstances, but by faith in God in all aspects of his life (even if we don't fully understand God's ways).

Rejoice in the Lord always! In the good times and in the bad times.

ZEPHANIAH

Author
Zephaniah

Date
About 630 BC

Main Theme
"The Day of the Lord" – judgment for some, joy for others

Key Verse
"The Lord your God in your midst, the Mighty One, will save; He will rejoice over you with gladness, He will quiet with His love, He will rejoice over you with singing (3:17)."

Key Phrases
"In the day of the Lord's wrath"
"The Lord your God in your midst"

Key Words
(Divine) Jealousy (God loves His children so much that He will not tolerate a rival, and He desires their whole-hearted devotion; He will do everything to secure His relationship with His children)

Setting
Zephaniah was a contemporary of Jeremiah, and ministered during the reign of king Josiah. Many scholars suggest that Zephaniah prophesied early in the reign of Josiah before the discovery of the Book of the Law, which ignited a sweeping spiritual revival in Judah. Zephaniah doesn't mention this revival. The corrupt influence of the wicked kings Manasseh and Amon, who ruled prior to Josiah, must still have been in the order of the day; therefore Zephaniah denounced Judah's sins (1:4-13; 3:1-7). However, Zephaniah's powerful prophecy may have been a factor that contributed to the reforms that would have taking place (about 628 BC).

Purpose
To announce God's plans to judge Judah as well as the surrounding nations because of their refusal to walk in His ways, and to hold out hope by promising the Jews that a Day will come that God will restore His people for good. Zephaniah's prophecy focuses on the final Day of the Lord.

Synopsis
In the midst of wickedness and moral decay Zephaniah repeatedly and strongly emphasized his message that the Day of the Lord, Judgment Day, is coming when God will finally deal with rebellious mankind and sin.

DISCOVERING THE MOST AMAZING BOOK   233

We divide the Book of Zephaniah into two main sections:

1. The Day of the Lord will bring Judgment to many (1:2-3:8)
Zephaniah declares that in the Day of the Lord, God "*will utterly consume everything from the face of the earth (1:2).*" God's judgment against Judah includes people from all walks of life: religious leaders (1:4-7); political leaders (1:8, 9); business leaders (1:10, 11); and unbelievers (1:12, 13). The great Day of the Lord is certain and imminent (1:14-18). In chapter 2:1-3, the gracious God calls all to seek him and repent. God declares judgment on all nations (2:4-15), including rebellious Jerusalem (3:1-7) and the whole earth (3:8).

2. The Day of the Lord will bring Salvation to many (3:9-3:20
The Day of the Lord does not only mean punishment, but will usher in a glorious time of salvation and joy when God Himself will rejoice over the faithful remnant (both Jew and Gentile) with gladness and quiet them with His love, He will rejoice over them with singing (3:17). Hallelujah! What a glorious promise.

Noteworthy
The name Zephaniah means "Yahweh has hidden." Having been born during the latter part of the reign of the wicked king Manasseh (before his repentance), Zephaniah's name may be indicative that he was hidden from Manasseh's atrocities. Zephaniah's name also give spiritual significance to 2:3; those who seek the Lord, righteousness and humility "*will be hidden in the day of the Lord's anger.*"

Zephaniah points out his royal lineage by tracing his ancestry back four generations, making him the great-great-grandson of King Hezekiah (1:1).

Personal Application
Among other things, we learn the following from Zephaniah:

- God is perfect in righteousness and love (3:5). He will continually and graciously call people to repentance, however, those who continually ignore Him will face the consequences of their rebellion.

- God does not desire to punish people, He loves them (John 3:16). However, people by their own choosing punish themselves in the end of the day.

- God is gracious, He offers last-minute repentance even to the most rebellious (2:1-3).

- Remain zealous for God, and be careful of complacency and spiritual laxity.

HAGGAI

Author
Haggai

Date
520 BC

Main Theme
Rebuilding the Temple

Key Verse
"Now therefore, thus says the Lord of hosts: Consider your ways (1:5)!"

Key Phrases
"The Word of the Lord"
"The Lord's House"

Key Words
Consider, Glory

Setting
Haggai prophesied during the second year of king Darius I, which was 520 BC. As we have seen, the first return from Babylonian captivity to Jerusalem, under the leadership of Zerubbabel, to rebuild the temple was in 538BC. In 536 BC the returned exiles began

restoring the altar of sacrifices and laying the foundation of the temple. The rebuilding of the temple was met with strong political opposition from the neighbouring Samaritans and other Gentiles. The returned exiles were so threatened by the hostile opposition that they stopped working on the temple in 534 BC. No work was done on the temple for sixteen years. Discouraged and distracted from their mission objective, the returned exiles became absorbed by their own personal affairs, particularly building for themselves comfortable houses (1:4, 9). Thus, God called the prophets Haggai and Zechariah to minister His message to them.

Purpose

Haggai prophesied to encourage the people to make the rebuilding of the temple their priority; he particularly encouraged Zerubbabel, Judah's governor, and Joshua, the high priest, to lead the Jews in their work of rebuilding the temple.

Synopsis

God used Haggai to preach four great sermons that would exhort the people to renew their commitment to rebuilding the temple.

1. Haggai's 1st Sermon: Put God First and Build the Temple (ch. 1) Date: August 29th 520 BC. In his first message Haggai challenged the people to: *"Consider your ways* (1:6)." He essentially said to the people "consider your priorities – you have time for building your comfortable homes, but you have no time to build God's house." Because of their misplaced priorities, their crops failed and their material possessions did not satisfy (1:6, 10). The people responded eagerly by resuming work on the temple.

2. Haggai's 2nd Sermon: The Glory of the Latter Temple (2:1-9) Date: October 17th 520 BC. Zerubbabel's temple is compared to Solomon's temple. Solomon's temple was glorious because it was built with very costly materials, such as gold, silver and precious jewels during a time of great wealth. Now, the returned Jews did not have all the resources that Solomon had, only the rubble of the original temple and whatever was supplied by Cyrus the Great. Perhaps the older people who had seen the original temple (also known as the former temple) wept over the second temple (also known as the latter temple) that would never be as glorious as the first one.

By the mouth of the prophet Haggai the Lord reminded the people that the significance of the temple is spiritual and not physical. He assured them that, based on His covenant with Israel, by His Spirit He was with them, and they need not fear. The Lord also promised that *"The glory of this latter temple shall be greater than the former (2:9),"* and that glory will be accompanied by peace. (Scholars disagree on how this prophecy of the "greater glory of this temple" may have been fulfilled. Some suggest that Herod the Great spent years enlarging and enriching this temple, and it was filled with the glory of God incarnate every time Christ came to Jerusalem. Others suggest that it prophesies God's indwelling of human temples through Jesus Christ. However, this promise of God encouraged the Jews to complete their task.)

3. Haggai's 3rd Sermon: Questions to the Priests (2:10-19)
Date: December 18th 520 BC. By asking the priests certain questions Haggai reminded them of sin's corrupting nature, and warned the people against becoming spiritually contaminated through close association with ungodly practices and people.

Holiness is not transferable; it comes from God when you personally commit yourself to Him. However, a dirty object causes uncleanness in whatever it touches. Thus, Haggai illustrated that the people's return to consistent sinful practices had defiled them and everything they touched.

Haggai's third message ends with a promise of blessing based on the obedience of the people.

4. Haggai's 4th Sermon: A Promise to Zerubbabel (2:20-23)
Date: December 18th 520 BC. Through Haggai's final message the Lord made two promises: (1) after seventy years of Babylonian captivity, the Jews feared that they could be taken captive again by other nations, the Lord promised to overthrow the nations that the Jews feared; and (2) He promised to re-establish the Davidic line in Jerusalem after the disruption of the Babylonian exile, ensuring the Messiah's lineage. Zerubbabel is a descendant of David, mentioned

in the genealogy of Jesus in Matthew 1:12, and here in Haggai 2:23 he is called "God's signet ring" as a sign of authority.

Noteworthy
The Book of Haggai is the second shortest in the Old Testament, and Haggai only prophesied for three months and twenty-four days.

Personal Application
Never place your personal affairs above God, and never allow circumstances to get you under. In the face of challenges remain faithful. Prioritize your life and put God first always.

Are you in a spiritual dry place? If yes: "Consider your ways," and "Consider God's ways."

ZECHARIAH

Author
Zechariah

Date
520-475 BC

Main Theme
The Lord Loves and Remembers His People

Key Verse
"And the Lord shall be King over all the earth. In that day it shall be – the Lord is one and His name one (14:9)."

Key Phrases
"The Day of the Lord"
"The Lord of hosts"

Key Words
Jerusalem, Jealous, Zealous

Setting

Zechariah was a younger contemporary to Haggai, and began prophesying to the returned exiles two months after the beginning of Haggai's ministry. The historical setting for chapters 1-8 of Zechariah is the same as that of Haggai. Based on stylistic differences and references such as Greece (9:13), scholars reckon that chapters 9-14 were written between 480-470 BC, during the reign of Xerxes (486-464 BC).

Purpose

Like Haggai, Zechariah encouraged the people to rebuild the temple, and he also revealed the First and Second Coming of Christ.

Synopsis

The prophet Zechariah is one of the greatest examples of a "seer" in the entire Bible. He saw what the people could not see because, as a seer, he not only saw God, but vividly saw in visions what God wanted to communicate to His covenant people.

God gave Zechariah eight visions, and several messages to portray His future plans for His people. The first eight chapters were primarily written to encourage the people in rebuilding the temple; the last six chapters were written after the temple was completed to anticipate Israel's coming Messiah. In these chapters the rise of Greece, the advent and rejection of the Messiah, and the final triumph of the Messiah are foretold.

We divide the Book of Zechariah into the following five main sections:

1. Introduction and the Call to Repentance (1:1-6)

After we are introduced to Zechariah and the historical setting in verse 1, the Lord reminds His people why the Babylonian captivity took place and encouraged them, *"Return to Me and I will return to you."*

2. The Eight Visions of Zechariah (1:7-6:8)

Through these visions God assured the people of His love, care, and future plans for them. These visions gave encouragement, strength, and hope to the despairing people of God.

Vision	Significance
Man and horses among the myrtle trees (1:7-17)	Although Judah suffered seventy years in exile, God will again be merciful to Judah and restore her. And, although wicked nations prosper, God will bring judgment upon them. The Angel of the Lord is a Theophany of Jesus Christ in the Old Testament.
Four horns and four craftsmen (1:18-20)	The four horns most likely represent Egypt, Assyria, Babylonia, and Mede-Persia that scattered Judah, Israel, and Jerusalem. The four craftsmen represent those who terrified and punished the four horns.
A man measuring Jerusalem (2:1-5)	Revealing the glorious prosperity of Jerusalem as a result of the overthrow of her enemies. God will be a protective wall of fire around Jerusalem. May also be indicative of the future New Jerusalem.
Cleansing of Joshua the high priest (ch. 3)	God cleansed Joshua as a symbol that He will remove the sin of the people and restore the priesthood of the nation. Both the Branch (see Jer. 33:15), and stone represent Christ, who in one day brought peace and removed sin for all who accept Him. Christ is the ultimate High Priest.
Vision of the lampstand and olive trees (ch. 4)	The two olive trees represent Zerubbabel and Joshua who were empowered by the Holy Spirit to empower the people. The Holy Spirit is symbolized as olive oil (constant fuel or empowerment). The end result is that Israel will be God's light bearer to the world.
Flying scroll (5:1-4)	The flying scroll is symbolic of God's judgment on those who sin. The focus is individual sin and not that of a nation. God's curse is a symbol of destruction.

Woman in a basket (5:5-11)	This vision promises the removal of wickedness. The woman represents the wickedness. The woman tried to escape; the angel put her back into the basket and sent her to Shinar (Babylonia). A sinful land like Babylonia was a fitting place to send evil. After the return of the Jews and under the revival of Ezra and Nehemiah, Israel was cleansed of much sin.
Four chariots (6:1-8)	God sent His angels of war and judgment against enemy nations. The horses represent God's judgment upon those who oppress His people. Red represents war; black represents famine and death; white is for conquering; and dappled represents pestilence. The black horses went north, the direction from which most of Judah's enemies came; the white horses went after the black ones; the dappled went to the south countries, while the others patrolled the earth, ready to execute judgment at God's command. Judgment on Babylonia caused God to rest.

3. The Crowning of the High Priest, Joshua (6:9-15)
This is a prophetic symbolic act, expanding on the vision of the Branch and pointing to Jesus Christ who will be the ultimate Priest, Prophet, and King. *"He shall build the temple of the Lord* (v. 13)." Christians are the spiritual temple of the Lord.

4. The Fasting Question (7:1-8:23)
Here a question is raised about the annual fast that commemorates the temple's destruction. Since the temple is rebuilt, should the people continue to fast? God's answer makes it clear that their fasting was selfish, but He desires obedience, faithfulness, and justice above ritual fasting. Fasting should be approached with the correct motive and attitude.

In chapter 8 God encouraged the people again, promising that He will return to His people and dwell in their midst, prospering them.

5. Prophecies about Israel's enemies, Israel's Restoration and the Coming Messiah (9:1-14:21)

Chapters 9-11 are called a "burden" or "oracle" (a revelation coming from God) about Israel's neighbouring nations (9:1); and chapters 12-14 are an oracle about Israel (12:1). The prophetic messages in this section are an expansion and continuation of the messages revealed through the eight night visions.

Zechariah announced that God will judge and destroy the heathen nations that are Israel's enemies (see 9:1-8; 12:1-6; 14:1-2). He also predicted the coming of the Messiah, the One whom God would send to deliver His people from sin and to reign over all the earth.

Zechariah's Messianic prophecies indicate that the offices of Prophet, Priest, and King will be united in the reign of the Messiah, the King of kings.

Prophecies concerning Christ in Zechariah	
Prophecy	**Reference**
His shed blood, the only means to remove sin	3:8-9; 13:1
Builder of the spiritual temple of the Lord	6:12
His universal reign as King and Priest	6:13; 9:10
His Triumphal Entry into Jerusalem	9:9, quoted in Matthew 21:5
His betrayal for 30 pieces of silver	11:2; quoted in Matthew 27:9-10
His deity	12:08
His hands pierced	12:10; 13:6, quoted in John 19:37
The stricken Shepherd	13:7, quoted in Matthew 26:31

Noteworthy

Zechariah is known as "the prophet of Visionary Encouragement." He was born to a priestly family in Babylon during the Captivity and returned to Jerusalem with his grandfather Iddo (Neh. 12:6) and the first group of exiles. Like Jeremiah and Ezekiel he was both a priest and a prophet.

Zechariah has the second highest number of Messianic prophecies in the Old Testament, Isaiah being first.

The *"Spirit of grace and supplication (12:10)"* refers to the Holy Spirit that will bring conviction and repentance, and regenerate those who embrace Jesus Christ as Saviour.

Personal Application
Take your eyes off your current circumstances and behold the glory of the King of kings and your glorious future in Him, "then the things of the earth (and your circumstances) will grow strangely dim."

MALACHI

Author
Malachi

Date
About 432-425 BC

Main Theme
Reassurance of God's Love and Justice

Key Verse
"The Sun of Righteousness shall arise with healing in His wings (4:2)."

Key Phrases
"Yet You say"
"Sun of Righteousness"
"Day of Judgement"

Key Words
Messenger, Priests

Setting
The historical background of Malachi involves the political, social and religious conditions that existed after the Exile. The remnant of Jews that returned from Babylon had been home for about 100 years. God had kept His promises, but the people were still disobedient. Although

the Babylonian Exile cured them of their idolatry, the Jews once again became spiritually lethargic and adulterous. They neglected the house of the Lord, worship was decaying because of the laxity of the priests, and the Jews were divorcing their wives and marrying idolatrous neighbours. In general, they did not honour the law of the covenant. For a full picture of the conditions in Judah during the days of Malachi read Ezra 7-10 and the Book of Nehemiah. Malachi's message addressed the same problems that Nehemiah faced: corrupt priests, neglect of tithes and offerings, and intermarriage with pagan wives.

Purpose
Malachi's purpose was to call God's people, especially the spiritual leaders, back to spiritual vitality, and to announce the coming of the Lord.

Synopsis
In order to fulfil his purpose Malachi emphasized the nature and attributes of God, the keeping of the covenant, and the importance of faithful commitment to God.

The Book of Malachi has a notable dialogue style. The content of the book is structured around six disputes between God and His people – God makes a statement, then He mentions what the response of the people is, by stating "yet you say," and then He explains to the people the reasons why He made that statement. These disputes centre on ten questions asked by the people in response to God's statements.[30]

Typical of backslidden people is their tendency to be seemingly innocent, and hypocritical. The Jews were in a cold spiritual condition, they were indifferent to both God and His law, consequently they questioned everything about God – wondering if God's messianic promises would ever be fulfilled and whether it was worth serving Him. The sins listed by Malachi are outward manifestations of their inward spiritual condition.

With the above in mind we divide the Book of Malachi into seven main sections.

---

[30] Global University, *Old Testament Survey*, p. 214

1. God's first statement: He has loved Israel (1:2-5).
   Israel's first question: *"In what way have you loved us* (1:2)?"

2. God's second statement: Israel has dishonoured God and the priests despised His name.
   Israel's second statement: *"In what way have we despised your name* (1:6)?"
   Israel's third question: *"In what way have we defiled You* (1:7)?"

3. God's third statement: Judah has been unfaithful in divorcing Israelite wives and intermarrying with pagan women (2:10-16)
   Israel's fourth question: *"For what reason* (2:14)?"

4. God's fourth statement: The Lord will suddenly come to His temple (2:17-3:6).
   Israel's fifth question: *"In what way have we wearied Him* (2:17)?"
   Israel's sixth question: *"Where is the God of justice* (2:17)?"

5. God's fifth statement: *"Return to Me, and I will return to you* (3:7-12)."
   Israel's seventh question: *"In what way shall we return* (3:7)?"
   Israel's eight question: *"In what way have we robbed You* (3:8)?"

6. God's sixth statement: Israel has said harsh things against the Lord (3:13-18).
   Israel's ninth question: *"What have we spoken against You* (3:13)?"
   Israel's tenth question: *"What profit is it that we have kept His ordinance, and that we have walked as mourners before the Lord* (3:14)?"

7. God's seventh statement: *"The Sun of Righteousness shall arise"* (4:1-6)

Noteworthy
The last two chapters of the last book of the Old Testament contain dramatic prophecies of the coming of the Lord and of John the Baptist. About four hundred years later Israel flocked to the Jordan River when *"the voice of one crying in the wilderness: 'Prepare the way of the Lord; make His paths straight'* (Matt. 3:3; Mal. 3:1)

DISCOVERING THE MOST AMAZING BOOK   245

appeared.[31] Thus, the Old Testament ends on a note of expectancy for the promised Messiah, Jesus the Christ who *"will save His people from their sins* (Matt. 1:21)."

Personal Application

The following are *Seven Whispers of a Heart Growing Cold toward God* based on the studies of *Calvary Academics, Old Testament Survey, Part 3,* pages 95-102:

1. To doubt God's love – do you doubt God's love. Ask yourself the following question: "If you are not as close to God as you once were, who moved?"

2. To Despise the Name of God – Do you despise the name of the Lord by not fearing Him, respecting Him, by not giving anything valuable to the Lord?

3. A Broken Commitment to God – Are you indifferent to God and His Word?

4. Broken Marriage Commitments – If married, are you in everything faithful to your spouse? If not married, are you in everything faithful to God?

5. Relative Morality – Does everything go in your life? Do you live according to Christian values?

6. Robbing God – Do you rob God in anything, time, money, natural and spiritual talents, service, and worship.

7. Unbelief – When you keep on listening to the previous six whispers and give in to them, then you will sadly end up in unbelief; you will be spiritually, and morally corrupt.

---

[31] *Nelson's Complete Book of Bible Maps & Charts,* p. 285

Part Four

Survey of New Testament Books

Chapter Eight

Differences between the two Covenants and a Survey of the Gospels

Introductory

The Old Covenant ends incomplete, still looking eagerly forward to the achievement of its purposes and the fulfilment of its prophecies and promises. If God's revelation to man had ended here, then all hope would have been lost. On the other hand, if there had been the revelation of the New Covenant without that of the Old, there would have been an end without a beginning, a fulfilment without a promise, a supply without a need, a superstructure without a foundation, a consummation without a commencement.[32] Now, looking back we can clearly see that the Old Covenant is predictive and preparative, and it creates expectation, while the New Covenant is realization and fulfilment. Undoubtedly the Old Covenant is the historical basis for the New, and we cannot truly understand the New Covenant without the background of the Old.

The New Covenant, as the fulfilment of the Old Covenant, declares: Jesus, the Saviour, came! Praise God! Now salvation is possible by grace through faith – no more striving and self-effort. Jesus, by His blood, paved a new and living way so that everyone who believes in Him can enter the presence of God (see Heb. 12:19-22).

The New Covenant is the fulfilment of the promise in Jesus Christ of Nazareth (Luke 1:31-33), who, by His godly life, ministry, death, and resurrection established and sealed the New Covenant

---

[32] Graham Scroggie, The Unfolding Drama of Redemption, p. 75

(Luke 22:20; Heb. 9:12). The 27 Books that make up the New Covenant are written testimonies to the truthfulness and faithfulness of God, and the Good News of Jesus Christ. They declare God's plan for the salvation of mankind as well as the restoration of all things. These Books not only introduce but make love, grace, hope, salvation, peace, good will, and freedom personally known. If rightly understood and believed they give great consolation, direction and encouragement. And if you rightly respond to their message, you will be established in love, hope, identity and purpose.

The New Covenant builds further on the foundation of the Old Covenant and throws a bright and marvellous light on the fulfilment of the Old Covenant prophecies. Therefore, we must let the New Covenant interpret the Old.

Having said that, it is of utmost importance to understand the difference between the Old and New Covenant in order to interpret the message of the Bible correctly. Therefore, we will now look at the differences between the two Covenants before we journey into the New Covenant.

Main differences between the Old and New Covenant

Many Christians struggle with questions such as: Is the Old Covenant still relevant to our lives today? In view of divine inspiration of all Scripture, how do believers determine what Old Covenant principles and commands apply today? The key to answering these questions is: the difference between the Old and New Covenant.

We have already seen in the Old Covenant that God promised to make a New Covenant with Israel. By the mouth of the prophet Jeremiah God declared: *"Behold, the days come, says the Lord, that I will make a new covenant with the house of Israel and with the house of Judah – not according to the covenant that I made with their fathers in the day that I took them by the hand to lead them out of the land of Egypt, My covenant which they broke, though I was a husband to them, says the Lord. But this covenant that I will make with the house of Israel after those days, says the Lord: I will put My law in their minds, and write it on their hearts; and I will be their God, and they shall be My people. No more shall every man teach* his neighbour, and every man his brother, saying 'Know the Lord' for they all shall know Me, from the least of them to the greatest of them, says the Lord. For I will forgive their iniquity, and their sin I will remember no more (Jer. 31:31-34; emphasis mine)." This passage is quoted in its entirety in the New Covenant (Heb. 8:8-12).

The promise that God gave Israel through the prophet Ezekiel is similar in concept to Jeremiah 31:31-34. *"A new heart also I will give you, and a new spirit I will put within you: and I will take away the stony heart out of your flesh, and I will give you a heart of flesh. And I will put My Spirit within you, and cause you to walk in My statutes, and you shall keep My judgments, and do them. And you shall dwell in the land that I gave to your fathers; and you shall be My people, and I will be your God (Ez. 36:26-28)."*

Both these prophecies obviously refer to the promise of the New Covenant that would be established by Jesus Christ, the One promised by God to deliver and restore His people. And without any doubt they reveal that the two covenants would be completely different. The new heart and the new spirit clearly speak of the new birth and the reception of the resident Holy Spirit.

We should keep in mind, if a New Covenant was promised, then it obviously means the Old was only temporary. Hebrews 8:13 confirms this: *"By saying, a new covenant, He has declared that the first is old. And what is old and aging is about to disappear."*

The following chart summarizes the difference between the Old and New Covenants according to Jeremiah and Ezekiel's prophecies.

The difference between the Old and New Covenants according to Jeremiah 31:31-34 and Ezekiel 36:26-28	
Old Covenant	**New Covenant**
Written on stone (material)	Written on people's heart (spiritual)
Based on the law/works	Based on the love and grace of God
Must be taught	Known by all
Works-obedience based relationship with God	Personal relationship with God, led by the Holy Spirit
Temporary	Eternal

Furthermore, when we study the Book of Hebrews, then we find conclusive evidence of the fulfilment of the Old Covenant in Christ.

The writer of Hebrews shows clearly the differences between the Old and New Covenants. He proves that the Old Covenant was a shadow of Jesus Christ.		
Reference	**The Old Mosaic Covenant**	**The New Covenant in Christ**
Heb. 8:3-4	Gifts and sacrifices by those guilty of sin	Self-sacrifice by guiltless Christ – He is the final gift and sacrifice
Heb. 8:5-6, 10-12	Focused on a physical place of worship	Focuses on the reign of Christ in believers' hearts (compare John 4:23-24)
Heb. 8:5-6, 10-12	A shadow and temporal	A reality and eternal
Heb. 8:6	Limited promises	Limitless promises
Heb. 8:8-9	Failed agreement by people	Faithful agreement by Christ
Heb. 9:1	External standards and rules	Internal standards – a new heart
Heb. 9:7	Limited access to God	Unlimited access to God
Heb. 9:9-10, 13	Outward, temporary, legalistic cleansing	God's cleansing by the blood of Jesus is complete
Heb. 9:11-14, 24-28	Continual sacrifice	Christ's sacrifice was perfect and complete
Heb. 9:22, 24-28	Forgiveness earned; only temporary, once a year	Forgiveness true and complete and freely given; Christ's death applied to our sin
Heb. 9:22	Available to some	Available to all

Additionally, when we continue to examine different passages in both the Old and New Covenants, then we gain more insight as to the differences between them.

In Exodus 19:4-6 God proposed His covenant for Israel to Moses. After Moses came down from the mountain, he presented it to the leaders and elders of Israel. In verse 8 we read that the people accepted the covenant of God and promise to abide to it. Herein we see that the Old Covenant was an agreement between God and Israel.

The track record of Israel throughout the Old Covenant, a period of about 1000 years, clearly shows that they could not keep their part of the covenant. By the mouth of various prophets God encouraged His people to remain faithful to Him, and He promised them that a set time, during which He will deliver and restore them, will certainly come. Our journey through the Old Covenant makes not only Israel, but mankind's desperate need for a Saviour evident. Man cannot save himself, and man cannot keep covenant with God.

When we study Isaiah 42 we realize that it is a conversation between God the Father and God the Son. Verse 6 makes it obvious that Jesus Christ, the Son of God is *a covenant to the people.*" In other words, the New Covenant is an agreement (covenant) between God the Father and God the Son. In the New Covenant, Jesus Christ upholds the covenant, not man, because 1000 years of Israelite history proves that man cannot keep covenant with God.

Jesus Christ came to fulfil the Old Covenant, to destroy the curse of the law, and to seal the New Covenant with His blood so that everyone who believes in Him may have everlasting life.

Based on what we have said above and what we have learned from the Old Covenant law in the Chronological Survey we suggest the following chart that contrasts the main differences between the Old and New Covenant.

Summary of the main differences between the Old and New Covenants	
Old Covenant	**New Covenant**
1. An agreement (covenant) between God and Israel (Ex. 19:4-6)	1. An agreement between God the Father and God the Son (Is. 42).
2. To distinguish Israel from other nations and to identify them as God's people; the OC was embodied in the nation of Israel and was exclusive.	2. Salvation is now available to everyone who believes in Jesus Christ (Jew and Gentile). The NC is embodied in Christ and His Church; it is inclusive.
3. To emphasise the holiness of God and man's inability to save himself	3. To reveal Jesus Christ as the only Saviour (Gal. 3:19-25; John 14:6)
4. To look forward to the coming Saviour	4. To look back at what the Lord has done
5. Given for temporal and material blessings	5. Given for both material and spiritual blessings
6. Based on works/self-effort	6. Based on Jesus' performance on our behalf and His work of Atonement – now by grace through faith one can be saved (Eph. 2:8, 9)
7. Not given for salvation	7. Given for the salvation of humanity
8. Only Jesus Christ could fulfil the Old Covenant (Matt. 5:17).	8. In the NC love fulfils the law of the OC (Matt. 22:37-40; Rom. 13:8-10), and the indwelling Holy Spirit is the norm for Christian living (Rom. 8:4, 14; Gal. 5:18). Now the righteous – those who are declared righteous as a result of their faith in Jesus Christ – will live by faith, not by law (Rom. 1:16, 17; 3:28; 4:13).

The apostle John summarizes not only the entire Biblical revelation, but also the difference between the two Covenants when he declares: *"The law was given through Moses [Old Covenant], but grace and truth came through Jesus Christ [New Covenant] (John 1:17)."* Therefore, Christians are not under the law but under the grace of God (Rom. 6:14), and *"Christ is the end of the law for righteousness to everyone who believes* (Rom. 10:4)." Once you believe in Jesus Christ as your Saviour, you are declared righteous, thus, it is *"the end of the law"* (also see Rom. 3:20, 28).

Finally, Jesus said: *"For all the prophets and the law prophesied until John* (Matt. 11:13)." The law and the prophets (Old Covenant) pointed to the Messiah (New Covenant). Although John the Baptist's ministry was still part of the Old Covenant, his ministry prepared the way for the Lord, and thus, served as the culmination of Old Covenant prophecy that looked forward to the coming of the messianic kingdom and the realization of the New Covenant. For that reason, the ministry of John the Baptist is the dividing line between the Old and New Covenant. (Also see Addendum: *Questions concerning Law keeping.*)

Synopsis of the Gospels and the Book of Acts

Now let us turn to the Gospels that will introduce the long-awaited Messiah to us.

The Four Gospels

Many people would wonder why the New Covenant contains four different Gospels (accounts) of the one authentic Gospel (the good news of salvation in Christ Jesus). The main reason is that any one of these Gospels alone would not do justice to Jesus' life and ministry; on their own they are merely "leaflets" and not full accounts. The most important life ever lived should be seen from different perspectives. Each Gospel writer wrote about Jesus to a different audience for a different purpose to give a unique perspective on His life and ministry. Together, the four Gospels give us a complete picture of who Jesus is and what He accomplished during His ministry.

The first three Gospels – Matthew, Mark, and Luke – are called the Synoptic Gospels, meaning that these three gospels see things in much the same way. Although there are many similarities in these Gospels, they vary in what material they include and in the arrangement of specific events to serve their purpose. In the Synoptic Gospels, Jesus' principal teaching is on the kingdom of God, which is mentioned more than fifty times in these three books. The Gospel of John was written much later than the Synoptic Gospels and differs from the Synoptics in a number of ways. It deals largely with matter unrecorded in the others: (1) John emphasises the Deity of Jesus Christ; (2) John reports the early Judean ministry of Jesus; (3) instead of the familiar parables, John has lengthy private discourses, for the most part not included in the Synoptics – only the feeding of the five thousand and Jesus walking on water are in all four; (4) instead of the many miracles and healings in the Synoptics, John uses seven carefully selected miracles, which serve as "signs;" (5) the ministry of Jesus revolves around three Passover Feasts, instead of the one cited in the Synoptics; (6) The seven *"I Am"* sayings are unique to John; (7) and also unique to John is the designation of the Holy Spirit as "Comforter" or "Helper" (14:16).

Different symbols for the Gospels are used to communicate the distinctive of each account. These symbols are not man made, but are prophetically pronounced in the Old Covenant. Ezekiel's vision of the four living creatures (1:5-11) has reference to the attributes of God, yet these attributes are centred and summed up in the Person of Christ. Each living creature had four faces, a lion's, king of the beasts; an ox's, king of cattle; an eagle's, king of birds; and a man's, crown of all creation.

Matthew is symbolized by a lion which represents strength and royal authority; the emphasis is on Jesus as Messiah-King. Mark is symbolized by an ox which portrays lowly service and power; the emphasis is on Jesus as God's Servant who came to make atonement for mankind. The figure of a man, for Luke, symbolizes the perfect manhood of Jesus, as well as Jesus as the universal Saviour; He paid the price for the whole of humanity. And an eagle, John's symbol, represents deity; the emphasis is on the Godhead of Jesus.

Also, the Mighty King of Matthew's Gospel is revealed in Jeremiah 13:5: *"Behold, the days are coming says the Lord, that I will raise to David a Branch of righteousness; a King shall reign and prosper and execute judgment and righteousness in the earth."* The Humble Servant of Mark's Gospel is in Zechariah 3:8: *"Behold, I am bringing forth My Servant the Branch."* The Ideal Man of Luke's Gospel is in Zechariah 6:12: *"Behold, the Man whose name is the Branch."* The Divine Son of John's Gospel is in Isaiah 9:6: *"For unto us a Child is born, unto us a Son is given; and the government will be upon His shoulder. And His name will be called Wonderful, Counsellor, Mighty God, Everlasting Father, Prince of Peace."*

All four aspects are needed to bring out the full truth about Jesus Christ. As the Sovereign King He came to rule and reign. As Servant He came to serve and suffer. As Son of Man He came to share and sympathise. As Son of God He came to reveal and redeem. These four outstanding characteristics form a marvellous fourfold blending – *sovereignty and servant hood; humanity and deity.* The four Gospels are four in one, and one in four.

The following chart summarizes the unique characteristics of each Gospel.

- Evangelistic – to proclaim the Good News of salvation in Jesus Christ
- Apologetic – to defend and explain the Gospel and Christianity
- Preservation – to preserve the message by writing it down, and
- To encourage and stimulate the faith of their readers.

The following summaries of the Gospels should help you to understand the unique characteristics of each.

Matthew:

- Written to a Jewish audience to show that Jesus was the promised Messiah-King of Old Testament prophecy. "Written by a Jew to Jews about a Jew."
- Key expression is *"that it might be fulfilled."*
- Quotes more from the Old Testament than any other Gospel.
- Uses *alternating* sections of didactic (giving instruction) and narrative (story telling) material to emphasize Jesus as the Rabbi (Teacher).
- Matthew emphasizes what Jesus *said*.
- A major theme is the kingdom of heaven or the kingdom of God – God's rule in the world and in human hearts.
- Other dominant themes are the Sermon on the Mount (chs.5-7), the Church (16:18; 18:19), the End Times and Second Coming of Christ (chs. 24, 25).

Mark:

- Probably the first Gospel written; Matthew and Luke may have used Mark as their source.
- The shortest Gospel; written to a gentile audience, particularly Roman citizens.
- The Gospel of Mark emphasizes what Jesus *did*.
- Mark focuses on Jesus as Servant who ministers to the physical and spiritual needs of others.
- Mark's account is vivid and short, with rapid movements to give a sense of urgency to the gospel message
- His key expression is "immediately"
- Mark's purpose was to show that Jesus was the Son of God; a Roman soldier declared at Jesus' death: *"Truly He was the Son of God* (15:39)."

Luke:

➤ Written by a Gentile writer, for Gentiles, to give the full story of Jesus' life, from His birth to the birth of the Church.
➤ Records many of Jesus' parables not found in the other Gospels.
➤ Portraying Jesus as the universal and compassionate Saviour of the world, with love for all people, whether rich or poor, Jew or Gentile; He reaches out especially to women and the poor and outcast of society.
➤ Emphasizes what Jesus *felt*.
➤ Also emphasizes the work of the Holy Spirit and the central place of prayer in Jesus' life and ministry.
➤ Key expression is "it happened" or "it came to pass."

John:

➤ Focuses on the theological meaning of Jesus' actions, rather than on the actions themselves
➤ Emphasizes who Jesus *is*, rather than what He did.
➤ Uniquely introduces the Holy Spirit as the "Comforter" or "Helper" who will lead the believer into all the truth and extends Jesus' ministry through believers.
➤ Uses many key words, such as *life, light, believe, love, witness, glory, water* and *truth*, to portray Jesus as God's eternal Son.
➤ John presents Jesus as God incarnate through seven miraculous signs
➤ Key expressions are "believe" and "I Am"
➤ John pronounces his intended purpose in writing this Gospel: *"that you may believe that Jesus is the Christ, the Son of God, and that believing you may have life in His name (20:31)."*

Now, let's look at each Gospel individually.

MATTHEW

Author
Matthew, meaning "Gift of the Lord," was also known as Levi (Mark 2:14).

Date
Late 50's early 60's

Main Theme
Jesus is the fulfilment of Old Testament prophecies regarding the Messiah King. His disciples are called to a New Covenant, to live at an exceedingly higher dimension than the Old ever realized.

Key Verse
"This is Jesus the King of the Jews (27:37)."

Key Phrase
"Son of David" (7 times)

Key Words
"fulfilled" (38 times), "Kingdom," "righteous," and "righteousness"

Setting
The Gospel of Matthew, like the other two Synoptics, was written during Roman rule against the backdrop of the early Church when there was ongoing tension between Judaism and Christianity, and much misunderstanding concerning Jesus Christ as the Messiah-King and the law of the Old Covenant.

Purpose
Matthew wrote his Gospel to encourage and confirm the persecuted Jewish Christians in their faith, to silence their opponents, and to prove that Jesus Christ of Nazareth is the fulfilment of the promised Messiah and King of the Old Covenant. Furthermore, Matthew wrote his Gospel to preserve written eyewitness testimony about Jesus' mission – who He really is, His ministry, and His Messianic purpose.

Synopsis
Matthew divided his book into three major sections: An introduction (1:1-4:16), the main body of Jesus' ministry (4:17-16:21), and a conclusion (16:21-28:20). His major divisions are marked by introducing them with the words *"from that time Jesus began to* (4:17; 16:21)." Matthew also divided his book into four blocks of major teaching, each of which concludes with a summary statement (8:1; 11:1; 13:53; 19:1; 26:1).

For the purpose of our study we divide the book of Matthew into three main sections:

1. The Coming of the Messiah-King and His Preparation for Ministry (1:1-4:16).
Matthew begins his book fittingly by immediately connecting Jesus with David and Abraham, demonstrating the royal messianic line of Jesus and His relevance to the Jews. In so doing Matthew also highlights that Jesus is the foretold divine-human Messiah – the King of the Jews. He then continues telling of Jesus' supernatural birth as fulfilment of Old Testament prophecies, the flight to Egypt in order to escape the murderous Herod, and the return to Nazareth. Matthew continues announcing the ministry of John the Baptist as forerunner of Jesus Christ, how he baptized Jesus in the Jordan (3:16-17), and how Jesus defeated satan in the wilderness. Jesus as the sinless God-Man had to face His adversary right at the outset of His ministry to demonstrate His victory over temptation and the schemes of the devil.

2. The Powerful Message and Ministry of the Messiah-King (4:17-25:46).
Jesus' powerful ministry began after His baptism and after He was led into the wilderness for forty days by the Spirit of God. His first message was short, yet thought provoking: *"Repent, for the kingdom of heaven is at hand* (4:17)." Jesus' public ministry took off when He called His first disciples and later gave His most elaborate teaching recorded in Scripture, the Sermon on the Mount (chs. 5-7), which is seen as the Constitution of the Kingdom of God.

Matthew demonstrates Jesus' divine authority by reporting His miracles of healing the sick, casting out demons, and even raising the dead.

Jesus experienced much opposition from the Pharisees and others in the religious establishment, however He continued to teach concerning the Kingdom of Heaven, making use of parables (chs. 13-14). (Here we have to keep in mind that the Jews expected an earthly king that would have liberated them from Rome and helped them to restore their hold on the land.)

The opposition from the religious establishment, the rejection of Jesus by His fellow citizens (13:54-58), the threat of Herod in the death of John the Baptist (14:1-12), and His disciples' lack of understanding His mission (16:13, 14) led Jesus to reveal His Messianic purpose to His disciples – to *"suffer ... and be killed, and be raised the third day* (16:21)." Jesus revealed His true identity to Peter, James, and John (17:1-5), and continued His ministry of healing and teaching.

The conflict of Jesus with His opponents led to a divinely ordained purpose – the crucifixion. Opposition against Jesus soon increased in intensity after His triumphal entry into Jerusalem (ch. 21). We see this in definite events, such as the debates with the Herodians, the Sadducees, and the Pharisees (22:15-40), and His denunciation of the scribes and Pharisees (ch. 23). Jesus knew that His death was near, so He taught His disciples about the future – He revealed to them the end time events (chs. 24, 25).

3. The Death and Resurrection of the Messiah-King (26:1-28:20). Here Matthew focuses on Jesus' final days on the earth – His Last Supper with His disciples, His prayer in Gethsemane, the betrayal by Judas, the flight of the disciples, Peter's denial, the trials before Caiaphas and Pilate, His crucifixion, His last words on the cross, and His burial in a borrowed tomb. But praise God, the story does not end here.

Matthew's Gospel ends with the triumphant Resurrection, as the decisive act of God's sovereign power, proving that Jesus Christ is the Messiah-King, the Risen Saviour.

After His resurrection Jesus gave His Church the Great Commission, a clarion call to spread the Good News of salvation to a lost world, and He promised: *"I am with you always, even to the end of the age."*

Noteworthy

Matthew was placed first in the canon of New Testament books by the early Church because it is a natural bridge between the two Covenants. He linked his Gospel with the Hebrew Scriptures, thus introducing the New Covenant as the fulfilment of the Old.

By making use of carefully selected Old Testament quotations Matthew proves that Jesus is the King of the Jews, the long-awaited Messiah, and he also explains God's Kingdom. Matthew uses approximately 130 Old Testament quotations and allusions, more than any other New Testament book. The phrase *"that what was spoken through the prophet might be fulfilled,"* appears nine times in Matthew and not once in the other Gospels. The emphasis on Jesus as the fulfilment of prophecy shows that Jesus' life and ministry were part of the single plan of God throughout the history of Israel, and not an act of desperation. Matthew shows how Jesus fulfilled not only the Old Testament prophecies, but also the Old Covenant and how the law finds new meaning in the Person, words and work of Christ.

Matthew's use of the title "Son of God" clearly underscores Jesus' deity (1:23; 2:15; 3:17; 16:16).

Matthew is the only Gospel to mention the Church (16:18; 18:17), and the phrase "kingdom of heaven" (which is equal to kingdom of God) occurs thirty two times in this Gospel but nowhere else in the New Testament. Only Matthew tells about the visit of the wise men (2:1-12), the flight to Egypt (2:12-23), Judas's repentance (27:5-10), of the Jews request that Christ's blood be upon them and upon their children (27:25), of the sealing of the stone, the setting of the guard, and the fabrication of the story that the disciples came and stole the body while the guard slept (27:62-66; 28:11-15), and of the rising of many of the saints after Christ's resurrection (27:51, 52).

Matthew also emphasizes Jesus as Lord and Teacher of the Church, the called-out community, which is called to be God's selective instrument for fulfilling the purposes of God on Earth.

Matthew includes fifteen parables, ten of which are found only in his book – the tares (13:24-30, 36-43), the hidden treasure (13:44), the pearl of great price (13:45, 46), the dragnet (13:47), the unmerciful servant (18:23-35), the labourers in the vineyard (20:1-16), the two sons (21:28-32), the marriage of the king's son (22:1-13), the ten virgins (25:1-13), and the talents (25:14-30).

Only three miracles are peculiar to Matthew: the two blind men (9:27-31), the dumb demoniac (9:32, 33), and the coin in the fish's mouth (17:24-27).

References to Jewish tradition, which would have meant nothing to Gentiles, and other references such as, 10:5-6, and 15:24 ("the lost sheep of the house of Israel") are also indicative that Matthew wrote primarily to a Jewish audience.

The Resurrection of Jesus Christ is a cardinal truth to Christian faith. The following chart shows Jesus' appearances after His resurrection, clearly confirming the truthfulness of this event.

Jesus' Appearances after His Resurrection
To Whom
• To Mary Magdalene (Mark 16:9; John 20:11-18)
• To the other women (Matthew 28:8-10)
• To Peter (Luke 24:34)
• To ten disciples (Luke 24:36-43; John 20:19-25)
• To the Eleven, including Thomas (Matthew 28:16-20; Mark 16:14; John 20:26-29)
• At His ascension (Mark 16:19, 20; Luke 24:50-53; Acts 1:4-12)
• To the disciples on the road to Emmaus (Mark 16:12, 13; Luke 24:13-35)
• To five hundred people (1 Cor. 15:6)
• To James and the apostles (1 Cor. 15:7)
• To Paul on the road to Damascus (Acts 9:1-6; 18:9, 10; 22:1-8; 26:12-18; 1 Cor. 15:8)

Personal Application
Jesus is the Risen Saviour! He lives, He has risen, so that those who believe in Him will also live eternally.

Jesus' teaching in Matthew is as relevant today as it was back then. He calls you to a higher dimension of living, a blessed life that can only be lived by the grace and Spirit of God.

This life of ultimate righteousness is pronounced and stipulated in the Jesus' Sermon on the Mount. In a small nutshell it means:

Christianity is a counter culture, don't imitate the world, follow Jesus and make a definite difference.

The Sermon on the Mount declares the following:

- There are blessed rewards for living as citizens of His Kingdom (5:3-12).
- Christian living will have a definite effect on the world (5:13-16).
- Keeping the law does not make you righteousness; Christ is the fulfilment of the law, you can only uphold the law in Christ, by loving God and others with His love. (5:17-48).
- Be careful of hypocrisy, watch your attitude and motives in giving, praying, and fasting (6:1-18).
- Prioritize your life: put God and His kingdom first (6:33).
- Don't judge others harshly and wrongfully (7:1-6)
- The blessings and privileges of prayer; keep asking, seeking, and knocking (7:7-11).
- Do to others as you would have them do unto you (7:12).
- Choose the narrow way, not the broad way that leads to destruction (7:13-14)
- *"By their fruits you will know them (7:15-20)."*
- To obey God, doing His will, is far more important than talking about it (7:21-29).

Worship Him as King of your life, and proclaim the Good News of salvation which is only to be found in Jesus Christ, because He is the promised Messiah who sacrificed His life in order to redeem mankind.

MARK

Author
John Mark a close associate of the apostle Peter. Papius, bishop of the church at Hierapolis (about AD 135-140) described Mark as "the interpreter of Peter."

Date
Mid to late 50's

Main Theme
Jesus Christ, the Son of God and the Son of Man is the Suffering Servant of God.

Key Verse
"For even the Son of Man did not come to be served, but to serve, and to give His life a ransom for many (10:45)."

Key Phrases
"Son of Man," "Son of God," "the Lord working with them and confirming the word (16:20)."

Key Word
"immediately" or "straightway" (42 times)

Setting
The Gospel of Mark was written during Roman rule under Herod the Great against the backdrop of the early Church in a time of opposition to the Gospel, fearful persecution, and misunderstanding regarding Christianity and the Gospel of Jesus.

Purpose
To clearly demonstrate to his Gentile Roman audience that Jesus Christ is the Son of God who triumphed over sin and satan, and who brought everlasting salvation. Mark wants his readers to draw encouragement and strength from the life and example of Jesus.

Synopsis
Mark, the shortest and simplest of the Gospels, tells us about the actions rather than the teachings of Jesus. He gives us a vivid and fast-moving account of the powerful ministry of Jesus in order to establish his purpose. The works of Jesus is the main focus, and His death and resurrection bring this Gospel to a thrilling climax.

We divide the Gospel of Mark into three main sections:

1. The Birth of God's Servant and His Preparation for Ministry (1:1-13)

The Gospel of Mark has no genealogy, because it was of no importance to Mark's purpose, which was to present Jesus as the Servant of God (who gives a pedigree of a servant?).

Mark's opening verse is an appropriate introduction to the content of his book: *"The beginning of the gospel of Jesus Christ the Son of God."* He then quotes from the Old Testament telling about the ministry of John the Baptist, and then referring shortly and swiftly to Jesus' Baptism and His temptation in the wilderness.

2. The Powerful Message and Ministry of God's Servant (1:14-13:37)

Here Mark takes us directly to Jesus' public ministry in Galilee: Jesus called His first disciples, cast out demons, healed Peter's mother-in-law and many others.

Mark continues by revealing the opposition that Jesus began to experience: he shares the controversy over Jesus' friendship with sinners (2:13-22), the controversy over Sabbath-Work and Sabbath-Healing (2:23-3:5), the Pharisees' council to destroy Jesus (3:6-12).

Jesus drew many people by His miracles (3:7-10). *"And the unclean spirits, whenever they saw Him, fell down before Him and cried out, saying, "You are the Son of God (3:11)."*

Next, Mark tells us about Jesus' selection of His twelve disciples (3:13-19). However, Jesus experienced opposition from His own people (3:20, 21), and the scribes falsely accused Jesus and, thus, committed the unpardonable sin by their unbelief (3:22-30). Afterwards Jesus made it clear that spiritual kinship with Him goes beyond blood relationships (3:31-35).

In chapter 4, Mark lists some of Jesus' parables – the parable of the sower (4:1-20), the parable of the lamp (4:21-25), the parable of the growing seed (4:26-29), and the parable of the mustard seed (4:30-34). About a third of Jesus' teaching was by parables. The word "parable" literally means "a casting alongside." A parable is a brief story told by way of analogy to illustrate a spiritual truth.

After sharing some of Jesus' teaching, Mark again dashed enthusiastically into sharing the wonderful miracles in the Servant of God's ministry: Jesus calmed the great windstorm (4:35-41), He cast out demons from a demoniac into swine (5:1-20), He restored Jairus' daughter to life and healed a woman who suffered from a flow of blood for twelve years (5:21-43).

Opposition against the Servant of God increased. He was rejected in Nazareth; opposition from Herod and the Pharisees increased, and John the Baptist was beheaded (6:1-6, 14-29). In the meantime Jesus sent out His twelve disciples on a missionary journey (6:7-13), and He continued His powerful ministry – feeding the five thousand, walking on the sea, and many who merely touched Him were made well (6:30-56). Later He miraculously fed four thousand (8:1-10), and healed the blind man of Bethsaida (8:22-26).

Jesus' disciples were a bit confused regarding His mission. Peter by divine revelation confessed Jesus as the Christ, but shortly afterwards showed that he didn't understand Jesus' mission. Then Jesus revealed His death and resurrection, and the cost of discipleship to His disciples (8:31-38).

In chapter 9 Mark records Jesus' Transfiguration, a visible experience of the power of God's kingdom that served as a foretaste and sign of both the Resurrection and the Second Coming.

From chapter 10-13 Mark records events that took place during Jesus' ministry in Judea. Among other things, Jesus taught His disciples about different concerns of Kingdom living, and end time events, while he continued healing the sick, and confronting the Pharisees about divorce and taxes, and the Sadducees about the resurrection, and one of the scribes about the greatest commandment.

3. The Triumph of God's Servant (14:1-16:20)
Mark devoted much time detailing the account of the last eight days of Jesus' life, quickly moving to a climax – the Last Supper, the betrayal, the Crucifixion, and the Resurrection are dramatically portrayed. In so doing Mark emphasises the Passion and Resurrection that underscore the essence of Jesus' ministry. (The word "passion" comes from a Greek word which means "to suffer.") The crucifixion of the Servant of God was His highest service – He died for the salvation of sinful humanity; He died so that we can live!

As in Matthew's gospel Mark records the Great Commission; Jesus' disciples are commissioned to *"Go into all the world and preach the gospel to every creature* (16:15)". Furthermore, Mark lists four specific signs that will follow those who believe: (1) In Jesus' name, they will cast out demons; (2) they will speak with new tongues; (3) they will be divinely protected; (4) they will lay their hands on the sick, and the sick will recover (16:17, 18).

The Gospel of Mark ends with the ascension, glorifying the Servant who suffered severely and highlighting His deity.

Noteworthy

The heroic figure of the perfect servant, the ideal worker, would have had a peculiar fascination for Roman Christians, because the Romans were people of action.

The explanation of Jewish words (3:17; 5:41; 7:11, 34; 14:36), Jewish customs (7:3, 4; 14:12; 15:42), and the use of Latin words are further indications that Mark wrote to a Gentile, Roman audience.

In this Gospel the dual focus of Christ's life and ministry unfolds clearly: service and sacrifice.

Mark highlights the power and authority of Jesus, the eternal Son of God, as a teacher (1:22), and over satan and unclean spirits (1:27; 3:19-30), sin (2:1-12), the Sabbath (2:27, 28; 3:1-6), nature (4:35-41; 6:45-52), disease (5:21-34), death (5:35-43), legalistic tradition (7:1-13, 14-20), and the temple (11:15-18).

Some of the earliest manuscripts, Sinaiticus and Vaticanus, do not include the last twelve verses of Mark (16:9-20). However, early church fathers such as, Irenaeus were familiar with these verses, and their content relates to the general teaching of the New Testament. Therefore, no point of doctrine is affected by the absence or presence of this longer ending of Mark.

We find what is called the "Messianic Secret" in the Gospel of Mark. On several occasions Jesus tells someone not to tell, either who He is or what they have seen that would demonstrate who He is. Why did Jesus want to keep His identity as the Messiah secret? We suggest the following: (1) to avoid being considered just a "miracle worker" – Jesus didn't want them to follow Him only to see Him doing miracles. He came as the Son of God to bring forgiveness from sin and salvation. (2) To avoid undue publicity which would have hindered His mobility and ministry to His disciples. (3) To avoid the mistaken notion of the type of Messiah He came to be. He came

270 CHARLES STEBBING

to suffer and serve and sacrifice Himself, not simply to display His power (see 10:45). (4) To avoid the premature death that increased popularity could bring.

Personal Application

When you stand for the Truth and proclaim the Gospel of Jesus Christ, you will experience opposition, resistance, and rejection. Jesus experienced the same. However, *"Whoever desires to come after Me, let him deny himself, and take up his cross, and follow Me. For whoever desires to save his life will lose it, but whoever loses his life for My sake and the gospel's will save it (8:34-35)."*

Have faith in God. Jesus says: *"If you can believe, all things are possible to him who believes (9:23)."*

Jesus is always willing and able to help those in need; if you are in need, turn in faith to Jesus; He will certainly help you. Furthermore, ask Him to enable you so that you can help others.

Preach the Word of God in season and out of season, believing and expecting that He works with you confirming the Word through accompanying signs (16:20).

Jesus ministered in both Word and Deed, you should do the same.

LUKE

Author
Luke, a Gentile physician (Col. 4:14) and a missionary companion of Paul (2 Tim. 4:11), also known as Luke the evangelist.

Date
AD 59/60 before he wrote the Book of Acts

Main Theme
Jesus the Saviour of all people, whether Jew or Gentile

Key Verse
"for the Son of Man has come to seek and save that which was lost (19:10)."

Also notable is: *"So when the centurion saw what had happened, he glorified God, saying, "Certainly this was a righteous Man (23:47)!"*

Key Phrases
"Son of Man" (26 times), *"It came to pass"* (40 times)

Key Words
"Pray," *"Temptation,"* *"Repentance,* *"Redemption"*

Setting
The Gospel of Luke was written during Roman rule against the backdrop of the early Church in a time of opposition, and misunderstanding regarding Christianity and the Gospel of Jesus Christ.

Purpose
Luke pronounces clearly that his purpose in writing this Gospel is to present *"an orderly account* (1:3)" about what *"Jesus began both to do and teach* (Acts 1:1)".

Synopsis
The Gospel of Luke is the first of a two-part work (the Book of Acts is the second), both are addressed to "most excellent Theophilus," apparently a high official who was most likely already a Christian. *Theo* means God, *philo* means love; thus, Theophilus means "one who loves God." Since Luke and Acts are written to one who loves God, each believer can feel included.

Although Luke's Gospel is addressed to one individual, its intent is to give all believers the full assurance that Christianity is completely truthful.

The Gospel of Luke is the longest, most comprehensive and most literary of all the Gospels. However, the general composition of Luke's Gospel follows the main sequence of events as given in Matthew and Mark, but with many unique additions; about half of Luke's material is exclusively his own. Luke organized his material around the central theme of Jesus Christ, a member of humanity who lived the perfect and representative life of the Son of man through the power of the Holy Spirit.

We divide the Gospel of Luke into four main sections:

1. The Coming of the Son of Man (1:1-2:52)

As a doctor, Luke was a man of science, and as a Greek, he was a man of reason and detail. Furthermore, Luke was an eyewitness to many of the events in the early Church, and as a missionary companion of the great apostle Paul, and an early Church historian, Luke was well able to compile and present an orderly and logical account that would best carry out his theme. He carefully researched and investigated eyewitness accounts of everything that happened from the beginning of the Christian movement (1:1-4). For that reason, Luke's Gospel is a reliable historical account.

After his introduction and the dedication of his book to Theophilus, Luke gives an account of both John the Baptist, and Jesus' birth. While Matthew records the birth of Jesus from Joseph's viewpoint, Luke does it from Mary's viewpoint. The birth of John the Baptist is unique to Luke's gospel.

Soon after John's birth, Caesar Augustus declared a census, and so Joseph and Mary had to travel to Bethlehem, the city of David, because Joseph was of the house and lineage of David. It was while they were there that Mary gave birth to Jesus.

Because this is the Gospel of the perfect humanity of Christ, our Lord is presented as having the development, feelings, sympathies, and traits of a man. Luke gives us details of the actual birth of Jesus, his childhood, growth, domestic and social life (chapter 2).

2. His Preparation for Ministry (3:1-4:13)

In this section Luke records the ministry of John the Baptist as the forerunner of Jesus. Next, Luke traces the genealogy of Jesus right back to Adam, connecting Him to the entire human race and presenting Him as the "Son of man," the ideal Man; the Friend of sinners and the Friend of the friendless, the Saviour of the world who walks within our human story.

The account of Jesus' temptation is much the same as Matthew. Luke insists that *"the devil had ended every temptation* (4:13),*"* indicating that Jesus met with all the temptations of humanity.

3. His Ministry (4:14-19:27)

After His temptation Jesus returned in the power of the Holy Spirit to begin His Galilean ministry. In Nazareth, He ministered from the Book of Isaiah, revealing His relation to the prophetic Word, and proclaiming the purpose and the extent of His mission, which would take place in the power of the Holy Spirit (4:18, 19). Apart from a few individual changes, the subsequent material up to Luke 9:50 is quite similar to that which is found at this point in the other Synoptics.

The section from Luke 9:51-19:27, known as the "travelogue," is found only in Luke (except 18:15-43). This special section particularly highlights Jesus' final journey from Galilee to Jerusalem, and begins with the words: *"Now it came to pass, when the time had come for Him to be received up, that He steadfastly set His face to go to Jerusalem* (9:51)." It contains many parables not recorded by the other Gospels – the parables of the Good Samaritan (10:25-37), the lost sheep, the lost coin, and the prodigal son (15:1-32), the unjust steward (16:1-13), the rich man and Lazarus (16:19-31), the Pharisee and tax collector (18:9-14), and the story of Zacchaeus (19:1-10). These parables are illustrative of the meaning of Jesus' mission. They underscore the universality of Luke's gospel – Jesus is the Saviour of all kinds of people.

4. His Triumph (19:28-24:53)

Luke's account of the Passion is basically similar than the other Synoptics. However, Luke emphasises the human sufferings and sympathies of Jesus by rearranging the order of events and supplementing his narrative with events such as Jesus' bloodlike sweat (22:43, 44), His address to the women of Jerusalem (23:27-31), and the penitent thief (23:39-43). This all brings the Passion to a pinnacle without changing the real meaning of it.

The resurrection account of Luke is strikingly different. Jesus' appearance to the two men on the way to Emmaus, which is unique to the Gospel of Luke, together with the revelation that He is the fulfilment of Old Testament prophecy, makes it crystal clear that He is the promised Saviour of the world, and the Christian message is truthful. Thus, the revelation through Jesus Christ is the Biblical basis for the preaching of repentance and of forgiveness of sins in His name to all nations (24:44-48).

Furthermore, before His ascension Jesus encouraged His disciples with the promise of the soon-coming Holy Spirit, who will empower them to be genuine witnesses of the Risen Saviour.

Luke, the Gospel of the sympathetic-hearted ideal Man, ends with the ascension and Jesus' disciples worshipping and praising Him with great joy.

Noteworthy

The Gospel of Luke was directed to the contemplative minds of the Greeks, who were philosophical and people of reason. This Gospel account will also serve the intelligent and curious minds in our day well.

Luke emphasises the following in his Gospel:

- **Jesus, the universal Saviour** – Jesus Christ, by means of the miraculous virgin birth, became the sinless Federal Head of mankind; He is our Kinsman-Redeemer; He is the Friend and Redeemer of all men. It is in the Gospel of Luke that we, for the first time in the New Testament, find with the word "redemption (2:38; 21:28)." Luke portrays Jesus Christ as one of kin to us in the work of redemption.

  In presenting Jesus as the Saviour of all kinds of people, Luke pays particular attention to Jesus' ministry to the poor, the outcasts, and to women. In so doing he includes material not found in the other Gospels, such as: the account of the sinful woman (7:36-50).

  In order to portray Jesus as the universal Saviour, Luke omits much material that is strictly Jewish in character. For example, he does not include Jesus' pronouncement of condemnation upon the scribes and the Pharisees (Matt. 23), nor the discussions about Jewish tradition (Matt. 15:1-20). He also excludes the teachings of Jesus in the Sermon on the Mount that deal directly with His relation to the Jewish law (see Matt. 5:21-48; 6:1-8, 16-18), and Jesus' instructions to the Twelve to refrain from ministering to the Gentiles and Samaritans (Matt. 10:5). Further, Luke included the pardon of the thief on the cross (23:39-43).

- **Prayer** – there are more references to prayer in Luke than in the other Gospels. Luke emphasises the prayer life of our Lord, recording seven occasions on which He prayed that are not mentioned elsewhere: (1) after John the Baptist baptized Jesus, *"while He prayed, the heaven was opened (3:21);"* (2) Jesus *"often withdrew into the wilderness and prayed (5:16);"* (3) Jesus *"went out to the mountain to pray, and continued all night in prayer to God (6:12);"* (4) Jesus *"was alone praying (9:18);"* (5) *"As He prayed, the appearance of His face was altered, and His robe became white and glistening (9:29);"* (6) *"Now it came to pass, as He was praying in a certain place, when He ceased, that one of His disciples said to Him, 'Lord, teach us to pray ... (11:1);"* (7) while hanging on the cross Jesus said (prayed): *"Father, forgive them, for they do not know what they do (23:34),"* and He said just before He died: *"Father, into Your hands I commit My spirit (23:46)."* Luke also shares teaching on prayer, which is not found in the other Gospels (e.g., 11:5-13; 18:1-8; 21:36).

- **The Presence and Ministry of the Holy Spirit** – There are seventeen explicit references to the Holy Spirit in Luke, emphasising His activity in the life and ministry of Jesus, and the continuing ministry of the Church (e.g., 1:35. 41, 67; 2:25-27; 3:22; 4:1; 4:14; 4:18, 31-44; 10:21; 24:49).

- **Praise and Thanksgiving** – We find many references to "rejoice," "praise," and "thanksgiving" in Luke (e.g., 1:28, 46-56, 68-79; 2:14, 20, 29-32; 5:25, 26; 7:16; 13:13; 17:15; 18:43).

Personal Application
Jesus is the Saviour of the world, *"a light ... to the Gentiles (1:32);"* your Saviour and your light in a dark world. Luke gives enough details so that you can believe in the reliability of Jesus and His message. Jesus is more than a good Teacher, He cares for you and because of His deep love for You, He can satisfy your deepest needs.

Reflecting on the emphases of Luke, you should realize that:

1. The Gospel is a universal message. It is trans-cultural. So spread the Gospel wide.

2. Jesus' mission is the mission of the Church, and for that matter, your mission (Luke 4:18, 19). The Church, which includes you, is called and equipped (anointed by the Holy Spirit):

- To preach the gospel to the (spiritually) poor
- To heal the brokenhearted ("shattered minds" in the original Greek)
- To proclaim liberty to the captives
- To proclaim recovery of sight to the blind
- To set at liberty those who are oppressed, and
- To proclaim the acceptable year of the Lord

3. Jesus' ministry is a perfect example of a ministry in the power of the Holy Spirit – the Holy Spirit desires to be actively involved in every aspect of your life; yield to Him and cooperate with Him.

4. Prayer, Praise and Worship are supposed to be a lifestyle.

   a. Prayer was Jesus' communication link to God while He was on earth. In the same way prayer is our communication with God. As you ought to know, the life blood of any relationship is communication; if there is no or very little communication in a relationship, then that relationship will certainly deteriorate. Your relationship with God will deepen as you invest time in sharing with Him in prayer. By prayer we make our requests known to God, then He can sovereignly act on our behalf. Prayer is also a way of joining God in His ministry.

   b. Praise means to commend, to approve, to give a favourable report, to glorify and to esteem. Praising God means you take the focus off your life and circumstances, and turn it onto God. It means you honour Him and express your admiration for Him. You praise Him for what He did, what He is doing, and for what He will be doing. Praise proclaims the goodness and greatness of God. Praise is the language of God's Kingdom.

   c. Worship is much more than a couple of songs of adoration. The Greek word used for worship implies to kiss the hand

and originally referred to the labour of slaves for the master. Worship refers to the supreme honour or veneration given to a person. True worship involves at least four important elements:

- Worship requires **reverence** (holy respect). This includes the honour and respect directed toward the Lord in thought, word and feeling. Jesus said that those who worship God must do so "in spirit and truth (John 4:24)." The term "spirit" speaks of the personal nature of worship. It is from my person to God's person and involves the intellect, emotions and will. It also speaks of the "presence dimension"; I can only worship God fully when I am in His presence. The term "truth" speaks of the content of worship: God is pleased when we worship Him truthfully, understanding His true nature.

- **Intimacy** – worship should lead to a time of real intimacy with the Father, when you share with and experience God in an intimate way. It is during times of genuine worship and intimacy that God's character "rubs off" on us.

- Worship includes **public expression**. It is not sufficient to express our worship privately but we must do so publicly and corporately also.

- Worship means **service**. The concept of worship must not be limited to the singing of worship songs, but should embrace an entire life of service and obedience to God.

5. Never limit an unlimited God. Mary could not understand or believe that she would give birth to the Messiah. However, the angel told her in no uncertain terms: *"For with God nothing is impossible* (1:37)." Believe, and let it be to you according to *His Word* (1:38).

JOHN

Author
The apostle John, the "disciple whom Jesus loved (John 21:7)," brother of James and son of Zebedee (Matt. 4:21)

Date
AD 85-90

Main Theme
Jesus Christ of Nazareth is God incarnate, the only Saviour of humanity

Key Verse
"but these are written that you may believe that Jesus is the Christ, the Son of God, and that believing you may have life in His name (20:31)."

Key Phrase
"I Am"

Key Words
God as *"Father"* (122 times); *"believe"* (100 times); *"love"* (57 times); *"glory"* (33 times); *"verily, verily"* (25 times)

Setting
The Gospel of John was written against the backdrop of the nation of Israel being a confirmed enemy of the Church (we deduce this from the manner in which John refers to "the Jews" throughout his book), and misunderstanding regarding the deity of Jesus Christ.

Purpose
The apostle John announced the purpose for his Gospel in John 20:30, 31: *"And truly Jesus did many other signs in the presence of His disciples, which are not written in this book, but these are written that you may believe that Jesus is the Christ, the Son of God, and that believing you may have life in His name."* Under the inspiration of the Holy Spirit John selected episodes from all the available material

to demonstrate that Jesus is the Son of God so that readers will put their trust in Him and receive life. In other words, he wants to lead his readers to faith in Christ, and so to eternal life. In a broader sense, John wrote his Gospel to supplement the Synoptic Gospels and to provide Christians with a deeper understanding of the deity of Jesus Christ.

According to Merrill Tenney the three words – *signs, belief,* and *life* – provide logical organization for John's Gospel. In the *signs* is the revelation of God; in *belief* is the reaction that they are designed to produce; in *life* is the result that belief brings.[33]

Synopsis

The first three Gospels prepare us for the fourth that interprets the divinity of Jesus in a deeper way, thus completing the full Biblical portrayal of Jesus. Having said that, it shows us that the Gospels, in their current order in the Bible, is not by chance but actually by divine inspiration. That which has been rightly said from the reports of the first three is now clearly declared in the review of the fourth: the historical Jesus is the Eternal Son; He is God. He who is Israel's Messiah-King is Himself God. He who is the Servant of God is Himself God. He who is the Saviour of the world is the world's Creator. He imparts life because He is life.

We divide the Gospel of John into the following six main sections:

1. The Word Became Flesh (1:1-18)

John, who emphasises the deity of Jesus, did not make use of a genealogy, but rather declares: *"In the beginning was the Word, and the Word was with God, and the Word was God ... And the Word became flesh and dwelt among us (1:1, 14)."*

The words "In the beginning" remind us of the first and foundational verse of the Bible, Genesis 1:1, which reveals the Eternal-Triune-Creator-God (Elohim) to us. In his first verse John links Jesus back to eternity, to His pre-existence as part of the Godhead.

The Greek word for "Word" that John uses is *logos,* which, in general is a philosophical term referring to reasoning and the expression of thoughts into words; a statement; a spoken word. However, John uses this term in a much deeper sense: to convey

---

[33] Merrill Tenney, *New Testament Survey,* p. 191

the idea of divine self-expression; that Jesus Christ is the expression of Divine Reason, who is God; that Jesus Christ is the complete and ultimate expression of God Himself; that Jesus Christ is God's Word to the world – God's Word is effective, He speaks and things come into existence (Gen. 1:3, 9; Ps. 33:6; 107:20), and by speech God relates personally to His people (Gen. 15:1).

In his Prologue John reveals seven things about the Word, laying a solid foundation for the rest of his message:

1. *"In the beginning was the Word* (v. 1)." The Word is eternal. While other things have a beginning the Word was.

2. *"And the Word was with God* (v. 1)." The word "with" in Greek means "face-to-face" – the Word was in eternal active fellowship with God.

3. *"And the Word was God* (v. v. 1)." The Word is distinct from God, yet the Word is also God. Here we identify the personal distinctions within the Godhead.

4. *"Through Him all things were made* (v. 3)." The Word is the Creator God.

5. *"In Him was life* (v. 4)." The Word is the source of life. This answers the question about the origin and continuance of life – life is given and maintained by the Word.

6. *"And that life was the light of men* (v. 4)." His life is light; it gives revelation and illuminates our hearts and minds.

7. *"The Word became flesh* (v. 14)." Here we have the Word incarnate. Jesus Christ born of the Virgin Mary is none other than the eternal Word of God. Thus He came to be the Living Word to a dying world.

Furthermore, the apostle John tells us about John the Baptist who witnessed about Jesus as the true Light of the world. This shows us that faith in Jesus Christ is not blind, it is based upon evidence.

Although there was substantial evidence to prove His truthfulness, *"His own did not receive Him* (1:11)." The Jews did not accept Jesus Christ as the Messiah.

Nevertheless, John declares: *"But as many as received Him, to them He gave the right to become children of God, to those who believe in His name: who were born, not of blood, nor of the will of the flesh, nor of the will of man, but of God* (1:12, 13)."

"Received Him" implies not merely intellectual acknowledgement of Jesus but also welcoming Him into your life and submitting to His Lordship. *"Believed in"* implies personal trust. *"Born not of blood ... but of God"* reveals to us that neither physical birth nor ethnic descent nor human effort can make people children of God, but only God's supernatural work in the new birth (see 3:3, 5). This also extends the possibility of becoming children of God to Gentiles, not only to Jews.

2. Jesus' Public Ministry (1:19-12:50)

This section opens up with the ministry of John the Baptist preparing the way for the Lord, making it clear that Jesus as "the Lamb of God" procured the redemption of mankind, and directing his disciples to follow Jesus.

In recording the public ministry of Jesus, the apostle John chose 7 of Jesus' miracles to reveal His divine nature and His life-giving mission. By means of these miracles Jesus demonstrated His inherent power and authority over things such as: the laws of nature, men, institutions, and religious laws. In every instance Jesus' deity is revealed. As the apostle John says about Jesus' first miracle: *"This beginning of signs Jesus did in Cana of Galilee, and manifested His glory; and His disciples believed in Him* (2:11)."

In chapter 3 we find Jesus' discussion with Nicodemus about the New Birth. Nicodemus was an influential and respected member of the Sanhedrin. As a Pharisee he was thoroughly trained in the law of the Old Covenant. Jesus therefore called him a teacher of Israel (3:10). After Nicodemus proposed that no man could do all these signs that Jesus did unless God was with him. Jesus answered him: *"Most assuredly, I say to you, unless one is born again, he cannot see the kingdom of God* (3:3)." Nicodemus did not understand, and asked if a person can enter a second time into his mother's womb and be born? Then Jesus answered him: *"Most assuredly, I say to you, unless one is born of water and the Spirit, he cannot enter the kingdom of God. That which is born of the flesh is flesh, and that which is born of the Spirit is spirit. Do not marvel that I said to you, 'You must be born again.' The wind blows where it wishes, and you hear the sound of it, but cannot tell where it comes from and where it goes. So is everyone who is born of the Spirit (3:5-8)."*

Jesus' explanation to Nicodemus reveals the following to us:

- The Greek word translated *again* can also be translated as "from above."

- If you want to see (perceive, understand) the kingdom of God you must be born again, or born from above, from God. Thus you must be made spiritually alive by God.

- If you want to enter (become part, experience) the kingdom of God you must be born from above.

- *"Born of water"* in verse 5, and *"that which is born of flesh is flesh* (v. 6)" are indicative that Jesus compared the natural birth to the spiritual birth. Just before a woman gives birth to a child, "her water will break."

- Verse 8 (about the wind) compares the Holy Spirit to wind. You cannot see the wind, but you can see the effect it has on, for instance trees when it blows through them – the branches and leaves will move. Although one cannot see the Holy Spirit, you will certainly see the affect He has on a person who is born from above.

The greatest miracle of Jesus is the resuscitation of Lazarus (we refer to it as resuscitation, because Lazarus was brought back to life only to die again. Only Jesus was resurrected; He was raised from the death to live eternally). Here Jesus claimed that He is the resurrection and life. By raising Lazarus from the death, Jesus undoubtedly, in the midst of many eyewitnesses, proved that His claim was truthful. What is striking about this miracle is: when Jesus heard that Lazarus was sick, He stayed two more days in the place He was (11:6). That resulted in Jesus' arrival in Bethany when Lazarus had been four days in the grave. Imagine that: four days in the grave; that body was badly decomposed. The resuscitation of Lazarus after being dead for four days served a divine purpose. Firstly, it was to destroy the Jewish myth in which some Jews believed: that the soul hovered over the dead body for three days, hoping to re-enter it, but after three days the soul would give up and depart (this, in their opinion meant that all hope was gone, the person was dead-dead). Secondly, we realize that God has an appointed time, a set time, to fulfil His purposes. And, thirdly, the end result was a greater display of God's glory so that the people could see *"His glory, the glory as of the only begotten of the Father, full of grace and truth* (1:14)."

As Jesus worked miracles we realize that belief and unbelief clashed; conflict and opposition increased, especially the venomous opposition of the Jewish religious leaders.

Throughout Jesus' public ministry we see that: (1) He consistently revealed His deity by the miracles that He worked and the claims that He made, (2) He revealed the Father by word and deed, and (3) He pointed beyond Himself to the Father who had sent Him.

3. Jesus' Private Ministry (13:1-17:26)

Up to this point Jesus' ministry was public, but from here on the apostle John records Jesus' private ministry to His disciples. This section, called by some "the period of conference," consists of final instructions and encouragement to His disciples – Jesus gave them a new commandment (13:34, 35); He encouraged them to believe and promised that when He departed from them, He would go and prepare a place for them, and that He would return to receive them to Himself (14:1-3); Jesus assured the doubting Thomas: *"I am the way, the truth, and the life. No one comes to the Father except through Me* (14:6)." He further encouraged His disciples by emphasising His genuine love for them, and telling them: *"These things I have spoken to you, that My joy may remain in you, and that your joy may be full* (15:11)." Jesus also promised His disciples that He would not leave them as orphans, but would send another (another of the same kind) Helper, the Spirit of truth, to guide them in all truth and tell them of things to come. Thus, Jesus prepared His disciples for the shock of His crucifixion.

His High Priestly Prayer for His disciples and report to the Father that He had finished His work concludes the earthly ministry of Jesus.

4. Jesus' Arrest, Trial, Death, and Burial (18:1-19:42)
In spite of the overwhelming evidence of Jesus' miracles the religious establishment would not believe in Jesus as the Messiah. This section brings the tension between belief and unbelief to an ultimate high point. The betrayal of Judas, Peter's denial of Jesus, the jealous malice of the priests, and the cowardice of Pilate show how unbelief manifests itself. While the crucifixion unveiled unbelief, Jesus' final words declared resounding victory: *"It is finished* (19:30)!"

5. Jesus' Resurrection (20:1-31)
The resurrection is the final death blow to unbelief, the justification of faith, and the final vindication of the revelation that Jesus Christ, the Son of God, is God Himself. His resurrection fully established His claim to deity. He is the Resurrection and the Life, those who believe in Him shall live eternally.

After His resurrection Jesus commissioned His disciples, saying "As the Father has sent Me, I also send you (20:21)." He afterward *"breathed on them, and said to them, 'Receive the Holy Spirit* (20:22)." This reminds us of Genesis 2:7 where God breathed natural life into Adam. Jesus breathed spiritual life into His disciples. From that moment on they were "born again;" they were made spiritually alive by the resident Holy Spirit.

6. Jesus' Post-resurrection Appearances to His Disciples (21:1-25)
After the disciples had breakfast with Jesus by the sea, He restored Peter who denied Him. Peter denied Jesus three times, and in this section Jesus asked Peter three times, *"do you love Me."* Jesus used the verb *agapao* which expresses God's kind of love: "self-sacrificial love." The three times Peter responded to Jesus, he used the word *phileo*, which signifies affection, as in brotherly love. The third time Jesus asked Peter, *"Do you love Me,"* He used the same word that Peter used *(phileo)*. Peter was grieved because the third time Jesus actually questioned what Peter had just affirmed twice. Peter continued telling Jesus, *"Lord, You know all things; You know I love You."* Here

Peter affirmed Jesus' omniscience, which is consistent with His deity. Jesus's response to Peter was *"Feed My sheep,"* thus, as the Chief Shepherd, Jesus appointed Peter (and the other disciples) to be subordinate shepherds (see 1 Peter 5:1-4). Peter will demonstrate his love for Jesus by *"feeding His lambs* (21:15)," *"tending His sheep* (21:16)," *"feeding His sheep* (21:17)," and *"following Jesus* (21:19)."

The apostle John ends his Gospel rightly with the promise of the Lord's return, and that *"there are also many other things that Jesus did, which if they were written one by one, I suppose that even the world itself could not contain the books that would be written. Amen."*

Noteworthy

Instead of the many miracles and healings in the Synoptics, John uses seven carefully selected miracles, which he calls "signs." A "sign" is a miracle with a message that reveals something about Christ, and His Kingdom; the message is more important than the manifestation. These signs illustrate different areas of Jesus' power, and collectively bear witness to the central doctrine of John's Gospel, the deity of Jesus Christ. The signs with their messages lead to faith which in turn lead to life.

The Seven Signs of Jesus		
The Sign	**Meaning (message)**	**Reference**
The Changing of Water into Wine	Jesus is the Source of life	2:1-11
The Healing of the Nobleman's Son	Jesus is Master over distance	4:46-54
The Healing of the Impotent Man	Jesus is Master over time.	5:1-9
The Feeding of the Five Thousand	Jesus is the Bread of life.	6:1-14
The Walking on Water	Jesus is Master over nature.	6:16-21
The Healing of the Blind Man	Jesus is the Light of the world.	9:1-12
The Raising of Lazarus	Jesus has Power over death.	11:1-46

Altogether twenty-three times we find Jesus' meaningful *"I Am"* statements in the Gospel of John. Seven of these *"I Am"* statements are joined with significant metaphors, which illustrate Jesus' saving relationship to the world, boldly underline His deity (He was without beginning), and strengthens John's main theme:

1. *"I Am the Bread of life (6:35, 41, 48, 51)."*
2. *"I Am the Light of the world (8:12)."*
3. *"I Am the Door of the sheep (10:7, 9)."*
4. *"I Am the Good Shepherd (10:11, 14)."*
5. *"I Am the Resurrection and the Life (11:25)."*
6. *"I Am the Way, the Truth, the Life (14:6)."*
7. *"I Am the true Vine (15:1, 5)."*

The message of John's Gospel centres on these seven signs and statements of our Lord.

The longest recorded prayer of Jesus, called the "High Priestly Prayer," is found in John 17:1-26. After His triumphant declaration of victory in 16:33, *"I have overcome the world,"* Jesus proceeds to pray for Himself, His disciples, and for future believers. Facing His hour of deepest travail, Jesus looks forward to the blessed results of His victory over sin and death – the gathering of the redeemed, and the love and unity that God and the redeemed will share (17:20-26).

Some of the distinctive differences between John and the Synoptics are: (1) Instead of the familiar parables, John has lengthy discourses, for the most part not included in the Synoptics – only the feeding of the five thousand and Jesus walking on water are in all four; (2) Instead of the many miracles and healings in the Synoptics, John uses seven carefully picked miracles, which he calls "signs;" (3) The ministry of Jesus revolves around three Passover Feasts, instead of the one cited in the Synoptics; (4) The seven "I Am" sayings are unique to John, and the designation of the Holy Spirit as "Comforter" or "Helper" (14:16).

John has at the utmost an account of about 20 days of our Lord's ministry. Chapters 13-19, 237 verses out of 879, cover only one day in the life of Jesus.

Personal Application

Jesus came so that you may have life and have it more abundantly. Embrace the New Life that Jesus gave you, and live life to the full in Him. As someone once said: "Live full and die empty." Make the most of your Christian life, you only live once on this earth.

The Holy Spirit is your Comforter, and Helper. The Greek word translated as "Comforter" is *Parakletos,* which literally means "called to one's side, that is, to one's aid." You are not alone, the Holy Spirit is with you and within you; He is walking alongside you to help you in and through this life, while He guides you in the truth.

Jesus gave us a new commandment: to love one another.

The New Testament begins with wise men asking the question, "Where is He?" If you want to discover where He is today, look where the love of the risen Christ is being channelled to the hurting people of this world. – Paul Banting

---

The Exemplary Life of Jesus

Having journeyed through all four Gospels, let us look what we have learned from the life and ministry of Jesus. What core values do we identify in His life?

Living in a postmodern world, we often hear of an absence of values, or what some may call "a values vacuum." Many evils in our day are the result of the absence of a true Standard and a set of God-given values.

We should be the love of Christ in this world.

Jesus came into this world not only to die for our sins, but also to show us how to live and minister. One way He did that was to teach and exemplify an absolute set of values. Jesus says: *"Follow Me* (Mark 1:17)." And the apostle Paul says: *"Imitate me just as I also imitate Christ* (1 Cor. 11:1)." Jesus is our perfect role model. He is the Standard for Christian living. Jesus modelled the perfect life in the Spirit. We are to live out the same values Christ lived. We should:

CHARLES STEBBING

- Believe as Jesus believed
- Live as Jesus lived
- Love as Jesus loved
- Minister as Jesus ministered
- Lead as Jesus led

What follows is the clear example Jesus came to demonstrate for us, which will certainly give us insight into Christ-like living and ministry.

1. **Jesus demonstrated Agape** (self-giving, unconditional, sacrificial love).

    a) He loved His Father – *"... the world may know that I love my Father* (John 14:31)."

    b) Because of His love for the Father He lived fully dependent on His Father and in obedience to Him (see John 5:19, 20, 30; 8:29). Obedience is the sign of love – love is expressed through obedience (John 14:23).

    c) Because of His love for the Father He lived in harmony and communication with the Father (see John 10:30; 17:21; Mark 1:35; Matt. 26:36-46).

    d) Because of Agape Jesus had compassion for the lost and broken hearted (see Matt. 9:36), He laid down His life for others (see John 3:16; 1 John 3:16), and He went about doing good and healing all who were under the devil's power (see Acts 10:38). He was even a friend of sinners (Luke 5:27-32). Jesus demonstrated the priority of people – He placed a great value on lost and hurting people. Jesus expressed dynamic love in all His interactions with people – they could see and experience love in Him.

    e) Jesus truly loved His disciples – "Now before the Feast of the Passover, Jesus knowing that His hour had come that He would depart out of this world to the Father, having loved His own who were in the world, He now showed them the full extent of His love (John 13:1)." Jesus challenged His disciples (and challenges you today) to establish a new covenant when He gave them a new commandment: *"A new commandment I give to you, that you <u>love one another,</u> even <u>as I have loved you,</u> that you also love one another* (John 13:34; emphasis mine)." Jesus clearly identified the quality of love with which we should love one another.

> "Jesus loves me; this I know. For the Bible tells me so."

Points to Ponder: Do you live out this value? Do you love the Father? Do you appreciate the incredible value of fellowship with the Father? Does the love of God compel you to be obedient to God and to love your fellow Christians genuinely? Do you have a heart for the lost?

2. **Jesus placed a great value upon the Word of God (Scriptures).** Three times, in both the Gospel of Matthew and Luke He said: *"It is written."* Often Jesus referred to the Scriptures (the Old Testament). One of His favourite questions for religious leaders such as the scribes and Pharisees was: *"Have you never read the Scriptures* (Matt. 21:42)." Through His life and ministry Jesus expressed His burden that the Scriptures should be understood and correctly applied.

> The Word of God should be the final authority in all matters of faith, teaching, ministry and living.

Points to Ponder: Do you share Jesus' burden? Is the Word of God the final authority in your life and ministry?

3. **Jesus modelled for us that His food, His nourishment, His fulfilment came from doing the work the Father sent Him to do** (John 4:34). Jesus pronounced His mission statement when He said in Luke 2:49: *"I must be about My Father's business."* He also said: *"I must work the works of Him Who sent Me while it is day. The night is coming when no one can work* (John 9:4)." Like Jesus, we must delight to do God's will (Ps. 40:8).

> Real success and fulfilment can only be accomplished by being in God's will.

Points to Ponder: Have you discovered your ministry gift(s), and God-given mission yet? Do you live out your ministry?

4. **His teaching was the teaching of God.** *"Then the Jews were amazed and asked, 'How did this man get such learning without having studied?' Jesus answered, 'My teaching is not My own. It comes from Him Who sent Me. If a man chooses to do God's will, he will find out whether My teachings come from God or whether I speak on My own (John 7:15-16).'"* In John 7 Jesus challenges us to believe that His teaching is the teaching of God. Jesus didn't speak on His own authority, but only what His Father told Him to say (see John 12:49-50), in so doing He was ministering the will/word of God. People were even astonished at His teaching, *"because He was teaching them like one who had authority (Matt. 7:29)."* You should receive your directives from God and your words should be inspired by the Holy Spirit.

> Jesus' words are spirit and life. – John 6:63

Point to Ponder: Do you put the teaching of Jesus into practice in your life?

5. **Jesus placed a high value on the importance of knowing God**. He says: *"And this is eternal life, that they may know You, the only true God, and Jesus Christ whom You have sent (John 17:3)."* We understand that this "knowing" is not to know a few facts about God, but to know Him personally. Through His teachings on the Holy Spirit Jesus emphasised the vertical relationship with God, which will have a dynamic influence on all other relationships.

> When your relationship with God is in order then everything else will fall into the right place.

DISCOVERING THE MOST AMAZING BOOK   291

Points to Ponder: Are you in an active relationship with God? Do you frequently read your Bible, invest time in prayer, praise and worship, and fellowship with other Christians?

6. **Jesus ministered in the power (fullness) of the Holy Spirit** (Matt. 12:28; Acts 10:38). To be both an effective servant-leader and a powerful minister who ministers to those who are under the devil's power, you need the grace of God and the empowerment of the Holy Spirit. Our relationship to the Holy Spirit makes all the difference in our lives and ministries. You should treasure the Holy Spirit's presence. Your being should be saturated and controlled by the Holy Spirit. His presence is more important than principles.

    The Holy Spirit makes Jesus a greater reality in our lives and continues His ministry through us (see Acts 4:13).

Not by might nor by power, but by My Spirit, says the Lord of hosts. – Zechariah 4:6

Points to Ponder: Are you Spirit filled? Are you sensitive and responsive to the dear Holy Spirit? Do you really treasure the Holy Spirit's presence? Do you demonstrate the love and the authority of God's kingdom through your ministry?

7. **Jesus accomplished His mission completely** (John 19:30). He was rejected, scorned, mocked, and severely persecuted but, through it all He endured in love to fully accomplish His God-given mission.

But endurance must do its complete work, so that you may be mature and complete, lacking nothing. – James 1:4

Point to Ponder: Are you following Jesus in such a way that you will accomplish your God-given mission? What changes could you make to streamline the accomplishment of your mission?

Chapter Nine

Survey of the Book of Acts

ACTS

Author
Luke

Date
AD 61/62

Main Theme
The Acts of the Holy Spirit in and through the early Church

Key Verse
"But you shall receive power when the Holy Spirit has come upon you; and you shall be witnesses to Me in Jerusalem, and in all Judea and Samaria, and to the end of the earth (1:8)."

Key Phrase
"Filled with the Holy Spirit"

Key Words
Holy Spirit, Apostles

Setting
The Book of Acts was written during first century Roman rule against the backdrop of the growing Spirit-empowered Church in a time of opposition mainly from Judaism.

Purpose

To record: (1) the establishment of the Church on the Day of Pentecost (AD 30), and (2) the development and swift spread of the Church (Christianity) throughout the Roman Empire in a single generation. In other words, to record what Jesus continued both to do and teach through His Spirit-Empowered Church.

Synopsis

Because of the importance of the Book of Acts as a historical overview of the early Church, which gives us a framework for understanding the Letters to the different churches, we will do a more elaborate summary.

After His resurrection Jesus told His disciples to wait in *"Jerusalem until you are endued with power from on high* (Luke 24:49)," *"to wait for the Promise of the Father* (Acts 1:4)." His disciples did wait with one accord in prayer, for ten days, in the upper room (1:12-14), and then it happened as promised – the Holy Spirit was poured out on the Day of Pentecost (fifty days after the Passover) and *"they were all filled with the Holy Spirit and began to speak with other tongues, as the Spirit gave them utterance (2:4)."* That was the moment when the disciples were *"endued with power from on high."* Now the Spirit of God was *on* them, *in* them, and would be ministering *through* them. They needed supernatural power for the task that was lying ahead of them – to establish a Church, one birthed and empowered by the Spirit of God.

The outpouring of the Holy Spirit accompanied by supernatural phenomena such as the rushing wind, the tongues of fire, and the speaking with other tongues, clearly announced the dawn of a pertinent new era, not only in history, but in God's relationship with people who believe in Him.

Now, the Book of Acts records the intimate and personal relationship of God with believers through His Spirit, and the fulfilment of our Lord's prophetic words in Acts 1:8; the Spirit-empowered disciples spreading the Gospel of Jesus Christ *"in Jerusalem, and in all Judea and Samaria, and to the end of the earth."* In addition it clearly demonstrates what Christianity is – the meaning, the function, the message, and the purpose of the Church.

We follow our Lord's prophetic statement as the structure for the book of Acts and therefore divide it into three main parts, which focuses mainly on a key personality, a particular audience, and a significant phase in the expansion of the early Church.

1. Peter's Ministry mainly to the Jews in Jerusalem (chs. 1-7, covering 2 years)

In this section we have the establishment of the New Testament Church, marked by the Jewish period of the Church's witness mainly in Jerusalem. The apostle Peter is the main minister in this section.

Peter, before he was baptized in the power of the Holy Spirit, denied Jesus and was afraid of the Jews (John 20:19). Now, after he received the power of the Holy Spirit he preached his first sermon. His listeners were cut to the heart (2:37) and they asked the apostles, *"What shall we do to be saved from this perverse generation (2:40)."* Peter answered them: *"Repent and let every one of you be baptized in the name of Jesus Christ for the remission of sins; and you shall receive the gift of the Holy Spirit (2:38)."* *"Then those who gladly received his word were baptized; and that day about three thousand souls were added to them (2:41)."* Thus the Church was established in the power of the Holy Spirit.

Once planted, verses 42 to 47 tell us of the growth of the early Church. This passage could be seen as a summary of what took place in the daily life of the early Church.

In chapters 3 and 4 the young Church experienced opposition. Luke tells us about Peter and John's arrest, by the religious establishment, after a lame man was miraculously healed. However, Peter continued preaching the gospel of Jesus. Filled with the Holy Spirit, Peter defended their case before the Sanhedrin and made it clear that *"there is no other name under heaven given among men by which we must be saved (4:12)."* *"Now when they [the religious leaders] saw the boldness of Peter and John, and perceived that they were uneducated and untrained men, they marvelled. And they realized that they had been with Jesus (4:13)."* Eventually Peter and John were released.

Chapter 5 informs us of the death of Ananias and Sapphira who lied to the Lord. This is a puzzling event for many. In my opinion, it is a once off statement made by God to arrest the attention of the early

DISCOVERING THE MOST AMAZING BOOK 295

Christians – it is a very serious matter, particularly for Christians, to lie to God.

The Church continued in power, *"through the hands of the apostles many signs and wonders were done among the people* (5:12)." Signs and wonders characterized the ministry of the early Church to confirm the message of the Gospel, and it should do the same today.

Chapter 6:1-7 gives us some insight into the administration of the early Church – the need for deacons. Seven deacons were chosen to serve the Gentile widows, showing us that the apostles were keen to minister to all and that there was no distinction between Jews and non-Jews.

Stephen (one of the seven deacons) was *"full of faith and power [and] did great wonders and signs among the people* (6:8)." Religious leaders of the so called *Synagogue of the Freedmen* challenged Stephen, but *"they were not able to resist the wisdom and the Spirit by which he spoke* (6:10)." The religious leaders falsely accused Stephen and brought him before the council. Stephen defended himself by referring back to the origin and history of Israel. In so doing, Stephen showed that Jesus Christ and His mission rest on the history of the Israelites.

The religious leaders were cut to the heart and furious, while Stephen had a glorious vision of heaven (7:54-56). They cast Stephen out of the city and stoned him; he became the first martyr of the Church. In his death the saying, "the blood of the martyrs is the seed of the Church," has its first illustration as we will see in what followed afterward.

2. Peter and Philip's Ministry in Samaria and the Conversion of Paul (chs. 8-13, covering 13 years)

This section is seen as the transition period of the Church's witness when the gospel was carried out to the Gentiles and the city of Antioch became the new headquarters of Christian preaching and evangelistic missions. The main ministers in this section are the apostle Peter and Philip the evangelist.

Saul, before he became Paul, was present at Stephen's martyrdom (Saul was Paul's Jewish name, and Paul was his Roman name). Afterward, he began persecuting the Church, creating havoc, entering every house, and dragging off men and women, committing them to prison, possibly thinking that he did God a favour. The persecution of the Church gave rise to the scattering of Christians. However, praise God! The scattered Christians moved out *"everywhere preaching the word* (8:4)."* Instead of stopping Christianity, the persecution led to widespread evangelism.

Philip went to Samaria and preached Christ to them. Many came to faith in Jesus and many signs and wonders took place. After hearing the good news that the people in Samaria received the Word of God, Peter and John were also sent to Samaria (8:14-25). Later, Philip in the midst of a flourishing ministry in a city, is commanded to leave it and go to a desert road to talk to a single person. One would wonder if it was worthwhile? It definitely was! By leaving the city he reached a continent; through the Ethiopian, Philip gave the Gospel to Africa. The command was simple: *"arise and go."* Philip immediately responded in obedience; without any hesitation or questioning he *"arose and went* (8:26, 27)."* Obedience is always worthwhile.

In chapter 9 we read of the conversion of Saul on the Damascus Road where he was confronted in person by Jesus who spoke to him (vv. 1-9); in a flash of revelation Paul realized that Stephen the martyr was right, and that they (Paul and the Jews) had been completely wrong all the while. Luke continues telling us of Saul's baptism (vv. 10-19), how he immediately preached Christ in the synagogues, "the Church's greatest opponent became her greatest advocate" (vv. 20-22). And "after many days" – Paul was in Arabia for three years (see Gal. 1:18) – the Jews plotted to kill him (vv. 23-25). Paul's faith in Jesus as the Messiah brought him into a clash with his former Jewish colleagues in Damascus.

Peter went on a second missionary journey to Lydda, Joppa, Antipatris, and Caesarea (9:32-10:48). Again many believed as a result of the powerful ministry of Peter. The conversion of Cornelius, the Roman Gentile, is particularly worthy of mention, because it now revealed that God's provision for salvation was not only to the Jews, but to the Gentiles as well (10:1-48). And Cornelius' conversion opened the door widely for bringing Gentiles into the Church.

Acts 11:19 and 20 informs us: *"Now those who were scattered after the persecution that arose over Stephen travelled as far as Phoenicia, Cyprus, and Antioch, preaching the word to no one but Jews only. But some of them were men from Cyprus and Cyrene, who, when they had come to Antioch, spoke to the Hellenists [Greek speaking Jews], preaching the Lord Jesus."*

The church in Jerusalem heard about the ministry in Antioch and delegated Barnabas to visit Antioch, where he ministered, and then went to Tarsus to ask Paul to become his assistant (11:22-26). They ministered together for at least a year, and it was during this time that the disciples of Jesus Christ *"were first called Christians (11:26)."* This name was most likely given in a scornful way. However, Christian means "belonging to Christ," indicating that they were not merely a sect, but a group of people who firmly believed in and belonged to Christ.

Verses 27 to 30 tell us about the need in Jerusalem and how the church in Antioch raised offerings that Barnabas and Saul brought to Jerusalem. This is the first instance of one church raising a relief offering for the members of another church. That's a clear expression of their mutual love and unity.

3. Paul's Ministry mainly to Gentiles (chs. 13-28, covering 14 years)
This section is seen as the Gentile period of the Church's witness when the gospel was mainly preached by Paul to the Gentiles during his three missionary journeys.

Formerly a persecutor of the Church of Christ, now a zealous apostle defending the Gospel of Justification by faith in Jesus Christ alone. During the course of three missionary journeys and his journey to captivity in Rome, Paul took the message of the gospel throughout much of the Roman Empire and even to its very heart – Rome, the capital city. Paul extended the Church's boundaries extensively. It was during his missionary journeys that Paul wrote most of his books.

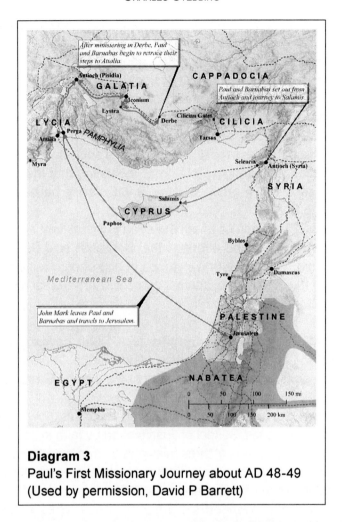

Diagram 3
Paul's First Missionary Journey about AD 48-49
(Used by permission, David P Barrett)

This section, beginning with Paul's First Missionary Journey, opens up with Barnabas and Paul back from Jerusalem. Under the leading of the Holy Spirit they were commissioned by the church in Antioch and sent out to witness on the Island of Cyprus (Barnabas' home; Acts 13:5), and the southern cities of the Roman province of Galatia. John Mark joined them on this journey for a while (13:13). Chapters 13 and 14 relate Paul's First Missionary Journey, which was marked by Paul's powerful teaching of the Lord (13:12). In Acts 13:46 and 47 we identify a transition: because of the Jews resistance to the message of Paul, the preaching of the gospel began to turn away from them and turned to the Gentiles of whom many believed

(13:48). At the city of Iconium many believed both Jews and Gentiles and the Lord granted signs and wonders to bear witness to His Word (14:3). At the city of Lystra Paul healed a man who was crippled from his birth, and later they ran into a mob who stoned Paul and dragged him out of the city supposing him to be dead. However, after the disciples prayed over him, he stood up and went into the city (14:19, 20). The next day Paul and Barnabas went to the city of Derbe where they preached the gospel and made many disciples. They returned to Lystra, Iconium and Antioch (in Pisidia) where they encouraged the disciples *"to continue in the faith, and saying, 'We must through many tribulations enter the kingdom of God (14:22).'"*

Chapter 15 deals with the conflict over circumcision and keeping the law of Moses; the controversy threatened to divide the Church. So all the principle leaders of the early Church agreed to meet in Jerusalem to resolve the conflict between legalistic Jewish Christians and Gentile Christians. After much dispute, the Jerusalem Council agreed on what has become the doctrinal foundation of the Christian faith: salvation is by grace through faith alone (v. 11). Christians, both Jews and Gentiles, are free from the law of Moses.

After the Jerusalem Council Paul and Barnabas returned to Antioch and spent some time in teaching and preaching (15:35). Most likely their teaching centred on careful instruction concerning the dispute over the question of circumcision and law-keeping.

Paul and Barnabas disagreed regarding the inclusion of Mark on the mission team, so Paul chose Silas to accompany him on his Second Missionary Journey (15:39-18:22).

The second journey was Paul's idea and it discloses an important aspect of his missionary strategy: *"Let us now go back and visit our brethren in every city where we have preached the word of the Lord, and see how they are doing (15:36)."* It is important to follow up: evangelization should be followed by encouragement in faith, having fellowship with new believers, and consolidating them through instruction and prayer.

Starting in Jerusalem, Paul and Silas travelled through Syria and Cilicia, and revisited the churches of Galatia where Paul had preached on his first journey. They visited Derbe, Lystra (where Timothy joined them), and Antioch in Pisidia, and *"the churches were strengthened in faith and increased in number daily (16:5).*

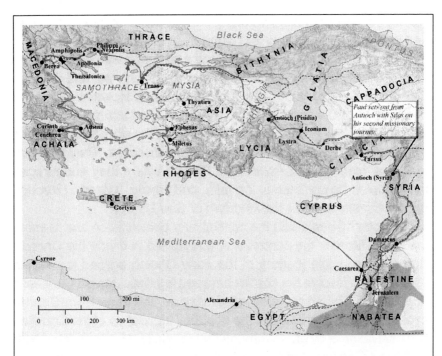

Diagram 4
Paul's Second Missionary Journey about AD 50-53 (used by permission, David P Barrett, www.biblemapper.com)

From there they travelled to Troas, because the Spirit of God forbade Paul to preach the word in Asia and Bithynia. In Troas Paul received the vision of a man from Macedonia calling to them (16:9). Herein we realize that Paul's journey was directed by the Spirit of God, and he obeyed every direction given to him. At Troas they were joined by Luke, the writer of Luke/Acts. The tenth verse makes this clear: *"Now after he had seen the vision, immediately we sought to go to Macedonia ... (emphasis mine)."* By obeying the call, Paul proclaimed the gospel farther into the world, into Europe.

In Philippi Paul cast out a spirit of divination from a slave girl. That led to the beating and imprisonment of Paul and Silas. However, they were miraculously released from jail, and eventually the Philippian jailor, together with his family, got saved (16:33). The "we-section" in the writing ends here, but resumes at a later date when Paul returned to Philippi. We suppose that Luke remained in Philippi possibly to

DISCOVERING THE MOST AMAZING BOOK

pastor the new church and perhaps to serve as an evangelist for Macedonia.

From Philippi, Paul and Silas travelled to Thessalonica where Paul reasoned with the Jews from the Scriptures – the Old Covenant – *"explaining and demonstrating to them that the Christ had to suffer and rise again from the dead, and saying, 'This Jesus whom I preached to you is the Christ* (17:2, 3).'" There was a division of opinion. Only some of the Jews were persuaded, while a great multitude of Gentiles joined Paul and Silas. The Jews who were not persuaded gathered a mob and attacked the house of Jason (one of the believers). Their complaint was: *"These who have turned the world upside down have come here too* (17:6)." The opposition was so intense that Paul and Silas fled by night to Berea.

The people of Berea *"were more fair-minded as those in Thessalonica, in that they received the word with all readiness and searched the Scriptures* (17:11)." Silas and Timothy remained in Berea, while Paul continued to the province of Achaia (modern Greece), visiting the city of Athens, the intellectual and religious centre of the Greco-Roman world. Here Paul addressed the intellectuals of Athens on their religiosity and their "unknown god," while he made it clear that there is a God who is personally knowable: *"for in Him we live and move and have our being* (17:28)." Paul had very little response in Athens (intellectuals tend to dismiss the simplicity of the Gospel).

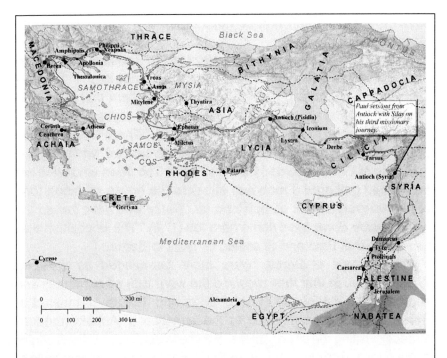

Diagram 5
Paul's Third Missionary Journey about AD 53-57 (Used by permission, David P Barrett, www.biblemapper.com)

From Athens Paul went to Corinth and settled there for a year and a half (18:11). He found employment at his old trade of tent-making, shelter, and fellowship with Aquila and Priscilla. During Paul's stay in Corinth, he wrote the two letters to the Thessalonians.

Acts 18:23-21:16 recount Paul's Third Missionary Journey, which followed much the same route as his second. Paul visited the churches of Galatia for a third time, and then settled in Ephesus for more than two years, preaching, teaching, and writing, and *"the word of the Lord grew mightily and prevailed (19:20)."* Then he travelled again through Macedonia and Achaia (Greece), strengthening the believers in their faith, and then finished with a visit to Jerusalem. Because *"Paul purposed in the Spirit ... to go to Jerusalem, saying, 'After I have been there, I must also see Rome (19:21)."* Paul's desire was to visit the church in Rome. It was on his third journey that Paul wrote 1 Corinthians from Ephesus, 2 Corinthians from Macedonia, and the letter to the Romans from Corinth.

Paul's glowing farewell address at Ephesus concludes the missionary focus of his ministry (20:17-37). Once back in Jerusalem, Paul delivered the offering that he had collected for the Jerusalem church, and he shared in detail with the elders of the Jerusalem church what God had done through his ministry. They rejoiced! But Paul's presence soon stirred up the Jews, who persuaded the Romans to arrest him. A plot to kill Paul was uncovered, so he was taken by night via Antipatris to the provincial prison in Caesarea, where he was imprisoned for two years. After Paul appealed to Caesar, he was sent by ship to Rome. Paul and his party were shipwrecked on the Island of Malta by a great storm. Three months later Paul arrived in Rome (in a different way that he had anticipated, but under divine providence).

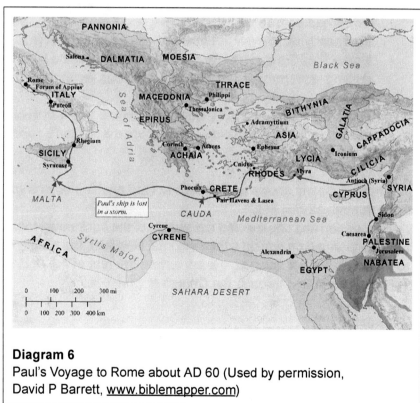

Diagram 6
Paul's Voyage to Rome about AD 60 (Used by permission, David P Barrett, www.biblemapper.com)

Paul lived in house arrest (28:16) for *"two whole years in his own rented house, and received all who came to him, preaching the kingdom of God and teaching the things which concern the Lord*

Jesus Christ with all confidence, no one forbidding him (28:30-31)."
It was during these two years that Paul wrote his so called Prison
Epistles: Philippians, Colossians, Ephesians, and Philemon.

Acts chapters 24-28 represent a significant portion of the book.
All the events recorded in this section of the book resulted from a
single cause – intense Judaic hostility towards Paul, his message
of Justification by Faith, and his Gentile mission. Why did Luke (or
rather, the Holy Spirit) dedicate so much to this phase of Paul's
life?

Among many other things, we learn the following:

- God used this hostility to accomplish His plans for Paul and
  the Church (everything worked together for good). Christianity
  did spread from Jerusalem to Rome, and it made a transition
  from nearly exclusively Jewish to a hope for all nations (v. 28).
- It gave Paul the opportunity to witness to some of the highest
  ranking government officials and religious leaders in the
  region.
- The trials revealed Paul's clear conscience and Christ-like
  character, and it confirmed his innocence and God's calling
  on his life.

Finally, it clearly shows us that faith in God enables us to stand
strong through storms in life.

The sudden and unexpected conclusion of the book could mean
that Luke planned on writing a third volume. However, the history of
the Church is not yet finished, we are writing the rest of the Acts of
the Holy Spirit in and through the Church of Christ.

Noteworthy

Most Greek manuscripts designate this book by the title "Acts," or by
an expanded title such as "Acts of the Apostles." While the apostles
are mentioned collectively, this book really records mainly the acts
of Peter (1-12), and of Paul (13-28). Considering the prominence of
the Holy Spirit in this book, a proper title for the Book of Acts could
be "The Acts of the Holy Spirit in and through the Early Church."

In the Old Covenant the Jewish people celebrated Pentecost
(also known as the Feast of the Weeks because it came seven

weeks after Passover) to commemorate the great events of Mount Sinai. During that time there were supernatural phenomena – *"thunderings and lightnings, and a thick cloud on the mountain ... the Lord descended upon it in fire ... the whole mountain quaked greatly (Ex. 19:16-18)."* Afterwards Moses went up the mountain again to receive the law which was written on tablets of stone with the finger of God (Ex. 31:18). As we know now, the law was, among other things, given to guide the Jewish people. When Moses came down the mountain he found the people worshipping a golden calf. Moses was furious (Ex. 32:19). He commanded the Levites to kill those who had committed idolatry and about 3,000 men were put to death that day (Ex. 32:28). During the Feast of Pentecost in Acts chapter 2 we read also of supernatural phenomena that took place – a rushing mighty wind, tongues of fire, and God the Holy Spirit came down to be their guide as Jesus promised. Strikingly enough: that day 3,000 people were made spiritually alive. The Holy Spirit also wrote the law of the Spirit of life on their hearts.

The apostle Paul's conversion is mentioned three times in the Book of Acts (9:1-9; 22:6-16; 26:12-18), indicating the importance of this event in Christian history. Paul wrote nearly two thirds of the New Testament, in the face of the fiercest persecution he remained faithful to Jesus; he is seen as the greatest Christian who ever lived.

The following are some of the outstanding values of the Book of Acts:

- It forms a natural bridge between the Gospels and Paul's letters. Acts is a true transition from the message of the Kingdom of God in the four Gospels to the mystery of the Church in Paul's letters. The Four Gospels relate the things which "Jesus began both to do and teach, until the day in which He was received up." The Book of Acts tells us what "Jesus began both to do and to teach" through the Spirit-empowered early Church – Jesus Christ, our Lord, continues His ministry through His Church. The Gospels reveal the Good News of salvation, while the Book of Acts proclaims the

Gospel; as witnesses of Christ the early Christians delivered the message in Word and Deed.

- Acts traces the growth of the early Church, showing us that the Church grew in numbers (2:41, 47; 4:4; 5:14; 6:7; 9:31, 42; 11:21; 16:5), and spread geographically while expanding its mission (starting in Jerusalem and ended in Rome).

- Acts guides faith and apologetics; it gives us guidance, not only in the lifestyle of the Church, but in what the Church should believe and do. Acts clearly illustrates what the Church is – not dead religion, but a living, dynamic organism. In so doing Acts lays a foundation for the development of doctrine and theology.

- Acts 2:38-47 give us insight into the life and ministry of the early Church that serve as an example to us today: (1) they preached the gospel; (2) baptized those who gladly received the Word; (3) they were devoted to (a) the apostles' doctrine, (b) fellowship, (c) breaking of bread or communion, and (d) prayer; (4) they Feared the Lord (the fear of the Lord is not to be afraid of God, but to revere Him, to have a holy respect for God); (5) were generous; (6) worshipped corporately; (7) ate together with gladness and sincere hearts. In doing all of that they had favour with the people (of course those who respected their lifestyle), *"and the Lord added to the church daily those who were being saved."*

- Acts emphasises the ministry of the Holy Spirit through believers; we need the empowerment of the Spirit to be powerful and effective witnesses for Jesus Christ, and we need to be guided by the same Spirit.

- Therefore, Acts reveals the Baptism in the Holy Spirit to us. Although it is mentioned in other books of the New Testament, Acts explains what it really means to be baptized in the Holy Spirit. In the following passages we see what it means to receive the power, or to be baptized in the power of the Holy Spirit: Acts 2:1-4; 8:14-19; 9:17-19; 10:44-46; and 19:1-7.

- Acts shows us that the Christian Church's main focus is missionary, because her message is for the whole world *"to the end of the world."* Herein we see that the Church is dynamic, never static. The Book of Acts serves as a missionary manual, showing us how we should spread the gospel to the ends of the earth: (1) send out ministers to preach the pure gospel of Jesus Christ, the Risen Saviour; (2) reach cities, beginning with your own city first; (3) make disciples by teaching new converts the Word of God; (4) plant churches in key and strategic areas; and (5) appoint competent spiritual leaders that can lead by example and shepherd the people.

The following chart shows us the five stages of Church growth in Acts.

Five Stages of Church Growth In Acts				
Stage	**Acts**	**Geographical area/s**	**Main Witnesses**	**Date**
1	1:1-9:31	Throughout Judea, Galilee, and Samaria	Peter, Stephen, and Philip	AD 35
2	9:32-12:25	As far as Phoenicia, Cyprus, and Antioch	Peter, Barnabas, Saul, and scattered disciples	AD 40
3	13:1-15:35	Throughout the region of Phrygia and Galatia	Paul, Barnabas, and John Mark (1st Missionary trip)	AD 48
4	15:36-21:16	Macedonia	Paul, Silas, and others (2nd Missionary trip)	AD 52
5	21:17-28:31	Rome	Paul and Luke (trip to Rome)	AD 60

The love, unity, and the power of the Holy Spirit through the early Church are the most striking features in this book.

The Book of Acts is the only authentic record of Apostolic history that we have, covering the history of the first thirty years of the early Church. It also gives us much insight into the lives of the apostles Paul and Peter.

The resurrection of Jesus Christ was the primary doctrine in the teaching of both Paul and Peter.

The supernatural character of the Church is clearly revealed by the variety of miracles recorded in the Book of Acts. That shows us: Christianity is supernatural, it astonishes people, and it is beyond understanding. As Martyn Lloyd-Jones said it well: "If you can understand your religion, that is proof it is not Christianity."[34]

The following chart gives us an indication of the different miracles that took place in the Book of Acts.

Miracles in the Book of Acts	
Acts	**Miracle**
1:03	The visible appearance of Jesus Christ after His resurrection.
1:09	Jesus, before the eyes of His disciples ascended into heaven.
2:03	The visible miraculous outpouring of the Holy Spirit.
2:04	The disciples, baptized in the power of the Holy Spirit spoke with other tongues.
2:43	Many signs and wonders done through the apostles.
3:7-11	The wonderful healing of the lame man at the temple gate.
4:31	God answers prayer by an earthquake.
5:5-10	Ananias and Sapphira died.
5:12	Signs and wonders by the apostles continued.
5:15-16	Many people healed by Peter's shadow.
5:19	Prison doors are opened by an angel.
6:08	Stephen performed great wonders and signs
8:6-7, 13	Philip did great miracles and sings in Samaria, and many believed.

---

[34] Martyn Lloyd-Jones, *Authentic Christianity*, p. 31

8:39, 40	Philip was supernaturally transported by the Holy Spirit.
9:3-9	Saul is confronted by a direct voice from heaven.
9:17-18	"Something like scales" fell from Saul's eyes after Ananias laid hands on him.
9:32-35	Aeneas was miraculously healed, and the whole region was converted to Christ.
9:40-42	Peter raised Dorcas from the dead, and many believed on the Lord.
10:3, 46	Cornelius was converted by the appearance of an angel and he spoke in tongues.
10:9-22	A vision and voice from heaven led Peter to Cornelius.
12:10	The prison's gate opened supernaturally.
13:11-12	The blinding of a sorcerer led the proconsul of Cyprus to believe.
14:3-4	People did signs and wonders in Iconium, and many believed.
14:8-18	The healing of a cripple, in Lystra, made the crowds to think Paul is a god.
15:12, 19	God worked many miracles and wonders through Barnabas and Paul.
16:18	Paul cast out an evil spirit from a slave woman.
16:26	Paul and Silas were miraculously set free from prison.
19:6, 7	In Ephesus about twelve men spoke in tongues.
19:11, 12	God worked unusual miracles by the hands of Paul.
20:8-12	In Troas, Paul raised a young man from the dead.
28:3-6	Paul miraculously healed from a deadly snake bite.
28:8-9	Paul healed many on the Island of Malta.

The early Church was a praying Church as the following chart indicates.

Prayer in the early Church	
Event	**Reference/s**
They prayed in one accord in the upper room.	1:14
They prayed before they chose an apostle to replace Judas.	1:24
They prayed daily corporately; as a way of life	2:42
They prayed on their way to a prayer meeting.	3:01
They prayed when they were threatened and persecuted.	4:24-31
The apostles gave themselves continually to prayer.	6:04
They prayed for the deacons.	6:06
Stephen prayed while he was dying.	7:59
They prayed for new believers to be filled with the Holy Spirit.	8:15; 9:17-19; 19:6
They prayed before eating.	10:09
They prayed for believers who were locked up in prison.	12:05
They prayed for those they sent out.	13:03
They prayed when they chose church leaders.	14:23
They prayed while in prison.	16:25
They prayed when they said good-bye to friends.	20:36
They prayed for the sick to be healed.	20:08

Personal Application

The message of the Book of Acts should: (1) reveal authentic Christianity to you, (2) awaken you to the reality of what is possible when you fully surrender yourself unto the Lord and yield to and cooperate with the Holy Spirit, and (3) encourage you to live fully for our Lord in the face of challenges and even persecution.

As you read the Book of Acts realize that you are part of the same Church. Put yourself in the place of the apostles: let their dedication be yours, have unwavering faith in Jesus Christ, proclaim the pure Gospel, give generously of your time, talents, and resources as the opportunity arises, expect the unexpected, and allow the Holy Spirit to live in and through you; He makes Jesus a greater reality in your life.

If you are a leader or maybe an aspirant leader consider the following outline of "power principles":

1. Leaders need an encounter with the Holy Spirit (Acts 2:3, 4), they should be full of the Holy Spirit (Acts 1:8; Eph. 5:18), and must be directed by the Holy Spirit, just as the Lord Jesus was (Matt. 12:28; Acts 1:2).

2. Leaders need to be full of faith and power, and they should demonstrate it (Acts 6:8; 11:24). They should strengthen others in faith (Acts 16:5). It is obvious that if you are full of the Holy Spirit then you ought to be full of faith.

3. There should be unity and harmony among leaders, and they should pray together in harmony (Acts 1:14; 2:1).

4. Leaders need to incorporate the following elements into their congregation's life:

    a) Sound Teaching (the apostle's doctrine)
    b) Genuine Fellowship (ponder on what genuine fellowship means)
    c) Breaking of Bread (communion and eating together)
    d) Prayer – purposeful, consistent individual and corporate prayer ... then the rest could follow (Acts 2:42-47).
    e) The fear of the Lord (the correct view on it)
    f) A lifestyle of praise & worship
    g) Body life and lifestyle ministry

5. Leaders should reflect the Presence and Power of Christ in and through their lives (Acts 3:6; 4:13, 14, 33).

6. Leaders together with congregants should frequently pray in harmony (Acts 4:24-31).

7. Leaders must be sensitive to the Holy Spirit and obey God rather than man (Acts 5:29).

8. Leaders have to share the ministry load. Do not weaken your life and ministry by doing work that others should do (Acts 6:1-6).

9. Leaders must give prayer and the ministry of the Word the central place in their lives and ministry (Acts 6:4).

10. Leaders should trust God and rely fully on Him (Acts 11:12).

11. Leaders must, with joy, encourage their people to remain faithful and serve the Lord with purpose of heart (Acts 11:23, 24).

12. Leaders have to set the example and encourage their congregants to a lifestyle of prayer (Acts 12:5), and believe that God will answer (v. 13, 14).

13. Leaders should submit to the Holy Spirit's guidance in decision making. Call leadership to fasting and prayer in such times. Listen to the Holy Spirit and release ministry freely when asked to do so by the Holy Spirit (Acts 13:1-3).

14. Leaders should always guard against inordinate praise from people. Dispel unrighteous adulation by admirers (Acts 14:14-18).

15. Leaders should strengthen their followers faith in the face of tests, trials and tribulation (Acts 14:22).

16. Leaders should personally train young men who are called to ministry. The development of leaders should be part of the leadership culture of any congregation (Acts 16:1-5). Kind produces after the same kind.

17. Leaders should live lives of praise and worship (Acts 16:25).

18. Leaders' messages, inspired by the Holy Spirit, should defeat the prevailing culture and turn the world upside down (Acts 17:5-6).

DISCOVERING THE MOST AMAZING BOOK   313

19. Leaders should encourage their followers to "examine the Scriptures daily (Acts 17:11)."

20. Leaders must proclaim the real God with boldness (Acts 17:22-34).

21. Leaders must be fervent in the spirit (Acts 18:25, 28).

22. Leaders should impart the ministry of the Holy Spirit to others who do not have it (Acts 19:6).

23. Leaders should keep nothing back that is helpful (Acts 20:20).

24. Leaders should be fully equipped in the whole counsel of God and teach that to their people (Acts 20:27).

25. Leaders should always guard against disloyalty. Leaders are not self-made, they are appointed by the Holy Spirit. Remember it is the Church of God. Ensure that no one is making disciples for himself. Leaders should take on the responsibility of guarding the flock of God from "savage wolves" (Acts 20:28-32).

❖ Characteristics of wrong kind of leadership (wolves) in the Church:

   a) They are more interested in themselves than the care of the flock (20:29; John 10:12, 13). They like attention and adulation – the spotlight on themselves.
   b) They will draw people after themselves (20:30).
   c) They will look for quick results that require little sacrifice (20:31).

Chapter Ten

Survey of Paul's Letters

We divide Paul's Letters into two groups:

1. Nine Letters to Churches: Romans to 2 Thessalonians

2. Four Letters to Individual Pastors: 1 & 2 Timothy, Titus, Philemon. The first three Letters are specifically called Pastoral Letters based on their content that focuses on pastoral responsibilities.

The following chart gives us a quick glance at the Letters of Paul.

Paul's Letters				
Letter	Place written	Date written	Audience	Emphasis
Paul's Nine Letters to Churches				
Romans	Corinth	AD 57	Christians in Rome	Doctrinal – Faith
1 Corinthians	Ephesus	AD 54/55	Corinthian church	Doctrinal/ Pastoral
2 Corinthians	Macedonia	AD 55/56	Corinthian church	Biographical
Galatians	Antioch	AD 48/49	Churches in Galatia	Doctrinal
Ephesians	Rome	AD 60/61	Ephesian Christians	Church of Christ

Philippians	Rome	AD 61	Philippian Christians	Christ & Church
Colossians	Rome	AD 60/61	Colossian Christians	Christ of Church
1 Thessalonians	Corinth	AD 50/51	Thessalonian Christians	2nd Coming
2 Thessalonians	Corinth	AD 51/50	..	2nd Coming
Paul's Four Letters to Individuals				
1 Timothy	Macedonia	AD 64	Timothy	Church Order
2 Timothy	Rome	AD 67	Timothy	Encouragement
Titus	Macedonia	AD 65	Titus	Church Order
Philemon	Rome	AD 60-63	Philemon	Brotherly Love

We will now look at Paul's Letters to the different churches, and then in the following chapter at his letters to individuals.

ROMANS

Author
The apostle Paul

Date
AD 56/57

Main Theme
The Righteousness of God

Key Verses
"For I am not ashamed of the gospel of Christ, for it is the power of God to salvation for everyone who believes, for the Jew first and also for the Greek. For in it the righteousness of God is revealed from faith to faith; as it is written, 'The just shall live by faith' (1:16, 17)."

Key Phrase
"the righteousness of faith"

Key Words
Righteousness, Faith, Justification, Redemption, Propitiation

Setting
Paul wrote his Letter to the Romans from Corinth near the end of his third missionary journey. Rome was the epicentre of the powerful Roman Empire, a city in need of a proper statement of the principles of the Christian faith. We do not know who founded the church in Rome, most probably Jews who returned from Jerusalem after Pentecost. However, the church in Rome was a mixed community consisting of both Jews and Gentiles, and there was considerable conflict between these groups. The conflict was primarily theological (different views about salvation and the law of the Old Covenant), and secondary ethnic (different cultures).

Purpose
Paul had never visited the church in Rome, but eagerly looked forward to meeting with and having fellowship with the Christians in Rome. He planned on going to Spain in order to continue his missionary work, and most likely thought that he would visit Rome on his way to Spain. Paul wrote this letter to the Romans not only to introduce himself, but mainly to set forth a comprehensive, logical and orderly account of the great principles of the gospel that he preached, showing how sinful men and women can receive the righteousness of God through faith in Jesus Christ.

Synopsis
While the four Gospels present the life and ministry of Jesus Christ, Romans records the most systematic presentation of the significance of His sacrificial death and glorious resurrection.

Paul's central theme is *"the righteousness of God* (1:17)." Within the context of his overarching theme of the righteousness of God, we divide Romans into four main sections:

1. The Universal Need for God's Righteousness (1:1-3:20)

After a brief introduction and sharing his desire to visit Rome, Paul declares his allegiance to the gospel of Christ, because *"it is the power of God to salvation for everyone who believes (1:16)."* And God's righteousness is revealed in the gospel (1:17). Paul continues by discussing mankind's universal need for the righteousness of God, *"There is none righteous, no, not one ... for all have sinned and fall short of the glory of God* (3:10, 23). Because God is righteous He condemns sin and He is righteous in His judgment. And, if all are helpless and condemned, then both legal and personal righteousness must be divinely provided for them.

2. The Manifestation of God's Righteousness (3:21-8:39)

After Paul established the universal need for God's righteousness, he continues to explain how God, in His grace, made His righteousness available to mankind. *"But now the righteousness of God apart from the law is revealed, being witnessed by the Law and the Prophets, even the righteousness of God, through faith in Jesus Christ, to all and on all who believe ... being justified freely by His grace through the redemption that is in Christ, whom God set forth as a propitiation by His blood, through faith, to demonstrate His righteousness, ... that He might be just and the justifier of the one who has faith in Jesus* (3:21-26)."

The words *"But now"* show us that Paul moved from judgment to justification. Justified means to be declared righteous in God's sight – restored to the right position before God through the grace manifested in Christ. Propitiation means the appeasement of God's wrath by Christ's sacrificial death – His death on the cross satisfied God that the righteous demand of the penalty for sin has been paid. The righteous demand is that the soul who has sinned must die. Jesus as our sinless Kinsman-Redeemer took our sin upon Himself and died on our behalf. Sending Jesus to die for our sins was God's amazing solution to the problem of how He could remain just (by punishing sin) and still justify us (declaring us righteous in His sight). Now, since the sinner cannot earn his salvation, the righteousness of God must be accepted in faith – by believing in Jesus Christ, who shed His blood for the salvation of mankind, one is justified (3:22,

24). Justification cannot be earned, or received by keeping the law (3:28); it is a gift of God, so that no one can boast.

Paul, then illustrates his teaching by referring to Abraham who was justified by his faith, even before his circumcision and before the law was given (4:1-25).

Next, Paul recites the benefits of justification. Among other things, justification means peace with God, access to grace in which we stand, rejoice in hope, and saved from the wrath of God (5:1-11). He contrasts Adam and Christ (5:12-21). Adam represents the condemnation of all people, while Christ represents the believer's justification.

In chapters 6 through 8 Paul deals with sanctification – the believer's union with the life of Christ through the indwelling Holy Spirit. To sanctify (verb) and sanctification (noun) are related terms referring to the setting apart, of the sinful person from sin, into a relationship with God who is holy. Justification, Sanctification, and Redemption are inseparable. Once you are redeemed, you are both justified and sanctified (see 1 Cor. 1:30). They are all three gifts of God. Therefore, sanctification is not a process as some would propose, but rather, the state (of holiness) into which God, in grace, calls sinful human beings based on their faith in Christ, so that they can manifest the life which is inside them.

Since we are saved by grace, and Paul previously stated that *"where sin abounded, grace abounded much more* (5:20)," he now asks the question: *"Shall we continue in sin that grace may abound* (6:1)?" Then answers: "Certainly not! *How shall we who died to sin live any longer in it* (6:2)?"

Paul uses four analogies to explain the Christian's relationship to sin and the Law: baptism (6:1-14), slavery (6:15-23), marriage (7:1-6), and personal experience (7:7-25). We will touch on one of these: baptism.

In his example of the baptism, Paul makes it clear that through our faith in Christ, we are united with Him. Our *"old man* (v. 6)," which is our unregenerate self before we trusted Christ as Saviour, was put to death with Christ the moment we had put our trust in Christ. The *"body of sin* (v. 6)" that Paul refers to is not our physical body, but the sinful nature that we have inherited from Adam. *"Done away with* (v. 6)" does not mean completely destroyed or annihilated, but "rendered powerless." Now, this means that sin's power over us had been broken. Sin has no control over us anymore. Union with Christ sets us free from the penalty and power of sin. This means that *"we should no longer be slaves of sin* (v. 6)." Based on knowing and believing who you are in Christ and that sin has no dominion over you, you can say no! to sin. You could sin, but you don't have to. What you rather should do is: *"present your members as instruments ... of righteousness to God* (v. 13)." Then you will have no problem with sin.

Chapter 8 of Romans is the most outstanding chapter in the Bible about the Holy Spirit as the agent of sanctification who sets us free from the law of sin and death (v. 2), and enables us to live a life pleasing to God (vv. 4-5), because He Himself lives in us (v. 9), gives life to our mortal bodies (v. 11), leads us (v. 14), testifies with our spirit that we are children of God (v. 16), and guides us in prayer (v. 26-27).

Faith in Jesus Christ and what He had done for us on the cross, sets us free from condemnation, the dominion of sin, and the dominion of the law.

3. The Relation of God's Righteousness to the Jews (9:1-11:36)

In this section Paul discusses God's righteousness as revealed in His faithfulness to His covenant promises that He made to Israel.

Paul shares his concern for Israel, and upholds the righteousness and sovereignty of God by answering questions such as, "Is God unjust in His choices?" God has made the way to righteousness for Jews and Gentiles the same: faith in Christ. Israel's unbelief had forfeited her standing with God; her choice to seek righteousness *"by the works of the law* (9:31)." However, God is sovereign and just in His choices.

Although Israel rejected God by their unbelief, God never rejected them. All is not lost for Israel, *"there is a remnant according to the election of grace* (11:5)." Israel's rejection is not total and final, someday full salvation will come to Israel (11:26).

Paul concludes this section by praising God for His wisdom (11:33-36).

4. The Application of Righteousness (12:1-16:27).

The Letter to the Romans could be divided into two main parts. The first part is doctrinal. Paul builds an airtight case, particularly for the doctrine of Justification by Faith Alone (1:1-11:36). The second part deals with the practical side of that doctrine: the lifestyle of those who are justified (12:1-16:27). It is not good enough to merely know the gospel, our lives should reflect it.

Romans 12:1 and 2 are seen as the gateway to effective Christian living. When you fully surrender yourself to God, then He can work in and through you. Paul continues by explaining what it means to live in complete submission to God: using your spiritual gifts to serve others (12:3-8), genuinely love and live at peace with others (12:9-21), and be a good citizen (13:1-14).

Freedom does not mean licence; it must be guided by love. We should be walking in love with our fellow Christians, building each other up in the faith, while we are sensitive and helpful to those who are weak (14:1-15:6).

In Romans 15:5-13 Paul encourages unity, especially between Jews and Gentiles, to the glory of God.

Paul concludes his letter to the Romans by reviewing the reasons for his writing, and his desire to visit Rome (15:14-33), and commending sister Phoebe (who most likely delivered the letter to the Christians in Rome), sending his regards to friends, and warning the Roman Christians to avoid divisive persons (16:1-20)."

Noteworthy

The Letter to the Romans is Paul's greatest work, and the most influential letter ever written. Professor FF Bruce wrote: "there is no saying what may happen when people begin to study the letter to the Romans."

Romans is Paul's most comprehensive and logical explanation of the significant message of the Gospel – God's saving grace in Jesus Christ.

Personal Application

You should at least receive the following from the message of Romans:

DISCOVERING THE MOST AMAZING BOOK 321

- All of humanity is sinful and in desperate need of salvation.

- Faith in the Crucified and Risen Saviour is the only means to be justified – declared righteous – by God. Law keeping, good works, and self-effort cannot save you, because then you can boast. Salvation, justification, and sanctification are gifts of God. You receive it by putting your trust in Him who died on the cross so that you might be saved.

- *"The just shall live by faith"* – all that God expects of you is to believe Him, to put your full trust in Him in every aspect of your life. God wants to bring all His children to the point where they would fully trust Him.

- Walk according to the Holy Spirit – allow the Holy Spirit to lead you in the will of the Father. Be sensitive to Him. He is residing in you.

- Surrender yourself fully unto God, then you will experience His *"good and acceptable and perfect will (12:2)."*

- Live like a Christian ought to live (12:9-21).

- Let your faith and obedience be known to all (1:8; 16:19).

1 CORINTHIANS

Author
The apostle Paul

Date
AD 54/55

Main Theme
Resolving doctrinal and practical church problems in the light of the relevance and sufficiency of Jesus Christ for every area of the Christian's life

Key Verse
"Do you not know that you are the temple of God and that the Spirit of God dwells in you (3:16)?"

Key Phrase
"Lord Jesus Christ" mentioned six times only in the first ten verses. It has been said that all the disorders that had crept into the lives of the Corinthian Christians had arisen through their failure to recognize Jesus Christ as Lord.

Key Words
The Cross, Spiritual Gifts, Love, The Resurrection

Setting
The church at Corinth was founded by Paul in AD 51/52 when he spent eighteen months there on his second missionary journey. Corinth was an important trade centre, strategically located between the Aegean and the Adriatic Sea in the Roman province of Achaia, and multicultural (Romans/Italians, Greeks, and Asians). There was gross immorality, and the many pagan temples encouraged a licentious way of life. The inhabitants worshipped the gods of Greece and Rome. The huge temple of Aphrodite, the goddess of love, housed many priestesses who were involved in temple prostitution. Even the name of the city became a notorious proverb: "to Corinthianize" meant to practice prostitution. The Corinthian Christians were surrounded by every conceivable sin and many gave in under its pressure.

Paul lists the sorts of sins that were part of the Corinthian Christians' former way of life. They had been *"sexually immoral ... idolaters ... adulterers ... male prostitutes ... thieves ... greedy ... drunkards ... slanderers ... swindlers* (1 Cor. 6:9-10)." Some of these practices were still a problem among church members.

During his three year ministry in Ephesus, on his third missionary journey, Paul received a bad report about immorality among the members in the Corinthian church. He sent the church a letter (now lost) to address the situation (5:9-11). Soon afterward, a delegation sent by Chloe, a member of the church, reported to Paul about divisive factions within the church. Before Paul could write a letter

DISCOVERING THE MOST AMAZING BOOK

to address the issue, another delegation arrived with a letter, asking him certain questions (7:1; 16:17). Paul immediately sent Timothy to Corinth to look into the situation (4:17), since Timothy was involved in founding the church (Acts 18:5). Paul then wrote this letter, which we know as First Corinthians.

Purpose
Paul wrote this letter to respond to several issues brought to his attention in order to resolve doctrinal and practical problems within the church.

Synopsis
The letter consists of Paul's response to ten different problems: a sectarian spirit, incest, lawsuits, fornication, marriage and divorce, eating food offered to idols, wearing of the veil, the Lord's Supper, spiritual gifts, and the resurrection.

We divide First Corinthians into three main divisions:

1. The Answer to Chloe's Report of Divisions (chs. 1-4)
After a brief introduction and thanking God for the grace of Christ Jesus and spiritual gifts at work in the church (1:1-9), Paul turns to the question of unity (1:10-4:21). He emphasizes the message of the cross; that Christ is the power and wisdom of God. They should embrace the message of the cross, reject worldly wisdom, and glory only in the Lord, because they are in Christ Jesus, who became for them *"wisdom from God – and righteousness and sanctification and redemption* (1:30)."

Paul also stresses that spiritual things must be spiritually discerned, and that division is a result of carnality. For the division among them Paul's remedy was spiritual maturity (3:1-9), and to avoid worldly wisdom (3:18-23). (Remember, these Christians were among the Greeks who were people of reason. Paul prepared his letter to meet the Greek mind. He, therefore, stresses that selfish and self-centred human wisdom is futile. The heart of true wisdom is knowing God and His will, and this can only be known when you have the Spirit of God.)

2. The Answer to the Report of Fornication and Disorder (chs. 5-6)
Paul continues to the next problem: severe sexual immorality of certain church members and lawsuits among Christians (5:1-6:8). Paul instructs the Corinthian Christians to exercise church discipline until the offenders repent and are restored, and referring to his previous letter (which is now lost), *"not to keep company with sexually immoral people* (5:9)." Because so many problems in the Corinthian church involved sex, Paul denounces sexual sin in the strongest possible terms (6:9-20). Sexual sin, in any day and age, will cause severe and increasing problems, and should be immediately and firmly addressed.

Concerning the lawsuits, Paul emphasize that they should not take their cases to heathen judges, but should instead settle their disputes themselves (6:1-6)

3. The Answer to the Letter of Different Questions (chs. 7-16).
Paul continues, answering the questions that the Corinthians Christians asked him in the letter they wrote to him. Because of the prostitution and sexual immorality marriages were under pressure, and the Christians were not sure what to do. Paul gives them clear advice and instructions concerning marital matters. In the case of marriage between a believer and an unbeliever, the concern of the believer is to influence the unbeliever in such a way that salvation becomes probable, not to reject him or her (7:16). Paul was also clear that a believer should not marry an unbeliever. Paul's instruction for the unmarried virgins was self-control or lawful marriage (7:36, 37).

Concerning meat sacrificed to idols, Paul tells them that the heart of the matter is to realize that there is really only one God, they should be completely committed to Him and should show sensitivity to other Christians, especially weaker brothers and sisters (ch. 8). Paul, then uses himself as a pattern of self-denial and selfless service to all kinds of people (ch. 9).

In chapter 10 Paul explains to the Corinthian Christians that what is written in the Old Covenant, concerning Moses and the Israelites, *"became our examples, to the intent that we should not lust after evil things as they also lusted* (10:6)."

Chapters 11 to 14 cover three problems related to public worship: the wearing of the veil, the Lord's Supper, and spiritual gifts.

The wearing of the veil was a first century Roman cultural tradition as a sign of marriage. (Today we have the wedding ring.) Paul's main concern here is with the relationship between husband and wife – the husband is the head of the house and the wife should be submissive to him.

The church mainly consisted of the poorer class, including slaves (1:26-28; 7:21). Apparently the wealthier members, unwilling to share their food, took the supper ahead of others and shamed those who had nothing (11:21-22). This serious problem was caused by their lack of understanding the meaning of the Lord's Supper and to observe it in an unselfish, and un-divisive way. Paul corrects this by reminding them of the solemn meaning behind and the purpose of the Lord's Supper.

The Spirit of God was active in the Corinthian church, but the members were ignorant concerning the spiritual gifts. Paul dedicates two chapters in dealing with this problem (chs. 12 and 14). It seems that the Corinthians Christians have placed too much emphasis on certain gifts, especially the speaking in tongues (considering its prominence in the discussion). They also, most likely, misunderstood the way that the Holy Spirit operates through believers, viewing gift-operations of the Spirit as a compulsive possession, negating the will (14:32). Paul corrects this problem by making it clear that the spiritual gifts are actually manifestations of the Spirit given to each one for the benefit of all (12:7), and *"the same Spirit works all these things [gifts], distributing to each one individually as He wills* (12:11)." By making use of the body analogy, Paul illustrates the need for multiple and varied manifestations (12:12-27). Sandwiched in the middle of the two chapters on the spiritual gifts, is Paul's epic chapter on love (ch. 13). This is certainly indicative that all gifts should operate in love and unselfish motives. Paul also underscores the need for self-control, and being orderly and edifying in the corporate services.

In chapter 15 Paul declares the gospel that he preaches (15:1-11). Paul continues by emphasizing the importance of Christ's resurrection, and discusses the resurrection of the dead and the incorruptible bodies they would receive (15:12-58).

Finally Paul refers to the question concerning the collection as a gift to the Jerusalem church (16:1-4). Paul then concludes his letter by sharing some of his personal plans, some final exhortations, and greetings (16:5-24).

Noteworthy

First Corinthians reveals the problems, pressures and struggles of a church called out of a pagan society. This letter gives us the best picture of the life and problems of a pioneer church in a multi-cultural environment.

Chapter 13 contains the most extensive and profound teaching on the self-giving character of God's love. The Greek word that Paul uses for love is *agape*, which refers to God's self-giving and unconditional love. And as we know, God is love (1 John 4:8). Therefore, in the context of this chapter we have to understand that love is not merely a feeling, it is a Person. Only God can love in such a way as 1 Corinthians 13 describes. When you read this chapter put God or Jesus in the place of the word "love."

First Corinthians contains extensive doctrinal instructions on the place and function of spiritual gifts in the local church (chs. 12-14), and on the nature of the resurrection body (ch. 15).

Personal Application

Paul's straightforward instructions concerning the different issues in the Corinthian church are applicable to every church or individual who struggles with the same.

Reflect on the following:

- If Jesus is not Lord of all in your life, then He is not Lord at all. Live a Christ-centred life.

- Your body is the temple of the Holy Spirit who is in you, and you are not your own. Look after your body; treasure what you have inside you; and when you are sexually tempted, do what Joseph did – flee from it!

- You are a member of the One Body of Christ. Discover your function in His body, support the other members, while you function in harmony with them to keep the body healthy.

- Don't only seek the gifts, seek the Giver of the gifts first, then the gifts will manifest through you when needed.

Love is the Greatest Gift. Because God loves you so much, He gave you what you need most – the Gift of Love – Jesus Christ (John 3:16).

2 CORINTHIANS

Author
The apostle Paul

Date
AD 55/56

Main Theme
Comfort in Powerful Persevering Ministry

Key Verses
"For the love of Christ compels us, because we judge thus: that if One died for all, then all died; and He died for all, that those who live should live no longer for themselves, but for Him who died for them and rose again (5:14, 15)."

Key Phrase
"the ministry of the Spirit"

Key Words
Comfort, Suffering, Ministry

Setting
Paul's first letter to the Corinthian church was not as successful in settling the issues at Corinth as he hoped. And in the meantime the church had been swayed by false teachers who denied the authority of Paul and stirred the people against him. When Paul heard of this he immediately travelled to Corinth from Ephesus in an attempt to resolve the issues. His visit turned out to be very painful (2:1; 12:14, 21; 13:1, 2). He experienced open rebellion from the leader of the opposition against him (2:5-8; 7:12). Paul decided to rather suffer humiliation by returning to Ephesus with the issues unresolved. Once

back in Ephesus Paul wrote a severe letter (now also lost), warning the church of God's judgment if they did not repent (2:3-4; 7:8-16). Paul sent this letter by Titus back to Corinth. Later, in Macedonia, Paul met Titus who had an encouraging report (7:5-16). To Paul's great joy, the majority of the Corinthians did repent, but there was still a minority who, under the influence of Paul's opponents (11:12-21), continued to reject Paul and his gospel.

Purpose
Paul wrote this letter that we know as Second Corinthians to express his thanksgiving for the repentant majority and to defend his apostleship to the minority as well as to remind the members that, as the founder of the church, he has a right to have a say in its life and ministry.

Synopsis
Second Corinthians differs much from First Corinthians in that Paul shares mainly his personal matters rather than doctrinal teaching or church order. Paul's ministry, feelings, desires, dislikes, ambitions, and obligations are the focus of this Letter.

We divide Second Corinthians into three main parts:

1. Paul's Explanation of His Ministry (chs. 1-7)
In these first seven chapters Paul gives his defence for his conduct and ministry. He reminds the Corinthian Christians of his relationship to them, he had always been honest and straightforward with them (1:12-14). Paul explains the reason for his delay in visiting them, and responds to the attack on his character, forgiving the rebel who led the opposition against him. Paul emphasizes that all should forgive, *"lest satan should take advantage of us; for we are not ignorant of his devices* (2:11)." Paul then continues reviewing his ministry in order to demonstrate the Nature of Christian Ministry:

- Our triumph is in Christ (2:14-17).
- We are living letters, read by all people (3:1-3).
- Our sufficiency is in God (3:4-6).
- We are ministers of the New Covenant of which the Holy Spirit is the Administrator (3:7-18).

- We preach Christ, not ourselves (4:1-6).
- We are dying and living with Jesus (4:7-15).
- We are assured of our glorious future in Christ, therefore we walk by faith, not by sight (5:1-11).
- We are reconciled to God, therefore, we are ministers of reconciliation (5:12-21).
- Paying the price to minister (6:3-10).
- Paul urges the Corinthian Christians to live holy lives (6:11-18).

After his long digression on ministry, Paul continues sharing about his travels, the repentance of the Corinthian church, and the joy of Titus who was refreshed in the spirit by them all (7:1-16).

2. The Collection for the Saints (chs. 8-9)
This section deals with the offering being raised by Paul for the poor Christians in Jerusalem. He tells the Corinthian Christians about the Macedonian churches that were financially poor, yet they had great joy and liberality in their giving. Paul shares a model for all Christian giving: *"they first gave themselves to the Lord* (8:5)." When you belong to God, then your finances belong to Him as well. He continues by telling that Jesus Christ is our pattern in giving (8:8, 9). Paul also urges the Corinthian Christians to be generous and cheerful in their giving, because *"God loves a cheerful giver* (9:7)."

3. Paul's Vindication of His Apostleship (chs. 10-13).
This last section of Paul's letter contains a rebuke to his remaining opponents. Paul responds to their false accusations and teachings. There is a change in Paul's tone, he gives a strong and severe defence of his authority as a genuine apostle, while pointing out the deceptive influence of the false teachers.

Paul concludes this letter with powerful greetings, highlighting the important themes he has covered, and a powerful Trinitarian benediction, emphasizing that grace, love, and fellowship with one another come from God in Christ through the Holy Spirit (13:11-14).

Noteworthy
Second Corinthians is mostly autobiographical, containing numerous references to the hardships Paul endured in the course of his ministry,

and revealing the depth and strength of his character. It reveals that Paul's life was completely sold out to the Lord and his converts; he was not a cold hearted professional, but a man with a deep love for Christ and His Church (see 1:6; 2:4; 5:13; 7:3-7; 11:2; 12:14, 15).

Chapter twelve reveals a secret Paul kept for fourteen years – he was caught up into the third heaven.
The last verse of Second Corinthians boldly underscores the Trinity in the Godhead.

Personal Application
While reading Second Corinthians examine your own motives for serving the Lord, whether as layperson or as an ordained minister.

Do you give: (1) yourself, and (2) finances generously and cheerfully for the work of the Lord, if it is in your means?

GALATIANS

Author
The apostle Paul

Date
AD 48/49

Main Theme
Justification by Faith Alone

Key Verse
"This only I want to learn from you: Did you receive the Spirit by the works of the law, or by the hearing of faith (3:2)?"

Key Phrase
"Walk in the Spirit"

Key Words
Grace, Liberty, Gospel, Faith, Justified, Promise

Setting

Paul's letter is set in the context of conflict and controversy, which followed Paul's preaching in Galatia. Both the truth of the Gospel and Paul's right to preach it was being challenged. Although the Galatian churches consisted mostly of Gentile Christians, there were some Jews among them. The legalistic Jews (known as Judaizers), did not deny that faith in Jesus is necessary for salvation, but they believed that Christianity is the fulfilment of the Jewish hope and in order to receive salvation, Gentiles need to become part of Israel. Therefore they taught that, to experience salvation, the Galatian Christians must also be initiated into Israel by the rite of circumcision and then, like all true Israelites, they must keep the obligations of the law. The Galatian Christians who were still young in their faith and vulnerable to any teaching, were confused when they were confronted by this "new" message. Furthermore, the Judaizers discredited the teachings of Paul and demeaned him as an apostle. They propagated that he was a compromiser who made the gospel more attractive to Gentiles by removing the valid legal demands of the law.

Purpose

Paul wrote this letter, with a tone of severity, to forcefully counter the false teachings of the Judaizers.

Synopsis

Paul's Letter to the Galatians is addressed to a group of churches in the region of Galatia, which would have included towns such as, Antioch, Iconium, Lystra, and Derbe (Paul, together with Barnabas founded churches in these towns on his first missionary journey, Acts 13:14-14:23).

The Letter to the Galatians can be divided into three main sections – biographical, doctrinal, and practical – consisting of two chapters each:

1. Paul's Biographical Argument: An Independent Revelation (chs. 1-2)

In this section Paul defends his apostolic independence to establish the divine origin of his message.

In his brief introduction Paul makes it clear that his apostolic authority is not from any human source but from Jesus Christ and God the Father (1:1-5). Paul then addresses those who are accepting "a different gospel," not another, because there is no other gospel. There is only one true gospel: *"even if we, or an angel from heaven, preach any other gospel to you than what we have preached to you, let him be accursed (1:8)."* Paul continues, summarising the controversy, including his personal confrontation with Peter and other church leaders (1:10-2:15). Paul made it abundantly clear *"that man is not justified by the works of the law but by faith in Jesus Christ ... for if righteousness comes through the law, then Christ died in vain (2:16, 21)."*

2. Paul's Doctrinal Argument: Justification by Faith Alone (chs. 3-4)

Here Paul presents a series of masterful arguments and illustrations to prove the inferiority of the law to the gospel and to establish the true purpose of the law.

Paul appeals to the Galatian Christians' own experience of the gospel, reminding them that their Christian life began with faith in the crucified Christ, and that they received the Holy Spirit upon hearing the message of faith; they would be foolish to abandon faith and try to reach perfection by their own efforts (3:1-5). Paul continues, showing how Abraham, in the Old Covenant, was justified by his faith, and making it clear that Christ has redeemed us from the curse of the law (3:6-20). Next, he explains the purpose of the law and the relationship between law, God's promises, and Christ (3:21-4:31).

3. Paul's Practical Argument: The Fruit of Freedom (chs. 5-6)

In this section Paul encourages the Galatian Christians to use their Christian liberty properly and not to abuse it.

He encourages the Galatians to stand fast in their freedom and to know that *"in Christ Jesus neither circumcision nor uncircumcision avails anything, but faith working through love (5:6)."*

Paul continues, encouraging them: *"walk in the Spirit, and you shall not fulfil the lust of the flesh (5:16)."* And he tells them that their freedom means that they are free to love and serve one another (6:1-10).

In chapter 6 verses 11-15 Paul tells the Galatians that *"not even those who are circumcised keep the law, but they desire to have you circumcised that they may boast in the flesh."* He makes it clear that he can only boast in the cross of our Lord Jesus Christ, because of that cross his interest in the world has been crucified. Paul then concludes his letter with a blessing and a plea that nobody would trouble him again with these things.

Noteworthy

The Letter to the Galatians is Paul's great declaration of religious freedom – a freedom that involves independence from self and men, and dependence on God.[35]

The doctrine of justification by faith is stated more emphatically in Galatians than in any other of Paul's letters.

This was Martin Luther's favourite letter, and it played a very important part in the Reformation.

Personal Application

Human beings have a natural tendency to be independent of God's grace – whenever a man becomes convicted of his sinful condition, usually his first reaction is to seek some means by which he can cure himself of that condition, and make himself righteous by his own efforts without relying on God's grace. However, it is only by the grace of God and faith in what Jesus had accomplished on the cross for yourself that you can find spiritual freedom.

For freedom Jesus Christ has set you free. Stand fast in that freedom, and don't allow anyone, not even yourself, to entangle you again with a yoke of bondage.

You were set free from the curse of the law, the power and penalty of sin, and your own self-effort in order to worship and obey God, not to misuse your freedom.

---

[35] Maxie Dunnam, *Galatians*, p. 9

EPHESIANS

Author
The apostle Paul

Date
AD 61

Main Theme
The Glorious Church

Key Verses
"And He put all things under His feet, and gave Him to be head over all things to the church, which is His body, the fullness of Him who fills all in all (1:22, 23)."

Key Phrase
"in Christ" (35 times)

Key Words
Blessed, Glory (80 times), Body, Walk

Setting
Ephesus was a wealthy and leading port city on the west coast of the Roman province Asia (modern Turkey), renowned for the temple of Diana (Artemis). Paul had a significant and powerful time of ministry in Ephesus for nearly three years (Acts 19). Luke notes in Acts that Paul performed unusual miracles in Ephesus (19:11, 12), and *"the word of the Lord grew mightily and prevailed (19:20)."* So many had believed that idolatry was in danger of falling into disrepute (19:26, 27). The church in Ephesus became a missionary centre and was apparently for centuries one of the strongholds of Christianity in Asia. Ephesus was one of the seven churches to whom Jesus addressed His letters in Revelation 2 and 3.

Paul developed a healthy relationship with the Ephesians as we can clearly see in his farewell address to them (Acts 20:17-38).

While imprisoned in Rome, a mature Paul wrote his Letter to the Ephesians. By now Paul had much experience and revelation in the

DISCOVERING THE MOST AMAZING BOOK   335

purposes of God and the meaning of the new organism that had come into being. Paul wrote this letter to be an encyclical letter – one that should be read by several congregations – to make his revelation and wisdom, which he received from the Lord, known to the churches.

Purpose

We identify a twofold purpose in Ephesians: Firstly, Paul wrote Ephesians to unveil the "mystery" of the Church. He reveals God's vision and intended purpose for the Church in this letter: (a) to form a spiritual body of which Christ is the head to express Christ's fullness on the earth (1:15-23; also see Heb. 10:5-7); (b) by uniting one people – Jew and Gentile – in Christ; and (c) equipping and empowering this Body of people as the main "instrument" that will make the manifold wisdom of God known while manifesting throughout the earth what He has already accomplished in Christ (3:10-20). Secondly, Paul wrote Ephesians to make Christians aware of who they are in Christ, and to motivate and challenge them to live up to their heavenly calling while functioning as the Body of Christ on earth.

Synopsis

Paul leads his readers logically from an understanding of the origin of salvation to the purpose and practice of that salvation.

The Letter to the Ephesians divides naturally into two main sections:

1. The Christian's Position in Christ (chs. 1-3)

After a brief introduction (1:1-2), Paul immediately reveals our wonderful and privileged redemption in Christ. How we are chosen before the foundation of the world to be accepted in Christ, to be blessed with every spiritual blessing in the heavenly places, sealed and empowered by the Holy Spirit, set free from the bondage of sin, and brought near to God so that we *"are no longer strangers and foreigner, but fellow citizens with the saints and members of the household of God* (2:19)." We have received it all by grace through faith (2:8, 9). In Christ we have and are all.

In chapter 3 Paul reveals the mystery of the Church and God's intended purpose for her. In deep appreciation of this revelation from God, Paul challenges and prays for the Ephesians to live in an intimate faith relationship with Christ (3:14-21).

2. The Christian's Practice in Christ (chs. 4-6).

In this section Paul turns to the implications of being in the Body of Christ. He uses the word "walk" to refer to their conduct. Paul implores the Ephesians to walk worthy of the calling with which they were called, to be humble, gentle, loving, patient, understanding, and peaceful; Christ must be seen in them (4:1, 2). Paul insists on unity in the Body of Christ. Instead of concentrating on what divides them, they should focus on what unites them: there is only one body, one Spirit, one hope, one Lord, one faith, one baptism, and one God and Father (4:4-6).

Next, Paul reveals to the Ephesians how the saints will be equipped for the work of ministry and for the edification of the Body of Christ – Jesus gave gifts to men, some apostles, some prophets, some evangelists, some pastors and teachers. They are called, graced, and have the responsibility to equip the saints correctly (4:7-16).

Paul continues asking the Ephesians to live in the newness of life, which they have in Christ, and to lay down the wicked habits of the old life (4:17-32).

In chapter 5 Paul encourages the Ephesians to walk in love as Christ has loved them (5:2), to walk in the Light as children of the light (5:8), and, being filled with the Spirit of wisdom, to walk in wisdom (5:15-21). He, then shares about marriage as a mirror image of Christ's relationship to His Church (5:22-33).

In chapter 6 Paul asks children to obey their parents and parents to take gentle care of their children (6:1-4). Before Paul closes his letter he reminds the Church that, precisely because of her calling and purpose, she is in a spiritual battle. Although the victory is already won by Christ, the enemy is in a tactical battle against the Church, trying to frustrate her purpose. The wrestling is not against other human beings, but against evil spiritual forces. But, in Christ, the Church is well equipped with the full armour of God. The

Ephesians, and for that matter, all Christians should stand, in faith, with Christ in the victory that He accomplished.

Paul closes his letter, asking for prayer, informing them of Tychicus' visit, and blessing them in the authority of God the Father and the Lord Jesus Christ.

Noteworthy

Ephesians has been called the "Alps of the New Testament," "The Grand Canyon of Scripture," and "The Royal Capstone of the Epistles."

Ephesians unfolds the way by which God is bringing the Church to its destined purpose in Christ (to be a glorious Church): (1) She *sits* (is seated) with Christ in the heavenlies far above principalities and powers; (2) she *walks* in unity, love and wisdom; and (3) she *stands* strong in the power and the might of the Lord. Thus, fulfilling her purpose in the power of the Spirit.

Personal Application

Do you know who you are in Christ? Your definition is in Christ. Your position in Christ gives you a new identity, destiny, and purpose. According to Ephesians 1, in Christ you are:

- Blessed (1:3)
- Chosen (1:4)
- Blameless (1:4)
- Predestined (1:5)
- Adopted (1:5)
- Accepted (1:6)
- Redeemed (1:7)
- Forgiven (1:7)
- Enlightened (1:8, 9)
- Given an inheritance (1:11)
- Sealed (1:13)
- Assured (1:14)
- Seated with Christ in the heavenlies far above principalities and powers (1:20, 21)

You are part of the Body of Christ, which means Jesus wants to express Himself through you to the world.

Also, the Body of Christ is diverse but a unit, though you may disagree with others, in love make room for them, draw close to other Christians, and pray for all your brothers and sisters throughout the world. We need each other, and should support each other in love.

PHILIPPIANS

Author
The apostle Paul

Date
AD 61

Main Theme
Christian unity and Joy in Christ

Key Verse
"For we are the circumcision, who worship God in the Spirit, rejoice in Christ Jesus, and have no confidence in the flesh (3:3)."

Key Phrase
"that I may know Him"

Key Words
Joy (5 times), to rejoice (11 times)

Setting
The city of Philippi in Macedonia was named after its founder, the father of Alexander the Great, Philip of Macedon. Philippi was a leading city of its district, located on an important trade route, the Egnatian Way.

Paul founded the Philippian church during his second missionary journey about AD 51 (Acts 16:12-40). It was in Philippi that Paul made his first convert in Europe, where he cast out a spirit of divination from the slave girl, where he and Silas were flogged, imprisoned and miraculously released from prison, resulting from which the jailor and his household were saved. This church displayed a strong missionary zeal and was consistent in supporting Paul's ministry (4:15, 16; also see 2 Cor. 11:8, 9). As the content of this letter clearly reveals, Paul had a much closer relationship with the Philippians than with any other church.

During Paul's first Roman imprisonment, about AD 61, he wrote this warm, affectionate, and joyful letter, to the Philippian Christians who were near his heart. Epaphroditus brought a financial gift to Paul from the Philippian church. He had nearly lost his life on the journey. After he recovered (2:25-30; 4:18), Paul sent this letter back to the Philippians with him.

Purpose

Paul wrote this letter to the Philippian Christians to: (1) acknowledge the gift sent by them, (2) to appeal for a spirit of unity and steadfastness among them, and (3) to warn them against dangerous heresies that were threatening them, such as Judaism.

Synopsis

Philippians is Paul's letter of joy and encouragement in the face of tests and trials. Although Paul is in prison, he's full of the joy of the Lord. Throughout this letter there is an exuberant joy of faith, especially in eager expectation of the near return of the Lord (1:6, 10; 2:16; 3:20; 4:5). Philippians makes it evident that true joy does not depend on favourable circumstances. Christian joy, according to Paul, is independent on outward conditions, and is possible even in the midst of the hardest circumstances. The joy that Paul speaks of is only to be found in a personal relationship with the risen Christ, and being in active fellowship within the Body of Christ.

We divide Philippians into four parts based on the focus of each chapter:

1. Partnership in the Gospel (ch. 1)

After a brief greeting from him and Timothy, Paul expresses his thankfulness towards God for the Philippian Christians, and shares his confidence in God, who will complete the good work that He has begun in them (1:6).

In the first chapter, Paul refers not less than five times to the gospel. He speaks of the "fellowship of the gospel (1:5)," "the defence and confirmation of the gospel (1:7)," "the furtherance of the gospel (1:12)," "be worthy of the gospel (1:27)," and "striving together for the faith of the gospel (1:27)." In so doing Paul demonstrates that the Philippians were his partners in proclaiming the gospel, and that the gospel is communicated through people who, in the face of danger, have confidence in the gospel. In spite of being shackled because of the gospel, Paul's hope is unshaken. He declares: *"I know that this will turn out for my deliverance ... Christ will be magnified in my body, whether by life or by death. For to me, to live is Christ, and to die is gain (1:19, 20, 21)."*

2. Servants of the Great Servant (ch. 2)
Paul begins this chapter by calling the Philippians to unity through love and humility, and sharing their common life in Christ. Verses 5-11 are an outstanding passage in this letter, expressing the supreme obedience of Christ to the will of God the Father. Paul did not write this passage to explain the incarnation, but rather to illustrate the nature of Christ's humility, using it as an example to encourage the Philippians to humility and unselfishness. For he says to them, *"Let this mind [attitude] be in you which was in Christ Jesus (2:5)."*

Paul tells the Philippians that their salvation must be seen in genuine Christian living and upright character, living as lights in the world and holding fast to the word of life (2:12-16).

Next, Paul shares his desire to send his spiritual son, Timothy, a trustworthy man with a proven character, to them. Then, Paul mentions that Epaphroditus, *"my brother, fellow worker, and fellow soldier, but your messenger"* is *"longing for you all"* and *"for the work of Christ he came close to death (2:25, 26, 30)."* This passage gives us a description of the fellowship of servants.

3. The Ultimate Goal (ch. 3)
Chapter 3 verses 2-15 are another outstanding passage in this letter. Here Paul makes it crystal clear that, for him, all of life is summed up in Christ. Therefore, he announces: *"what things were gain to me, these I have counted as loss for Christ (3:7)."* Paul wants to gain Christ, his desire is to *"be found in Him,"* not by the self-righteousness

of the law, but by faith in Christ. Through this passage Paul proclaims his highest goal: to know Christ intimately and personally, no matter what. Knowing Christ implies knowing the power of His resurrection. As part of pursuing his goal, Paul says: *"but one thing I do, forgetting the things which are behind and reaching forward to those things which are ahead. I press toward the goal for the prize of the upward call of God in Christ Jesus* (3:13, 14)."

Philippi was a Roman colony. Many of the inhabitants were Roman citizens, most likely from the upper class. There was an intense pride in being a citizen of Rome (see Acts 16:20, 21). Some of these proud Roman citizens had become Christians. Were they been accused of belonging to a fellowship disloyal to Rome and the Emperor? Paul encourages them by declaring *"our citizenship is in heaven* (3:20)." They have a higher citizenship and much to look forward to.

4. The Uniqueness of the Christian Life (ch. 4).
With the eager hope of the coming of their Lord and Saviour, and that *"He is able to subdue all things to Himself,"* Paul requests the Philippians earnestly to stand united in the Lord for the sake of the gospel.

There are distinct qualities that mark the lives of Christians who know their Lord, and that their citizenship is in heaven, and who live in expectation of their coming Lord. Paul joyfully exhorts the Philippians: *"Rejoice in the Lord always. Again I will say rejoice!"* Paul calls the Philippians to rejoice in faith, and to let their gentleness be known to all people.

In verses 6 and 7 Paul gives the perfect antidote for anxiety: in faith, entrust yourself into the hands of your loving and all powerful God, then His peace will guard your heart and mind in Christ Jesus.

Paul asks the Philippians to discipline their minds, because their actions are affected by what they dwell on in their thoughts. He lists eight things on which they should meditate, which will inspire worship of God and service to others (4:9). He continues challenging them to practice what they have seen him doing, then they will find that it is not simply the peace of God, but the God of peace Himself who will be with them (4:10).

Paul rejoiced greatly for the financial gift that the Philippians sent him. However, whatever the circumstances, Paul had learned to be content (4:11-15). He makes it evident that Christ is the source of his strength. And Paul assures the Philippians that, because they have sent him an offering, God will certainly supply all of their need.

Then, Paul closes his letter with final greetings.

Noteworthy

This letter is written to the first church founded in Europe.

Because Paul is closely associated with the Philippian church, his letter to them is the first one in which he does not insist on his authority as apostle. He simply begins his letter: *"Paul and Timothy, bondservants of Jesus Christ."* (Paul's introductions in the letters to the Thessalonians are also without the title apostle.)

Philippians is one of Paul's most personal letters. The first personal pronoun "I" appears about one hundred times in this letter (not in a boastful way; because of his relationship with the Philippian church, Paul merely speaks freely of his tribulations and spiritual ambitions.) And Paul shares his own deep personal experiences with Christ, among other things, he says *"for me, to live is Christ, and to die is gain* (1:21)."

Ironically enough, Paul's imprisonment was a great encouragement to many and led to the spreading of the gospel even further afield.

Personal Application

Paul says: *"Beware of dogs, beware of evil workers ... (3:2)."* By implication Paul says beware of anything or anyone that would divert you from knowing Christ personally and experientially. (The "dogs" and the "evil workers" refer to the Judaizers that were a potential threat to the Philippians.)

For Paul, Christ is the sum and substance of life. To preach Christ was his consuming passion; to know Him intimately was his highest goal; and to suffer for Him was his greatest privilege. What about yourself?

Don't get too attached to earthly things; your citizenship is in heaven. And be content, while you fully trust in Jesus Christ as the source of your joy and strength.

COLOSSIANS

Author
The apostle Paul

Date
AD 60/61

Main Theme
The Pre-eminent Christ

Key Verses
"Beware lest anyone cheat you through philosophy and empty deceit, according to the tradition of men, according to the basic principles of the world, and not according to Christ. For in Him dwells the fullness of the Godhead bodily; and you are complete in Him, who is the head of all principality and power (2:8-10)."

Key Phrase
"Hope of glory"

Key Words
Fullness, Wisdom, Knowledge

Setting
Colosse was a small town in the Roman province of Asia, about 100 miles east of Ephesus. Paul had never visited Colosse (2:1). Although the Colossian church was an outgrowth of Paul's three-year ministry in Ephesus (Acts 19:10; 20:31), he didn't found the church. It was most likely established by Epaphras, a native of the town and convert of Paul while in Ephesus (1:7, 8; 4:12, 13).

The Colossian Christians were Phrygian Gentiles, whose religious background was apparently highly emotional and mystical. They were seeking to attain the fullness of God. When false teachers came among them with a philosophy that promised a mystic knowledge of God and spiritual fullness, they were drawn to it. The false teachings, known as the Colossian heresy, included rigorous self-denial (which actually centred on false humility), the worship of angels, abstinence from certain foods and drinks, and the observance of feasts and ceremonial days (2:16, 18, 20, 21). The Colossian heresy was apparently a mixture of Gnosticism, pagan occultism, Judaism, and Christianity.

By their false teachings the heretics had denied the deity, sovereignty, and supremacy of Christ.

Apparently Epaphras visited Paul and informed him about the false teachings that threatened the Colossian church. Thus, Paul wrote his letter to the Colossians to address the issue at hand during his first Roman imprisonment, about AD 61. And Tychicus took the letter to the Colossians.

Purpose

Paul wrote this letter to: (1) faithfully portray the pre-eminent Lord Jesus Christ, emphasizing His Deity, Glory, and Supremacy; (2) to expose and refute heresies; (3) to warn the Colossians against error and heresy, while instructing them in the truth; (4) to express personal interest in the Colossians; and (5) to inspire them to Christ-centred living.

Synopsis

Under the inspiration of the Holy Spirit Paul nullifies the heresies of the false teachers by emphasizing Christ's deity, His relationship with the Father, and His sacrificial death on the cross. He builds a water tight case for firm faith in Christ. And then he informs the Colossian Christians of the practical implications of their union with the pre-eminent Christ.

The Letter to the Colossians divides naturally into two, the first part is doctrinal and the second practical:

1. The Supremacy and Sufficiency of Christ (chs. 1-2)

After his brief greeting and blessing, Paul thanks God for the Colossians' faith and their love in the Spirit. And he prays that:

- They may be filled with the knowledge of God's will (1:9)
- God may give them spiritual wisdom and understanding (1:9)
- They may walk (live) worthy of the Lord, fully pleasing Him (1:10)
- They may be fruitful in their Christian service (1:10)

DISCOVERING THE MOST AMAZING BOOK — 345

- They may increase in the knowledge of God (1:10)
- They will be strengthened with all might with God's power for endurance and patience (1:11)
- They will be filled with joy and thankfulness for their awesome inheritance in Christ 1:12, 13).

This is an appropriate and significant prayer considering the circumstances in which the Colossians were at that time. We should pray the same today.

Paul moves on and begins his doctrinal declaration of the pre-eminence of Christ (1:15-23). He states that Christ is:

- *"The visible image of the invisible God* (1:15)"
- *"The firstborn over all creation* (1:15)"
- The Creator of all things, visible and invisible. "All things were created through Him and for Him (1:16)."
- The Sustainer of all things (1:17)
- *"The Head of the Church"* (1:18)
- *"The firstborn from the dead,"* supreme over all who rise from the dead (1:18)
- The Great Reconciler (1:19-22)

By His death on the cross, Christ reconciled us to God and made it possible for us to stand in the presence of God (1:22).

Paul then expresses his concern for the Colossian and Laodicean Christians who are threatened by false teachers. He encourages them: *"As you therefore have received Christ Jesus the Lord, so walk in Him, rooted and built up in Him and established in the faith, as you have been taught, abounding in it with thanksgiving (2:6, 7)."*

Paul explains to them how the philosophies of the world and the false teaching to which they were open, are totally empty when compared with Christ in Whom *"dwells all the fullness of the Godhead bodily (2:9)."* And he assures them: *"you are complete in Him, who is the head of all principality and power (2:10)."* Christ's sufficiency lies in His sovereignty. Paul continues, challenging the Colossians to reject false teachings and shallow answers, and to live in union with Christ (2:11-23).

2. The New Life in the Pre-eminent Christ (chs. 3-4)

In the second half of his letter, Paul particularly explains the implications of the Colossians' union with Christ – what the deity, death, and resurrection of Christ should mean to all Christians.

Paul instructs the Colossians to have a proper focus: Christ. As with all Christians, they should switch the focus of their minds to Christ and His reign; their minds should be filled with thoughts of heaven and Christ, then they will live Christ-centred lives (3:1-4). Somebody once said: "Where the mind leads, man follows." Sexual impurity and other worldly lusts should not even be named among them (3:5-8). They should live holy lives consistent with their new life and identity in Christ. Their lives should be marked by truth, love, and peace; their lives should reflect the new life which they have in Christ (3:9-15). Because He is their life. They should give the Word of God their undivided attention, and everything that they do should be God-honouring (3:16-17).

Now, Paul gives specific instruction for various members of the Christian household – wives, husbands, children, fathers, and slaves. He roots his instructions in Christ to emphasize the importance of Christ-like living (3:18-25). To live a life that centres on Christ and honours God, Paul says your motto should be: *"Whatever you do. Do it heartily, as to the Lord and not to men (3:23)."*

Paul encourages the Colossians to a lifestyle of prayer, since it is their communication with God, and to live wisely toward non-Christians, manifesting a Christ-like testimony (4:1-6).

The long list of greetings to a church that Paul did not establish is indicative that he wanted to strengthen his ties with the Colossians (4:7-14).

Noteworthy

Colossians is most probably the most Christ-centred Book in the Bible – Paul emphasizes the deity and supremacy of Christ and the completeness of salvation in Him. The focus of Colossians is the Christ of the Church.

Colossians and Ephesians share a great resemblance in language and subject matter. Over 70 of the 155 verses in Ephesians contain expressions echoed in Colossians.[36] While Ephesians portrays the "Church of Christ," Colossians portrays the "Christ of the Church."

Personal Application

In this humanistic postmodern world in which we live the deity and sovereignty of our Lord are constantly under attack. Your confession should be: "Jesus is Lord." And your lifestyle should confirm your confession.

While reading Colossians, especially the first two chapters, ask God for a fresh revelation of Christ, and what it should mean to you.

1 THESSALONIANS

Author
The apostle Paul

Date
AD 50

Main Theme
The Second Coming

Key Verse
"and to wait for His Son from heaven, whom He raised from the dead, even Jesus who delivers us from the wrath to come (1:10)."

Key Phrase
"The Day of the Lord"

Key Words
Coming, Faith, Hope

Setting
Thessalonica was the capital of the Roman Province of Macedonia, and was located on a natural harbour along the busy Egnatian Way, an important Roman route.

---

[36] Trevor L Grizzle, *Spirit Filled Life Bible: Colossians*, p. 1810

Paul established the church in Thessalonica (modern Salonika in Northern Greece) during his second missionary journey. This was the second church that Paul founded on the European Continent.

Because of the great stir that Paul caused in Thessalonica, he could not stay long enough to fully instruct the church. During his brief ministry in Athens, Paul was concerned for the infant church. So he sent Timothy back to Thessalonica to encourage the church (3:1, 2). Timothy brought back a good report. The Thessalonian Christians were thriving in their faith and were also concerned for Paul. During Paul's ministry and year-and-half stay in Corinth, he wrote 1 Thessalonians.

Purpose
Paul wrote First Thessalonians for the following reasons: (1) to commend the Thessalonian Christians for their faith and steadfastness; (2) to encourage them; (3) to defend himself against the charges of the enemies; (4) to strengthen the bonds between himself and the Thessalonian church; (5) to encourage them to moral purity, brotherly love, and diligent application to their daily work; (6) to offer consolation concerning their loved ones who had died in Christ; (7) to esteem and support their leaders; and (8) to be patient and helpful towards the varieties of human need.

Synopsis
Paul was blessed and filled with joy after hearing the good report of this young growing church. He took the opportunity to encourage them affectionately to persevere in their newfound faith in the face of persecution. He also gave them instructions on practical implications of faith and reminded them of their hope in the return of their Lord.

We divide First Thessalonians into two main section:

1. Thanksgiving and Comfort (chs. 1-3)
Paul opens his letter with greetings from himself and his associates – Silas and Timothy – who helped him to establish the Thessalonian church. He then expresses his thankfulness to God for the strong faith and good reputation of the Thessalonians (1:2-10). Paul uses three key words: faith, love, and hope, which formed a summary of Christian teaching in the early church (these words are used

elsewhere in Paul's letters). The Thessalonian church was an example to all of Macedonia and Achaia, of perseverance under persecution and of genuine Christian conduct (1:7).

This passage profiles an effective church:

- Persevering and energetic (v.3)
- Established by God's will (v. 4)
- Embracing the Full Gospel (v. 5)
- Receive the word with joy, while afflicted (v. 6)
- Exemplary in Christian conduct (v. 7)
- Evangelistic (v. 8)
- Not compromising, worshipping the living and true God (v. 9)
- Expectant (v. 10)

Next Paul reviews their relationship – how he and his associates brought the gospel to them (2:1-12). Here Paul mainly defends himself and his fellow labourers against the charges of their enemies. In so doing he actually profiles an effective ministry:

- In the face of persecution, preach the gospel courageously (v. 2)
- Preach with pure motives the true gospel (v. 3)
- Be a trustworthy minister, not seeking the praise of men, but the glorification of God (v. 4, 6)
- Avoid using flattery, and do not be greedy (v. 5)
- Do not be a burden (v. 6)
- Be gentle (v. 7)
- Minister with affection (v. 8)
- Labour in love (v. 9)
- Be devoted, just, and blameless (v. 10)
- Encourage, comfort, and urge in love (vv. 11, 12)

Then Paul shares how they, the Thessalonians, accepted the Word of God in faith (2:13-16), and how he eagerly longed to see them again (2:17-20).

Paul was deeply concerned for the young Christians in Thessalonica. For that reason he sent Timothy back to encourage them in their time of persecution (3:1-10; also see Acts 17:15; 18:1,

5). As we know now, Timothy returned with good news which gave rise to this letter.

This section ends with a prayer of Paul for the Thessalonians that they may increase and abound in love to one another and that God may establish their hearts blameless in holiness (3:11-13).

2. Instruction and Second Coming (chs. 4-5)

This section actually forms the main body of the letter, consisting of exhortation and comfort. Paul gives them instruction on living God-honouring lives by avoiding sexual immorality (4:1-8). We have to keep in mind that these young Gentile Christians were new to Christianity and not aware of the ethical code of Christianity. Furthermore, Paul challenges them to love each other, work for a living, and to live respectable lives in order to have a good testimony (4:11-12).

The Thessalonian Christians did not understand what happens to Christians who die. Here Paul comforts them by sharing the glorious hope of the resurrection of which Jesus' resurrection is the basis of all hope (4:13-18). Paul's main point is that those Christians who have "fallen asleep" (or died), their spiritual-souls will be with Jesus when He returns at His Second Coming (remember at the time of death, the body dies, but the spiritual-soul – the real you – goes to be with the Lord, 2 Cor. 5:1-8). In verses 16 and 17 Paul explains how it will take place. Jesus will descend from heaven with a "commanding shout, with the voice of an archangel, and with the trumpet of God." Then their dead bodies will be resurrected. Then, together with them (the resurrected bodies), those Christians who are still alive on the earth will be caught up to meet the Lord in the air, and at that moment the resurrected bodies will be reunited with the spiritual-souls, and so we will always be with the Lord.

In chapter 5 verses 1 to 11 Paul reassures the Thessalonians that they are aware of the day of the Lord (Second Coming) and that they are children of light, God's children, and God has not destined them for wrath, but for salvation. They don't need to worry unnecessarily. However, Paul reminds them to be prepared.

Then he gives them a long list of instructions from respecting leaders to community life and relationships (5:12-22). Paul closes his Letter with a blessing, a prayer request and a request to circulate the Letter.

Noteworthy
First Thessalonians is significant because: (1) it is one of Paul's earliest writings (most likely second to Galatians); (2) it gives us a clear picture of Paul's ministry and the life of an early church; and (3) it is the first letter that clearly speaks of the Second Coming.

Although 1 Thessalonians 4:13-18 specifically refers to the Second Coming of Jesus Christ, every chapter in this letter refers to it: 1:10; 2:19; 3:13; and 5:23.

Personal Application
Be greatly encouraged and rejoice in the reality of Jesus' return, resurrection, and eternal life.

2 THESSALONIANS

Author
The apostle Paul

Date
AD 50

Main Theme
The Second Coming of Christ

Key Verses
"Let no one deceive you by any means; for that Day will not come unless the falling away comes first, and the man of sin is revealed, the son of perdition, who opposes and exalts himself above all that is called God or that is worshipped, so that he sits as God in the temple of God, showing himself that he is God (2:3, 4)."

Key Phrase
"The Day of the Lord"

Key Word
Traditions

Setting
A few weeks after Paul wrote First Thessalonians, while he was still in Corinth, he received word from Thessalonica that a forged letter and a false verbal message (2:2), stating that they were now passing through the great Tribulation (because of the persecution they went through), and that the Day of the Lord had come, caused distress and confusion about the Day of the Lord. Some of the Thessalonians even quitted working because of the false teaching. Paul then wrote Second Thessalonians.

Purpose
To correct misunderstandings, to encourage the church, and to admonish the disorderly and idle to a quiet and orderly lifestyle.

Synopsis
In this letter Paul sets the minds of the Thessalonians at rest by revealing to them that certain events must first take place before the Day of the Lord will take place. In his first letter Paul taught that the Second Coming will be sudden, but in this letter he points out that "sudden" does not mean "immediate."

We divide this letter into three sections:

1. Encouragement in Persecution (1:1-12)
Again Paul begins his letter with a greeting from himself, Silas and Timothy, a blessing, and a statement of thanksgiving to God for the faith and love of the Thessalonians even while they are suffering persecution. For Paul, the fact that the Thessalonians are deepening in faith and love while they are enduring persecution is a clear sign that God is at work in their lives. He encourages them that one day the present situation will be reversed; they will be at rest while their persecutors, if they don't repent, will suffer tribulation with everlasting destruction (vv. 5-10). This shows us that not everybody on the earth will be saved. By reminding them that they are praying for them, Paul further encourages the Thessalonians (vv. 11, 12).

2. Explanation of the Day of the Lord (2:1-12)

In chapter 2 Paul answers the misunderstanding concerning the timing of the Day of the Lord, also known as the Second Coming of Jesus Christ. He tells the Thessalonians not to be quickly shaken or alarmed. Then Paul lists two specific events that must first occur before the Day of the Lord can take place:

- The falling away must come first – a great apostasy, and
- The man of sin must be revealed – refers to a man of eminent wickedness, the antichrist (2:3).

Then Paul refers to the antichrist and reminds them that when he was with them, he did tell them about these things. This is important for us to keep in mind when we interpret this passage. Paul merely refers to the antichrist and to that which restrains him, he does not explain it fully, because he expected that his readers, the Thessalonians, would already have known what it all entail (because he had given them instruction when he was with them). So, we should be careful not to be too dogmatic in our interpretation of this specific passage, particularly verses 6 and 7. (There are a variety of interpretations on this passage which do not really make any sense.)

However, what is important to know is that satan is the power behind the antichrist who empowers him to do mighty but deceptive wonders. Those who refuse to believe in God, and don't want to embrace the gospel, are those who will be perishing. Because by their own choosing they reject the truth, God sends them strong delusion so that they should believe the lie and be condemned (2:8-13).

3. Exhortation and Closing (2:13-3:18)

Now Paul reassures the Thessalonians that they are destined for glory (2:13-14), and calls on them to stand fast and hold the traditions which they were taught, whether by word or by letter (2:15). "Traditions" here refers to fixed Christian beliefs and practices which Paul taught them.

Next Paul prays for the Thessalonians to be divinely comforted and established in every good word and work (2:16-17). And then he requests the Thessalonians to pray for them that the Gospel will spread swiftly, and that the Lord will strengthen and protect them (3:1, 2). Again Paul reassures them concerning God's faithfulness and prays that the Lord will give them guidance.

Paul then strongly commands the Thessalonian Christians to discipline by not associating themselves with those who live disorderly lives and who are idle (3:6-15). There is no certainty concerning the reason for some of the Thessalonians being idle. Some suggest that they stopped working to await and proclaim the Lord's coming. While others believe the problem was merely one of lazy Christians who did not want to work.

Paul closes his letter with greetings and a benediction.

Noteworthy
Paul gave the Thessalonians a token whereby they may distinguish his letters from those of forgers – the salutation of Paul in his own hand (3:17). This appears also at the end of 1 Corinthians, Galatians, Colossians, and Philemon.

Personal Application
Although end time events are hard to interpret, and we cannot put a date to when the Second Coming will take place, the following is of real importance: you are destined for glory! Remain faithful to the Lord, live in expectancy, and tell others the Good News – eternal life is available in Christ Jesus.

Chapter Eleven

Paul's Letters to Individuals

The first three of these letters – 1 Timothy, 2 Timothy, and Titus – as we have mentioned, are referred to as Paul's Pastoral Letters. There is an affinity between these letters, especially 1 Timothy and Titus. These letters are written to two young apostolic representatives of Paul, who were sent out by Paul to churches that shared much the same problems. It seems as if there was a leadership vacuum, and for that reason concerns such as church order, leadership, and church conduct needed to be addressed. The instructions in these letters are still applicable today, especially to younger churches that deal with typically the same problems.

1 TIMOTHY

Author
The apostle Paul

Date
AD 64

Main Theme
Sound Advice to a Young Pastor

Key Verse
"but if I am delayed, I write so that you may know how you ought to conduct yourself in the house of God, which is the church of the living God, the pillar and ground of the truth (3:15)."

Key Phrase
"the pillar and ground of the truth"

Key Words
Godliness, Watchfulness, Strength, Commitment, Sound, Doctrine

Setting
Timothy was born in Lystra to a Greek father and a Jewish mother. He was brought up in the Old Covenant Scriptures (2 Tim. 3:14, 15), and was, apparently at age fifteen, converted during Paul's first missionary journey while Paul ministered at Lystra (Acts 14). Timothy had a clear calling of God on his life (1 Tim. 1:18). He joined Paul on his second missionary journey (Acts 16:3), and thus became an associate of the apostle, remaining with him ever after.

The aged and experienced Paul most likely wrote First Timothy during his fourth missionary journey (about AD 63-67), which is not recorded in the Book of Acts. While on this journey, Paul was not able to stay long at Ephesus, so he appointed Timothy to take charge of the church (1 Tim. 1:3). Afterward Paul writes to his much younger associate who was facing much responsibility at Ephesus.

Purpose
Paul wrote to the young Timothy mainly: (1) to encourage him in ministry, and (2) to give him detailed instructions for church organization, life, and ministry.

Synopsis
Timothy was a trustworthy man but not a forceful character. Paul, who appointed him to the pastorate at Ephesus, now writes, in effect, a challenge to Timothy to fulfil the task before him. In this letter Paul encourages him to combat false teaching with sound doctrine, develop spiritual leadership, teach apostolic faith, and encourage Christian conduct.

Because of its conversational style and personal tone, it is hard to break the Letter to Timothy down into proper sections. However we divide First Timothy into four sections dealing with specific topics:

1. The Need for Sound Doctrine (ch. 1)

In the opening of his letter we recognize Paul's relationship with Paul: "a true son in faith (1:2)." Paul was Timothy's spiritual father and pastor.

False teaching had been sown in the church. From what follows we gather that the false teaching came from legalists. Paul urges Timothy to deal with the false teachers and to make sure that only sound doctrine is taught. He then briefly enlightens Timothy about law versus grace and states *"that the law is not made for the righteous person, but for the lawless and insubordinate, for the ungodly and for sinners ... (1:9)."*

Paul then gives thanks to Jesus who has enabled and called him to proclaim the glorious gospel of grace (1:12-17). Subsequently Paul restates his charge to Timothy to take specific action against the false teachers and to hold on to his faith and good conscience (1:18-20).

Paul's instruction that Timothy should preserve genuine Christian faith by teaching sound doctrine and modelling right living, shows us that right teaching, rightly applied, will produce right results.

2. Public Worship (chs. 2)

After Paul denounced the false teachings, he turns to the importance of public prayer (2:1-7). He makes it clear that prayer for all people should be the first priority of any church. It should be the primary ministry of a local congregation. The local congregation should be a centre of prayer, a powerhouse from which effective intercessory prayer goes forth into the world (see Is. 56:7). Because people in authoritative positions have an influence on the quality of life, Paul specifically asks that the church should pray for those who are in civil authority.

Paul then, moves on to men and women in the church; he addresses particular concerns in regard to each gender. Perhaps the specific concerns regarding men were anger, doubt and not surrendering onto God (2:8). And concerning women the concerns were modesty and submission. Paul says that women who profess godliness should maintain a modest conduct; they should be dressed properly, not seductively. In view of the Creation, Adam being formed first, Paul indicates a priority of responsibility. The man is first in

358 CHARLES STEBBING

responsibility, therefore, he is the head of the family, and the wife is not to usurp his authority. On the other hand, the man in fulfilling his role, should not be a tyrant but a servant and subject to the will of God.

3. Church Leadership (ch. 3)
Paul's previous statements lead to a discussion of the qualifications of church leaders – elders and deacons (3:1-13). (The terms bishop, overseer, and elder are used interchangeably to refer to the same position.) He lists specific qualifications for each office.
Qualifications of the elder:

- Blameless (3:2)
- Husband of one wife, meaning faithful to his wife (3:2)
- Temperate (3:2)
- Sober-minded (3:2)
- Good behaviour (3:2)
- Hospitable (3:2)
- Able to teach (3:2)
- Not a drunkard (3:3)
- Not violent, but gentle (3:3)
- Not a lover of money (3:3)
- Not quarrelsome (3:3)
- Manage his own household well, care for God's church (3:3-4)
- Keeping his children submissive (3:4)
- Not a new convert (3:6)
- Good testimony among those outside the church (3:7)

Qualifications of deacons:

- Dignified (3:8)
- Not double-tongued (3:8)
- Not addicted to wine (3:8)
- Not greedy for dishonest gain (3:8)
- Clear conscience (3:9)
- Must be tested (3:10)
- Blameless (3:10)
- Husband of one wife (3:12)
- Managing children and household well (3:12)

DISCOVERING THE MOST AMAZING BOOK

Paul then shares the mystery of godliness:

- God was manifested in the flesh
- Justified in the Spirit
- Seen by angels
- Preached among the Gentiles
- Believed on in the world
- Received up in glory (3:16).

4. Spiritual Duties and Motives (chs. 4-6)

Paul returns to the challenge of false teaching, telling Timothy how to identify and respond to them (4:1-5). Paul insists that Timothy, by his teaching of sound doctrine and his godly lifestyle, can help the church to persevere in the face of heresies (4:6-16).

Now Paul gives practical advice on pastoral care as to how specific groups in the church should be taken care of – young and old (5:1-2), widows (5:3-16), elders (5:17-25), and slaves (6:1-2).

In the concluding section of the letter, Paul again confronts false teachers. All teaching is to be judged by its agreement with the words of our Lord Jesus Christ, says Paul. In contrast to the false teachers, Timothy is exhorted by Paul to guard his motives (6:3-10), to fight the good fight of faith, meaning to stand firm in his faith in the face of opposition and persecution (6:11-12), to be exemplary in the confession of his faith in Christ (6:13-14), and to help the rich people to have a proper Christian perspective on wealth (6:17-19).

In his brief closing, Paul reiterate Timothy's calling.

Noteworthy

The usage of the words "doctrine" and "sound doctrine" is striking in the Letter to Timothy (1:10; 4:1, 6, 13, 16; 5:17; 6:1, 3). False teaching was a constant threat for the early church as it is to the present-day church.

We find three, what Paul calls, "faithful sayings" in First Timothy (1:15; 3:1; 4:9). These faithful sayings were Christian household proverbs and expressions that they generally used in their meetings.

The phrase "man of God" is familiar in the Old Testament, but is only found twice in the New Testament, once in First Timothy (6:11), and once in Second Timothy (3:17). By using this term Paul confirms the authority of Timothy in contrast with the false teachers, who are not men of God.

Personal Application

Do you believe the Bible is the Authoritative Word of God? Do you uphold the teaching of sound doctrine, that is, the apostolic teaching that we find in the New Testament?

Do you pray frequently for those in civil authority? Paul says: *"For this is good and acceptable in the sight of God our Saviour* (2:3)."

If you are in leadership or desire to be, measure yourself against the qualifications that Paul gives for elders and deacons.

Right belief leads to right behaviour. By living a godly life and upholding Christian values, you can make a difference in the lives of others.

2 TIMOTHY

Author
The apostle Paul

Date
AD 67/68

Main Theme
Commitment to the Lord and Ministry

Key Verses
"Be diligent to present yourself approved to God, a worker who does not need to be ashamed, rightly dividing the word of truth (2:15)."

"All Scripture is given by inspiration of God, and is profitable for doctrine, for reproof, for correction, for instruction in righteousness, that the man of God may be complete, thoroughly equipped for every good work (3:16, 17)."

Key Phrase
"Not ashamed"

Key Words
Fight, Instruct

Setting
Paul wrote Second Timothy during his second Roman imprisonment which is not mentioned in the book of Acts. Paul's second imprisonment was completely different to his first one. He was confined to a dungeon, consequently he did not have the freedom he had during his first imprisonment, and he was lonely. Paul also knew that his death was near (4:6).

Purpose
This letter is seen as a "farewell letter" from Paul to Timothy in which we identify a twofold purpose: (1) to urge Timothy to stand firm in the face of hardship while living out his calling, and (2) to come as soon as possible to Rome for one final visit (1:4; 4:9, 11, 13, 21).

Synopsis
In Second Timothy, Paul writes as one who knows his days on earth are counted. Through this letter the mature and godly apostle seeks to both challenge and strengthen his faithful but somewhat timid associate in his difficult ministry in Ephesus.

Despite Paul's bleak circumstances – imprisoned, awaiting execution – this is a letter of encouragement that urges Timothy on to steadfastness in the fulfilment of his divinely appointed task.

We divide the Second Letter to Timothy into two main sections:

1. Perseverance in Present Hardships (chs. 1-2)
Paul opens this letter slightly different than his others. As a man who knows his end is near, reminds Timothy his apostleship is *"according to the promise of the life that is in Christ Jesus."*

After expressing his thankfulness to God as he does usually in his letters, Paul reminds Timothy *"to stir up the gift of God"* which is in him. *"For God has not given us a spirit of fear, but of power and of love and of a sound mind (1:7)."* Thus, Paul encourages Timothy, as a young minister, to the fullest use of his spiritual gift with boldness in the face of opposition. Paul continues, encouraging

Timothy not to be ashamed of the Gospel, and he uses himself as an example (1:8-12). (In those days of persecution, Christian leaders who remained faithful to Christ almost certainly would have been fiercely persecuted.) Next, Paul challenges Timothy to hold fast to sound doctrine in faith and love, and by the power of the indwelling Holy Spirit (1:13-14). And to be strong in grace while he prepares faithful men to follow him in ministry (2:1-2).

Paul illustrates Timothy's strenuous duties as a Christian minister by making use of three metaphors: a good soldier, an athlete competing according to the rules, and a hardworking farmer (2:3-6). In so doing he encourages Timothy to be disciplined and ready to endure hardship, while he remains faithful for the sake of Christ and those who need Him (2:7-13).

Paul asks Timothy to remind the congregation about the previous things he told him and to reject meaningless argument. He then challenges Timothy to rightly handle the Word of God, which will nullify the meaningless disputes of the false teachers (2:15). And to live a pure life by fleeing from youthful lusts and pursuing righteousness, faith, love, and peace with genuine Christians (2:22). Also to avoid foolish and ignorant disputes that will only cause strife.

Next Paul gives Timothy five characteristics of a servant of the Lord:

- Must not quarrel – share the truth in love
- Be gentle – compassionate and trustworthy
- Able to teach – the ability to make truth applicable
- Be patient when wronged
- Humbly correcting those who are in opposition, so that he could lead those who are in error to repentance (2:24-26).

2. Perseverance in Future Hardships (chs. 3-4)

Paul warns Timothy about perilous times that will be evident in the last days. The term "in the last days" refers to the coming of the Holy Spirit at Pentecost through to the Second Coming of Christ. That means the prediction of "perilous times" was beginning to be fulfilled even in the present situation of Timothy. These "perilous times" or "times of difficulty" will be marked by all kinds of self-centred and unnatural perversions of people. Paul says they have a form of

DISCOVERING THE MOST AMAZING BOOK 363

godliness but deny the power thereof. In other words, they have an outward pretence, but inward they are empty, because they deny the heart (power) of Christianity – the reality of the Risen Saviour, the truth of the Word, and the indwelling and overflowing power of the Holy Spirit. Turn away from such people says Paul, because they are led away by their lusts and resist the truth (3:1-9).

After focusing on the false teachers, Paul now addresses Timothy directly on how he should respond and resist the opponents while he remains faithful to sound doctrine (3:10-17). Paul reminds Timothy of his example how the Lord delivered him, and that everyone who desires to live a godly life will suffer persecution. Then he encourages Timothy to continue in the face of opposition from evil imposters, finding strength and power in the Scripture. Paul also reminds Timothy of the divine origin, power and sufficiency of Scripture (3:16, 17).

Then Paul gives Timothy a powerful charge: To preach the Word at every opportunity (4:1-4), and to be watchful, to endure afflictions, and to fulfil his ministry until the end (4:5).

Now Paul gives a moving farewell message. Somebody once said it is "the grandest utterance of the grandest mortal man who ever lived." Paul reflects on his life being poured out as a drink offering for the purpose of the cross. After a long and hard fight for faith, Paul could shout out in exultation: "mission accomplished!"

In his conclusion, Paul closes with some personal instructions to Timothy, giving God again all the glory, and greetings to dear fellow ministers.

Noteworthy
Second Timothy was the last letter written by Paul, and is of an intensely personal character, because it contains his last words to his beloved spiritual son.

Paul's instructions to Timothy (particularly as summed up in 2 Tim. 4:1-5) provide an appropriate summary of the essential conduct of a minister of the Gospel.

Central to everything in Second Timothy is the sure foundation of the Word of God.

Personal Application

As you read Second Timothy realize that you read the final words of the "greatest Christian" who ever lived. A man whom God used to write nearly two thirds of the New Testament. A man of unwavering faith, deep love for Jesus and His disciples, profound revelatory insight, intense zeal to proclaim the Gospel, and willing to die for the name of Jesus. Commit yourself to stand courageously for the truth, study and know the Word of God as your final authority against which you measure all things in life, and make yourself available as an instrument through whom the Holy Spirit can minister. Don't ever be ashamed of the Gospel, and don't quit in difficult times.

If you are a parent, remind yourself what a profound effect a Christian household can have on family members, friends, and neighbours. Timothy's godly grandmother and mother had a great influence on his life (1:5), which in turn helped to change the lives of many other people.

TITUS

Author
The apostle Paul

Date
AD 65

Main Theme
Sound Doctrine, Sound Church, Sound Conduct

Key Verses
"For the grace of God that brings salvation has appeared to all men, teaching us that, denying ungodliness and worldly lusts, we should live soberly, righteously, and godly in the present age, looking for the blessed hope and glorious appearing of our great God and Saviour Jesus Christ (2:11-13)."

Key Phrase
"Sound doctrine"

Key Words
Diligence, Commitment, Order

Setting
Titus was a Greek (Gal. 2:1-3), converted under Paul's ministry (1:4), and like Timothy, a younger associate of the apostle Paul.

During Paul's fourth missionary journey, soon after he had written First Timothy, Paul journeyed to the Island of Crete. Apparently Paul's visit was short, so he left Titus on Crete to set in order the things that are lacking in the churches and to appoint elders (1:5). (The church at Crete was not established by Paul, but probably by those who were at the great Pentecostal Feast, where the Holy Spirit was poured out, Acts 2:11. The content of the Letter indicates that the church was established long before Paul's visit mentioned in Titus 1:5. During his short visit Paul obviously identified specific concerns in the church, such as lack of leadership, sound doctrine, and order.)

Paul had great faith in the wisdom and abilities of Titus, because he already had entrusted delicate missions to him (see 2 Cor. 2:13; 7:6, 7; 8:6, 23).

Purpose
Not long after Paul's departure from Crete, he wrote this letter, possibly from Nicopolis (3:12), to encourage and assist Titus in his task of organizing the churches.

Synopsis
In this brief letter Paul emphasizes sound doctrine and warns against those who distort the truth. And he focuses on Titus' role and responsibility in the organization and supervision of the churches on the island of Crete. This letter serves as a conduct manual that emphasizes the inward discipline and outward duty of the Church.

We divide the Letter to Titus into three sections based on the emphasis of each chapter:

1. The Order of the Church (ch. 1)
The emphasis in this chapter is on church order, the elders' task.

After a longer than usual introduction, Paul instructs Titus concerning leadership in the church, showing, first of all, the nature

366 CHARLES STEBBING

of it (1:5-9), and then, the necessity for it (1:10-16). In so doing, Paul lists the qualifications for elders, basically the same as we find it in First Timothy, and contrasts faithful elders with false leaders and teachers, particularly those of Judaism.

2. The Sound Church (ch. 2)
In this chapter the emphasis is on sound doctrine that will lead to sound behaviour.

Here Paul, in contrast to false teachers, tells Titus how to instruct the various age groups in the church so that their lives will reflect godliness (2:1-6). He urges Titus to be exemplary in his conduct; to teach and lead by example (2:7-8), and that the lifestyle of the church must highlight the attractiveness of the gospel (2:9-10).

Next Paul gives the solid basis for the lifestyle he has described: the grace of God that saves and also instructs and empowers you to live such lives, while you are looking forward to *"the blessed hope and glorious appearing of our great God and Saviour Jesus Christ"* (2:11-13). The transformation of your life is rooted in what Jesus did on the cross for you (3:14).

Paul then encourages Titus to teach these things with courage and conviction (2:15).

3. The Practical Church (ch. 3)
In this chapter the emphasis is on the practical life of the church.

Paul discusses godly living and obligations of Christians towards civil authorities and all their fellow citizens outside the church, and asks Titus to remind the Cretans of these (3:1-2). He states two motives for proper conduct towards those who are outside the church: to remember their own worldly behaviour before their conversion, and to realize the love and kindness of God towards them (3:3-7). Paul then instructs Titus to avoid foolish disputes (particularly from false teachers), which are unprofitable and foolish, and to reject a divisive person (3:9-11).

Paul closes his letter to Titus with final instructions and greetings (3:12-15).

Noteworthy

This is the last letter that Paul wrote during his final days of freedom, because shortly afterward he was re-arrested and taken to Rome, this time to die.

The only time that Paul calls himself "a bondservant of God" is in this Letter (1:1).

Personal Application

As you read through the Letter to Titus, value godly leadership, sound doctrine, and Biblical church order.

If you are a leader choose to be an exemplary one who trains up men and women to lead and teach by example.

Remember: right doctrine, rightly applied, produces right results, which include right relationships. And a life that is transformed by Christ will lead into doing what is good for all, making the gospel attractive.

PHILEMON

Author

The apostle Paul

Date

AD 60-63

Main Theme

Brotherly love

Key Verse

"no longer as a slave but more than a slave – a beloved brother, especially to me but how much more to you, both in the flesh and in the Lord (v. 16)."

Key Phrase

"Beloved brother"

Key Words
Brother, Receive

Setting
Philemon was a wealthy Christian of Colosse, a convert and friend of Paul (vv. 4, 5, 19). The church of Colosse met in his house (v. 2).

Onesimus was one of his slaves, who had fled to Rome, apparently after damaging or stealing his master's property (vv. 11, 18). In some way he came in contact with Paul in Rome, and was converted (v. 10). Realizing the need for forgiveness and reconciliation, Paul sent him back to Philemon with this letter.

Purpose
Paul wrote this Letter to Philemon to appeal to him to lovingly embrace the fugitive slave – Onesimus – as a brother in Christ. He also expressed joy in Philemon's ministry and encouraged him to continue (vv. 4-7).

Synopsis
This brief letter of Paul is a perfect picture of Christian forgiveness. We find all the elements of forgiveness in Paul's letter (or as some said "postcard") to Philemon:

- The offense (vv. 11, 18)
- Compassion (v. 10)
- Intercession (v. 4, 10, 18, 19)
- Choice to forgive (v. 14)
- Forgiveness (v. 12, 15, 17)
- The need for substitution (vv. 18, 19)
- Restoration to favour (v. 15)
- Elevation to a new relationship (v. 16)

Noteworthy
Philemon is the shortest (only 334 words) of Paul's Letters. However, it is a revelation of Paul's godly character, we sense his warmth, friendship, love, humility, tactfulness, courtesy and unselfishness.

This letter gives us an illustration of the reforming influence of the Gospel on social life, and serves as an analogy of our redemption.

We were the runaway sinners, who, by the grace of God, were forgiven and reconciled with Him, and our reconciliation with God makes reconciliation with others possible. As Paul offered to pay the debts of Onesimus, so Christ paid our debt of sin.

Personal Application
During your life, as a Christian, in this fallen world, you will need to forgive many people who would seemingly not deserve it.
In Christ there are no dividing walls of racism, social and economic status – we are One in Him.

Walk in love and forgiveness, and be a tactful minister of reconciliation.

Philemon illustrates how love works:

- Thankful for the best in others (vv. 4, 7)
- Seeks the welfare of others (vv. 10)
- Deals honestly with others (v. 12)
- Bears the burdens of others (v. 18)
- Believes the best of others (v. 21)

Chapter Twelve

Survey of the General Letters

Now we will turn to the General Letters (also known as the Christian Hebrew Letters).

These letters are called general, mainly because they are addressed to the Church in general or to groups of churches, (except Second and Third John that are addressed to individuals). They are called Christian Hebrew Letters to distinguish them from the Gentile emphasis of Paul's Letters. Also, Paul's Letters are named according to their recipients, while the General Letters are designated by the name of their author.

HEBREWS

Author
Unknown. Some argue, based on internal evidence of the Letter, that the apostle Paul wrote it, while others reckon that perhaps Apollos or Barnabas wrote it. Maybe we should agree with, Origen, who remarked, "Who the author of this Letter is, God only knows."

Date
AD 67-69

Main Theme
The Right View of the Glory, Work, and Ministry of Christ

Key Verses
"Now this is the main point of the things we are saying: We have such a High Priest, who is seated at the right hand of the throne of the

DISCOVERING THE MOST AMAZING BOOK 371

Majesty in heavens ... He has obtained a more excellent ministry, inasmuch as He is also Mediator of a better covenant, which was establish on better promises (8:1, 6)."

Key Phrase
"Let us"

Key Words
Better, Faith, Perfect, Heavenly, Eternal

Setting
The recipients of this letter were Christians (3:1) who had come to faith through the testimony of eyewitnesses to Christ (2:3, 4). They had endured persecution and loss of their possessions for the sake of the Gospel (10:32-34), which tested their faith and patience. In addition, many expected the soon return of Christ, when it didn't happen, their faith receded, while others, in view of persecution, reverted back to Judaism, because followers of Judaism were not persecuted.

The repeated discussions on the superiority of Christ and His sacrifice over Moses and the Old Covenant sacrificial system indicate that the recipients were mainly Jewish (Hebrew) Christians in danger of drifting back into Judaism.

Purpose
This letter was written to encourage the Jewish Christians who were wavering in their faith, to warn them not to turn away from Christ, and to exhort them to break completely with Judaism. The writer to the Hebrews does this by explaining to them the absolute superiority of Christ in His Person and Work over all that for which the Old Covenant stands.

Synopsis
The Letter to the Hebrews is actually an extended explanation of selected Old Covenant passages that the writer uses to demonstrate the superiority of Christ's Person (1:1-4:13) and Ministry (4:14-18:18), and then the writer applies these revealed truths in a practical way to show the superiority of the Christian's walk of faith (10:19-13:25).

372 CHARLES STEBBING

We divide the Letter to the Hebrews into two main sections:

1. The Superiority of Jesus Christ in His Person and Ministry (1:1-10:18)

After touching on God's supreme revelation in Jesus Christ, as a summary view of his main subject (1:1-4), the writer demonstrates how Jesus is superior to the angels (1:5-2:18), and to Moses, the founder of the Old Covenant and powerful leader of Israel (3:1-19), and then he challenges the Jewish Christians to enter by faith into the rest provided for them – this rest is not a place or a day, but a Person (4:1-11). Then the writer to the Hebrews reminds them that *"the word of God is living and powerful, and sharper than any two-edged sword, piercing even to the division of soul and spirit, and of joints and marrow, and is a discerning of the thoughts and intents of the heart* (4:12)." The writer continues by demonstrating that Christ is superior to the priests of the Old Covenant, and explains the need for the new Priesthood and the greatness of the new High Priest, who has become a guarantee of a better covenant, and *"He is also able to save to the uttermost those who come to God through Him (7:25)."* Next, the writer contrasts the sanctuary of the Old Covenant with that of the New, he then shows why Christ's death was necessary, and demonstrates the greatness of His sacrifice which fulfils God's will and perfects those who believe in Him (8:1-10:18).

3. The Superiority of Faith (10:19-13:25)

Having established the superiority of Christ and Christianity, the writer to the Hebrews moves on to the practical implications, the life one should live when you follow the superior Christ. He exhorts his readers to hold on to their new faith, to consider, love and encourage each other, and to look forward to Christ's return (10:19-25). His readers are warned about the serious consequences of rejecting Christ's sacrifice (10:26-31) and reminded of the rewards for faithfulness. Therefore they should not cast away their confidence (faith), which has great reward – the just shall live by faith (10:32-39). Then the writer explains what faith is – it consists of persistent trust in God. To illustrate how to live by faith, he gives examples of men and women in the Old Covenant (known as the Hall of Faith), how their faith endured through trust in God. Their triumphs and

DISCOVERING THE MOST AMAZING BOOK

accomplishments should encourage his readers to lives of faith and perseverance (11:1-40). The writer continues, giving encouragement and exhortation for daily living (12:1-29) – to run with endurance the race of faith, to realize that God disciplines His children for the good because He loves them, to set an example of encouragement for others by pursuing peace without compromising holiness, and he cautions his readers against rejecting the grace of God.

In his final chapter the writer to the Hebrews states some specific points of godly conduct – brotherly love, remembering those who are persecuted, the sacredness of marriage, not to be carried away by strange doctrines, to praise God continually, and to obey and be submissive to leadership (13:1-17). After a request for prayer (13:18-19), he closes his letter with a benediction and greetings (13:20-25).

Noteworthy

The writer to the Hebrews builds his entire theme around the word "better," which is used in a series of comparisons to demonstrate that Jesus Christ is better in every aspect – He offers a better revelation, a better sacrifice, a better salvation, a better covenant, a better priesthood, a better sanctuary, a better position, and better power.

Parallel with his warnings, the writer uses exhortations that serve as encouragement to his readers to strengthen them in their walk of faith:

- Let us fear ... (4:1).
- Let us therefore be diligent to enter that rest ... (4:11).
- Let us hold fast our confession (4:14).
- Let us therefore come boldly ... (4:16).
- Let us go on to perfection ... (6:1)
- Let us draw near with a true heart in full assurance of faith ... (10:22).
- Let us hold fast the confession of our faith ... (10:23).
- Let us consider one another ... (10:24).
- Let us Let us lay aside every weight ... (12:1).
- Let us run with endurance ... (12:1).
- Let us have grace ... (12:28).
- Let us go forth to Him ... (13:13).
- Let us continually offer the sacrifice of praise to God ... (13:15).

Personal Application
Jesus Christ is superior to everyone and everything. He is the brightness of God's glory and the express image of God who upholds all things by the word of His power (1:3).

Put your trust in Him and fix your eyes on Him *"the author and finisher of our faith* (12:2)," while you run with endurance the race of faith. You can have victory in your trials if you don't give up. Whenever you go through a hard time, consider Jesus *"who endured such hostility from sinners against Himself, lest you become weary and discouraged in your souls* (12:3)."

Hebrews shows you how faith works:

- Faith has confidence in God's power and certainty in His promises (11:1)
- Faith responds to God's promises (11:8-22)
- Faith overcomes trials (11:29-38)
- Faith esteems Christ above all (11:26)
- Faith believes and understands that God is the Creator (11:3)

JAMES

Author
The apostle James, brother of Jesus

Date
Most likely between AD 45-49

Main Theme
Genuine Faith Leads to Righteous Living

Key Verse
"But be doers of the word, and not hearers only, deceiving yourselves (1:22)."

Key Phrase
"Working together"

Key Words
Faith (12), Works (13), Doer (5)

Setting
James addresses his letter *"to the twelve tribes which are scattered abroad (1:1)."* Thus, he most likely wrote to predominantly Jewish house churches outside Israel; scattered throughout the Mediterranean world. From the content of the letter, it seems that the experiences, spiritual state, and doctrinal misconceptions of the Jewish Christians in the Diaspora (Dispersion) led James to write this letter. The Jewish Christians suffered from various kinds of trials and persecutions, such as unjust treatment by the rich, poverty, and physical afflictions. Therefore, their spiritual state was low, and they had a wrong attitude towards God and His gifts; they indulged in unbridled speech; strife and factions were among them; and they had a worldly spirit. They also laboured under great doctrinal misconceptions. Many acted as if knowing the truth was sufficient and their lives did not display the practical application of truth.

Purpose
James wrote his letter to call his readers and the church to full commitment to God, to comfort and encourage them in their trials and tribulations, and to challenge them to engage in right living, while they have concern for each other. He emphasizes that genuine faith must be evidenced by good works (Christian service).

Synopsis
It seems as if James was a practical person; he practised what he preached. In his endeavour to comfort and encourage his fellow Jewish Christians he writes with sternness and severity, typically like an Old Testament prophet. Because of the variety of topics that he covers, which do not follow any fixed pattern, it is difficult to outline his letter.

However, we divide James into three main sections:

1. The Test of Faith (1:1-27)
After a brief introduction, James urges his readers to take a right attitude towards trials and temptations, then they will profit from them

376 CHARLES STEBBING

(1:2-18). And to receive the Word of God with meekness, then obey it. Hearing the Word without putting it into practise is self-deceptive, while hearing that results in right responding leads to godly conduct and ministry (1:19-27).

2. The Nature of Genuine Faith (2:1-3:12)

James forbids his readers to show partiality; it is incompatible with genuine faith in our Lord Jesus Christ, and empty religion betrays itself in relationships (2:1-13). The "royal law" is "love your neighbour as yourself."

Then James explains the relationship between faith and works (2:14-26). Here James does not intent to teach that works is the basis for salvation. No! He suggests that works is the result of faith (see the point under "Noteworthy" for further explanation).

James moves on and warns his readers against the sins of the tongue which *"is a little member and boasts great things. See how great a forest a little fire kindles ... With it we bless our God and Father, and with it we curse men, who have been made in the similitude of God (2:5, 9)."*

3. The Nature of Genuine Wisdom (3:13-5:20

Next James distinguishes between two kinds of wisdom – heavenly and earthly (3:13-18). According to James heavenly wisdom consists of: purity, peace-making, consideration of others, mercifulness, good fruit, impartiality, and sincerity and issues into a harvest of righteousness. While earthly wisdom consists of: envy, selfishness, and (wrong) ambition, and issues into disorder and every evil practise.

James continues telling his readers that pride promotes strife, but humility sets you free from worldliness (4:1-10). He also instructs them not to judge a brother wrongfully, and not to boast about tomorrow, but they should rather submit to the will of the Lord (4:11-17).

Now James turns to the rich and scold them for misusing and abusing the poor (5:1-6). He then encourages his readers to be patient with each other and persevering in suffering until the coming of the Lord (5:7-12).

James then gives sound advice to meet specific needs: those who suffer should take the initiative and pray; those who are ill should take the initiative and call the elders of the church to pray over them after they have anointed them with oil (5:13-15). The prayer of faith will heal the sick. *"The effective, fervent prayer of a righteous man avails much,"* declares James. He uses Elijah as an example to drive his point on the power of prayer home (5:16-18). Elijah, in spite of his greatness as a prophet, was subject to the same feelings and weaknesses they experience. However, he prayed earnestly and it didn't rain for three and a half years, then afterwards he prayed again and it began to rain (see 1 Kings 17 and 18).

In his conclusion James calls his readers to bring back those who are in error (5:19, 20).

Noteworthy

The Letter of James is most likely the oldest of the New Testament Letters, and the most Jewish in the New Testament; written by a Jew to Jewish Christians.

James is primarily practical and ethical, emphasizing duty rather than doctrine; it deals with the practical and social aspects of Christianity. Faith is both spiritual and practical.

Because of James' assertion in 2:24 that *"a man is justified by works, and not by faith only,"* some church leaders have felt that James contradicts Paul's teaching of justification by faith. A careful reading of Paul and James reveals that the contradiction is only apparent. Paul, no less than James, realized that genuine living faith will issue in works of love (Christian service) and obedience (Gal. 5:6); the proof that I am justified by faith will be seen in what I do. The difference between Paul and James lies in the fact that Paul attacks the problem of legalism, while James opposes libertines who felt that the quality of a Christian's conduct is irrelevant. For Paul, the question is how genuine faith lays hold of the finished work of Jesus Christ – the contrast is between faith and works. For James, on the other hand, the question is how you demonstrate that your faith is genuine – the contrast is between living faith and dead faith. Living faith is more than mere knowledge – it transforms lives and includes heartfelt trust that endures and obeys God. Dead faith does not accomplish anything.[37]

---

[37] *Nelson's Complete Book of Bible Maps & Charts*, p. 456

Personal Application

We all go through trials and temptations in life, however, the way in which we respond to these things are important. Victor Frankl, a psychologist who survived a Wold War II death camp, believed that the last of the freedoms humans have is the freedom to choose one's attitude in any given circumstances.

Genuine faith is living; it expresses itself through acts of love. (We are not saved by good works, but once we are saved, then we want to do good to others.)

Watch your mouth, and remember that words are powerful – they can either bless the hearer or cause harm.

Remember: earnest heartfelt prayers are effective.

1 Peter

Author
The apostle Peter

Date
Possibly between AD 62-64

Main Theme
Hope in the midst Sufferings

Key Verses
"In this you greatly rejoice, though now for a little while, if need be, you have been grieved by various trials, that the genuineness of your faith, being much more precious than gold that perishes, though it is tested by fire, may be found to praise, honour, and glory at the revelation of Jesus Christ, whom having not seen you love. Though now you do not see Him, yet believing, you rejoice with joy inexpressible and full of glory, receiving the end of your faith – the salvation of your souls (1:6-9)."

Key Phrase
"Full of glory"

DISCOVERING THE MOST AMAZING BOOK
379

Key Words
Hope, Suffering

Setting
The apostle Peter wrote this letter towards the end of his life most likely from Rome, symbolically referred to as "Babylon" in 5:13. And he addressed the Christians who were scattered throughout Asia Minor (modern Turkey) in the Roman provinces of Pontus, Galatia, Cappadocia, Asia, and Bithynia.

Purpose
Peter wrote this letter to comfort and encourage the Christians who were suffering for their faith, and to show them how to live out their redemption in a hostile world.

Synopsis
As a Christian with first-hand experience regarding persecution, Peter wrote this letter knowing and believing that faith in and loyalty to Jesus Christ are the only antidotes to suffering and persecution. Although there is no hint of martyrdoms, imprisonments, confiscations, or demands of emperor worship, the content of the letter indicates that hostility and suspicion were increasing against Christians in the Roman Empire. And they were being reviled and abused for their lifestyles and talk about another kingdom. The stage were being set for severe persecutions and martyrdom in the near future during Nero's brutal persecution against Christians (AD 64-67).

We divide First Peter into two main sections:

1. The Christian's Heavenly Inheritance (1:1-2:10)
After his introduction Peter comforts his readers by reminding them of their heavenly inheritance, and explains to them that trials refine their faith (1:1-7). They should believe in spite of their circumstances, because salvation in Christ has been revealed even to the Old Covenant prophets (1:8-12). For that reason, they should live holy lives – live like people who are separated from the world to live for God only – because they are redeemed by the precious blood of Jesus (1:13-21). They also should live Christ-like lives (1:22-2:3). Although they are rejected by people, they should realize and believe

that they are chosen by God to be a royal priesthood, a holy nation, His own special people to proclaim the praises of Him who called them out the darkness into His marvellous light (2:4-9).

2. The Christian's Conduct in the midst of Suffering (2:11-5:12)
Now Peter explains to his Christian readers, who are like exiles in a world that rejects their message, how they should live during difficult times (2:11-4:11). He encourages them to live lives in submission to God's will. In so doing they will glorify God (2:12), silence foolish people by doing good (2:15), win spouses to Christ by their examples (3:1), and puzzle former companions (4:4). Peter says patience in the midst of unjust suffering is *"commendable before God* (2:20)," and it is better to suffer for doing good than for doing evil (3:17). He then uses Christ as a model for unjust suffering; He is their example and hope in times of suffering. And he urges his readers to serve one another for God's glory (4:1-11). Peter then outlines the right attitude towards suffering:

- Expect it (4:12).
- Rejoice in it (4:13). Even as Christ suffered and then glorified, so they should anticipate the glory ahead (4:13-18).
- Remain faithful to God through it (4:19).

Next, Peter gives instructions to the elders to take good care of the flock of God, serving willingly and selflessly as overseers, because of their own eagerness to serve God; they should be examples to the congregation, and not use their position of leadership to domineer (5:1-4). He exhort the younger people to be submissive to leadership and to be careful of pride, because *"God resists the proud, but gives grace to the humble* (5:5)." Peter gives further instructions that they should cast their burdens upon the Lord because He cares for them; to be vigilant, to resist the devil, and to know that all Christians are experiencing suffering (5:6-9). By rightly responding to suffering they magnify the grace of God, and Peter writes that *"this is the true grace of God in which you stand* (5:12)." He exhorts his readers to live in this grace daily.

Peter closes his letter stating that Silas was his amanuensis (the one who wrote the letter while he dictated), and greetings.

Noteworthy

This letter of Peter is a glorious testimony of the transforming power of the grace of God. We see the result of being *"born again to a living hope through the resurrection of Jesus Christ from the dead (1:3)"* transformed Peter's life so that he became completely hopeful, loving, patient, and restful in Christ.

Although suffering, as the main theme, pervades this Letter, we do identify a counter-theme *"the true grace of God (5:12)."* Suffering should be "confronted" with the grace of God and should strengthen grace in the individual.

Personal Application

Although Christians are not exempt from suffering, in the midst of suffering Christians should be a redeeming force. Choose to live differently from the corrupt society around you, while you remain faithful to God.

When suffering, <u>cast</u> your burdens upon the Lord, because you are not design to carry those burdens; Jesus as your Saviour wants to take care of you by carrying your burdens.

2 PETER

Author

The apostle Peter

Date

AD 65-67

Main Theme

Remaining Loyal and Pure in the midst of Corruption and Apostasy

Key Verse

"Grace and peace be multiplied to you in the knowledge of God and of Jesus our Lord, as His divine power has given to us all things that pertain to life and godliness, through the knowledge of Him who called us by glory and virtue, by which have been given to us

exceedingly great and precious promises that through these you may be partakers of the divine nature, having escaped the corruption that is in the world through lust (1:2-4)."

Key Phrase
"Knowledge of the Lord"

Key Words
Remembrance, Know, Knowledge,

Setting
This second letter of Peter was written during the time that Nero persecuted Christians, and if Peter was martyred in that persecution then he wrote it shortly before his death.

Purpose
Peter wrote his second letter to warn Christians against false teachers and to encourage them to grow in the grace and knowledge of Jesus Christ.

Synopsis
While First Peter encourages Christians to respond properly to external opposition, Second Peter focuses on internal opposition (in the church) caused by false teachers whose *"destructive heresies (2:1)"* can seduce Christians into error and immortality.

We divide Second Peter into three main sections:

1. The Grace and Origin of True Knowledge (1:1-21)
After a brief greeting to all Christians, Peter emphasizes that God's grace in Christ is the source of godly living and fruitfulness (1:1-11). He lists 9 qualities that belong to the Christian because of being a partaker in the divine nature. Peter continues and reveals to his readers that his end is near (1:12-15), and emphasizes that the prophetic word is trustworthy, because of its divine origin (1:16-21).

2. The Dangers of False Doctrine (2:1-22)
In his second chapter Peter warns against destructive doctrines, the doom of false teachers, their depravity and deceptions. He informs his readers that false teachers will become prevalent in the last days, they will use deceptive words to take advantage of Christians, and they will be boastful and will be despise the things of God, but they will utterly perish in their own corruption.

3. The Certainty of the Day of the Lord (3:1-18)
In the last chapter Peter warns against false teachers that will come in the last days to ridicule the prophetic promise of the Second Coming of Christ. He explains why this hope is yet unfulfilled: *"The Lord ... is longsuffering toward us, not willing that any should perish but that all should come to repentance* (3:9)." Peter assures his readers that the promise of the Lord's return will be fulfilled, and encourages them to be steadfast in living godly lives.

Noteworthy
2 Peter 1:19 to 21 agrees with 2 Timothy 2:15 and 3:16, and emphasizes that the written Word of the Old Covenant originates in God, and thus, it is authoritative and the accepted standard of faith, and doctrine.

"Knowledge" in Second Peter is much more than intellectual knowledge; it's experiential knowledge, knowing God and Christ by experience. The basis for that knowledge is Scripture, called the "prophetic word (1:19-21)" and the apostolic teaching (3:1, 2, 15, 16).

2 Peter chapter 2 is almost identical to Jude verses 4 to 18.

Personal Application
Second Peter provides a response to false teaching in our day of manmade philosophies, speculations, and typical "half-truths" that do not line up with true knowledge as we find it in the Bible.

Be careful of corrupt teaching because it produces corrupt practices; in love correct those who distort the truth.

A little knowledge could be dangerous; the best antidote for error is a mature understanding of true knowledge.

Know and believe that you are a partaker of the divine nature; remind yourself of this truth continually.

1 JOHN

Author
The apostle John

Date
About AD 90

Main Theme
A life of fellowship with God is joyful, victorious, guarded, and assures eternal life.

Key Verses
"If we say that we have fellowship with Him, and walk in darkness, we lie and do not practice the truth. But if we walk in the light as He is in the light, we have fellowship with one another, and the blood of Jesus Christ His Son cleanses us from all sin (1:6, 7)."

Key Phrases
"From the beginning," emphasizing that his readers should already be familiar with what he shares with them.

"We know," signifying the certainty that is achieved through experience.

Key Words
Love, Know, Life, Light, Fellowship

Setting
John wrote this letter apparently from Ephesus after error had crept in among the churches in Asia. These churches would have included: Ephesus, Smyrna, Thyatira, Pergamum, Sardis, Philadelphia, Laodicea, and Colosse. So this Letter was meant to be a circular letter. The false teaching in those days was a forerunner of the second-century Gnosticism that denied the incarnation of Christ (see Addendum for explanation).

Purpose

We identify five main reasons why John wrote this letter: (1) *"that your joy may be full (1:4);"* (2) *"that you may not sin (2:1);"* to expose and warn them against error (2:26); (4) that they will know the true character of worldliness and error; and (5) that they will know the true God and have full assurance of salvation (5:13). By writing this letter John addresses the doctrinal and practical needs of his readers, and reassures his readers in their faith.

Synopsis

The apostle John, now advanced in years and experience, wrote this fatherly letter out of loving concern for his "children." Their steadfastness in the truth was being threatened by the seduction of worldliness and the craftiness of false teachers. In a simple yet profound way, John presents God as light, as love, and as life, and explains what it means to have fellowship with Him.

We divide First John into two main sections:

1. The Basis of Christian Fellowship (1:1-2:27)

John begins his letter as an eyewitness, emphasizing the deity and incarnation of Christ, and stating his desire for his readers to experience fullness of joy (1:1-4). He then presents God as light, symbolizing absolute purity and holiness (1:5). Since John's desire for his readers is to have fullness of joy, he points out to them that it is a result of walking in the light; having your sins forgiven and fellowshipping with the Father and the Son and fellow Christians. However, if they do sin, Christ is their Advocate (2:1-2). *"He Himself is our propitiation for our sins."* Propitiation simply means that God is satisfied that the penalty for sin was paid by Jesus Christ. For that reason, if anyone sins grace and forgiveness are available in Christ.

John continues, challenging his readers to remain faithful to Christ, because it is the mark of someone who loves and knows Christ. And he urges them to love one another as everyone who walks in the light ought to do (2:3-17). He also commands his readers not to love the world or the things of the world. The word "world" does not refer to the physical creation, but to the sphere of evil operating in the world in which we live under the dominion of satan.

386   CHARLES STEBBING

Following his warning against the world, John now warns his readers against the coming of the antichrist and the spirit of the antichrist, which is already manifesting through the false teachers who deny Christ (2:18-27). Nevertheless, John encourages his readers by telling them that two things will protect them from falling victim to the seductive teachings of the heretics: (1) abide in the Truth (Christ is the personification of truth, they should remain faithful in their walk with Him), and (2) the anointing (illumination and empowerment) of the Holy Spirit will enable them to distinguish truth from error (2:24-29).

2. The Life of Christian Fellowship (3:1-5:21)

Now, John declares that God is love (3:1-4:21), and He loves us as His own children. That is one of the reasons why the world does not understand us; it does not have God and does not share in our experience. John then explains that those who are children of God do not practice sin, but rather righteousness (3:4-9). Coming from the same God, love and righteousness walk hand in hand.

Continuing with his theme of love, John uses the example of Christ to illustrate what love is: love is practiced in self-sacrifice, not mere profession. Possessing love and expressing that love towards others is a clear evidence that one is a Christian (3:10-23). Also, the indwelling Holy Spirit, manifesting His presence outwardly through the life and conduct of his readers is further evidence that they belong to God.

Again, John warns against false teachers, which include false prophets, and asks his readers not to *"believe every spirit, but test the spirits, whether they are of God* (4:1)." He then gives some of the marks of these false prophets: (1) they deny the incarnation of Christ; (2) they are worldly (sinful) and promote the things of the world; and (3) those who are like them, will listen to their heresies. But, children of God confess their faith in Christ and are submitted to His sovereignty.

Again, John emphasizes love as a test of the Christian life (4:7-21). Here he insists that God is the source of love – love is not a feeling but a Person. Those who do not know God (the unsaved), has a wrong view of love, and turns these words around "love is god." God made His love personally known to us by sending His Son into the world so that we might receive God's love through

Him. Christians show that they are belonging to God by manifesting sacrificial attitudes and actions in love. And the Holy Spirit gives them the power to love. John says love for God must express itself in love for fellow Christians. He also gives his readers the best antidote for fear: the perfect love of God.

In chapter 5:1-5 John shows how faith, love, and obedience are interrelated. Whoever believes in Christ will love God and his fellow Christian, and thus be obedient to God. It reminds us of what Paul teaches in Galatians 5:6, *"faith working through love."* Faith is the root, love is the fruit. John continues and says faith in Christ brings victory over the world.

In the last part of John's letter, he presents God as life (5:6-21). He first underscores the basis for his authoritative teaching by explaining that Jesus is really the Son of God – he based his teaching on the witness of God (5:9), and his own testimony. Because in those days there was a false teaching in circulation that Jesus was merely human until He was baptized, at which time "the Christ" then descended upon Him, but later left Him before His death on the cross. In other words, false teachers denied the deity of Jesus. John moves on and makes it clear that God's life, that is, eternal life is in His Son. *"He who has the Son has life; he who does not have the Son of God does not have life (5:12)."*

John also reminds his readers to have confidence in prayer: when they ask according to God's will, He hears them (5:14).

In his conclusion John emphasizes that his readers should know Him who is true, and reject the false. He ends his Letter with a declaration that Jesus the Son of God is *"the true God and eternal life (5:20)."*

Noteworthy

Because they are from the same author, there are obvious similarities between the Gospel of John and First John. Furthermore, the Gospel was written that people may believe (20:31); the Letter was written to those who had believed (5:13). The Gospel was written to show the way to eternal life; the Letter was written to assure those who had believe that they have eternal life (5:11, 12).

John is also known as the Apostle of love. In this Letter he reveals the nature and significance of love to his readers:

- God is love (4:8, 16).
- Love comes from God (4:7).
- Everyone who loves has been born of God and knows God (4:7).
- We ought to love one another (4:11)
- If we love one another, God lives in us (4:12).
- We should love one another (3:11).
- Anyone who does not love his brother is not a child of God (3:10).
- We know that we have passed from death to life, because we love our brothers and sisters (3:15).
- Whoever lives in love lives in God (4:16).
- Perfect love drives out fear (4:18).
- We love Him because He first loved us (4:19).
- If anyone says, "I love God," yet hates his brother, he is a liar (4:20).
- For anyone who does not love his brother, whom he has seen, cannot love God, whom he has not seen (4:20).

One of the keywords that John uses to underscore the assurance of salvation and eternal life is "know:"

- *"We know that we know Him, if we keep His commandments (2:3)."*
- *"We know that we are in Him (2:5)."*
- *"We know that when He is revealed, we shall be like Him (3:2)."*
- *"We know that we have passed from death to life, because we love the brethren (3:14).*
- *"We know that we are of the truth (3:19)."*
- *"We know that He abides in us (3:24)."*
- *"We know that we abide in Him (4:13)."*
- *"These things I have written to you who believe in the name of the Son of God, that you may know that you have eternal life (5:13)."*
- *"We know that He [God] hears us (5:15)."*
- *"We know that we are of God (5:19)."*
- *"We know that the Son of God has come and has given us and understanding, that we may know Him who is true (5:20)."*

Personal Application

Know and believe that you are truly loved by God. Also, God and salvation are great realities in your life as a result of your faith in Jesus Christ.

Walk in the light, love, and life of God, while you share it with those who are in need of it.

Don't love the world or the things in the world. Look at the following chart which illustrates three aspects of temptation. Both Adam and Jesus were tempted in the same way that we are tempted today.

Temptation: Contrasted		
Genesis 3:6 - Adam	**Luke 4:1-13 - Jesus**	**1 John 2:16 - Us**
"the tree was good for food"	*"command this stone to become bread"*	*"the lust of the flesh"*
"it was pleasant to the eyes"	*"the devil ... showed Him all the kingdoms"*	*"the lust of the eyes"*
"a tree desirable to make one wise"	*"throw yourself down from here"*	*"the pride of life"*

2 JOHN

Author
The apostle John

Date
About AD 90

Main Theme
Christian Faithfulness

Key Verses
"And now I plead with you, lady, not as though I wrote a new commandment to you, but that which we have had from the beginning:

that we love one another. This is love, that we walk according to His commandment, that as you have heard from the beginning, you should walk in it (vv. 5, 6)."

Key Phrase
"That we love one another"

Key Words
Love, Truth

Setting
In this letter John is concerned with the abuse of Christian hospitality extended to itinerant ministers, and to commend her for walking in the truth. False teachers, most likely from the same group that John referred to in his First Letter, were abusing the charity of a certain lady.

Purpose
John wrote this letter to a generous and influential lady to warn her against entertaining some false teachers. (Some scholars suggest that the address should be taken literally to a specific influential woman and her children, while others prefer to take it as a figurative description of a local church, whose members are her "children".) Genuine Christian ministers, who could be recognized by their sound teaching (v. 10), are worthy of support; but false teachers, those who denied the Incarnation (v. 7), are to be rejected, because they could bring harm to the church.

Synopsis
The apostle John had seen Truth and Love first-hand – he had been with Jesus. He was so affected by Truth and Love that all of his writings are filled with it.

In this letter, John encourages his readers to love truthfully, because *"truth abides in us and will be with us forever (v. 2)."* This shows us that faith in Christ should be shared, it is not only a personal conviction.

John insists that Truth is the basis, nature and test of all fellowship. When you walk in Truth, then you will inevitably walk in love, which will spontaneously result in obedience – truth and love are expressed through obedience (as we have seen before, these three are inseparable). For this reason John says to his readers to live in the truth, love one another and obey God (vv. 4-6), while watching out for deceivers (verse 7), and they should abide in the doctrine of Christ (v. 9). John also says that giving hospitality to the false teachers will encourage them to continue in their evil work (vv.10, 11).

John concludes his letter with an affectionate ending.

Noteworthy
Second John is the only letter exclusively addressed to a lady. Tradition suggests that the lady was Martha of Bethany.

Personal Application
Again, love Truth, your fellow Christians and God. Be a Christian who is *"walking in the truth, and abides in the doctrine of Christ."*

3 JOHN

Author
The apostle John

Date
About AD 90

Main Theme
The Duty of Hospitality towards Genuine Christian Ministers and the Danger of Domineering Leadership

Key Verse
"Beloved, do not imitate what is evil, but what is good. He who does good is of God, but he who does evil has not seen God (v. 11)."

Key Phrase
"Walk in truth"

Key Words
Love, Truth

Setting
In John's day Christian ministers travelled from town to town, helping to establish new congregations and encouraging existing congregations. They depended on the hospitality of fellow Christians such as Gaius. (In Second John itinerant false teachers disturbed local churches, in this letter genuine teachers of truth are travelling from church to church.)

Purpose
John wrote this letter to Gaius to commend him for his hospitality and to encourage him in his Christian life.

Synopsis
John begins his letter with heartfelt affection, a prayer for physical health, and commending Gaius for his exemplary walk in the truth (vv. 1-3).

The content of this short letter centres on three men: (1) **Gaius**, the example of one who follows Christ and loves others (vv. 1-8). John praises Gaius for his support of the itinerant ministers and encourages him to continue in hospitality, and walking in the truth. (2) **Diotrephes**, the self-proclaimed, and arrogant church official who does not reflect God's values (vv. 9-11). He was a domineering character, inhospitable, and back-biter, who did not want to acknowledge the authority of John. (3) **Demetrius**, who was praised by all for his good testimony as a follower of the truth (vv. 12).

Throughout this letter John emphasizes aspects of church life such as: enjoying and continuing to have fellowship, in truth and love, with fellow Christians, especially full-time Christian workers; the necessity of church discipline to promote healthy ministry; and integrity of faith is reflected through actions.

Noteworthy
In both Second and Third John, the author identifies himself as the "Elder," most likely suggesting that he is older both in years and experience.

As in Second John, we again see that Truth is the source and nature of love (v. 1), an inward presence and power (v. 3), that manifests itself in outward practice (vv. 3, 4). Exactly because Truth is a Person – Jesus says: *"I am ... the truth ... (John 14:6)."* (For that reason you can be certain that He does love you truly.)

In this letter we identify the beginning of arrogant and domineering church leadership, which is an "evil" that frequently surfaces in the Church.

Personal Application
The church is a family united by bonds of love with its members extending gracious hospitality to one another. There is no room for selfish ambition and factious jealousy in the fellowship of the church.

While you maintain a loving relationship with everybody, guard against selfish ambitions and attitudes.

JUDE

Author
Jude, the half-brother of Jesus

Date
AD 75-80

Main Theme
Keep the Faith and Oppose Heresy

Key Verse
"Beloved, while I was very diligent to write to you concerning our common salvation, I found it necessary to write to you exhorting you to contend earnestly for the faith which was once for all delivered to the saints (v. 3)."

Key Phrase
"Contend earnestly for the faith"

Key Word
Keep

Setting
As we have seen through other letters, the early Church was constantly threatened by false teaching. False teachers have gained entry to the church and were perverting the one true faith and the morals of the church with their false teaching.

Purpose
Jude wrote this letter to urgently warn Christians against the false teachers and calls the church to defend the truth aggressively against this infiltration.

Synopsis
Strikingly this letter begins and ends with tender affection and affirmation of God's gracious action on behalf of Christians, emphasizing divine preservation (vv. 1-3, 17-25). However, when Jude speaks of the false teachers and their heresies, he uses strong language to denounce them.

Through the content of Jude's letter the message is loud and clear: Although opposition would come and false teachers would arise, Christians everywhere should *"contend earnestly for the faith* (v. 3)" by rejecting all falsehood and immorality (vv. 4-19), remembering God's mighty acts of rescue and even punishment (vv. 5-11, 14-16), and the warnings of the apostles. Jude encourages his readers to build themselves up on their most holy faith by praying in the Spirit (v. 20), to keep themselves in the love of God and close to Christ (v. 21), to help others (vv. 21-22), and to hate sin (v. 23).

Jude concludes with a glorious benediction of praise to God (vv. 24-25).

Noteworthy
It appears that Jude was about to write a letter concerning salvation, when the Holy Spirit moved him to write this Letter (v. 3).

The letter of Jude gives us a history of apostasy from before time to the end of time, dealing with the ambitious angels, self-righteous

Cain, depraved Sodomites, rebellious Israel, greedy Balaam, presumptuous Korah, and the apostasy of his day and ours.[238]

It is only in the letter of Jude that we have a reference to the strife for the body of Moses (v. 9), and Enoch's prophecy (vv. 14, 15). (Concerning the body of Moses – this story has been lost to history. However, Deuteronomy 34:5 and 6 indicate that Moses' burial was divinely arranged.)

Personal Application
In our day false teaching abounds. Guard yourself with sound doctrine against false teachings, live in the love of God, and defend the true faith, while you build yourself up on your most holy faith praying in the Holy Spirit, relying on the mercy of Jesus, and showing mercy to everyone, even your opponents.

---

[38] Robert Lee, *The Outlined Bible*

Chapter Thirteen

Survey of Revelation

The Prophetic Book of the New Testament
The Book of Revelation refers to itself as a prophetic book (1:3; 22:7, 10, 18, 19).

REVELATION

Author
The apostle John

Date
AD 85-90

Main Theme
The Sovereign Kingship of the Lord God Almighty

Key Verse
"Write the things which you have seen, and the things which are, and the things which will take place after this (1:19)."

Key Phrase
"The revelation of Jesus Christ"

Key Words
Throne, Lamb, Seven (52 times)

Setting
Evidence within the Book of Revelation indicates that it was written during a period of persecution of Christians (1:9; 2:10, 13; 3:10), probably during the reign of Emperor Domitian (AD 81-96). John had been exiled to the island of Patmos where he had a vision of the glorified Christ and what would take place in the future.

Purpose
The Holy Spirit Himself declares the purpose of the book to be: *"to show His servants – things which must shortly take place (1:1)."* "Shortly" does not necessarily mean that the fulfilment will actually begin at once, but merely that the readers should expect it to begin to happen at any time in the future.

Involved in the general purpose are immediate aims such as to encourage the seven churches that were experiencing tremendous pressure from Roman culture, particularly emperor worship, and to warn them against careless living (and beyond them the whole Church); also to reveal the full identity of Jesus Christ, to give the Church hope, and to establish God's people in the belief of the ultimate triumph of Christ and His cause.

Synopsis
This book is *"The Revelation of Jesus Christ* (1:1)," and not Revelation**s**, or the revelation of John. The word "Revelation" is a translation of the Greek word *apokalypsis,* which means disclosure or unveiling of unseen realities. This Revelation came from God through Jesus Christ – unveiling God's redemptive purposes through His Son, Jesus Christ.

The type of literature to which Revelation belongs is known as "apocalyptic." Apocalyptic literature was usually produced during times of persecution and oppression as a means of encouraging those who were suffering for their faith. In this kind of writing the predictive (prophetic-revelation) element is prominent, symbolism is used extensively, and the visions become the vehicle of the message. The symbols are usually left unexplained; this makes it hard to interpret the message of the book. The Book of Revelation is related to the same type of prophecies that we find in Daniel, Ezekiel, and Zechariah. The prophecy of Revelation is not to be sealed up (22:10) because it is relevant to Christians of all ages.

Because of the rich symbolism and being hard to interpret, we have different views on this book, especially the visions of chapters 6:1-18:24. The following chart is a summary of the four most common approaches to the interpretation of Revelation:

Interpretive Approach	Basic View
Preterist (from the Latin term for "past")	All the events of Revelation were fulfilled during the period of the Roman Empire.
Idealist	Revelation is not a representation of actual events, but is rather a symbolic depiction of the spiritual warfare between good and evil.
Historical	Revelation is a panoramic outline of Church history from the apostolic era until the consummation.
Futurist	Beginning with chapter 4, Revelation describes future events that will occur at the end of the age.

Revelation 1:19 gives us the three-fold division of the book:

1. *"the things which you have seen"* (ch. 1). Main focus: The Glorious Christ
Here John explains to his readers how he received this revelation from God, and pronounces a blessing on those who read and hear the words of the prophetic revelation that he is about to share with them. He greets the seven churches in Asia and assures them of the love of Jesus Christ for them, who has paid the ultimate price for their redemption. John then reveals to them the glowing and glorious vision he had of the King of kings.

2. *"the things which are"* (chs. 2 &3). Main focus: The Church
In chapters 2 and 3 John records specific messages from the Lord Jesus to the seven churches in Asia. We may ask, why only these seven churches? Perhaps John was only acquainted with these seven. On the other hand, since the number seven means completeness, it appears that, by identifying only seven churches,

Jesus wants to suggest that the messages are intended for all churches, wherever they may be located.

The seven churches of Revelation were located on a major Roman postal route and are listed in the order in which a messenger would reach the towns, starting at Ephesus and ending at Laodicea, travelling in a semi-circle.

The following chart presents a summary of the letters to the seven churches.

The Letters to the Seven Churches			
Church	**Commendation**	**Criticism**	**Instruction**
Ephesus (2:1-7)	Hard working, rejects evil, patient	Have lost their first love	Repent, prioritize and put Christ first
Smyrna (2:8-11)	Gracefully bears suffering, poverty	None	Don't fear; be faithful unto death
Pergamos (2:12-17)	Remained loyal	Tolerates immorality, idolatry, and heresies	Repent
Thyatira (2:18-29)	Love, faith, service, endurance	Tolerates immorality and idolatry	Repent
Sardis (3:1-6)	Some have kept the faith	A dead church	Repent, be watchful, and strengthen what remains
Philadelphia (3:7-13)	Perseveres and Faithful	None	Hold on
Laodicea (3:14-22)	None	Lukewarm	Be zealous and repent

The Church today, in general, will have a mixture of the characteristics of these seven churches. So every local church should ask, To what extent does this situation fit our church? And should follow the instruction of our Lord: *"He who has an ear, let him hear what the Spirit says to the churches."*

3. *"the things which will take place after this"* (chs. 4-22). Main focus: The Consummation

"After these things I looked (4:1)," introduces a new vision and begins a new section. Now there is a great shift in scene, it moves from the things on the earth to that which is in heaven. John *"was in the Spirit"* and had a vision of God on the throne and of the worthy Lamb of God (chs. 4, 5).

A series of visions follow, revealing the struggle of the church in the midst of conflict and persecution, but also God's judgment upon His enemies. Here John portrays the future rise of evil, culminating in the antichrist (6:1-18:24). Throughout one is reminded that God is the sovereign King – he rules and overrules in the affairs of mankind.

Then John reveals the resounding final victory of the King of kings, the final judgment, and the glorious eternal state (19:1-22:5).

The Book of Revelation closes with the promise of the soon coming King (22:6-21). Having read the last chapter we realize: Glory to the Lamb that was slain for us, we win! And the last "Amen" in the Book of Revelation underscores and proclaims the complete revelation of the most amazing Book.

A Basic Outline of Revelation

he Book of Revelation is a very complex and intricately structured book. However, the following basic outline of Revelation will give us a glance of the events within the book.

Part One: *"The things which you have seen"* (1:1-20)
Christ in the midst of His Church

1. Introduction	1:1-8
2. Revelation of Jesus Christ in the midst of His Church	1:9-20

Part Two: *"The things which are"* (2:1-3:22)
Christ's letters to His churches

1. Message to Ephesus	2:1-7
2. Message to Smyrna	2:8-11
3. Message to Pergamos	2:12-17
4. Message to Thyatira	2:18-29
5. Message to Sardis	3:1-6

DISCOVERING THE MOST AMAZING BOOK   401

6. Message to Philadelphia	3:7-13
7. Message to Laodicea	3:14-22

Part Three: *"The things which will take place after this"* (4:1-22:21)
Christ's defence of His Church and the Destruction of His enemies

1. **Vision of God in Majestic Glory**	4:1-5:14
A. The Throne of God	4:1-11
B. The Lamb of God and the Sealed Book	5:1-14
2. **Visions of God in Judgment**	6:1-19:6

Visions of Conflict, Persecution, and Judgment

A. Seven Seals of Judgment	6:1-8:5
Interlude: saints on earth and in heaven	7:1-17
(i) The sealing of the 144,00	7:1-8
(ii) The great multitude	7:9-17
B. Seven Trumpets of Judgment	8:6-11:19
Interlude: prophecy and witness	10:1-11:13
(i) John and the little book	10:1-11
(ii) John measures the temple	11:1, 2
(iii) The two witnesses	11:3-13
C. Explanatory: great conflict described	12:1-14:20
D. Seven Bowls of Judgment	15:1-16:21
E. The Fall of Babylon	17:1-18:24
• Rejoicing in Heaven	19:1-5
3. **Visions of the Second Coming**	19:6-21
A. Marriage of the Lamb	19:6-10
B. Second Coming of Christ The Final Victory	19:11-21
4. **Visions of the Millennium***	20:1-15
A. Satan is Bound 1,000 years	20:1-3
B. Saints Reign 1,000 years	20:4-6

C. Satan is Released and Leads Rebellion	20:7-9
D. Satan is Tormented Forever	20:10
E. Great White Throne Judgement	20:11-15

1. **Visions of the Eternal State** 21:1-22:5

A. New Heaven and Earth	21:1
B. New Jerusalem Descends	21:2-8
C. New Jerusalem as the final Eden	21:9-22:5

2. **Conclusion** 22:6-21

*Different Views on the Millennium

Based on varying interpretation of the twentieth chapter of Revelation, we find three divergent views on the millennium.

1. The **Amillennial** view holds that the millennium is not a literal period of a thousand years, but only symbolic. Those who hold this view say there will be no literal earthly reign of Christ following His Second Coming; in their opinion He reigns now through His Church. The "millennium" is symbolic of the age-long struggle between good and evil. Christ may return at any time, when He will judge the wicked, and then usher in the eternal state. The advocates of this view argue that Revelation 20 is the only place in the Bible where the idea of a millennium or thousand year is mentioned, and most of the content of the book of Revelation is symbolic.

2. The **Premillennial** view holds that, at the time of the Second Coming, Christ will personally return to establish His millennial kingdom; satan will be bound for a thousand years; the dead in Christ will be raised; they will reign personally with Him on the earth for a thousand years. After the millennium satan will be released for a short while to lead a final rebellion, which will be immediately suppressed, the devil will be cast into the lake of fire, the wicked dead will be judged at the Great White throne judgment, and then the eternal state will begin. (Most evangelical mainline churches hold this view.)

DISCOVERING THE MOST AMAZING BOOK

403

3. The **Postmillennial** view holds that the millennium will not be established by Christ's coming, but by the Church. It will be a time that will be marked by victory of Christianity over the world during which the gospel will triumph as the Church exerts power over the wicked. Thus, a period of peace, realized by the Church, will precede the Second Coming of Christ.

Noteworthy

The Book of Revelation completes the Divine Library in an amazing way. The striking comparison and contrast between the Books of Genesis and Revelation emphasizes that.

Now, after we have journeyed through the Bible, let us look at the following comparison between the sinful world under the curse (Paradise lost) and the Eternal world (Paradise regained) after Jesus Christ has restored all things (Gen. 3:15; Acts 3:21).

World under the curse: (Genesis)	The Eternal world: (Revelation)
1) Evil triumph of serpent (3:13)	1) Ultimate triumph of the Lamb (20:10)
2) Judgment pronounced (3:15)	2) Judgment completely executed (20:10)
3) Cursed world (3:17)	3) No more curse (22:3)
4) Daily sorrow (3:17)	4) No more sorrow (21:4)
5) Thorns and thistles (3:18)	5) No more pain (21:4)
6) Sweat on the face (3:19)	6) Tears wiped away (21:4)
7) Eating herbs of the field (3:18)	7) Twelve manner of fruit (22:4)
8) Returning to dust (3:19)	8) No more death (21:4)
9) Man's dominion broken (3:19)	9) Man's dominion restored (22:5)
10) Paradise closed (3:23)	10) New Paradise opened (21:25)
11) Evil continually (6:5)	11) Nothing that defiles (21:27)
12) Coats of skins (3:21)	12) Fine linen, white and clean (19:14)
13) Satan opposing (3:15)	13) Satan cast into the lake of fire (20:10)
14) Kept from the tree of life (3:24)	14) Access to the tree of life (22:14)
15) Banished from the garden (3:23)	15) Free entry to the City (22:14)

The following comparison of the original world which God created, and the eternal world also emphasizes the striking balance between Genesis and Revelation, and illustrates the outcome of God's ultimate purpose.[39]

Original world (Genesis)	Eternal world (Revelation)
1) Division of light and darkness (1:4)	1) No night there (21:25)
2) Division of land and sea (1:10)	2) No more sea (21:1)
3) Rule of sun and moon (1:16)	3) No need for sun and moon (21:23)
4) Man in a prepared garden (2:8, 9)	4) Man in a prepared City (21:2)
5) River flowing out of Eden (2:10)	5) River flowing from God's throne (22:1)
6) Gold in the land (2:12)	6) Gold in the City (21:21)
7) Tree of life in the midst of the Garden (2:9)	7) Tree of life throughout the City (22:2)
8) Limited precious stones (2:12)	8) All manner of precious stones (21:9)
9) God walking in the Garden (3:8)	9) God in unbroken fellowship with His people

Furthermore:

The Book of Revelation is the only book in the Bible that pronounces a blessing for those who read, hear, and keep what is written in it (1:3). This makes it an important Book and worth studying.

As Genesis, the Book of Revelation is constantly under attack precisely because: (1) it is the *"Revelation of Jesus Christ,"* and (2) it illustrates the complete judgment and doom of satan.

---

[39] Henry Morris, *The Genesis Record*, pp. 33, 34.

Personal Application

While you read through the Book of Revelation, don't be discouraged or clouded by all the symbolism. Instead, be encouraged and take hope as you realize the following:

- The Book of Revelation is really a Revelation, an unveiling *of* your all powerful and glorious Saviour. He is the King of glory! In the gospels we see Jesus as meek and mild – the Servant King. In Revelation we see Him as the All-Conquering King.

- As the Revelation of Jesus Christ, this Book is an unveiling *by* Him, revealing how He is going to deal with the enemy of mankind and God, and making known the glorious future which God gave Him to give to us.

- God is sovereign. He is in control of history and what He promised in Genesis 3:15, He will certainly bring to full completion. He will restore Creation to its formal glory and bring all true believers in an eternal loving fellowship with Him.

Part Five

Bible Study

Chapter Fourteen

How to read and study the Bible

The Correct Approach

It is obvious that your approach to the Bible is of utmost importance; it will make all the difference in your understanding thereof. The following are a few suggestions that you should think about in order to approach the Bible correctly, and to make the most of your Bible study.

- Faith and Reverence. Realize that the Bible is truly the written Word of God and it has been divinely preserved throughout all the ages so that you are able to read it in your own language. What a privilege! Approaching the Bible with doubt or scepticism will obviously lead to wrong conclusions. What people see in the Bible and how they see it, is largely determined by what they believe about it.

- Honesty. You should be honest enough to agree that there are difficulties in the Bible (and expect difficulties). Even the apostle Peter agreed when he has said concerning some of Paul's teachings: *"There are, however, some points in them that are difficult to understand, which people who are ignorant and immature in their faith twist, as they do with the rest of the Scriptures, to their own destruction* (2 Peter 3:16)."

    However, difficulty does not equal falsehood or contradiction – a difficulty in a doctrine, or a fierce objection to a doctrine, does not, in any way, prove the doctrine to be untrue. Furthermore, things such as weaker translations and variations in the copies of the original Manuscripts do not mean that there are errors in the Bible.

- Diligence. Be determined to find a solution by diligently studying and examining the Scriptures while you prayerfully trust in God for answers. Also consult scholars. It is far better to seek for an honest answer to a difficulty than to attempt a solution that is evasive and unsatisfactory.

- What kind of "lenses" do you wear when reading the Bible? Receiving the correct message from Scripture depends largely on the "lenses" you look through. Do you look through legalistic or justification by faith lenses? Or, do you look through Old Covenant or New Covenant lenses? Or, do you look through self-effort or *"it is finished"* lenses? Or, do you look through lenses that only fit yourself? Have a teachable spirit. Guard against your own presuppositions and personal opinions that are not in line with the teaching of the Bible. (To have a presupposition means you suppose or assume your view is correct, while it is not, and you take only your view as the correct one.) Simply because we cannot understand everything absolutely, we need to learn as much as possible about reality, as presented by the Bible, and then adjust our perception of reality accordingly. To do this we must learn to be open to understandings that lie beyond those we now have. In this learning process the Holy Spirit must be the real Teacher.

- The Golden Key is always to look for the self-revelation of God, particularly in Jesus Christ, because He is the sum and substance of all revelation. We have seen that the Old Covenant is the Promise, specifically in Christ. Now when you read the Old Covenant, look for the Promise in the prophecies, symbols, and types. When you read the New Covenant look for the manifestation and realization of the Promise in Christ Jesus. Follow the storyline of Genesis 3:15 throughout the entire Bible, and look beyond the written Word, to Jesus Christ who is the living Word.

The Importance and Motivation of Bible Study

As we have seen throughout our studies, the Bible is unique among the books of the world. As the written Word of God, it is an expression of God Himself. This makes Bible study certainly important. We ought to be people of the Word: finding instruction, encouragement and spiritual nourishment in it, and then expressing the life, love, light and values of God in a fallen world that desperately needs God.

There are different motivations in Scripture that should encourage us to read and study the Bible frequently and consistently. We read and study the Bible ...

- To humble ourselves (discovering and realizing how awesome God is, and how frail mankind is, will cause you to humble yourself before Him)
- To hear from God and receive spiritual nourishment (Matt. 4:4)
- To stimulate our faith (Rom. 10:17)
- To experience consistent joy (Ps. 119:111)
- To stay on the right track (Ps. 119:105)
- To sort out our thoughts or motivations (Phil. 4:8; Heb. 4:12)
- To know the truth and think clearly about what God says is valuable (2 Pet. 1:21)
- To be built up as a community with other believers (Acts 20:31; Eph. 4:14-16)
- To find comfort, consolation and encouragement (Heb. 6:17-18)
- And ultimately, *"that I may know Him and the power of His resurrection, and the fellowship of His sufferings, being conformed to His death* (Phil. 3:10)." So that, *"you may walk worthy of the Lord, fully pleasing Him, being fruitful in every good work and increasing in the knowledge of God* (Col. 1:10)."

Different Types of Bible Studies

It is always wise for new converts to begin their Bible study in the New Testament, with the Gospels – where we meet Jesus the Saviour. The Gospel of John and the First Letter of John are always appropriate for beginners. However, as you advance in the Lord, you need to go deeper with Bible study.

There are a variety of ways to study the Bible. The following are a few suggestions:

- **Chronological** study of the Bible
  In this type of study you begin at the beginning of the Old Covenant, Genesis, and then work your way through the Bible. Or, you begin at the beginning of the New Testament, Matthew, and journey through to the end of the Book of Revelation. To make it more interesting some people will study the Bible in its historical chronological order, meaning they study it in the order of the dates in which the Books were written.

- **Devotional** study
  This study focuses on reading and studying a specific passage, or only a small portion of a passage, or a specific topic daily. This type of study would be related to a topical study.

- **Bible Book** study
  In this type of study you will take one Bible book at a time and do a thorough study on it.

- **Topical** study
  This type of study aims at studying great topics or subjects of the Bible such as: Bible prayers, Bible promises, Bible sermons, Bible songs, Love, Faith, Wisdom, Righteousness, and so on. For instance, take the Book of Proverbs and as you read through it, take notice of the word "wisdom." What do you learn about wisdom? How can you define wisdom? How do you get wisdom? What are the characteristics of wisdom? What is the value of wisdom? How does a person with wisdom act? And so on. Or, take a concordance and look up the word "love" (particularly in relation to God). What do you learn about God's love from all the different references to it?

- **Word** study
  Studying the meaning of specific and important words in the Bible by making use of Concordances and Bible Word Dictionaries, which will give you the different possible meanings of a word in the original language. For instance, the word "salvation" is translated from the Greek word *soteria,* which could mean "rescue, deliver, health, salvation, save, saving."

- Or, you can do a combination of the above.

Practical Suggestions

The following are several important and practical suggestions for sound Bible study:

- Begin your Bible reading with prayer. As you begin your Bible reading, ask God to give you a receptive heart and ask the Holy Spirit to speak to you through the words in the Bible. He is the author of the Book and knows exactly what He means by what He said. Ask Him to give you guidance and bring the Word to life.

- Read expectantly and joyfully. The Bible is an expression of God Himself – He expresses His desire to have relationship with mankind; He wants to share His life and love with human beings, who are the pinnacle of His Creation. When you read a letter from somebody, can't you "experience, or sense" what that person wants to communicate to you? Now, when reading the Bible expect to hear from God, being joyful and thankful for what you find in His Word to you.

- Read slowly through one chapter, or perhaps two or three chapters or perhaps just one paragraph at a time. After reading, ponder on it, and ask yourself, what does God want to say to me? What are the implications for belief and practice? Then you could reread it. Remember, it is not the amount of pages that you read at a time, but what you receive from the reading that is important.

- Take brief notes on what you read.

- Memorize key verses.

- Make use of highlighters to highlight words, phrases or passages that really speak to you. You can also use different colours to highlight verses/passages that speak of important doctrines. For instance: use red to highlight verses that refer to the blood of Jesus and yellow to highlight verses that refer to healing, and so on.

- When you read the Bible you have to interpret it. Interpretation means to explain the meaning of Scripture and to understand it in a specified way. The following 3 steps could serve as a good working model to interpret and apply Scripture correctly:

Observation – Determine what the original author actually wrote. Ask questions, such as: To whom was it written? Why? When? Where? What are the topics of concern? What was the historical context like?

Interpretation – This point is closely related to the previous one. Seek the meaning of the text in its original setting. The correct interpretation must be something the original author could have meant in order to address certain concerns in the recipients' lives.

Application. What are the implications? How does this relate to me and my circumstances? Make it applicable to your life, circumstances, and situation.

(The technical term for interpretation is hermeneutics – the principles that we use to explain Scripture. The word "hermeneutics" is derived from the Greek word *hermeneuo* which means to interpret or explain, as used in Luke 24:27, when Jesus walks to Emmaus with His disciples, and Luke records: *"Beginning with Moses and with all the prophets, He explained (hermeneuo) to them the things concerning himself in all the Scriptures."* Hermeneutics is broken down into exegesis, a word from the Greek which means literally to "read out of," that is, (1) to see what the passage said when it was written; and (2) application which looks at how the original meaning applies today. These two aspects of exegesis form the heart of Scripture interpretation. Thus, while you read a text or a passage you should always ask: (1) what was the intended meaning of the text when the writer wrote it? (2) What should the passage mean to a reader today?)

DISCOVERING THE MOST AMAZING BOOK 415

> Another Greek word that stands in contrast to *exegesis,* is *eisegesis,* which means "to read into." Don't make yourself guilty of *eisegesis.* Rather allow the Word to speak life into you instead of you speaking meaning into it.

- When you do a Book study you could do the following: determine the historical context (the circumstances — cultural, political, religious, and social — in which the Book was written), and the reason and purpose why the Book was written. Also determine what are the main themes and main subjects of the Book. Then you could divide the Book into main sections, the chapters into main subjects, and look for key thoughts and words. You could consider to do an outline of the Book and then develop the outline into a study that covers the main thoughts of your outline. (Look at the survey of Bible Books in this book.)

- The nature of the subject under discussion will obviously contribute to the correct interpretation thereof. The subject under discussion in John 3:1-6, for example, is birth. Thus, *"born of water"* in verse 5, is to be *"born of the flesh"* (verse 6) and it points to the natural birth; *"[born of] the Spirit"* in verse 5 is to be *"born of the Spirit"* (verse 6) and it refers to the spiritual birth, born from above, from the Spirit, or to be born-again.

- Often the way in which words are arranged to form the sentences of a passage is the key to the meaning of it. For example, sometimes the meaning of the sentence depends on something as simple as a preposition. It obviously matters a great deal whether a passage says *"till," "because of," "through," "into," "therefore,"* or *"with."* Here are a few examples:

"... for the equipping of the saints for the work of the ministry, for the edifying of the body of Christ, <u>till</u> we all come to the unity of the faith and of the knowledge of the Son ... (Eph. 4:11-13; emphasis mine)."

"I can do all things through Christ who strengthens me (Phil. 4:13; emphasis mine)."

"I beseech you therefore, brethren, by the mercies of God that you present your bodies a living sacrifice, holy, acceptable to God, which is your reasonable service (Rom. 12:1; emphasis mine)." The word "therefore" is used after a writer (or speaker) has made certain statements, then s/he introduces a logical conclusion. As we have seen in our study of the Letter to the Romans, Paul first explains his doctrine of the righteousness of God (Rom. 1-11), then in Romans 12:1 he says, *"therefore,"* introducing the logical conclusion that it is wise to commit your life fully unto God. So, whenever you see the word "therefore," find out why it is "there for."

- Read everything in the light of where you find it. What is the context of the passage? Context means the setting in which a word or verse or passage appears, and refers to the words that come before and after a particular word or phrase and help to fix its meaning. You should get the meaning of a passage from the context – every word you read must be understood in the light of the words that come before and after it, while you keep the circumstances in which it was written in mind. By complying with the rules of context you will safeguard yourself against: (1) isolating the text to arrive at a wrong view, and (2) taking the meaning out of context, which usually leads to twisted views.

  Also, when you do word studies, remember that usually a word, though it could have different meanings, can only have one meaning in a given passage. And normally the meaning of the word lies not as such in the word itself but in the context in which that word is used.

- Always keep the overarching theme and unity of the Bible in mind. Read book introductions noting where each book fits in the overall development of God's revelation to man. (If your Bible doesn't have Book introductions, make use of the survey of Bible Books in this book.)

DISCOVERING THE MOST AMAZING BOOK 417

- Read parallel passages. For example, the instance where David took the Ark of the Covenant to Jerusalem. We read about it in 2 Samuel 6 and also in 1 Chronicles 15. The reading of both passages will give you a clearer understanding of the meaning. Also, think of the four Gospels; we need to read all four in order to receive a proper understanding of Jesus' life and ministry.

- Nothing interprets Scripture as Scripture. This means that you need to interpret Scripture in the light of other Scripture on the same subject. Also, no part of Scripture should be interpreted in such a way that it will violate the teaching of the whole of Scripture. Take care not to build a doctrine on a single obscure or unclear text. If the Bible is God's Word, then it should be consistent with itself. He will definitely not disagree with Himself. One divine author inspired the whole Bible, so it has one marvellous, supernatural unity.

- When you read/study a passage that is specifically prophetic, keep the following in mind: (a) prophecy is given for a specific time and situation, for example Jeremiah's prophecy about the New Covenant (Jer. 31:31-34). (b) Prophecy is given for a reason: to give us guidance and to instruct us in what we are to do and what we are not to do (see Jer. 1:4-19; Matt. 24:19-20). (c) Although prophecy is sometimes given in symbolic language, its implication and fulfilment are always literal (see Jer. 13:1-14); so take care not to "spiritualize" it. (d) The spirit of prophecy focuses on Jesus (see Rev. 19:10); meaning He is the central theme of all biblical prophecy from Genesis to Revelation (see John 16:13-14). (e) Some prophecies will remain secret (see Deut. 29:29), because God is sovereign in His revealing and fulfilment of prophecy.

- Familiarize yourself with figures of speech, symbolism, and types that we find in the Bible.

- Discipline yourself to keep a reading/studying plan; be realistic about the goals you set.

- Make use of study helps.

It should be a great delight to do Bible study, and no book could be more deserving of dedicated, diligent, and determined study.

Study Helps
Nowadays there are a vast variety of resources on Bible study available. We are really spoiled for choice. Just as any job is accomplished more easily and with better results when the right tools are used, so your Bible study will be more effective when you use the resources available to you. To make the most of your Bible study it would be wise to have the following at hand:

- An English Dictionary – to look up definitions of difficult words.

- A Reliable Bible Dictionary – to look up the meanings of terms and names that we find in the Bible.

- A Good Concordance – to find the different references to the same topic in the Bible. Most Bibles have a concordance at the back of it.

- Sound Commentaries – will help you to find background information on Bible Books and give you outlines, illustrations, verse-for-verse, or section-by-section explanations. Hint: always compare different commentaries, because the commentators also have presuppositions!

- Reliable Bible Handbooks – will give an abundance of information on the Bible and its content.

- Other Translations – make use of different translations, especially if you are reading a passage that is hard to understand.

- Study Bibles can be helpful in that they give many explanatory notes and short commentaries on Scripture.

- Books by respected Bible teachers on specific Biblical topics that you feel you need to explore more. For instance, books on grace, faith, the Holy Spirit, the Church, the Interpretation of Bible symbols, and so on.

- A Notebook

- A pen/pencil and highlighters

Enjoy an exciting learning experience as you journey into the Most Amazing Book that has ever been written.

Addendum

A Suggested Chronology of New Testament Books According to Dates

The following chart is merely a suggestion of the chronology of the New Testament Books. The dates are approximate, and we have to keep in mind that the time of writing of some of the books overlapped.

Book	Date
James	AD 45-49
Galatians	AD 48/49
1 Thessalonians	AD 50
2 Thessalonians	AD 50
1 Corinthians	AD 54/55
2 Corinthians	AD 55/56
Romans	AD 56/57
Gospel of Mark	Mid to late 50's
Gospel of Matthew	Late 50's early 60's
Gospel of Luke	AD 59/60
Philemon	AD 60-63
Colossians	AD 60/61
Ephesians	AD 60/61
Philippians	AD 61
Acts	AD 63
1 Timothy	AD 64
Titus	AD 64
2 Timothy	AD 64/65

1 Peter	AD 65
2 Peter	AD 67/68
Hebrews	AD 67-69
Jude	AD 75-80
Gospel of John	AD 85-90
1 John	AD 85-90
2 John	AD 85-90
3 John	AD 85-90
Revelation	AD 85-95

Outstanding Chapters of the Bible

Chapter	Topic
Genesis 1	Creation, heaven and earth
Genesis 3	Fall and future
Genesis 22	Father of faith tested
Exodus 12	Passover
Deuteronomy 6	Commitment
Deuteronomy 32	God's faithfulness
Joshua 3	Possessing your inheritance by faith
Joshua 24	My house and I
Judges 16	In death victory
Psalm 22	Prophetic preview of crucifixion
Psalm 23	The Lord is my Shepherd
Psalm 27	Confidence in God
Psalm 51	A clean heart
Psalm 91	Fully covered by God
Psalm 103	All His benefits
Psalm 119	Walk in His ways
Psalm 150	Praise Him greatly
Proverbs 3	Trusting in the Lord

Proverbs 8	The excellence of wisdom
Ecclesiastes 3	Timing
Ecclesiastes 11	Bread upon water
Isaiah 6	Isaiah's vision
Isaiah 7	Sign of Immanuel
Isaiah 35	Glorious hope
Isaiah 40	God's Greatness
Isaiah 52:13-53:12	The Suffering Servant
Jeremiah 18	God's power
Jeremiah 31	New Covenant promise
Ezekiel 33	Israel's Watchman
Daniel 9	God's great mercies
Hosea 14	Healing of sins
Matthew 5-7	The Sermon on the Mount
Matthew 24	End times
Matthew 27	His trial, crucifixion and burial
Matthew 28	The Resurrection and Great Commission
Mark 5	Compassion healing
Mark 12	Greatest Commandment
Mark 15	The King forsaken for us
Luke 2	A Saviour born to us
Luke 15	Lost and found
Luke 23	Pilate to Paradise
Luke 24	Promise for witnesses
John 1	The Word became flesh
John 3	You must be born again
John 6	Jesus, Bread of life
John 14 and 16	The Holy Spirit
John 15	Abide in Me
John 17	Jesus' unifying prayer
John 19	The complete sacrifice

John 20	Sent by the risen Christ
John 21	Fishing and feeding
Acts 2	Holy Spirit poured out, power harvest
Romans 3	Justified by faith
Romans 8	Life in the Spirit
Romans 12	Complete surrender, Christian living
1 Corinthians 7	Married or single
1 Corinthians 12	Manifestations of Holy Spirit
1 Corinthians 13	Faith, Hope, LOVE
1 Corinthians 15	Resurrection explained
2 Corinthians 5	New creations in Christ
2 Corinthians 12	Dependence
Galatians	The just live by faith
Ephesians 1	Spiritual blessings, destination in Christ
Ephesians 2	Household of God
Philippians 2	Christ's humility
Philippians 3	The priceless value of knowing Christ
Colossians 1	Perfect in Christ
Colossians 3	Righteous living
1 Timothy 3	Leadership
1 Thessalonians 4	Always with the Lord
Hebrews 1	Jesus is superior
Hebrews 11	Faith
Hebrews 12	Endure the race of faith
James 1	Temptation
James 3	Controlling mind & mouth
1 Peter 4	Suffering
1 John 1	True fellowship
Revelation 1	Glorious Jesus who is to come
Revelation 5	Jesus alone is worthy
Revelation 21-22	We win! Heaven

Outstanding Verses of the Bible

Verse	Topic
Genesis 1:1	God Triune, the Creator
Exodus 14:14	God's protection
Deuteronomy 16:17	Giving
Deuteronomy 33:27	God's protection
Joshua 1:9	Courage
Joshua 24:15	Serving God
1 Samuel 15:22	Obedience
1 Samuel 17:47	The battle is the Lord's
1 Samuel 30:6	Strengthen yourself in the Lord
2 Samuel 22:31	God's protection
1 Chronicles 28:9	Seeking God
1 Chronicles 29:11	God's reign
2 Chronicles 7:14	Humility/Repentance
2 Chronicles 16:9	Commitment
Nehemiah 8:10	The Joy of the Lord is your strength
Nehemiah 9:6	God the Creator
Job 9:10	God's power
Job 36:26	Mystery of God
Psalm 3:3	God's protection
Psalm 8:1, 9	The excellence of His name
Psalm 9:1	Thankfulness
Psalm 16:8	God's presence
Psalm 18:19	God brought you out into a broad place
Psalm 19:1	Creation declares His glory
Psalm 19:14	Words & meditation
Psalm 23:1-6	The Lord our Shepherd
Psalm 24:1	God's reign
Psalm 30:4-5	God's forgiveness

Psalm 32:8	Guidance
Psalm 37:4	Delight yourself in the Lord
Psalm 37:7	Rest in the Lord
Psalm 40:8	Joy
Psalm 46:1	Strength
Psalm 55:16, 17	Prayer/Rescue
Psalm 56:3-4	Trust in God when fearful
Psalm 84:2	A hunger for God's presence
Psalm 86:11	Purity
Psalm 86:15	God is compassionate, gracious & merciful
Psalm 91:1	Rest in God
Psalm 92:1	Thankfulness
Psalm 96:3	Declare His Glory
Psalm 100:4	Approach God with gratitude and praise
Psalm 102:25-27	God is unchanging
Psalm 104:1-2	God is awesome
Psalm 106:1	Give thanks to God; He is good
Psalm 111:10	The fear of the Lord
Psalm 118:24	This is the day the Lord has made...
Psalm 119:9	Purity/God's Word
Psalm 119:89	God's Word is eternal
Psalm 119:105	God's Word/Guidance
Psalm 127:1	Unless the Lord builds the house
Psalm 139:13-16	You are fearfully and wonderfully made
Proverbs 1:7	Fear of God/Wisdom
Proverbs 1:8	Education/Obeying parents
Proverbs 3:5-6	Fully trust in God
Proverbs 4:23	Guard your heart above all else
Proverbs 11:2	Pride versus humility

Proverbs 11:3	Integrity/Guidance
Proverbs 11:25	Generosity
Proverbs 11:30	Soulwinning
Proverbs 15:1	Gentleness/Speech
Proverbs 18:21	Death and life in power of tongue
Proverbs 18:24	Friendship
Proverbs 19:1	Honesty
Proverbs 21:21	Life, Righteousness, Honour
Proverbs 28:20	Faithfulness
Proverbs 28:1	Courageous in Christ
Ecclesiastes 12:13	The Importance of the Fear of the Lord
Isaiah 26:3	Peace
Isaiah 40:31	Renewed Strength
Isaiah 53:4-6	Christ is Our Substitute
Isaiah 55:6	Seeking God
Isaiah 58:11	Guidance/Provision
Isaiah 65:24	God Answers Prayer
Isaiah 66:2	Awe for God's Word
Jeremiah 15:16	God's Word Precious
Jeremiah 29:11	God's Prosperous Plan
Jeremiah 31:3	God's Everlasting Love
Jeremiah 31:34	God Forgives and Forgets
Lamentations 3:22-23	Great is God's Faithfulness
Ezekiel 11:19-20	New Hearts
Daniel 11:32	Be Strong; Carry out Great Exploits
Joel 2:28	The Pouring Out of the Holy Spirit
Amos 5:24	Justice
Jonah 4:2	God is Gracious and Merciful
Micah 6:8	Justice, Mercy, Humility
Habakkuk 3:19	Confidence in God

Zechariah 9:9	Rejoice! Jesus is coming
Matthew 5:3-11	Blessings in Christ
Matthew 11:28	Jesus gives rest
Matthew 28:6	He is risen
Mark 5:36	Only believe
Mark 11:25	Forgiveness
Mark 16:17	Signs follow those who believe
Luke 1:37	Nothing is impossible with God
Luke 6:31	Loving others
Luke 11:2-4	Prayer
Luke 14:26-27	Following Jesus
John 1:12	To become a child of God
John 3:3-6	You must be born again
John 3:16	God's love
John 10:10	Life in abundance
John 11:25	Resurrection life
John 14:1	Trust in Jesus
John 14:6	Jesus Alone
John 14:16, 17	The Helper
John 14:23	Fellowship with God
John 14:27	Peace
John 15:11	Fullness of joy
Acts 1:8	Empowerment by the Holy Spirit
Acts 4:13	Boldness in Christ
Acts 16:31	Faith/Salvation
Acts 17:6	Turn the world upside down
Acts 24:16	Clear conscience
Romans 1:16	Not ashamed
Romans 3:23	Sin/Salvation
Romans 3:28	Justified by faith
Romans 5:1-2	Faith/Peace with God

Romans 8:1	No condemnation
Romans 8:28	All things work together for good
Romans 12:1-2	Complete surrender
1 Corinthians 4:20	Kingdom of God/Power
1 Corinthians 6:17	Joined to the Lord
1 Corinthians 13:13	Faith, Hope, Love
2 Corinthians 1:3-4	Comfort
2 Corinthians 4:7	God's power
2 Corinthians 5:17	New Creations
2 Corinthians 9:7	Giving cheerfully
2 Corinthians 12:9	Grace sufficient
Galatians 2:20	Crucified with Christ
Galatians 3:13	Redeemed from the curse
Galatians 5:22-23	Fruit of the Spirit
Galatians 6:9	Responsibility
Ephesians 1:3	Blessed
Ephesians 1:6	Accepted in the Beloved
Ephesians 2:8, 9	Saved by grace through faith
Ephesians 3:20	God's power in us
Ephesians 4:18	Be filled with the Holy Spirit
Ephesians 6:10	Be strong in the Lord
Philippians 2:5	Having Christ's attitude
Philippians 3:10	That I may know Him
Philippians 4:4	Rejoice in the Lord
Philippians 4:6, 7	Joy and peace
Philippians 4:13	Strength through Christ
Philippians 4:19	Needs fulfilled
Colossians 1:15-17	The Pre-eminent Christ
Colossians 3:2	Set your mind on Christ
Colossians 3:23	Motto/Lifestyle
1 Thessalonians 3:12	Abound in love

1 Thessalonians 4:3	God's will
1 Thessalonians 5:17-18	Prayer/Thanksgiving
Hebrews 2:18	Jesus our help during temptation
Hebrews 4:12	God's all powerful Word
Hebrews 4:16	Grace/Mercy
Hebrews 10:24-25	Encouragement
Hebrews 11:1	Faith
James 1:5-8	Wisdom/Pray
James 1:22	Doers of the Word
James 4:7-10	Humility
1 Peter 4:10	Serving one another
1 Peter 5:7	Burdens
2 Peter 3:9	None should perish
1 John 1:9	Confession/Forgiveness
1 John 2:3-6	Obeying God
1 John 3:16-19	Love in action
1 John 5:4, 5	Faith/Overcome
Revelation 3:20	Salvation

Where to turn when ....

You feel abandoned ...	Hebrews 13:5
You are afraid of death ...	Psalm 23
You are angry ...	Eph. 4:26-27
You are anxious ...	Philippians 4:6, 7; 1 Peter 5:7
You are anxious for those you love ...	Psalm 107
You are afraid ...	Psalm 24
You are prideful ...	Romans 12:3
You are in need ...	Phil. 4:19; Proverbs 3:5
God does not seem to act ...	Luke 24:13-35

DISCOVERING THE MOST AMAZING BOOK

You seek assurance of God's purpose for your life	...Psalm 138:7-8; Proverbs 19:21
You feel down ...	Psalm 42:5
Your hopes are dashed ...	Psalm 34:18
You are bored ...	Psalm 103
You feel burdened ...	Psalm. 55:22; 1 Pet. 5:7
God seems to delay ...	John 11:1-24
God seems far away ...	Psalm 139; Heb. 13:5
Nothing seems to be going right ...	Psalm 37:1-4
It seems as if everything is working against you ...	Rom. 8:28
Evil seems greater than God ...	Rev. 19:6
You are discouraged ...	2 Cor. 1:3-11
You need direction ...	Psalm 25:9
You doubt that God is able ...	Eph. 3:20; Rom. 4:21
You doubt your worth ...	Psalm 139:13-18; John 3:16
You doubt that God loves you ...	John 3:16; 1 John 4:8
You experience trouble ...	2 Cor. 1:3-11
You have failed God ...	Lam. 3:23; 2 Tim. 2:13
You need forgiveness ...	Psalm 51; 1 John 1:9
You need more than human help ...	Psalm 46
You need to get your head sorted out ...	Rom. 12:1, 2; Phil. 4:8; Col. 3:1, 2
You need guidance ...	Proverbs 3:5-6
You need wisdom ...	James 1:5-8
You fear failure ...	Psalm 37:23-24
Friends turned against you ...	Psalm 55
You're feeling bitter ...	Hebrews 12:15
You feel sick ...	James 5:14; Isa. 53:5
You feel like giving up ...	Luke 11:5-14
Your faith feels insufficient ...	Mark 9:14-24
You feel inadequate ...	Phil. 4:13

You feel weak ...	Proverbs 28:1; 2 Cor. 12:9; 1 John 4:4
You feel lonely ...	Psalm 13; Matt. 1:23
You feel sorry for yourself ...	Psalm 102
You don't feel like praising God ...	Psalm 103; Heb. 13:15
You feel the devil is behind you ...	James 4:7
You feel you are lacking in power ...	Zech. 4:6; Acts 1:8; Eph. 1:19-20
You feel less thankful ...	1 Thess. 5:18
You feel shame ...	Proverbs 28:13; Rom. 8:1
You see evil people prosper ...	Psalm 37:1-3; 78
You are tired ...	Psalm 127:1-2
Your past haunts you ...	Colossians 1:21-22
People come against you ...	Matt. 5:11-12
Someone has harmed you ...	Matt. 6:14-15; Mark 11:25
Selfishness gets you in its grips ...	Matt. 16:25
Temptation seems stronger than you are ...	1 Cor. 10:13
You are tempted to commit sexual sins ...	1 Cor. 6:18-20
You are tempted to look down on others ...	Matt. 7
You are experiencing various trials ...	James 1:2-4
Having trouble with your husband ...	Eph. 5:22-24
Having trouble with your wife ...	Eph. 5:25-30
You suffer for doing right ...	1 Pet. 1:6-7; 4:12-18
You think you're them only one suffering...	1 Pet. 5:9
You think God owes you mercy ...	Rom. 2:4
You worry ...	Matthew 6:34

Questions concerning law keeping

We have already referred to the difference between the Old and New Covenant and touched on the question if Christians are under the Law. The following two discussions will throw more light on whether Christians should keep the Law and the Sabbath.

1. Do Christians need to keep the Law?

There is much confusion among well-meaning Christians regarding the law and grace. The following short study will help us to clear up the confusion.

The complete law was given through Moses

"For the law was given through Moses, but grace and truth came through Jesus Christ (John 1:17; emphasis mine)." Take notice "the law," not "some laws," or "part of the law," but the law – complete and entire in one system – was given at one period in history through one man, Moses. This complete law consists of 613 "laws" which include the Ten Commandments.

Those who argue that Christians should still keep the law, or at least the Ten Commandments, divide the law for convenience sake into three categories: moral laws (Ten Commandments), civil laws (which regulate daily social and civil living), ceremonial laws (the sacrifices and religious ceremonies). And they insist that Jesus only fulfilled the ceremonial laws. However, the Bible never divides the law into three categories. The Bible refers to the law as "the law;" implying that it is a complete system of law that cannot be divided into different sections. William Mounce (a scholar in Biblical Hebrew and Greek) writes: "These laws regulate every aspect of Israelite life, from food to offerings to social interactions to warfare. It is impossible to divide these neatly into categories ... since the Old Testament does not make such distinctions and various types of law are all intertwined."[1]

Therefore, if you want to be justified by the law, then it is obvious that you must keep the complete law, all 613 of them. James confirms this for us when he says: *"For whoever shall keep the whole law, yet stumble in one point, he is guilty of all. For He who said, 'Do not*

---

[1] William D Mounce, *Mounce's Complete Dictionary of Old and New Testament Words*, pp. 392, 393.

commit adultery,' also said, 'Do not murder.' No if you do not commit adultery, but you do murder, you have become a transgressor of the law (James 2:10-11)." Those who want to keep the law cannot pick and choose which ones they want to keep and which not; they have to keep the complete law.

Moreover, Deuteronomy 4:1 and 2 tell us that the law was only given for Israel not for the Gentiles (compare Acts 15 especially verse 24, 28 and 29).

Christians are not under the law
Romans 6:14, which is addressed to Christians, says: *"For sin shall not have dominion over you, for you are not under the law."* Again, in Romans 10:4 Paul says: *"For Christ is the end of the law for righteousness to everyone who believes."* Our faith in Christ justifies us (Rom. 5:1). As soon as a person puts his faith in Christ for salvation, that is the end of the law for that person as a means of achieving salvation, because *"grace and truth came through Jesus Christ."*

Further, according to Paul Christians are guided by the Holy Spirit, not the law: *"But if you are led by the Spirit, you are not under the law (Gal. 5:18)."*

In Colossians 2:13-14 Paul also states that the law as a means of righteousness came to an end with the atoning death of Christ upon the cross. The word "requirements" in verse 14 could be translated as "ordinances" which would then include the whole system of law which God had ordained through Moses. Paul continues in Colossians 2:16 and says: *"Therefore let no one judge you in food or in drink, or regarding a festival or a new moon or Sabbaths."* Also compare Ephesians 2:14-15, 1 Timothy 1:8-10, Romans 8:14 and Galatians 5:18.

The Purpose of the Law
What is the purpose of the law then? We have mentioned this before, but let's look at it again. According to the New Testament the main purposes of the law are:

DISCOVERING THE MOST AMAZING BOOK 435

- To reveal sin – Rom. 3:19-20; 7:7, 13. Compare the law to a mirror – if you have dirt on your face and look into a mirror, you will see the dirt, but you cannot take the mirror, which revealed the dirt, to clean your face.

- To prove man's inability to save himself by his own efforts – Rom. 7:18-25.

- The law directed us to Christ; it is our *"tutor to bring us to Christ"* – Gal. 3:22-24.

In his Letter to Timothy Paul makes it crystal clear that the law is not for those who are justified by their faith in Christ, but for the sinner who is not yet justified. *"But we know that the law is good if one uses it lawfully, knowing this: that the law is not made for a righteous person, but for the lawless and insubordinate … (1 Tim. 1:8, 9)."*

What do we understand by the following phrase, *"the law is good if one uses it lawfully?"* It simply means that the law is good as a means to bring conviction of sin; then it is used lawfully. Therefore, the law is for the unrighteous, not for the righteous.

The law was perfectly fulfilled by Christ
Jesus Christ Himself sums up His attitude and relationship to the law in Matthew 5:17-18: *"Do not think that I came to destroy the Law and Prophets. I did not come to destroy but to fulfil. For assuredly I say to you, till heaven and earth pass away, one jot or one tittle will by no means pass from the law till all is fulfilled."*

Two questions arise from this text: (1) in what sense did Jesus fulfil the law? (2) After the law is fulfilled, is it still applicable?

The following is the answer to the first question:

- Jesus personally fulfilled the law, as a Jew born under the law, by His own life of spotless righteousness and by complete obedience to the law (Gal. 4:4-5).

- He fulfilled the law by His atoning death, through which He satisfied the law's just demand upon all those who had not perfectly observed it (1 Pet. 2:22, 24).

- He fulfilled the law by fulfilling all that the law foretold and foreshadowed concerning the Saviour and Messiah who was to come (John 1:45; Luke 24:44).

Here is the answer to the second question:

- A reading from the Amplified Translation throws more light on verse 18: *"For truly I tell you, until the sky and earth pass away and perish, not one smallest letter nor one little hook [identifying certain Hebrew letters] will pass from the law until all things [it foreshadowed] are accomplished* (emphasis mine)." First of all, we should realize that Jesus employs hyperbole to emphasize how strongly He felt about the complete fulfilment of the Law and Prophets. Secondly, the Law and Prophets remain valid until what they foreshadowed is completely fulfilled – Jesus was foretold and foreshadowed by the Law and Prophets. Now, after He fulfilled them, they are not applicable anymore to those who are justified by faith, because *"Christ is the end of the law."*

- Hebrews 8:13 confirms it: *"In that He says, 'A new covenant,' He has made the first obsolete. Now what is becoming obsolete and growing old is ready to vanish away."*

You may ask, but what about verse 19 where Jesus says: *"Whoever therefore breaks one of the least of these commandments, and teaches men so, shall be called least in the kingdom of heaven; but whoever does and teaches them, he shall be called great in the kingdom of heaven."* To which commandments does Jesus refer? The commandments of the Old Covenant? No! Firstly, Jesus does not mention any specific Old Covenant laws or commandments, such as the Ten Commandments or the Sabbath. Secondly, Jesus uses the Greek word *entolé* for "commandment." This word means authoritative prescription or instruction, and does not refer to the law of the Old Covenant. The Greek word used for "law" in the New Covenant is almost invariably *nomos*. If Jesus wanted to refer to the law of the Old Covenant, He would have used *nomos* and not *entolé*. Therefore, in verse 19 Jesus refers to His teaching, His authoritative instructions to His disciples in the Sermon on the Mount, not the laws of the Old Covenant.

Now, since Jesus fulfilled the law completely on behalf of all those who choose to believe in Him, Christians fulfil the law in Jesus Christ by living in love (Rom. 8:3-4; 13:8; Matt. 22:35-40; Gal. 5:14). Paul says that the love of God was poured into our hearts by the Holy Spirit who was given to us (Rom. 5:5). The pouring in of the love of God by the Holy Spirit empowers Christians to live by the law of love, which is the fulfilment of all the commandments (Matt. 22:37-40; Gal. 5:14). It is plain logic that if you love God, then you will obey Him; if you love your brother, then you will not do anything to his detriment.

2. Do Christians have to keep the Sabbath?

Jesus said: *"The Sabbath was made for man, and not man for the Sabbath. Therefore the Son of Man is Lord even of the Sabbath* (Mark 2:27, 28)."

Preliminary Notes

In order to understand the concept of Sabbath, it is important to have a basic understanding of:

- The difference between the Old and New Covenants

- The fulfilment of the Old Covenant by Jesus Christ

- Grace – God's unmerited favour; His desire to bless us, not on the basis of our performance, but on the basis of Jesus' performance on our behalf.

We are not going to examine the above, but we will touch on these points through our study.

The person who does not accept the truth that Jesus Christ fulfilled the Old Covenant, and does not understand grace in the New Covenant will naturally have a different view on Sabbath as that which follows.

Where does Sabbath come from?

The only really satisfactory answer is to be found in the Creation account in Genesis 2:1-3. In the Old Covenant God established the Sabbath as a day of rest commemorating creation: *"Thus the heavens and the earth, and all the host of them, were finished. And on the seventh day God ended His work which He had done, and He rested on the seventh day from all His work which He had done. Then God blessed the seventh day and sanctified it, because in it He rested from all His work which God created and made."*

When God established Israel as His covenant nation, He gave them the Law, which includes the Ten Commandments. The fourth commandment in the Ten Commandments stipulated the Sabbath (Ex. 20:8-11). (Here we have to keep the purpose of the law in mind in order to understand the real meaning of Sabbath. God gave Israel the law: (1) to single them out as His covenantal people; (2) to remind them of His holiness and their sinfulness; and (3) to direct their attention to the promised Messiah as the ultimate sacrifice and fulfilment of the law [Heb. 10:1-4; compare Gen. 3:15].)

What does Sabbath mean?

The Hebrew word used for "rest" is *shabbath* from which we have our English word "Sabbath." The word Sabbath means "to stop," "to cease" or "to rest." It **doesn't** mean Saturday or Sunday. (We don't even have certainty that our "seventh day" is the same as the original seventh day of Creation Week. So to argue about it is actually irrelevant.)

After God completed creation He didn't rest because He was tired. Since God doesn't require rest (see Isa. 40:28). His rest was not the result of exhaustion. Instead, it was a cessation of His work of creation. The word "Sabbath," in the context of our study, does not refer to remedying exhaustion after a tiring week of work. Rather, it describes the enjoyment of accomplishment, the celebration of completion. (Keep this point in mind; it is very important in understanding the real meaning of the Sabbath.)

Jesus said: *"The Sabbath was made for man, and not man for the Sabbath."* That is to say, God didn't create a Sabbath and then a man to keep it. As we know, He first created a human being, then knowing human beings would need rest and spiritual renewal, He

DISCOVERING THE MOST AMAZING BOOK 439

instituted the Sabbath for their benefit. In other words, God intended the Sabbath to be for man's physical and spiritual benefit and it should not be an impossible religious burden in striving to observe narrow man-made laws.

"Sabbath" in the New Covenant

When we carefully examine the New Testament, then it becomes crystal clear that Jesus Christ has fulfilled the law (Matt. 5:17; John 1:17; Gal. 3:13, 19-26; Rom. 10:4). And Christians "are not under law, but under grace (Rom. 6:14)." Meaning that Christians do not have to keep the letter of the law; they are under the New Covenant which is a Covenant of grace and in Christ they uphold the spirit of the law which is love (see Matt. 22:37-40; John 13:34; Rom. 13:8-10; Gal. 5:14).

The Sabbath and its fulfilment in Christ are discussed in Hebrews 4:1-10. Before we look at this passage, let's recall the reasons why the book of Hebrews was written. That will expand our horizon in understanding the passage under discussion. First of all, Hebrews is another word that is used to refer to the Jews. The book of Hebrews was written, among other things, to Jewish believers who were wavering in their faith: (1) to reveal to them the overwhelming superiority of Christ over all that they had experienced under the law: Christ is the perfect revelation of God, He is the Mediator of a better Covenant, the New Covenant, which was established on better promises; (2) to remind those, who had a tendency to backslide into Judaism, that Christ is supreme and completely sufficient for salvation: once and for all He offered Himself as the perfect sinless sacrifice; and (3) to encourage them to live by faith in the face of persecution (the Jewish Christians were persecuted for their Faith in Christ by their fellow countrymen who were not Christians).

Now let's read Hebrews 4:1-10: *"Therefore, since a promise remains of entering His rest, let us fear lest any of you seem to have come short of it. For indeed the gospel was preached to us as well as to them; but the word which they heard did not profit them, not being mixed with faith in those who heard it. For we who have believed do enter that rest, as He has said: 'So I swore in my wrath, they shall not enter My rest,' although the works were finished from the foundation of the world. For He has spoken in a certain place of the seventh day in this way: 'And God rested on the seventh day from all His works;' and again in this place: 'They shall not enter My rest.' Since therefore it remains that some must enter it, and those to whom it was first preached did not enter because of disobedience, again He designates a certain day, saying in David, 'Today,' after such a long time, as it has been said: 'Today, if you will hear His voice, do not harden your hearts.' For if Joshua had given them rest, then He would not afterward have spoken of another day. There remains therefore a rest for the people of God. For he who has entered His rest has himself also ceased from his works as God did of His."*

In verses 1 and 6 to 9 we are reminded that the promise of rest given to Israel is much more than entering the Promised Land. It is a promise which still stands, that is, it was not satisfied by entering Canaan, but still exists. This shows us that: there is a Higher Rest; the promise of rest in Canaan is a shadow of the better promise, a Higher Rest.

As we have said before, God rested on the seventh day, not because He was tired, but because Creation was completed – this rest of God is mentioned in verse 4 and is also a shadow of the rest that remains. In the New Covenant, we read that Jesus says: *"It is finished (John 19:30)."* Jesus' work of redemption is fully accomplished – He exchanged His heavenly glory to come and fulfil the Old Covenant; He paid the ultimate price for our salvation and sealed the New Covenant with His blood (Matt. 26:28; Heb. 9:12). In fact, Jesus completed the full potential of the new creation – now by grace through faith we can be saved; we can become new creations (Eph. 2:8; 1 Cor. 5:17). And, through His substitutionary death, Jesus reconciled us with God so that we can be at peace with God. Therefore, the accomplishment that we find in the New Covenant says to us that the promised rest which remains of which Hebrews 10 speaks can only refer to Jesus Christ – He is the fulfiller and fulfilment of all the promises of God (2 Cor. 1:20). So the promised rest is a spiritual rest, a rest in a **Person**, not in a **Place**, or a **Day**; a rest in a **Life**, not a **Land**! It is the rest experienced by Christians – both now (today) and in the future. Furthermore, now Christians can keep the Sabbath holy – by the holiness of Jesus Christ (1 Cor. 1:30).

The Sabbath of which Hebrews 10 speaks is exceedingly more meaningful than that of the Jews (under the law), because now it commemorates not only the completion of God's work in creation but also the completion of His work of salvation.

> In Hebrews 4 the author of Hebrews sees the invitation to a "Sabbath-rest" as an invitation to cease striving with God and to receive the salvation available by faith in Jesus Christ. – William Mounce

After examining Hebrews 4:1-10, we can say with full conviction that the Sabbath is not a specific day but a Person – Jesus Christ the Son of God. By faith in Him we are at peace with God and rest from the works of the law as well as our own efforts, because as Jesus says: *"it is finished."* Hebrews 4:10 confirms that: *"For the person who has entered His rest has rested from his own works, just as God did from His (emphasis mine)."* As Christians we can now cease (rest) from striving to please God – Jesus already pleased God completely. Hebrews 2:17 declares that Jesus made propitiation for the sins of the people. Propitiation means "to satisfy." The crucified Christ satisfied God completely that sin was punished.

All that God asks of us is to enter His rest – Jesus Christ – by faith and celebrate the completed work of creation and new creation (salvation).

Finally, keep in mind, "the righteous shall live by faith," not by the law, not by works, not by sight, not by feelings or thoughts, but by faith in Jesus Christ and His finished work. (We are reminded in Hebrews 4:2, 6 that the Jews in the wilderness didn't enter the rest of Canaan because of their unbelief. Faith is all that is required to enter God's rest.)

> Sabbath for the Christian is pre-eminently a life of rejoicing in the finished work of his Lord and Saviour, and it could be done any day and time.

Sunday Worship

Sunday is the day that most Christians will gather in their local churches to celebrate their salvation and worship God. This worship on the "first day of the week [Sunday] (Acts 20:7; 1 Cor. 16:2)" follows the practice of the early Christians. There is no example in Scripture of the early Church meeting on a seventh day Sabbath, that is, Saturday (although not all Jewish Christians abandoned the Sabbath immediately).

Christ was resurrected on a Sunday (Luke 24:1; John 20:19, 26), and that same day He met with His disciples. On the Day of Pentecost, which was also on a Sunday, the disciples of Jesus were together to be filled with the Holy Spirit (Acts 2:1-4). In Acts 20:7 we read: *"Now on the first day of the week, when the disciples came together to break bread."* First Corinthians 16:2 also indicates that the Church assembled on Sunday. These Scriptures are indicative that the early Church assembled on Sundays right from the beginning.

Even the writings of the early Church fathers confirm that they worshipped on Sunday. If you really research the early Church Fathers' views on Sunday worship you will find that there are numerous instances that they actually emphasized that Sunday is the day of Christian worship. We are going to refer to only two Church Fathers. **Justin Martyr** in the mid second century wrote in his apologies about the cessation of Sabbath observance and the celebration of the first day (or eighth day) of the week (not as a day of rest, but as a day for gathering to worship): "We all gather on the day of the sun", (recalling both the creation of light and the resurrection). He argued that Sabbath was not kept before Moses, and was only instituted as a sign to Israel and a temporary measure because of Israel's sinfulness, no longer needed after Christ came without sin. **Cyprian**, a 3rd-century church father, linked the "eighth day" with the term "Lord's Day" in a letter concerning baptism. "For in respect of the observance of the eighth day of the Jewish circumcision of the flesh, a sacrament was given beforehand in shadow and in usage; but when Christ came, it was fulfilled in truth. For because the eighth day, that is, the first day after the Sabbath, was to be that on which the Lord should rise again, and should quicken us, and give us circumcision of the spirit, the eighth day, that is the first day after the Sabbath, and the Lord's Day, went before in the figure; which figure ceased when by and by the truth came and spiritual circumcision was given to us." (Both quotations are taken from *Wikipedia, The Lord's Day.*)

All this makes Sunday the most appropriate day to corporately worship the Lord as well as to celebrate the completion of His great work of redemption that was demonstrated on a Sunday (Resurrection Sunday).

Furthermore, the idea that Sunday worship is pagan because Sunday is named after the "sun god" is irrelevant. Saturday is also named after a pagan god "Saturn" and so is every day of the week. If worship on Sunday makes Christians idolaters, then Saturday worship makes Jews also idolaters. In fact, if we consider "worship on a Sunday is pagan" and that every day of the week is named after a pagan god, then worship on any day would be pagan; that's absolutely ridiculous.

NB! Through this short study we realize that the idea that Constantine (AD 321) instituted Sunday worship is wrong. The Church already worshipped on a Sunday. Constantine's declaration that Sunday should be a holiday merely benefitted the Church, which already met for worship on Sundays. And, the idea that the Roman Catholic Church changed Sabbath worship to Sunday worship is not true; as we have already seen, the very first meeting of the Church was on a Sunday. In fact, the Church was established on a Sunday, which laid the foundation for corporate Sunday worship. We should further emphasize that Sunday is not the Christian Sabbath; Jesus Christ is our Sabbath – spiritual rest and eternal peace with God.

In Conclusion
Paul says: "*So let no one judge you in food or drink, or regarding a festival or a new moon or Sabbaths, which are a shadow of things to come, but the substance is of Christ* (Col. 2:16-17)." Meaning, the law with all its ordinances was a shadow or a representation of Christ who was to come and fulfil them. Christ is the Substance (only a substance can cast a shadow, and substance surpasses shadow); He is the substance of spiritual and heavenly things; the substantial things and doctrines of the Gospel are all of Christ, they all come by Him; all the truths, blessings, and promises of grace are from Him and by Him, and He Himself the sum of them all.

Praise God, Christ is our Sabbath! And it's Scriptural to have our corporate worship on Sundays.

Glossary

The following are simple explanations of various general and important expressions that we find in the Bible or used by Christians.

Agape – a Greek word that refers to the highest form of love: God's self-giving and unconditional love.

Agnostic – a person who believes that nothing can be known about the existence of God or of anything spiritual except material things.

Alfa and Omega – beginning and end; first and last. In the Greek alphabet, alpha is the first letter and omega is the last letter.

Allegorical – is an extended metaphor; a story or description in which the characters and events symbolize some deeper underlying meaning.

Amen – An expression of affirmation often spoken at the end of a prayer. It comes from a Hebrew word that means "it is true" or "so be it."

Anointing – in relation to the Holy Spirit it means the powerful in-working of the Holy Spirit on the life of the Christian. The Holy Spirit is also called the Anointing. Anointing could refer to the anointing (rubbing) of the sick with olive oil.

Antichrist – Anyone who is against Christ is an antichrist, but many Christians believe the book of Revelation teaches that a final Antichrist will appear in the end times.

Antinomian – the position which holds that believers in Jesus are discharged from all law

Apologetics – a reasoned explanation to defend one's faith or an idea or system of beliefs

Apostasy – a turning away from faith. Apostasy means literally: "to stand or fall away from a position that you have taken with God." An apostate turns away entirely and rejects identification with the faith.

Apostle – from the Greek word, *apostolos*, which literally means "sent one" or "delegate." In the New Testament it was used to refer specifically to Jesus' close associates whom He sent out with delegated authority to be His authorized representatives to proclaim the Gospel and to establish local congregations.

Armageddon – According to Revelation 16:16 a great battle between good and evil will be fought at "the place that in Hebrew is called Armageddon" (*NIV*). It would most probably take place at the plains of Megiddo, an area in Northern Israel. In this battle God will triumph over Satan and his evil forces.

Ark of the Covenant – the rectangular chest made of acacia wood; the most sacred of all the furniture in the tabernacle; it contained the tablets of the Ten Commandments; the Ark of the Covenant was symbolic of the presence of God's dwelling with the Israelites; the lid of the Ark was known as the mercy seat on which the high priest applied the sacrificial blood which annually gave Israel forgiveness on the Day of Atonement.

Asia – When we read of Asia in the New Testament, it refers to a province in the Roman Empire, in the western part of modern Turkey, and not the Continent as we know it today.

Ascension – going upward, especially Jesus rising to heaven from the earth.

DISCOVERING THE MOST AMAZING BOOK   447

Atonement – One of the central teachings of Christianity, referring to the reconciliation between God and sinners. This reconciliation is brought about through the death of Christ as a substitute for sinful man.

Baptism, baptize – The ordinance that shows publicly that the individual had repented from his/her sin, accepted Jesus as Saviour and is now a member of the body of Christ. It is also referred to as the believer's baptism or baptism in water. Baptize comes from the Greek word "baptizo," which means "to immerse, to dip under, to wash." Regarding the Christian baptism in water, it means that we immerse the person fully in water which signifies the cleansing from sin (Matt. 3:13-17; Acts 2:38).

Baptism in the Holy Spirit – an experience with the Holy Spirit during which a person is baptized in the power of the Holy Spirit.

Baal – the great fertility god of the Canaanites

Beelzebub – ruler of demons, satan

Believer – In Biblical context, a Christian; a person who believes in and confesses Jesus as the Son of God who died for him or her.

Bema – high judgment seat

Benediction – A blessing, usually pronounced by a minister of God's Word

Blasphemy – Insulting or mocking God. It can include using the Lord's name in vain, which is specifically prohibited in the Ten Commandments.

Body of Christ – The universal Church is called the Body of Christ (Col. 1:18). In 1 Corinthians 12, Paul describes the Church as a single body made up of many individual parts, each of which plays an important but different role.

Book of Life – A record kept in heaven listing all who have eternal life.

Born Again – The actual meaning is: born from above, from God, by His Spirit. It is the spiritual rebirth of a sinner that is separated from God. By means of the born again experience the person is made spiritually alive and reconciled with God.

Casuistic laws – laws describing specific cases or situations in the form of "If ... then ..."

Cherubim – plural for cherub; angelic beings, evidently guardians of God's holiness

Christian – One who believes in and confesses Jesus as the Son of God who died for him or her.

Church – The body of all Christians (born again believers).

Circumcision, circumcise – Cutting the foreskin from the penis of an infant boy. When the Lord made a covenant with Abraham, promising that Abraham would be the father of many nations, he also instituted the ceremony of circumcision (Gen. 17). That was only for Abraham's natural offspring; born again believers are "circumcise" in the heart.

Consecration – dedication to God's purposes

Counsellor/advocate – Holy Spirit

Covenant – a specific binding agreement between two parties

Confess, confession – to speak out in public; to verbally acknowledge a sin; to say the same as, for example: what God says about me in Scripture I "confess"

DISCOVERING THE MOST AMAZING BOOK 449

Demons – evil spirits; they are satan's agents opposing the will of God

Deliver, deliverance – to set free, as from bondage, misery or evil.

Disciple – the basic meaning of the word is "a student;" in Christianity a disciple is a follower of Jesus Christ who accepts the teaching of Christ, not only in belief but also in lifestyle.

Discern – to recognize and distinguish between right and wrong, or good and evil. The gift of discerning of spirits is a supernatural ability to separate, distinguish and evaluate the difference between spirit beings.

Divination – the pagan and occult counterpart of biblical prophecy

---

Edifies – builds up

Epicurean – a person that follows the philosophy of Epicurus (300 BC); a philosophy that denied the existence of gods, or if they did, they lived for pleasure; a philosophy that seeks freedom from anxiety and disturbance, their creed was "eat, drink, and be merry."

Epistle – a Letter written by early Christian writers and included as books of the Bible

Eternal, eternity, eternally – time that lasts forever.

Eunuch – a man whose sex organs have been removed or do not function

Evangelist – someone who is called to proclaim the gospel with conviction

Evangelize – to spread and share the gospel with people, particularly those who are not familiar with it

Exhortation – giving advice and encouragement earnestly

Faith – a conviction, trust, belief or assurance; to be fully convinced that God is well able to fulfil His promises.

Fallen angels – demons

Feast of Unleavened Bread – seven-day feast in which Jews eat bread made without yeast

Feast of Weeks – another name for the Feast of Pentecost

Fellowship – it is not merely having a chat over a cuppa; it implies sharing life together; fellowship demands commitment and tests one's loyalty and sincerity

Firstfruits – feast that marked the start of the barley harvest

Flesh – could have different meanings depending on the context. It could refer to the substance of the body, or the complete person, or the sinful nature of man. In Jesus' case, it refers to His holy humanity. In reference to human beings, it most often refer to the fallen, sinful nature of man.

Gentiles – heathen nations, especially people who are not Jewish.

Glory of God – the excellence and praiseworthiness of God which He displays through His Person, work and interactions with man. That leads Christians to glorify God by expressing honour and adoration in response to His glory.

Gnosticism – from the Greek word *gnosis* (knowledge). Gnostics claimed that they had superior and esoteric knowledge, and stressed salvation through *gnosis* and rigorous self-discipline. They asserted that God was completely separated from the material world and could not have created the world, because in their opinion matter was evil and spirit was good. Since God was spirit and therefore good, the evil material world could have no contact with Him. They also rejected the deity of Jesus and argued that if Jesus was God, He could not have lived in an evil material body. They, therefore, maintained that Jesus did not live as a man, His suffering on the cross was not real, and there was no Resurrection. Furthermore, they were convinced that the Holy Spirit hovered over Him from the time that He was baptized, but left Him at the time of His crucifixion.

Gospel – Good News.

Grace – the unmerited (undeserved) favour of God. Grace is also a power-word describing the Holy Spirit's operational means. Grace is a *force* and a *favour*, a verb as well as a noun.

Grecian Jews – Jews who spoke Greek and adopted the Greek culture

---

Hades – in the New Testament the Greek word *hades* refers to the place of the dead.

Hallelujah – praise the Lord

Hallowed – used to describe something or someone that is holy.

Hebraic Jews – Jews who spoke Hebrew, and who were very little influenced by the Greek culture

Hebrew – a Jew, or could refer to the language

Hellenist – a person who spoke Greek and adopted the Greek culture

Heresy – false teaching, an opinion that is contrary to what is normally accepted

Hosanna – means "save now;" it was originally essentially a plea from an oppressed people to their Saviour for deliverance (Psalm 118:25, 26). Later it became a shout of adoration.

Hypocrite – a person who says one thing but does another.

Immanent – of God, existing in time and space, permanently pervading the universe

Immortality – the state of living forever

Impart – giving or granting what one has. God imparts life to those who receives Christ into their lives as Saviour.

Imputes – credits to a person. God imputes or credits the righteousness of Christ to those who put their faith in Christ.

Incarnation – means "in flesh;" the act whereby the eternal Son of God united himself with human flesh in the person of Jesus – Jesus is fully Man and fully God simultaneously.

Incorruptible, incorruption – not able to be destroyed or spoiled

Intercession – pleading with God on behalf of another person or people group, usually for a serious need

Judaism – the apostle Paul refers to it as the religion of the Jews, with belief in one God and based on the Law of Moses (Acts 26:5).

Judaizer – Jewish Christians who still wanted to live according to Jewish customs, which included keeping the law; they insisted that Gentile converts adhered to Jewish cultural and religious practices

Judgment – making a decision, based on evidence that determines one's guilt.

Justification – to be free from a charge or accusation, declared righteous.

Last days – the period of time between the First Coming and Second Coming of Christ

Legalistic or legalism – when the focus is on the letter of the law, law keeping; legalism is based strictly on performance, self-effort

Leviathan – a large animal living in water, described at length in Job 41

Libertines – those who live without moral restraint

Licence – disregard of rules or standards of personal conduct; living irresponsible

---

Martyrs – those who died for their faith.

Meditate, meditation – to think often or deeply about something.

Mercy – love, kindness. A contrast between grace and mercy will throw light on both terms: The mercy of God withholds from us what we deserve. The grace of God lavishes on us the favour and blessings of God that we do not deserve.

Messiah – Hebrew for Anointed One; in Greek *Christos,* Christ

Messianic Jew – is a Jew who confesses Jesus as Saviour

Monotheism – belief in only One God; monotheism forms the basis of the Mosaic Covenant

---

Oppress, oppressed – to treat people cruelly so that they don't have the same freedom or benefits as others.

Pantheism – the belief that there is no difference between God and the material world, and that God is in everything

Passover – yearly feast to commemorate Israel's deliverance from Egypt and death

Peace – "to be united with" as well as "to bring an end to hostility."

Pentecost – from the Greek word for "fiftieth day." In the Old Testament the Feast of Pentecost was celebrated fifty days after Passover. In the New Testament the term Pentecost refers to the outpouring of the Holy Spirit approximately fifty days after Jesus' resurrection during the Feast of Pentecost which is also referred to as the Feast of Weeks.

Pharisees – a religious group that originated in the second century BC that were dedicated to the strict observance of the Mosaic Law. However they believed that the Law could be adapted to changing conditions after careful study; they developed the so called Oral Law, or Law of the Elders (man-made traditions), which was treated as equal to the Written Law. They laid the foundation for Orthodox Judaism. In Jesus' day the Pharisees were self-righteous and hypocritical religionists (see Matt. 23:13-36).

Polytheism – belief in or worship of many gods

Prophesy, prophesying – to speak forth, bring a word directly from the Lord, often about the future (see 1 Cor. 14:3 in the *Amplified*)

Prophecy – the actual words that are spoken forth

DISCOVERING THE MOST AMAZING BOOK

Prophet – comes from the Greek word *prophetes*, which literally means "one who speaks forth." The prophet speaks forth on behalf of God by the inspiration of the Holy Spirit.

Propitiation – from the Greek *hilasterion*, and means "that which expiates or makes propitiation." It is the satisfying of the righteousness of a holy God, so that it is possible for Him to show mercy without compromising his infinite holiness. This satisfaction was procured by Christ's death on the cross; He being perfect man and perfect God dying on behalf of mankind.

Rabbi – Teacher

Rapture – the doctrine that the Church will be "caught up" in the air to meet Christ (1 Thess. 4:16-17).

Recompense – something received as a payment or reward, to make compensation.

Reconcile – to unite with, to restore a relationship

Redemption – being set free because someone paid ransom, being delivered from evil and the penalty of sin.

Regeneration – the experiencing of new life; being spiritually born again

Remission (of sins) – a cancellation of all judgment or obligation.

Repent, repentance – a turning around; a change of mind and heart accompanied by a change of behaviour.

Resurrection – a restoration to life; rising from the dead.

Righteous, righteousness – the quality of being right because of the grace of God; a right standing with God.

Sadducees – they were followers of Zadok, mostly from the wealthy and powerful families. They had a powerful influence in the Sanhedrin. As opposed to the Pharisees they accepted the written law, but did not believe in bodily resurrection and the immortality of the soul (see Matt. 16:1-12; 22:23; Acts 23:6-8).

Saints – those who have experienced salvation in Christ and are committed to Him.

Salvation – rescue, deliverance; in Scripture it includes forgiveness, healing, prosperity, deliverance, safety, rescue, liberation, and restoration.

Scribes – Jewish experts in the Law of Moses (Matt. 2:4; 12:28-38; 15:1). They originated after the Exile and instituted the synagogue service. Some were members of the Sanhedrin (Matt. 16:21; 26:3). The scribes upheld the oral law and eventually claimed that the oral law was more important than the written law, and thus substituted human tradition for the Word of God (Mark 7:6-13).

Sanctify, sanctification – to set apart, dedicate, consecrate, make or become holy.

Sanhedrin – supreme Jewish legal, religious, and political council; the council that condemned Jesus

Sheol – a Hebrew word meaning "grave." In Scripture it denotes as a place of sorrow (Ps. 18:5; 116:3) to which the wicked are consigned while fully conscious (Ps. 9:17; Ez. 32:21). Sheol is the equivalent of hades in the New Testament (Luke 16:19-31).

Shema – the creed of Judaism: *"Hear, O Israel: the Lord our God, the Lord is one* (Deut. 6:4)"; recited by the Jews in daily prayer

Signs/wonders – miracles; signs are viewed as miracles with a message, and the message is more important than the miracle

Sin – is essentially rebellion against God

Sovereignty of God – meaning God has absolute power and authority

Spirit of God – the understanding of God's presence moving, in power, in a place to accomplish His purposes; the Holy Spirit is also referred to as the Spirit of God, particularly in the New Testament

Stoic – a stoical person believes that the only important thing in life is virtue, and that one should remain unmoved by external affairs, bearing difficulties or discomfort without any complaining. (Named after the Stoics, Greek and Roman philosophers of the 3rd century BC)

Synagogue – Jewish place of worship

Temptation – being tempted; arousing a desire in you or trying to persuade you into doing something wrong or unwise; the devil has no power over us Christians, therefore he tempts us, trying to lure us away from our relationship with God

Testimony – proof, evidence, or what someone can say from their personal experience to support what they believe to be true; also a praise-report to the faithfulness and goodness of God

Theology – from the Greek words *Theos* (God) *Logia* (utterances, sayings or oracles); theology could be defined as the systematic and rational study of concepts of God, His direct relation to the universe, and the nature of revealed truths as we find it in the Bible. Theology wants to understand why we believe what we believe in order to be certain of what we believe. (However, theology can never be complete, because we have only limited knowledge of God.)

Theophany – an appearance of God to man in which He shows Himself in some physical way that people experience by at least the senses of sight and hearing (Gen. 12:7; 18:1, 2); the appearance of the Angel of the Lord was a theophany of the pre-incarnate Christ.

Transcendent – exceeding beyond the limits of normal experience; of God, it means He exists apart from the material universe

Trinity – the term describing the Tri-une nature of God in three Persons: God the Father, God the Son, and God the Spirit

Typology – in the Bible are types and symbols to explain God's work in Biblical events, people, and institutions.

Transgression, transgressors – the breaking of a moral law or rule of behaviour.

Urim and Thummim – meaning "Lights and Perfections"; were in the breastplate of the high priest when he went in before the Lord (Ex. 28:30), and were used as a means of consulting with God in cases of doubt (Num. 27:21); but precisely what these were are unknown; probably precious stones that were divinely controlled in times of consulting, they either glowed or were thrown as lots.

World the – the Greek word *kosmos* could have different implications depending on the context in which it is used. At times it refers to the created universe and at other times it refers to the sphere of human life – the created world in which human beings live. This word is also used, especially by the apostles John and Paul to refer to the sinful and enslaving systems of this present world order that are under the influence of satan (see Gal. 4:3; 1 John 2:15). Sometimes the word "world" is used to refer to an evil "age" (space and time in which we live) that is opposed to God (see 2 Cor. 4:4).

Yom Kippur – the holiest day of the Jewish year, also called the Day of Atonement

---

Zealot – a member of a fanatical Jewish sect that opposed Roman rule during the first century.

Zionism – a movement that is focused on supporting the well-being of Israel.

Bibliography

Anderson Bernhard W. *The Living World of the Old Testament.* Harlow England: Longman Group UK Limited, 1957.

Baxter J Sidlow. Explore the Book, Vol. One. Grand Rapids Michigan: Zondervan Publishing House, 1960.

Baxter J Sidlow. *The Strategic Grasp of the Bible.* London: Marshall, Morgan & Scott, 1968.

Barrett David P. *"Chronological Survey of the Bible."* Chronological Life Application Study Bible. Carol Stream, Illinois: Tyndale House Publishers, 2007.

Calvary Academics. *Old Testament Survey, Part One.* Sinoville Pretoria South Africa: Calvary Academics, 2007.

Calvary Academics. *Old Testament Survey, Part Two.* Sinoville Pretoria South Africa: Calvary Academics, 2007.

Calvary Academics. *Old Testament Survey, Part Three.* Sinoville Pretoria South Africa: Calvary Academics, 2007.

Comfort Ray. *Scientific Facts in the Bible.* Alachua, Florida: Bridge-Logos, 2001.

Connor Kevin J. *Interpreting the Symbols and Types.* Portland Oregon: City Bible Publishing, 1992.

Cotton Roger. *Pentateuch.* Springfield MO: Global University, 2010.

Dennis Lane T, et al. *ESV Study Bible*. Wheaton Illinois: Crossway, 2008.

Drane John. *Introducing the Old Testament*. Littlemore, Oxford, England: Lion Publishing, 1987.

Drane John. *Introducing the New Testament*. Littlemore, Oxford, England: Lion Publishing, 1986.

Dunnam Maxie D. *The Preacher's Commentary, Vol. 31: Galatians, Ephesians, Philippians, Colossians, Philemon.* Nashville Tennessee: Thomas Nelson, 1982.

Ferguson Sinclair B, et al. *New Dictionary of Theology*. Leicester, England: Inter-Varsity Press, 1988.

Freeman James M. *Manners and Customs of the Bible*. Springdale PA: Whitaker House, 1996.

Global University. *Old Testament Survey*. Springfield Missouri: Global University, 2010.

Gould Dana. *Shepherd's Notes, Acts*. Nashville Tennessee: B & H Publishing Group, 1997.

Gould Dana. *Shepherd's Notes, James*. Nashville Tennessee: B & H Publishing Group, 1998.

Hailey Homer. *A Commentary on the Minor Prophets*. Grand Rapids Michigan: Baker Book House, 1972.

Hale Thomas. *The Applied New Testament Commentary*. Eastbourne Sussex: Kingsway Publications, 1996.

Hammond Peter. *"The Greatest Man Who Ever Lived."* Joy! Magazine. Ed. Erin Georgiou. Somerset West South Africa: Independent Christian Media, 2006. 45.

DISCOVERING THE MOST AMAZING BOOK 463

Hampton Henry Halley. *Halley's Bible Handbook.* Grand Rapids: Zondervan, 2000.

Hayford Jack W, et al. *Spirit Filled Life Bible.* Nashville: Zondervan, 1991.

Horton David. *The Portable Seminary.* Grand Rapids: Zondervan, 2006.

Kee Howard Clark and Young Franklin. *The Living World of the New Testament.* London: Darton, Longman & Todd, 1960.

Keil & Delitzsh. *Commentary on the Old Testament: Genesis.* E-Sword. 2003.

Laymon Charles D, gen. ed. *Interpreter's Concise Commentary Vol. 4: Isaiah-Daniel.* Nashville: Abington Press, 1983.

Lee Robert. *The Outlined Bible.* Pickering & I, 1921.

Lloyd-Jones Martyn. *Authentic Christianity.* Wheaton Illinois: Crossway Books, 2000.

Marshall Howard I. *Tyndale New Testament Commentaries: Acts.* Leicester England: Inter-Varsity Press, 1980.

Metzger Bruce M. *Breaking the Code: Understanding the Book of Revelation.* Nashville: Abingdon Press, 1993.

Miller Stephen. *Shepherd's Notes: Daniel.* Nashville Tennessee: Holman Reference, 1998.

Morris Henry. *The Genesis Record.* Grand Rapids: Baker Book House, 2001.

Morris Henry M. *The Bible Has The Answer.* Grand Rapids Michigan: Baker Book House, 1971.

Mounce William D. *Complete Expository Dictionary of Old & New Testament Words.* Grand Rapids Michigan: Zondervan, 2006.

Osborne Grant. Baker Exegetical Commentary on the New Testament: *Revelation.*
Grand Rapids: Baker Academic, 2002.

Packer J I. *Knowing God.* London: Hodder & Stoughton, 1973.

Pawson David. *Unlocking the Bible.* London: HarperCollinsPublishers, 2003.

Phillips John. *Bible Explorer's Guide.* Grand Rapids: Kregel Publications, 2002.

Prince Derek. *Foundations.* Tamil Nadu, South India: Rhema Media Centre, 1993.

Scott Julius J Jr. *"The Time Between the Testaments."* ESV Study Bible. Wheaton Illinois: Crossway, 2008.

Scroggie Graham W. *The Unfolding Drama of Redemption.* Grand Rapids: Kregel Publications, 1994.

Stott John R W. *The Message of Romans.* Leicester England: Inter-Varsity Press, 1994.

Thiessen Henry Clarence. *Introduction to the New Testament.* Peabody, Massachusetts: Hendrickson Publishers, 2002.

Thomas Nelson Publishers. *Nelson's Complete Book of Bible Maps.* Nashville: Thomas Nelson Publishers, 1993.

Unger Merrill F. *Unger's Concise Bible Dictionary.* Grand Rapids, Michigan: Baker Book House, 1974.

Vine William Edwy. *Vine's Expository Dictionary of Old & New Testament Words.* Nashville Tennessee: Thomas Nelson, 1997.

Walker Derek. *The Gospel of John.* Oxford: Friends Print + Media, 2005.

Wood George O. *Acts: The Holy Spirit at Work in Believers.* Springfield Missouri: Global University, 2010.

www.biblemapper.com Maps used by permission, David P Barrett.

Young Douglas G, et al. *Bible Dictionary.* Wheaton Illinois: Tyndale House Publishers, 1989.

Lightning Source UK Ltd.
Milton Keynes UK
UKOW02f1058091114

241262UK00006B/99/P